THE MODEL RAILROADER'S GUIDE TO
FREIGHT CARS

JEFF WILSON

KALMBACH
BOOKS

Printed in the United States of America

05 06 07 08 09 10 11 12 13 14 10 9 8 7 6 5 4 3 2 1

Visit our website at
http://kalmbachbooks.com
Secure online ordering available

Publisher's Cataloging-In-Publication Data
(Prepared by The Donohue Group, Inc.)

Wilson, Jeff, 1964-
    The model railroader's guide to freight cars / Jeff Wilson.

    p. : ill. ; cm.
    ISBN: 0-89024-585-1

1. Railroads—Freight-cars—Models. 2. Railroads—Freight-cars—Design and construction. 3. Railroads—Freight-cars—History—20th century. I. Title.

TF197 .W55 2005
625.19

Managing Art Director: Mike Soliday
Book Design: Sabine Beaupré

CONTENTS

INTRODUCTION

Modelers have long paid special attention to locomotives and cabooses, but freight cars often don't receive the same care in modeling. That needn't be the case, as the last few years have seen an explosion in the number of highly detailed, realistic freight car models available in all scales.

With so many models available, it can be difficult to determine the types of cars appropriate for different eras or types of service. This goal of this book is to make freight car selection less of a mystery.

Each chapter provides a brief history of a type of freight car, then shows through photos how car designs have evolved from the World War I era to the present. This book is designed as a guide for modelers, illustrating the spotting features that make cars unique and making it easier to choose and detail appropriate models.

In addition to the cars themselves, the book also examines the evolution of freight car components: wheels, trucks, and brake equipment. An overview of how air brakes work.

This book is not meant to be a complete guide to every freight car ever produced, or to examine the myriad detail differences present on every sub-class of car—space simply doesn't allow that. Much of the information was culled from hundreds of articles in dozens of modeling, railfan, and trade magazines, including *Model Railroader*, *Trains*, *Freight Car Journal*, *Mainline Modeler*, *Modern Railroads*, *Model Railroading*, *RailModel Journal*, *Railroad Model Craftsman*, and *Railway Age*. Also invaluable were reference guides, including various issues of the *Car Builders' Cyclopedia* and the *Official Railway Equipment Register*, and books too numerous to mention.

Other sources include clinics and seminars, photographs, and personal observation. As with any work of this scope, sources sometimes conflict regarding dates, figures, and facts. I did my best to sort through these for the most accurate information; any mistakes made in sorting out this material are my own, and not of those who assisted me. I hope this book serves as a handy reference for your modeling and railfanning.

Projects like this would not be possible without the help and work of others. I would like to thank the many people who provided information and/or searched their photo collections to find materials, including Scott Chatfield, Bob Gallegos, Jim Hediger, Richard Hendrickson, J. David Ingles, Keith Kohlmann, Brian Kreimendahl, Marty McGuirk, Hol Wagner, and Jay Williams. I also want to thank the many photographers whose photos reside in the David P. Morgan Library at Kalmbach Publishing Co. Without that library's collection, this book would not have been possible.

Jeff Wilson
January 2005

BOXCARS

The ubiquitous boxcar was the dominant freight car throughout much of the history of railroading. Boxcars were *the* general-purpose car on the rails into the 1970s. Although today much of what was once carried in boxcars now rides in containers, plenty of boxcars remain in service carrying auto parts, paper, canned goods, and other products (fig. 1-1).

Boxcars have evolved significantly since World War I. Part of that evolution relates to size. The 40-foot, 40-ton cars of the 1910s grew longer and taller over the years, resulting in the 50-foot cars in the 1950s and the 86-foot excess-height cars introduced in the 1960s.

Materials played a big role in development as well. Wood gave way to steel. Improved designs for roofs, ends, and other components made cars stronger, more durable, and weather-tight.

1-1 Even though boxcars are no longer the most numerous freight car type on the rails, modern boxcars, such as this 60-foot TBOX car, still a play vital role in hauling freight. *Jeff Wilson*

ONE

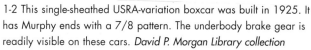

1-2 This single-sheathed USRA-variation boxcar was built in 1925. It has Murphy ends with a 7/8 pattern. The underbody brake gear is readily visible on these cars. *David P. Morgan Library collection*

1-3 Double-sheathed USRA cars had heavy fishbelly underframes and straight side sills. This car has the 5/5/5 Murphy ends found on true USRA boxcars, and it rides on Andrews trucks. *David P. Morgan Library collection*

1-4 The original deep fishbelly underframe is still visible on this rebuilt USRA boxcar. The wood sides have been replaced with steel, the Murphy ends extended to make the car taller, and a new power hand-brake (Miner) has been added. *David P. Morgan Library collection*

Regardless of the era you model, boxcars will be a key element of your mix of freight cars. To help you determine what cars are appropriate for your era and industries, we'll start by taking a look at how cars have evolved with the United States Railroad Administration (USRA), American Railway Association (ARA), and Association of American Railroads (AAR) standard designs. We'll then examine other significant railroad- and manufacturer-built designs. Space doesn't allow covering every variation of every boxcar type, but we'll look at representative samples of key types and at key differences in detail, including doors, roofs, ends, and brake equipment.

USRA designs

Prior to World War I, boxcars followed many designs. Each order—whether built by a manufacturer or a railroad—tended to be custom made, as each railroad had its own idea of what constituted an ideal car design.

That changed in 1917 with government control of the railroads during World War I by the United States Railroad Administration. The USRA developed standardized designs for several types of locomotives and freight cars, including boxcars. Railroads were for the most part against the idea of standardization, but the USRA deemed the concept necessary to increase manufacturing efficiency and speed delivery of needed cars for the war effort.

The USRA formulated two designs for 40-foot boxcars. Both were wood cars with steel underframes, but one was single-sheathed and the other was double-sheathed. Single-sheathed boxcars had exposed body framing, with a single layer of sheathing applied on the inside. Double-sheathed cars had two layers of sheathing—one inside, one outside—giving the car a smooth-sided appearance.

The USRA single-sheathed car (fig. 1-2) had a 50-ton capacity and used a Howe-truss design for the steel framing on its sides, with four panels on each side of the door and the diagonals meeting at the top of the door opening. These

cars had steel underframes, three-piece Murphy ends with a 5/5/5 corrugation pattern (see the sidebar on page 9 for more information on car end features), and vertical brake staffs.

About 25,000 USRA single-sheathed cars were built, and several thousand more cars were built to the same or similar design after USRA control ended.

The double-sheathed cars (fig. 1-3) had 40-ton capacities, with wood framing (instead of steel) inside the sheathing. This was an important distinction because double-sheathed cars tended to deteriorate much faster than the steel-framed single-sheathed cars.

The double-sheathed cars had distinctive steel fishbelly underframes, which were very strong (overly so) and made the double-sheathed cars prime candidates for rebuilding. As with single-sheathed cars, double-sheathed USRA cars featured Murphy 5/5/5 ends.

The designs proved themselves worthy, and many railroads built or bought copies of the designs into the 1920s. A characteristic of most of the copies—and a way to

1-5

1-6

1-7

1-5 Mather cars were 40-foot, 40-ton single-sheathed boxcars with wood ends. *David P. Morgan Library collection*

1-6 The Pennsy X-29 boxcar was the first mass-production steel boxcar built. This is a late X-29, built in 1934. It has a Youngstown door, AB brakes, and a power handbrake. *Pennsylvania RR*

1-7 This 1932 ARA boxcar (built in 1936) has early Dreadnaught 4/4 ends with square corner posts, Youngstown doors, and an earlier-style horizontal brake wheel. The tabs extending below the sides cover the ends of the bolsters and cross-bearers. *Pullman-Standard*

tell them from the original USRA cars—is their improved Murphy ends with the 7/8 pattern (fig. 1-3).

Many USRA cars were rebuilt with steel sides in the 1930s and 1940s. Some single-sheathed cars were rebuilt, but most of the rebuilds were double-sheathed cars because of their weaker all-wood body construction.

Figure 1-4 shows one of the rebuilt cars. Rebuilds generally retained their deep fishbelly underframes and Murphy ends (although the ends were often extended to make a taller car), both of which are good spotting features. Another feature to look for is the side sill, which is set in from the bottom of the sides.

Rebuilds received various types of roofs, doors, and ladders, and had either eight- or ten-section side panels. Most had their older K style brake equipment replaced with AB brakes, and many had their vertical brake staffs replaced with vertical brake wheels on the car ends.

Another common wood boxcar that lasted through the steam era was the Mather patent car, shown in fig. 1-5. The Mather Co. built

and leased these cars to many railroads. Although dated (the cars looked older than they actually were), Mather cars were simple and inexpensive to build. They were single-sheathed, with three panels on each side of the door, and had wood ends.

Many other styles of single- and double-sheathed boxcars were built through the 1920s, including many that were unique to a single railroad. Spotting features to watch for include number and spacing of the vertical posts; type of truss (direction of the diagonal members); car height and width; roof, door, and end type; ladder or grab iron style; side sill; and underframe type.

Standard steel cars

Steel gained in popularity as a building material in the early 1920s and had been widely used for other car types—such as hoppers—since the turn of the century.

An ARA design of 1923 proposed a steel car, and although resistance among some member railroads kept it from becoming a standard, the design became the

first widely used steel boxcar.

The most famous of these was the Pennsylvania Railroad's X-29 boxcar (fig. 1-6). The Pennsy built about 30,000 X-29s through the early 1930s, making the design significant because so many of the cars could be found traveling on railroads throughout the country. In addition, another 21,000 cars based on the ARA design were built by or for other railroads.

The original X-29s were 8'-7" inside height (IH) cars, with an 8'-9" inside width (IW). They had lap-seam roofs, and most were built with flat riveted-plate ends, Creco doors, and K brakes with vertical brake staffs. Starting in 1928 most new X-29s received Youngstown doors.

The last few thousand cars, built in the early 1930s, had Dreadnaught ends (see sidebar on page 9), AB brakes, and Ajax hand brakes. Also, many of the earlier cars were eventually rebuilt with AB brakes and power hand brakes. (See chapter 8 for more information on brake equipment.) Most cars rode on Pennsy's own 2D-F8 trucks.

1-8

1-9

1-10

1-8 The AAR 1937 cars were taller than the 1932 cars, as witnessed by their 4/5 Dreadnaught ends. This car has square corner posts—note the sharp angle of the corner. Vertical brake wheels were now standard on these cars. *W.C. Whittaker*

1-9 Later AAR 1937 cars had improved W corner posts, which resulted in ends with rounded corners as on this M&StL car. *Minneapolis & St. Louis*

1-10 Modified 1937 cars, such as this 1942-built Southern car, had 5/5 Dreadnaught ends and an increased IH of 10'-6". The car has a Murphy panel roof and steel running board. *Don Phillips*

1-11 Cars began appearing with improved Dreadnaught ends in 1944. On these the small triangular protrusions are replaced with long slender corrugations. Monon No. 1 has Superior seven-panel doors and eight-rung ladders. *David P. Morgan Library collection*

1-11

The cars proved to be solid but had a design flaw in that moisture could be trapped behind the sides at the floors, causing the lower areas of the sides to rust out over time. Most of these cars that were still in service in the 1950s and later were modified with thin plates over the lower sides to fix this problem.

The 1932 ARA steel boxcar
In 1932 the American Railway Association (ARA) introduced a standard design that ranks among the most revolutionary in the evolution of the boxcar. It was the first steel car accepted as a standard by American railroads, and its design would lead directly into the next generation of standard cars (fig. 1-7). The car introduced the basic appearance that all ARA/AAR cars would follow for the next 25 years, with tabs extending below the sides to hide the ends of the boxcar's underframe crossbearers.

The design relied on steel sheathing—the carbody itself—for strength, whereas earlier cars relied more on their underframes. This allowed the car to be lighter than previous designs. It was also larger than the older cars, with a 9'-4" interior height and 8'-9" interior width standard (although some cars varied from these dimensions).

The design was a standard, but it allowed for many options in components—a factor that helped increase its popularity. Most 1932 cars had Dreadnaught 4/4 ends and panel roofs, although some were equipped with lap-seam, radial, or Viking roofs and 4/5 Dreadnaught, Murphy, or flat plate ends.

About 14,000 cars were built to the 1932 design, and, even with the upgraded standard that came in 1937, some cars were built to the 1932 design into the early 1940s. Major builders of 1932 cars were American Car & Foundry

(ACF) and Pullman-Standard, but several other companies also built cars to this design.

Later AAR steel cars
The 1937 Association of American Railroads (AAR) standard design was based heavily on the 1932 design, but was taller and wider: 10'-0" and 9'-2", respectively (fig. 1-8). A spotting feature of these cars was their 4/5 Dreadnaught ends, which allowed for the increased height.

Another spotting feature was the corners on the Dreadnaught ends. The 1932 cars and the first 1937 cars had ends (figs. 1-7 and 1-8) that wrapped at a right angle around square internal corner posts. The corner posts were later changed to a W shape, which resulted in a rounded corner as fig. 1-9 shows.

Other details to watch for are the ladders, which have seven or eight rungs. There were also several different designs and patterns

Boxcar ends

Several types of steel ends were used on boxcars and other house cars (reefers and stock cars) from World War I to the present. Among the earliest was the Murphy design, which had thin horizontal corrugations (as in figs. 1-1 and 1-3).

Since ends are made of two or three panels that are riveted or welded together, the number of corrugations on each panel is an identifying feature. Thus, a Murphy end with 7 ribs on the top section and 8 on the bottom has become known as a Murphy 7/8 end.

The other main type of end is the style made by the Standard Railway Equipment Mfg. Co. called "Dreadnaught" (see photo at right). This distinctive design originally had a series of heavy corrugations (thicker than the Murphy) with a series of small triangular shapes—often called "darts"—at the ends. The number of corrugations varied with the height of the car, with 3/3 ends common on refrigerator cars, moving to 4/4, 5/4, and 5/5 on AAR boxcars.

A spotting change occurred in 1940. Earlier ends had sharp angles at the corners, as seen in the photo of the Soo Line car in fig. 1-7. Later cars had rounded corners (fig. 1-9), as the

Dreadnaught ends were the most commonly used through the 1960s. This is a 4/4 pattern end on a boxcar built in 1942. ACF

end wrapped around a newly designed W-shaped corner post.

In 1945 the design changed again, with the introduction of the improved Dreadnaught end. With these, as fig. 1-11 shows, the small triangles were replaced by long narrow corrugations. In 1948 this was further modified with an additional thin corrugation at the top (which became heavier in later years), as fig. 1-18 shows.

For a time in the early 1950s the thin corrugations were eliminated, creating what many modelers have termed the "Dartnaught" pattern (fig. 1-12).

The Dreadnaught end continued to evolve. The design was used on some cars until the 1970s (by then Standard Railway Equipment had become Stanray, part of Abex Corp.), as fig. 1-32 shows.

When Pullman-Standard introduced its

PS-1, it used its own proprietary steel end. The PS end is marked by several wide corrugations of a different shape when compared with Dreadnaught ends as fig. 1-13 shows. PS ends originally featured poling pockets, which were eventually eliminated. Until the mid-1950s, the top and bottom sections of the ends were riveted together (fig. 1-13); after that they were welded (fig. 1-14).

Slab ends—with two or more flat pieces of steel riveted together—were popular on some early boxcars (fig. 1-16) including notables such as Pennsy's early X-29 and some early AAR steel cars.

Most modern boxcars have corrugated ends with overlapping sides (called non-terminating ends), as fig. 1-27 shows. These can be found with varying number (and size) of corrugations.

Many other end patterns—too many to describe here—have also been used over the years, but are in the minority.

1-12

1-13

1-14

1-12 This Missouri-Kansas-Texas car, built by ACF in 1950, has welded side panels, a diagonal-panel roof, and Dreadnaught ends without the small corrugations (a version sometimes called the "Dartnaught" end. *ACF Industries*

1-13 Pullman-Standard's PS-1 had welded sides and the company's own ends and roof. This 1951-built 40-foot car has Youngstown doors and a Miner brake wheel. *Pullman-Standard*

1-14 Later PS-1 ends were welded together instead of riveted. This 50-foot car, built in 1955, has Youngstown doors with eight-foot-wide openings. *Pullman-Standard*

of steel (rather than wood) running boards.

The AAR standard cars were built by a number of manufacturers, notably ACF and Pullman-Standard (PS), but also Bethlehem, General American, Magor, Mt. Vernon Car Mfg. Co., and Pressed Steel Car Co. In addition, several railroads built their own cars to the standard design, many using kits available from ACF and PS.

In 1941, the AAR modified the 1937 car design, creating what became known as the 1937 ARA Modified car. The main difference was an increase in interior height to 10'-6" (although many 10'-4" cars were also built), with 5/5 Dreadnaught ends (fig. 1-10). However, many 10'-0" IH cars continued to be built.

Another update came in 1944 with the introduction of the improved Dreadnaught end (fig. 1-11). As the sidebar on page 9

explains, the small triangular protrusions between the main ribs of the Dreadnaught ends were gone, replaced by long slender corrugations.

The last AAR standard for boxcars, calling for a lightweight welded car, came in 1951, but none were actually built. By the late 1950s production of 40-foot cars was declining as 50-foot cars became more popular. Wider doors and welded construction were the norm as 40-foot production wound down. Figure 1-12 shows a late AAR 40-footer with a diagonal-panel roof and Dreadnaught ends without small corrugations.

Pullman-Standard's PS-1

A revolution was brewing in the boxcar world in the late 1940s. Pullman-Standard, which had built a large number of AAR-design cars, had pioneered many concepts for welded construction.

Based on those techniques, in 1947 the company unveiled its welded PS-1 boxcar (fig. 1-13).

The PS-1 was based on the latest AAR design, with inside heights of 10'-5" or 10'-6" and a 9'-2" inside width. However, the PS-1 used ends and roofs of Pullman-Standard's own design. About the only notable differences among orders of PS-1 box-cars were the doors—with Youngstown, Superior (seven- and five-panel), and (after 1956) PS's own design—and the type of brake used. The PS-1 featured welded construction (although some riveted cars were built).

Key spotting features are the ends and roof. The ends consisted of several wide horizontal corrugations, without the intermediate corrugations of the Dreadnaught ends. Some features on the ends

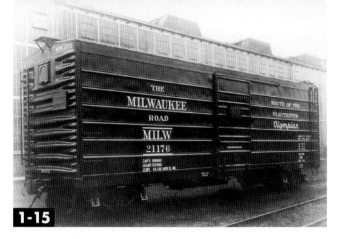

1-15

1-15 Milwaukee Road's rib-sided boxcars are tough to miss. This 1940-built car has straight side sills, the early rib pattern that extends to the end of the car, and the small end (lumber) doors used on some cars. *Milwaukee Road*

1-16

1-16 Baltimore & Ohio's wagon-top boxcars had side panels that wrapped around to the roof, with no seam between roof and side. Note the flat slab steel ends on this car, which was built in 1938. *Roy H. Hammond*

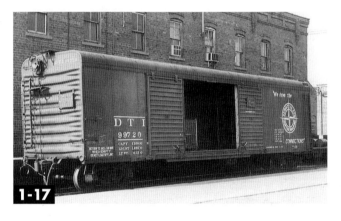

1-17

1-17 This DT&I car has a separate round roof. It is a former automobile-service boxcar. *Jim Hediger*

1-18

1-18 ACF built this 50-foot AAR car for Atlantic Coast Line in 1960. The car has improved Dreadnaught ends and a nine-foot Youngstown door. Note the roller-bearing trucks. *Atlantic Coast Line*

changed over time. Ends initially featured poling pockets in the lower corners, which were eventually eliminated. Until the mid-1950s, the top and bottom sections of the ends were riveted together (fig. 1-13); after that they were welded as fig. 1-14 shows.

Milwaukee Road's rib-sided cars

Another series of cars that deserve special mention are the welded rib-side boxcars built by the Milwaukee Road (fig. 1-15). These cars were notable for their welded construction when first built in 1937. Their distinctive appearance (with horizontal ribs) makes them stand out among other boxcars.

The railroad built more than 13,000 40- and 50-foot versions of these cars through 1949, and they could be found across the country. Early cars had ribs extending to the ends of the car sides; after 1944 the ribs stopped short of the sides. Early cars had Hutchins roofs and a 10'-6" interior height; later cars had Murphy panel roofs and were taller (10'-9"). The cars used a variety of doors, including Youngstown and Creco.

B&O wagon-top cars

Round-roof cars stand out in trains. There were two types: Baltimore & Ohio's cars (fig. 1-16) were known as "wagon-tops," because the side panels continued uninterrupted to the roof. This style is distinguished from round-roof cars, such as the Detroit, Toledo & Ironton boxcar in fig. 1-17.

On round-roof cars (also owned by the Pennsylvania RR, Northern Pacific, and others) the roof is a separate piece, with a seam between the sides and roof.

50-foot cars

Before World War II, most 50-foot cars were dedicated-purpose cars used for automobiles, lumber, and furniture. Not many were in general service. In fact, there was no AAR 50-foot standard until recommendations were issued in 1942.

The AAR cars of 1942 followed the general appearance of contemporary 40-foot cars. Plans allowed both single- and double-door ver-

11

1-19

1-20

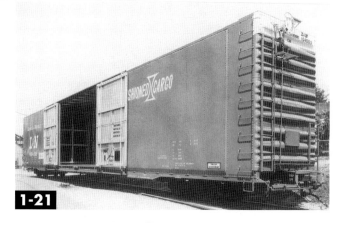

1-21

1-19 This 40-foot double-door car was built for automobile service in 1937. It has straight side sills and 4/5 Dreadnaught ends with square corner posts. It was in general service by the time of this 1959 photo. *Jeff Wilson collection*

1-20 This end-door, double-door boxcar was built in 1944 for auto service but, by the late 1960s, was in service hauling cereal out of Battle Creek, Michigan. *Jay Williams collection*

1-21 High-cube 86-foot cars were built specifically for carrying auto parts. Greenville was the major builder of these cars, including this 70-ton double-door car. *Louisville & Nashville*

sions, with 16-panel sides, tabs extending below the sides at the crossbearers as with the 40-foot cars (although many 50-foot cars were built with straight side sills or dropped sills), 5/5 Dreadnaught ends, panel roof, and door openings 6, 7, or 8 feet wide (fig. 1-18).

The 1950s saw a growing use of 50-foot cars, especially late in the decade. By this time, cars typically had 4/3/1 improved Dreadnaught ends, diagonal panel roofs, and welded sides. Single-door cars had wide doors—usually 8 or 9 feet.

Pullman-Standard's PS-1 production also shifted to a 50-foot design, with about 24,000 built through 1961, when the car's design changed (fig. 1-14).

Automobile cars

Through the 1950s boxcars provided the primary means of hauling new automobiles from assembly plants to their final destinations. Into the 1930s cars used for this purpose were primarily 40-foot wood single- or double-sheathed cars (single-sheathed 50-footers began appearing in the late 1920s) with double doors to make it easier to load and unload. Both full double-door and door-and-a-half designs were used.

Steel cars became more common in the 1930s, following basic ARA patterns but taller (fig. 1-19). Many cars used Evans auto racks, which allowed two levels of autos to be loaded in each car. These racks folded to the roof when not

in use, so the cars could be used in general service on return trips.

End doors were common on auto boxcars, especially into the 1930s (fig. 1-20). These were a mixed blessing: They made it easier to load autos into the cars but, since cars had doors on one end only, required a great deal of switching to get each boxcar into position for loading. The doors could also be maintenance headaches, especially after a car had been in service for a few years. Many of these cars eventually had their end doors welded shut.

Auto cars usually had special markings to indicate their service: generally they were stenciled "automobile" with a white stripe on the right-hand side doors.

Roofs and running boards

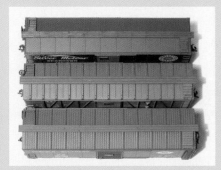

Early boxcar roofs (from the top) included flat seam (as on this HO Red Caboose X29 car), Hutchins (on an Accurail single-sheathed boxcar), and Viking (on a Red Caboose boxcar). *Jeff Wilson*

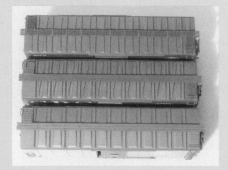

The most popular roofs from the late steam era through the 1960s were (from top) Pullman-Standard PS (on an HO Kadee PS-1 boxcar), diagonal panel (on an InterMountain AAR boxcar), and Murphy panel (on an InterMountain car). *Jeff Wilson*

Modern roof styles (from top) include the X-panel (on an Athearn HO SIECO boxcar), Pullman-Standard (on an Athearn PS 5,344 car), and diagonal panel (on an Accurail exterior-post 50-foot car). *Jeff Wilson*

Early boxcar roofs were made of wood covered with tarpaper and were prone to leaking and rotting. Metal roofs were the answer to both of these problems.

Roofs were applied in panels that were riveted together. Popular early designs (used into the 1930s) included flat panels of various types: the Viking, with its corrugated panels, and the Hutchins, which had a raised ridge in the middle of each panel.

The roof that would become most common was the Murphy panel roof. Introduced in 1932, it was used through the 1940s. It is characterized by raised seams joining the panels and raised sections in each panel.

An improvement on the Murphy was the diagonal-panel roof, which first appeared in 1948 and can still be found today. This design provided greater

strength for the roof.

As with its boxcar ends, Pullman-Standard came up with its own roof design with the introduction of the PS-1. At first glance, the roof looks like a Murphy, but the raised sections are narrower and taper in at the roof peak.

A modern roof design that debuted in the 1980s is the Stanray X-panel roof, which uses an X pattern instead of diagonal raised panels.

Roofs are typically made of galvanized steel. Most modern roofs are unpainted; many early cars had roofs painted the car color, or painted black (or coated with black roof cement). Peeling paint was common, as paint does not adhere well to galvanized metal.

Roofs are probably the most difficult car feature to identify, simply because most photos are taken from track level. If you're

concerned about accuracy on a model, track down the most reliable information possible, whether it be prototype photos, books, or magazine articles.

Running boards

Running boards (not roofwalks) on house cars were once made of wood, with three stringers down the center of the car and panels, called laterals, reaching to side ladders at two corners. These were generally painted the car color.

As they were exposed to the elements, running boards wore out quickly and required a great deal of maintenance. Thus new boards can often be found on older cars. Steel running boards came into use in the late 1930s and became mandatory on new equipment starting in 1945.

Steel running boards came in various patterns, the most common of

which was a rectangular grid. Some running boards had a diagonal grid, and others had perforated holes.

Running boards fell out of favor and were no longer required on new cars as of 1966 (although high-cube boxcars had been exempted from the requirement in late 1964). All running boards were to be removed from existing cars by 1974, although this date was extended to 1979.

As cars came in for servicing, their running boards were removed. At the same time, their ladders would be cut down to four rungs. Moving the brake wheel down was optional; if it was left in the high position, the ladders on that corner would remain in place.

Cars so modified are noticeable, as they generally kept their running board supports and ladder brackets.

1-22

1-22 Sixty-foot cars in auto parts service carry higher-density items such as castings. *David P. Morgan Library collection*

1-23

1-23 Thrall was second in 86-footer production. Note the recessed side sills on this four-door car built in 1966. *Thrall*

1-24

1-24 Pullman-Standard modified its PS-1 with a continuous-tapered sill in the early 1960s. This 50-foot car has the company's Hydroframe-60 cushioned draft gear and nine-foot-wide doors. *Milwaukee Road*

As auto racks began taking over auto service in the early 1960s, most double-door cars were reassigned to general service.

Auto parts boxcars

In the early 1960s the auto industry, looking for better and more efficient ways of shipping parts to assembly plants, worked with railroads and car builders to develop new freight cars. The goal was to build a boxcar that could handle a variety of parts, without custom-built loading racks or permanent interior fixtures.

The result was the massive 86-foot high-cube boxcar (fig. 1-21) and its little brother, the 60-foot auto parts car. The big cars were designed to carry low-density items, like stampings, while the 60-foot cars (fig. 1-22) carried heavier, higher-density parts like engines, transmissions, and other castings.

Large doors enable easy loading. The racks are unloaded by forklift and often taken directly to the assembly line. Various parts are made to fit in the standard-sized racks, thus the cars can carry racks holding any type of part.

The 89-foot cars first hit the rails in 1964, and more than 11,000 were built through 1978—mainly by Greenville, Thrall, and Pullman-Standard. The cars have either double doors (fig. 1-21) or four doors per side (fig. 1-23). Most of them are 70-ton cars, although some have 100-ton capacity. Greenville and Thrall cars both used Dreadnaught ends, while Pullman used a version of its PS-1 end. Thrall cars had a recessed straight side sill (fig. 1-23), while Greenville cars had a stepped/tapered sill (fig. 1-21).

The 60-foot cars were built by Pullman, ACF, and other manufacturers. Key spotting features include the type of end, side sills, and door style and number.

Modern boxcars

The 1960s saw changes in boxcar design and a move away from the general-purpose AAR boxcars that had dominated the market since before World War II. The overall trend toward larger cars, seen in dramatic fashion with auto-parts cars, would apply to general service and other boxcars, with larger door openings to accommodate forklifts. Pullman-Standard kept making its PS-1, but modified the design, as fig. 1-24 shows.

Specialized boxcars began appearing in larger numbers. One of these types was the short high-cube boxcar (fig. 1-25), a 40-foot cousin of the 86-foot auto-parts car. These shorter cars were often used in appliance service in dedicated service for specific shippers.

Another specialized boxcar was the all-door car, shown in fig. 1-26. These cars, built mainly by Thrall (as the Thrall-Door car) and Evans (as the Side Slider), facilitated loading and unloading of lumber and lumber products while protecting loads from the elements. The Evans cars are slightly longer (52'-5" IL) than the Thrall cars (50'-6" IL), and they differ slightly in design as well. The cars were built from the late 1960s into the 1970s.

Insulated boxcars with plug doors came into wide use through-

1-25

out the 1960s. Although they didn't have refrigeration equipment, many were classified as refrigerator cars (RBL). You can read about them in chapter 4.

The 1970s saw a shift in general-purpose boxcars to 50-foot exterior-post designs, typified by the Railbox car shown in fig. 1-27, with door openings to ten feet. Railbox provided a pool of cars to member railroads, and although it's tempting to lump them together, the company's cars had many differences as they were built by several companies.

Railbox cars were grouped in three basic classes: XF10 were plate B cars (fig. 1-27); XF20 were plate C cars; and XF30 cars were plate C cars (lettered ABOX) with combination plug/sliding

1-25 Short high-cube boxcars, such as this Pullman-Standard 40-footer, were often in appliance service. *Russ Goodwin*

doors (fig. 1-28). In addition, Railbox cars were built by several companies, including American Car and Foundry, Pacific Car & Foundry, Pullman-Standard, and FMC.

1-26

1-27

1-28

1-26 All-door boxcars, such as this Thrall-Door car, greatly simplified the process of loading and unloading lumber products compared with standard boxcars. *Jeff Wilson collection*

1-27 ACF built this Railbox class XF10 car, a Plate B car. Note the non-terminating ends: corrugated ends with the sides extending past the corrugations. *S.H. Mailer*

1-28 This former Railbox (ABOX) car has a combination plug door and sliding door. *Jeff Wilson*

1-29

1-30

1-29 The Pullman-Standard 5,344 cubic-foot boxcar was a common 1970s car. It had a flat roof that wrapped around the tops of the sides and posts, and non-terminating ends with closely spaced corrugations. *Jeff Wilson collection*

1-30 This FMC-built car has non-terminating ends, a peaked roof, and a different sill design than the ACF car in figure 26. *Jim Hediger*

Along with Railbox, several railroads bought 50-foot cars, including many short lines trying to capitalize on incentive-per diem (IPD) regulations that made investing in boxcars attractive.

Many details of Railbox (and other cars) varied among builders: the number, style, and spacing of side posts; side sill style; ends; roofs, whether flat or peaked, diagonal panel, X-panel, or PS pattern; and door style.

A number of manufacturers built cars during this time, including ACF (fig. 1-27), Pullman-Standard (fig. 1-29), FMC (fig. 1-30), Pacific Car & Foundry (fig. 1-31), Southern Iron & Equipment Co., or SIECO (fig. 1-32), and others.

A variation on these cars was the "waffle-side" car (fig. 1-33), with stamped protrusions in the steel between the exterior posts.

Most of the above companies produced variations of their cars to match either Plate B or Plate C clearances. Plate C cars could be taller (often just over 11 feet). Spotters should check the *Official Railway Equipment Register* for details on individual car dimensions and capacity to verify the specific model of a boxcar.

Boxcars today

The recession of the late 1970s and early '80s created an overabundance of boxcars. Along with a shift to container traffic, this caused boxcar production to drop substantially from the pace of the late 1970s, a trend that continues to the present. For example, in 1977 more than 450,000 boxcars were in service; that number dropped to 190,000 by 2003, placing boxcars behind covered hoppers, tank cars, and gondolas in number.

1-33 Waffle-side cars, like this 1973-built PS car, were built with many waffle pattern variations. This car has non-terminating ends and Pullman's modern sliding doors. *Jeff Wilson*

1-33

1-31

1-32

1-31 Pacific Car & Foundry built this Plate C car for Boston & Maine with a flat roof and non-terminating ends. The car has 14 posts per side. *Tom Nelligan*

1-32 This SIECO car has Dreadnaught ends, a Superior Door, and a straight sill with squared-off ends. Raritan River was one of many short lines to acquire large fleets of boxcars in the 1970s. *George Drury*

Many of the boxcars in service today are the 50-footers of the 1970s, many of which have been rebuilt and refurbished. Some earlier specialized cars, such as the 60- and 86-foot auto parts cars, also still ride the rails.

Although they've slipped in number, boxcars are still being built to replace older cars that are scrapped or no longer fit for paper loading, which requires clean, weather-tight cars (fig. 1-34). With their external-post design, new cars resemble the cars of the 1970s but are larger. Among the newest cars on the rails are TTX's TBOX cars (fig. 1-35), built by Gunderson and National Steel Car, which hearken back to the Railbox cars of the 1970s.

Paper and wood products, as well as food and other packaged products, are the most common loads for boxcars today.

1-34

1-34 Gunderson built several excess-height 60-foot cars in the 1990s, including this Norfolk Southern car. *Jeff Wilson*

1-35

1-35 Among the newest cars on the rails in 2005 are TTX's TBOX cars, such as this one built by National Steel Car. They're primarily used to transport paper and paper products. *Jeff Wilson*

Standard sliding doors

As steel cars grew in popularity, so did several major types of doors. The most popular was the Youngstown door, identified by its numerous horizontal ribs. Early Youngstown doors had a 5/7/5 rib pattern (fig. 1-9); this was changed to a 4/5/4 pattern in 1946 (fig. 1-12). Some doors had an alternate 3/5/5 pattern.

Another popular door type was the Superior, marked by its wide panels with fewer horizontal partitions (fig. 1-11). These doors originally had seven panels, with the spacing even on early cars and then uneven on later cars. Starting in 1952, five panel doors were frequently used.

Although rarer, Creco doors also deserve mention. Used mainly in

Creco doors were similar in appearance to Superior doors, but had three panels. *J. Parker Lamb Jr.*

Pullman's own PS doors had five raised panels, giving them a different appearance from Superior doors. *Pullman-Standard*

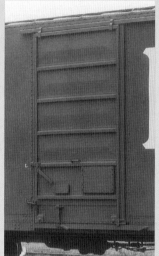

the 1920s and '30s, these look like a three-panel Superior door (see photo above left).

Most PS-1 boxcars had Youngstown or Superior doors, but many were also equipped with Pullman-Standard's proprietary PS door (shown above right). At first glance these look like Superior doors, but the panels are raised slightly, giving them a unique appearance.

Capacity and Gross Rail Load

It's common to refer to car size in terms of capacity, such as a 50-ton boxcar or a 70-ton boxcar. Each car's rated capacity was once stenciled on the car; this hasn't been required since the 1980s. Instead, the stenciled load limit indicates the maximum weight allowed for the load itself.

Gross Rail Load (GRL) is the maximum weight for the car allowed on the rail, figured by adding the car's light weight to the weight of the load. The current maximum GRL for unrestricted interchange of cars is 263,000 pounds (nominal 100-ton cars), although since the late 1990s most major

routes have allowed a GRL of 286,000 pounds (110-ton cars).

For example: Look at the TTX boxcar in fig. 34. It has a load limit of 207,600 pounds and its light weight is 78,400 pounds. By adding the two we find that this is a 286,000 GRL car.

For more on freight car data and lettering, see page 89.

Cushioning and load restraints

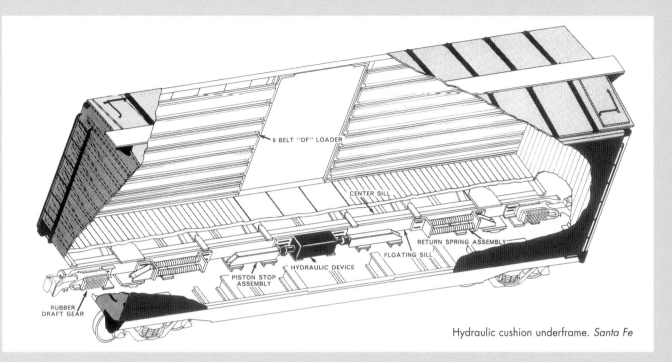

Hydraulic cushion underframe. *Santa Fe*

A problem that grew along with train size in the early 1900s was shifting or damage to loads caused by rough slack action or by hard coupling during switching. A solution to this was the cushion underframe, which became popular in the late 1940s and into the 1950s, first on boxcars, then other freight cars.

The drawing above shows how a cushion underframe system works. There are two types: Some have sprung draft gear that moves in and out; others, as depicted in the drawing, have a hydraulic device in the center sill that absorbs the shock instead of the car itself. The photo below left shows how the couplers on these cars extend from the car end. You can identify cushioned cars by these extended draft gear housings, and many cars have lettering indicating these devices (see figs. 1-22, 1-23, and 1-24).

Cushion underframes are found on many boxcars, auto-rack cars, piggyback flats, and coil cars. They are not used on cars carrying bulk products, such as tank cars, hoppers, and covered hoppers.

Load restraining devices are another common way of preventing damage to lading in boxcars and reefers. The illustration below right shows how these systems use moveable walls, partitions, belts, or other devices to hold loads securely in place inside the car. As with cushion underframes, lettering and stenciling on the car often indicate their presence.

The draft gear on cushion underframe cars extends from the body, allowing for spring travel as the coupler and draft gear travel in and out. *Linn Westcott*

Adjustable partitions and dividers are used to hold loads securely in place. *Evans Products*

USRA, ARA, AAR

You'll find frequent references to the USRA, ARA, and AAR throughout this book and in other freight car literature. The United States Railroad Administration (USRA) took control of the country's railroads during and just after World War I: from December 1917 to March 1920. During that time the USRA developed standard designs for several locomotives and freight cars. Several of these were quite successful, and many cars and locomotives were built to USRA or similar designs well after USRA control had ended. These USRA cars were common sights on railroads throughout the steam era.

The American Railroad Association (ARA, later the American Railway Association) was created in 1918 as a result of combining several railroad associations, including the Master Car Builders Association, which had been responsible for car standards. In 1934 the ARA was combined with other groups to form the Association of American Railroads (AAR), to which individual railroads belong. Among other responsibilities, the ARA and AAR have been responsible for research and development of various car types, as well as setting standards for safety and performance.

Boxcar classifications

The AAR car mechanical designation—often stenciled near the capacity data on a car and listed in the Railway Equipment Register—will tell you the type of service a boxcar is in. The most common classes include:

XM—General service boxcar

XAP—Boxcar with permanent racks for carrying auto parts

XMP, XP—Boxcar equipped for a specific commodity

XML, XL—Boxcar equipped with loading devices

XMR, XAR, XR—Boxcar with automobile loading racks or devices

The letter "I" appearing after the above codes indicates an insulated car

2-1 Tank cars have evolved from simple petroleum carriers into specialized cars that carry hundreds of petroleum, chemical, and food products. This modern car is carrying asphalt. *Jeff Wilson*

Tank cars have been part of railroading since the 1860s. Their numbers have grown since then to make them the second-most-common car type on the rails today, trailing only covered hoppers. By World War I, tank cars had taken on the basic look that they have today. However, they have evolved significantly, with larger tank sizes, welded instead of riveted construction, and the use of the tank itself for structural strength instead of a separate underframe.

Tank car uses have also changed dramatically. In the early 20th century, the primary job of tank cars was carrying refined oil products such as gasoline, motor oil, and lubricating oil. Today pipelines carry much of that traffic, but tank cars carry hundreds of products, including petroleum, solvents, food products, sulfur, clay slurry, acids, ethanol and methanol, and many other chemicals (fig. 2-1).

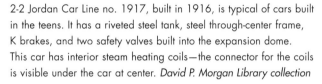

2-2 Jordan Car Line no. 1917, built in 1916, is typical of cars built in the teens. It has a riveted steel tank, steel through-center frame, K brakes, and two safety valves built into the expansion dome. This car has interior steam heating coils—the connector for the coils is visible under the car at center. *David P. Morgan Library collection*

2-4 The X-3, a non-pressure, uninsulated ICC103 tank car, was the mainstay of the UTLX fleet from the 1930s through the 1960s. This car, built by ACF, has a 12,000-gallon capacity; X-3s come in other sizes as well. *Richard H. Hendrickson*

Regardless of the era or region you model, tank cars should be a vital part of your traffic mix. Understanding the differences among the various types will help you more accurately model both the cars and operations.

Early tank cars

Figure 2-2 shows a state-of-the-art car for the World War I era. It follows the basic construction pattern of cars built into the 1950s. The main feature is the riveted steel tank, with an 8,000-gallon

size the most common into the 1920s, and 10,000-gallon tanks becoming more widely used in the 1930s and later.

Figure 2-3 illustrates the major components of a typical riveted tank car. Through the 1950s, tank cars had steel underframes, with the tank resting in saddles above each truck. A series of steel bands passed over the tank to secure it to the frame. Running boards (wood into the 1940s; steel thereafter) were located around the car, including the sides and ends.

Large domes were prominent features on tank cars through the 1950s. These allowed for expansion of the liquid. Safety valves allowed venting of internal pressure. These valves were outside the dome on early cars (as in fig. 2-2), and built into the dome on later cars.

Tank cars were (and still are) either insulated or uninsulated, and tanks could have either internal (inside the tank itself) or external (outside the tank but covered by the outer shell) steam heating coils.

DOME PLATFORM — SAFETY VALVE — MANWAY COVER — EXPANSION DOME — TANK HEAD — DOME LADDER — TANK BANDS — HANDRAIL — HANDRAIL BRACKET — P.S.P.X. 909 CAPY 10076 GALS — PLACARD HOLDER — BRAKE WHEEL — PLACARD HOLDER — UNDERFRAME — RUNNING BOARD — TANK BAND ANCHOR — RIVETED SEAM — TANK CRADLE (SADDLE)

2-5

2-6

2-7

2-5 Texaco no. 6811, built in 1929, is a 10,000-gallon ACF Type 21 tank car. It was one of the most popular tank cars built through the 1920s. Type 21s are shorter with larger-diameter tanks than the later Type 27s. *Frank Taylor*

2-6 Shippers no. 6028 is a 6,000-gallon ACF Type 27 car. Type 27 cars were built from the late 1920s through the 1940s, with 8,000- and 10,000-gallon tanks common. *Roy C. Meates*

2-7 This ICC103 car was built by General American in 1930. Note the visible ends of the bolsters and the different style of saddle compared to the ACF-built cars. *Rail Data Services collection*

Uninsulated cars without heating coils are used for loads not affected by outside temperatures and ones that flow freely in normal temperatures. Cars carrying thick, heavy liquids that don't flow readily ride in insulated cars with heating coils. These include products such as heavy oils, asphalt, and corn syrup.

Ownership and builders

Many companies have built tank cars over the years. American Car & Foundry (ACF) has been a significant builder, supplying its own Shippers' Car Line as well as cars for Union Tank Line (UTLX) and many other companies. In 1955 Union, which until that time had designed its own cars but had other companies build them, bought Graver Tank Co., of East Chicago, Ind., and began building its own cars. Another major builder was General American (GATX), which built thousands of tank cars for its own GATX fleet as well as for other owners through 1984. Current tank car builders include ACF, Union, and Trinity.

Most tank cars were (and still are) privately owned. Railroads were reluctant to build cars for specialized service, leaving it to the shippers and leasing companies to supply the cars. Railroads do own some tank cars, but these are non-revenue cars used for fuel and other company service.

Currently the largest tank car owners include UTLX and its Canadian subsidiary, Procor, as well as GATX, both of which lease cars to many different companies. Other major owners over the years have included ACF's Shippers' Car Line (SHPX) and North American, now part of GE Railcar Services. Many petroleum and chemical companies have operated their own large fleets of cars over the years.

Tank cars are classified by type, which specify the kinds of products they are allowed to carry. The sidebar on page 30 explains tank car classifications, from the early American Railway Association (ARA) standards through the current Department of Transportation (DOT) classes.

Common early designs and spotting features

Over the years tank cars have been built to many different designs, some based on builders' standards, some on users' specifications. The most visible variations include the tank length and diameter, along with the dome and top fittings. Underframes also vary widely in design. A USRA tank car design was developed, but no cars were built to the design—either during or after USRA control.

Figure 2-4 shows a Union Tank Line X-3 car, which—because of the sheer number of cars operated by UTLX—was the most common tank car in service from the 1930s through the 1960s. This car was designed by Union, but since Union didn't build its own tanks at the time, it was built by several manufacturers. The X-3 was built with several sizes of tanks.

The other most common early tank car designs were ACF's Type 21 (fig. 2-5) and Type 27 (fig. 2-6) cars. Type 21 cars (so named because they were designed in

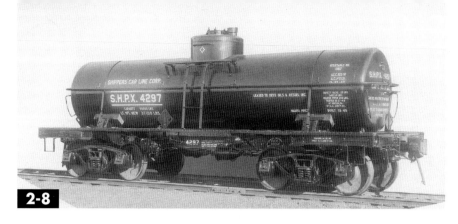

2-8

2-8 This 4,000-gallon welded (ICC103W) car, built by ACF in 1949, was designed for hauling vegetable oil. Note how small the tank appears compared to the trucks.
American Car & Foundry

War II, although 10,000-gallon cars were built in the 1920s and later (and 12,000-gallon tanks in the 1930s). In addition, some cars were (and are) built with much smaller tanks to haul small lots or heavier (denser) products. Figure 2-8 shows one example.

Cars with multiple compartments were also common through the 1950s (fig. 2-9). These were often used to ship multiple products (different grades of gasoline to a fuel distributor, for example). A detail to note is that the expansion dome for each compartment is smaller than the dome on a single-compartment car, because each compartment is smaller.

Many early riveted tank cars stayed in service into the 1960s and even into the '70s. Spotting features on these early tank cars include the tank length and diameter, rivet seams (tank courses)

1921), built through the 1920s, can be identified by their shorter, larger-diameter tanks compared with Type 27s, which were built from the late 1920s through the 1940s. They also had different styles of underframes and tank saddles. Each car was available with several sizes of tanks, with

8,000- and 10,000-gallon capacities the most common.

Figure 2-7 shows a car of the same period built by General American. Note the exposed ends of the bolsters and the different frame style compared with the ACF cars.

Tanks with 8,000-gallon capacities were common through World

2-9

2-9 Many early tank cars had multiple compartments, such as this ICC103 riveted car built by Pressed Steel Car Co. for Deep-Rock in 1930. Note the rivet lines showing the two bulkheads separating each compartment. The car's K brakes are quite visible.
Pressed Steel Car Co.

2-10 The first ICC103W (welded) cars, built starting in the late 1940s, looked much like earlier ICC103 cars, just without the rivets. Some were built quite late—this ACF diesel fuel car was built in 1957, after Union had introduced frameless/domeless cars.
Mike Small

2-10

and patterns, style of tank saddles, number and type of tank bands, underframe style, and styles of ladders and grab irons.

Through the 1940s most tank cars were riveted, though forge-welded tanks began appearing in the mid-1920s, almost exclusively for high-pressure cars. Fusion welding became more common in the 1940s, first on pressure cars, then on no n-pressure cars, and by the late 1940s welded cars had become standard (fig. 2-10). The first welded non-pressure cars looked much the same as the earlier riveted cars, but without the rivets. Not many welded non-pressure cars of this style were built, however, because of the surplus of tank cars after World War II and the dropoff in shipping refined petroleum products by rail due to the petroleum industry's growing pipeline network.

Pressure and insulated cars

The growth in use of propane and butane (now usually blended as liquefied petroleum gas, or LPG) for home heating in the 1930s led to a dramatic increase in the number of high-pressure tank cars, especially following World War II. Other products carried in these cars include anhydrous ammonia, chlorine, and methyl chloride.

Figure 2-11 shows a typical early pressure tank car. These cars had welded tanks, though the outside jacketing was sometimes riveted. They were insulated to protect the lading in case of an accident or external fire. The key spotting feature of early cars is the lack of a large expansion dome. Instead, the small housing atop the tank contained valves and fittings for loading and unloading.

Instead of going around the outside jacket, the tank bands pass through the outer jacket and through the insulation to wrap around the tank itself. Insulated cars built through the 1950s typically had a lip around the rim at each end. Into the 1950s these ICC-105 cars typically had capacities of 10,500 or 11,000 gallons.

Modern frameless cars

The modern tank car era began in 1954 when Union introduced its frameless tank car (fig. 2-12). Union called it the HD car, for "hot dog," because that's what it resembled. The car was revolutionary because it relied on the tank itself for strength and had no underframe. The idea of a frameless car actually dated back to the turn of the century, but it took Union's introduction of the HD car for railroads to buy into the idea.

The HD car also debuted without running boards, though the

2-11

2-11 ACF built this ICC105A300W car for Dow in 1949 to carry methlyl chloride. Similar cars were used for LPG, anhydrous ammonia, and chlorine. Note the lip around the end where the jacket overlaps the end. Pressure cars are often insulated but lack expansion domes, bottom outlets, or heating coils. *American Car & Foundry*

2-12

2-12 Union Tank Line ushered in the era of the modern tank car in 1954 with its frameless HD car. The car also did away with expansion domes. *Union Tank Car Co.*

2-18

2-19

2-20

2-18 This is an insulated non-pressure DOT111A100W3 car used for carrying asphalt (note the "HOT" placard). *Jeff Wilson*

2-19, This AAR 211A100W1 is a general-purpose uninsulated car. The "2" indicates a car for non-hazardous commodities; otherwise it conforms to DOT111 specifications. *Jeff Wilson*

2-20 Funnel-Flow and similar cars have ends that slope toward the middle of the car. This insulated car is in molten sulfur service. *Jeff Wilson*

or other sealed products), loading valves, and a cap for the bottom unloading valve. Many non-pressure cars have bottom unloading valves (with the exception of acid cars), and a connec- tor for heating line if the car is so equipped.

These cars come in a variety of styles and configurations for carrying various products. Figure 2-17 shows a modern non-pres- sure car designed for carrying corn syrup, and fig. 2-18 shows an insulated non-pressure car used to haul asphalt.

Figure 2-19 shows a general-purpose uninsulated car. Note

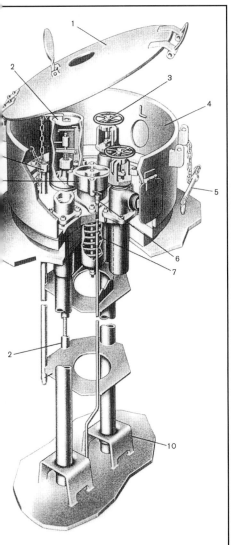

1	MANWAY BONNET COVER
2	GAUGING DEVICE ASSEMBLY
3	ANGLE VALVE
4	MANWAY BONNET
5	SEAL PIN
6	SMALL ANGLE VALVE
7	CHECK VALVES
8	THERMOMETER WELL
9	SAFETY VALVE
10	PIPE GUIDE

GATX Inc.

2-21

2-22

2-23

2-22 Pressure cars for chlorine are smaller than LPG cars. This DOT105J500W car has modern matrix stenciling as well as the appropriate placards for chlorine. *Jeff Wilson*

2-23 The biggest tank cars today are the 30,000- to 33,500-gallon cars carrying LPG and anhydrous ammonia. *Jeff Wilson*

how the tank saddles are welded directly to the tank, compared to the insulated car in fig. 2-18, where the saddle passes through the exterior sheathing (and has a plate above it to keep water out).

Union introduced the Funnel-Flow car in 1967 (fig. 2-20). These cars have bodies that slope down toward the middle from each end, giving them a swaybacked look. These non-pressure cars are designed to make unloading easier by routing liquid to the middle of the car. This design can be found in several car sizes, and with varying slope angles. Other manufacturers are now building their own versions of this design.

Pressure cars have a single housing on top of the tank to cover fittings (fig. 2-21). These cars don't have bottom outlets or heating coil connectors. Figure 2-22 shows a modern car designed for carrying chlorine.

The biggest tank cars in service today are pressure cars carrying anhydrous ammonia and liquefied petroleum gas (fig. 2-23), both of which are comparatively light. These cars have a capacity of 33,000 gallons and are 65 feet long.

All tank cars built in 1971 and later must have shelf-style couplers (see chapter 8). These are designed to keep couplers aligned in case of a derailment, preventing the coupler from an adjoining car from separating and then puncturing the end of a tank.

Spotting features and variations on modern tank cars include the styles of the various roof details; end shape; style of tank saddle; style of side safety railing supports; style of side ladder; location of brake gear; and style of top platform and railing.

You can often tell what a tank car is carrying by the stenciling found on its sides. See the sidebar on page 31 for more information.

Tank car classifications

Tank cars are classified by their construction. In 1917, the Master Car Builders Association (MCB), one of the predecessors to the American Railway Association, updated standards for tank cars. These became ARA classes in 1919. They were:

ARA I—Cars not built to the 1910 standard

ARA II—Cars built to the 1910 standard

ARA III—Cars built to the more stringent 1917 standard

ARA IV—Insulated, for flammable volatile liquids

ARA V—Insulated (pressure) heavy-duty for dangerous liquids

(Class I-IV cars were riveted; Class V were forge welded)

Cars built to the 1917 standards kept their ARA ratings, even after later ICC standards were adopted. All ARA tank cars were to be removed from service by January 1, 1975.

In 1927 the Interstate Commerce Commission redefined tank car classifications, which applied to cars built after that point. Classification numbers included the basic car type, special characteristics (letter suffixes), and, for pressure cars, psi rating. These would be modified over the years, but most remained in force through the 1960s.

The most common types were 103 (general purpose, non-pressure, with dome), 104 (insulated, non-pressure, with dome), and 105 (insulated, pressure, welded). Common letter suffixes included A (acid cars), AL (aluminum tank), C (corrosion-resistant), and W (welded).

Thus an ICC-103 car was an uninsulated, non-pressure, riveted general-purpose car, and an ICC-105W300 car was a welded, insulated high-pressure car tested at 300 psi.

The Department of Transportation assumed the role of issuing tank car classes in 1967. Common classes include DOT103 (non-pressure, can be insulated or uninsulated), DOT104 (non-pressure, insulated, carbon steel tank with dome), DOT105A (insulated pressure car), and DOT111A (non-pressure domeless car, insulated or uninsulated). The "A" after the number class has no significance. Special materials are indicated after the test pressure: CS (carbon steel), AA (aluminum alloy), N (nickel), AS (alloy (stainless) steel), and CSEL (carbon steel rubber or elastomer lined). A suffix W indicates a fusion welded tank, and F stands for a forge-welded tank.

Thus, a DOT-105A500W car is an insulated pressure car with a test pressure of 500 psi and a fusion-welded tank. Other letters (for example, the 105J chlorine car in fig. 2-22) indicate reinforced head shields and other features.

More information

For more information on tank cars, see the book *Tank Cars, American Car & Foundry Co., 1865 to 1955*, by Edward S. Kaminski (Signature Press, 2003). The book includes a history of tank cars with information on construction and use. Another handy reference is the *GATX Tank Car Manual* (General American Transportation Corp., 1972), which includes DOT and AAR data for commodities along with drawings of various tank equipment.

Tank car lettering

DOT 111A100W3

UTLX 67069	STATION STENCIL	QUALIFIED	DUE
TANK QUALIFICATION	UTCL	2002	2012
THICKNESS TEST	UTCL	2002	2012
SERVICE EQUIPMENT	UTCL	2002	2012
PRD: VALVE 75 PSI	UTCL	2004	2012
LINING			
88.B.2 INSPECTION	UTCL	2002	2012
STUB SILL INSPECTION	UTCL	2002	2012

HEATER PIPES 250 PSI
TESTED 2003 UTCX

ABD ABDW	LUB NO
BLT - 9-84	

SRR
PAINTED 4-02
UTC-L
SYSTEM 72
GAUGE TABLE NO. 2402

2 INCH HF COMP SHOE

Jeff Wilson

You can find a great deal of information on tank car types and loads in the lettering. Shortly after World War I, car class labeling (ARA, AAR, ICC, DOT) was required on the tank, usually on the right side. The builder's initials were also located here, along with other information, including pressure-test dates.

Today, tank cars carry this information in a tank qualification matrix as shown above. These began appearing around 2000.

Tank cars have hazardous-material placard holders on each end and side. Placards on loaded cars are color-coded based on lading, with numerical codes that identify the specific product in the car (for example, 1017 for chlorine and 1075 for LPG). You can see these in figs. 2-18, 2-20, 2-22, and 2-23.

Cars are often stenciled with their lading; examples are shown in figs. 2-8, 2-11, 2-17, 2-20, 2-22, and 2-23.

THREE

3-1 Covered hoppers revolutionized the handling of grain and many other dry bulk products. Covered hoppers have rooftop hatches and bottom outlets for easily loading and unloading lading. This modern cylindrical covered hopper is in potash service.
Brian C. Nickle

The covered hopper has grown from an experimental car in the early 1930s to the most common car type in service today. Covered hoppers haul almost any dry bulk commodity, including grain, fertilizer, plastic pellets, potash, lime, cement, sand, flour, sugar, carbon black, various chemicals, and many other products (fig. 3-1).

Grain and cement industries are popular subjects on model railroads, and modeling them accurately requires an understanding of the differences among various types of covered hoppers. We'll start with a history of the car type, then look at the various spotting features and show how covered hoppers have evolved over the years.

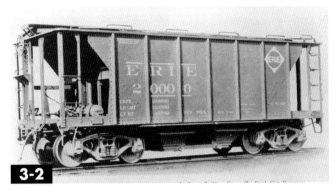

3-2

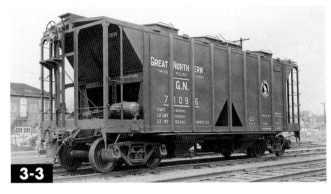

3-3

3-4

3-2 Among the first purpose-built covered hoppers was Erie 20000, a 50-ton, two-bay cement hopper built in 1934 by Greenville Steel Car Co. *Greenville Steel Car Co.*

3-3 Built by ACF from about 1940 through 1953, this car had eight roof hatches and a 1,958-cubic-foot capacity, the most common size for early two-bay cars. *ACF Incorporated*

3-4 The new PS-2 from Pullman-Standard featured welded construction, a staggered post pattern, round roof hatches, new roof design (overhanging the sides) and a unique end design. This 2,003-cubic-foot car was built in 1954. *Pullman-Standard*

Early covered hoppers

Bulk products not affected by the elements—such as coal and gravel—have been shipped in open-top hoppers or gondolas since the early days of railroading. Into the 1930s, moisture-sensitive bulk products like grain and flour were usually shipped in bags or other containers placed in boxcars, or they were loaded in the boxcars in bulk.

Bagging, loading, and unloading products this way was cumbersome and time-consuming, and railroads and shippers both began looking for ways to haul bulk products more efficiently. The answer was to add a roof with tight-sealing hatches to a hopper car and redesign the bottom outlets.

American Car and Foundry (ACF) began building covered hoppers in 1932, and Pullman-Standard, Greenville, and others soon followed. The first cars were largely for heavy, dense products such as cement, lime, and sand. These 50- and 70-ton cars generally had capacities from 1,700 to

1,900 cubic feet. Figure 3-2 shows an early car built by Greenville for the Erie RR in 1934. Some other early cars were larger, designed for hauling carbon black.

As more and more covered hoppers were built, standard designs and sizes began emerging. The most common size for a car became 1,958 cubic feet, with a 70-ton capacity. Cars generally had riveted steel construction (although some were welded), with two unloading bays, and square roof hatches (either 30" or 36" square). Figure 3-3 shows a common ACF car, built in 1951 and reflecting a style common from around 1940 through about 1953. Many early cars such as this one had triangular openings in the sides between the bays; later cars lacked these openings. Pullman-Standard built many cars to a similar design, but with side braces that were beveled on top.

Pullman-Standard revised and improved the covered hopper with the introduction of its PS-2. Pullman had been building cov-

ered hoppers for many years, and—as with its PS-1 boxcar—wanted to build cars using its own components in a standard design.

Introduced in 1952, the PS-2 covered hopper featured all-welded construction (see fig. 3-4). Cars had circular (30" diameter) roof hatches, and the roof extended over the sides. These 2,003-cubic-foot, 70-ton cars had a distinctive look, with a 4/4 side brace pattern.

Car size increases

By the mid-1950s, covered hoppers were no longer rare, but they hadn't yet been used much to haul the commodity that would eventually be transported primarily by them—grain. At the time, railroads were reluctant to invest in single-purpose cars, especially for a seasonal product. However, boxcars—although plentiful and relatively easy to convert to grain service—were labor-intensive to load and unload, and their relatively small capacity meant it took a lot of them to haul a bumper crop.

3-5 The first true grain covered hoppers were the three-bay 3,219-cubic-foot PS-2s (shown here) and the earlier and similar—but slightly shorter and narrower—2,893-cubic-foot cars. These 70-ton cars shared common details with their shorter two-bay cousins. *Pullman-Standard*

3-6 One of the most popular grain cars of the 1960s was the 100-ton, 4,427-cubic-foot PS-2. This car, built in 1964, has the tall sides of cars built until 1966. *Pullman-Standard*

3-7 Later versions of the 4,427-cubic-foot PS-2 had 13 side posts and smaller side sheets. These are known as "high-side" cars. Note how the bottom of the side is taller than the older 4,427-cubic-foot car at right. *Jeff Wilson*

A car that would help solve the problem was Pullman's 2,893-cubic-foot PS-2, introduced in 1953. (A later version of this car is shown in fig. 3-5.) These three-bay cars had a capacity of 70 tons, compared with 50 tons for most other boxcars of the time. Their increased capacity made them ideal for lighter-density products such as grain, feed, sugar, and potash. Plastic pellets—a fairly new product in the 1950s—could also be shipped in these larger covered hoppers.

Thousands of these cars would be built by PS (along with copies built by Greenville Steel Car and others) into the early 1960s. Key spotting features are the 4-3-4 side bracing pattern and a low profile compared with the more modern 100-ton cars.

This basic three-bay car grew over the years, to 3,219 cubic feet (thanks to a 5" increase in height and a 6" increase in width) in 1958 (fig. 3-5) and to 3,500 cubic feet in 1960. These latter cars were noticeably taller (by about a foot) than the 2,893-cubic-foot cars, but the basic design remained the same. These cars still had the round roof hatches, paired along the sides of the roof, with the running board down the center of the car.

The trend continued toward bigger cars with higher weight limits along with a corresponding increase in cubic capacity. In 1962, a 4,000-cubic-foot PS-2 debuted with a 190,000-pound capacity. The car still has the 4-3-4 rib pattern and three bays of earlier cars, but it was substantially larger than the earlier 2,893-cubic-foot and similar cars. It also introduced a center trough loading hatch, developed to make grain loading faster and easier (see the sidebar on page 39).

The 100-ton, 4,427-cubic-foot PS-2 (fig. 3-6), introduced in 1964, was among the most popular early grain haulers, with more than 23,000 purchased by several railroads and private owners. Later versions of this car had 13 evenly spaced side braces instead of the 4-3-4 rib pattern of earlier cars.

In 1966, the 4,427-cubic-foot model had its sides revised so that the bottom portion of the hopper bays were exposed (fig. 3-7). These later cars became known as "high-side" cars; earlier cars were termed "low-side" cars.

Among the most popular grain cars of the late 1960s and 1970s were the PS-2 4,740-cubic-foot

3-8 The 4,740-cubic-foot PS-2s, such as this former Union Equity car, can be spotted by their 16 evenly spaced side posts. *Jeff Wilson*

3-9 The best-selling PS-2 of all time was the 4,750-cubic-foot car, distinguished from others by its 18 side posts. This Milwaukee Road car was built in 1973. *David P. Morgan Library collection*

3-10 Later versions of the 4,750-cubic-foot PS-2, such as this former Peavey car built in 1979, have an angle piece across the middle 12 side posts. *Jeff Wilson*

(fig. 3-8), introduced in 1966, and 4,750-cubic-foot (fig. 3-9). The 4,740-cubic-foot cars can be distinguished by their 16 side braces; the 4,750-cubic-foot cars (the best-selling PS-2) have 18 braces. Later versions of the PS-2 4,750-cubic-foot car have a long, angled strip above the middle 12 braces as fig. 3-10 shows.

ACF Center Flow cars

As covered hoppers got larger in the early 1960s, ACF came up with a revolutionary design: the Center Flow car (see fig. 3-11). The first Center Flow cars looked almost

like tank cars, but their cross section was an inverted-pear shape. The goal of the design was to enable the cars to be loaded and emptied more readily than a conventional covered hopper with vertical sides.

ACF's cylindrical cars were built to a number of different sizes, with round or trough-style roof hatches and from three to six bays. The first cars in 1962 were 3,960-cubic-foot cars with three compartments and six bays, and 3,510-cubic-foot cars with three bays (both types had round 30" hatches). They had capacities

from 70 to 90 tons. Later cylindrical cars built into the mid-1960s were 3,700-cubic-foot, 100-ton cars with trough hatches.

As with the PS and other covered hoppers, Center Flows kept getting larger. To increase cubic capacity, ACF modified the design by flattening the car's sides more and extending the ends of the hopper bays.

Figure 3-12 shows a 4,650-cubic-foot Center Flow car, introduced in 1964. This car and the PS-2 4,750-cubic-foot hopper were the most popular grain cars of the 1960s and 1970s. ACF called these "high cubes" (referring to the cubic capacity). More than 15,000 4,650-cubic-foot cars would eventually be built.

ACF also made a 4,600-cubic-foot Center Flow car, which was popular for hauling grain. These cars, introduced in 1965, were longer but lower than the 4,650-cubic-foot cars, accommodating the tighter Plate B clearance (see explanation on page 16) desired by some railroads.

Figure 3-13, showing a later version of the 4,600-cubic-foot car, illustrates a spotting feature that differentiates early and late Center Flow cars. Center Flow cars built until August 1971 have a single long horizontal stiffener along the side, with a smooth area

3-11 ACF's first Center Flow cars were cylindrical, with an inverted pear shape cross section. This 3,960-cubic-foot car has six round roof hatches. *ACF Industries*

3-12 In 1964, ACF began offering a Center Flow that looked more like a conventional covered hopper. The three-bay 4,650-cubic-foot version, like this New York Central car, would be among the most popular grain cars of the 1960s. *ACF Industries*

3-13 The 4,600-cubic-foot Center Flow was longer and shorter than the 4,650-cubic-foot car. This is a late Center Flow (built in 1977), identified by the pair of ribs along the top where the roof meets the sides. *Jim Hediger*

3-11

3-12

3-13

where the side meets the roof (see fig. 3-12). Cars built later don't have this horizontal piece, but do have a pair of thin horizontal ribs where the side meets the roof.

Other types of Center Flow cars included the 4,460, which was the same length as the 4,650 but not as tall, and the 4,700, which had shallower end sheets. Always check the *Official Railway Equipment Register* if in doubt about a particular car type.

ACF also makes shorter versions of Center Flow cars for cement and other high-density products, as fig. 3-14 shows. It has the early single horizontal stiffener along the side, as well as a high brake wheel, marking it as an early car.

Other spotting features of Center Flow cars involve the number of pieces of steel used to form the sides (the seams are often visible in photos). On 4,650-cubic-foot cars, the sides were originally made of two pieces; later cars used four. In 1972 ACF went to six-foot-wide pieces for all cars, so 4,650-cubic-foot cars have six panels (plus end sheets); 4,600-cubic-foot cars have seven. These cars originally had 13 running board supports on each side, but after 1975, they had nine supports.

Through 1968, ACF cars had truck-mounted brake cylinders. After that, the cylinders could be truck- or body-mounted.

A late-1970s variation of the Center Flow is the Pressureaide

(see fig. 3-15). These cars, designed for flour and other powdered commodities, are pressure-differential cars that use an internal pressure of 15 psi to force lading out of the car. They look like standard Center Flow cars, but with additional piping along the unloading bays and with an extra-wide stiffener at the top of the sides.

Plastic pellet and chemical hoppers

Grain products will hit the 100-ton weight limit in cars of around 4,800 cubic feet, but other commodities—notably plastic pellets, carbon black, and some dry chemicals—are less dense and thus can fill a larger capacity car before they hit the car's weight limit.

3-14

3-15

3-16

3-14 Several two-bay Center Flow cars have been made for carrying cement, lime, and other dense materials. This Burlington Northern Santa Fe car has a 3,200-cubic-foot capacity and elongated roof hatches. The high-mounted brake wheel marks it as an early (1966 or before) car. *Jeff Wilson*

3-15 Pressureaide cars are Center Flow cars that use internal pressure to force the lading out of the car. Note the extra piping along the four bays of this 5,000-cubic-foot car. *ACF Industries*

3-16 This 5,250-cubic-foot Center Flow car is designed for carrying plastic pellets. Built in 1965, it has four pneumatic outlets and small round roof hatches. *ACF Industries*

3-17

3-17 Early single-bay Airslides had boxy ends with diagonal bracing from the bottom of the ends to the top of the body. This car was built in 1958. *Jim Hediger*

To more efficiently carry these commodities, companies began building jumbo covered hoppers with capacities of 5,000 cubic feet and larger. Figure 3-16 shows a 5,250-cubic-foot Center Flow car built in 1965. Typical of plastics cars from other manufacturers, it has individual round roof hatches and four pneumatic unloading outlets. (See the sidebar on page 42 for information on different types of outlets). The later 5,701-cubic-foot Center Flow was among the most popular cars for plastics service.

A spotting feature of all covered hoppers is the brake wheel location. Brake wheels on cars built until September 1966 were mounted high, as on the ACF two-bay car in fig. 3-14. Cars built after that date had brake wheels mounted low, as on the car in fig. 3-13. Older cars sometimes had their brake wheels relocated during rebuilding.

Airslide covered hoppers

Another covered hopper that deserves special mention is the Airslide, introduced in 1954 by General American Transportation Corp. (fig. 3-17). Airslides are specialized covered hoppers designed for carrying powdered or granulated commodities.

What sets an Airslide apart is its finely perforated fabric lining. When the car is unloaded, air flows through the lining, effectively "liquifying" the lading, enabling it to flow out completely and efficiently. Airslide cars are commonly used for flour and sugar, and have also been used for grain and other products.

Airslides were built in several sizes over the years, from small single-bay cars to larger double-bay cars (fig. 3-18). Early single-bay cars had open "porches" over each truck, with angled braces running from the end sills to the top of the end (see fig. 3-17). Cars

built in 1965 and later eliminated the angle braces and had triangular gussets added at the top of these openings, making the car look more like a conventional covered hopper from the side (see fig. 3-19). The vertical side braces also changed in shape and style over the years.

Other modern covered hoppers

Although Pullman-Standard and ACF captured the lion's share of covered hopper production through the 1970s, other companies also built large numbers of covered hoppers.

FMC Corp. built almost seven thousand 4,700-cubic-foot cars (fig. 3-20) between 1971 and 1981. At first glance, these look like PS cars, but they can be distinguished by their tall sides and the horizontal groove that runs down the center of the side. FMC also made a 4,692-cubic-foot car that looks like the 4,700-cubic-foot car,

3-18 Long two-bay Airslides are boxy, without the open end bracing of other covered hoppers. *Jeff Wilson*

3-19 Later single-bay Airslides had diagonal gussets at the top of the sides at the ends. This Union Pacific car was built in 1966, just before low brake wheels became mandatory. *Jim Hediger*

3-20 This 4,700-cubic-foot car was built by FMC. These tall-sided cars have a horizontal groove down the middle of each side. FMC also built a similar 4,692-cubic-foot car that had a staggered post pattern. *Jeff Wilson*

but has a 5/4/5 side brace pattern.

Thrall and Trinity both turned out large numbers of 4,750-cubic-foot cars that resemble PS cars. Figure 3-21 shows one such car built by Thrall. Spotting features include side braces (style and number) and the design of the end bracing, steps, and ladder.

Thrall also turned out many

Roof hatches

Most covered hoppers built through 1960 were equipped with round individual roof hatches for loading, as fig. 3-4 shows. Square on early cars and round starting in the 1950s, these hatches can be found in different sizes.

Individual hatches can be made to seal tightly and so do a good job of protecting the load. However, it can take a long time to load a car, as the loading spout must be positioned over each hatch in turn.

The solution was to equip cars with long, trough-style hatches on cars designed for grain and other commodities that don't need an air-tight seal, as the photo at right shows. Among the variations are multiple long openings or a single continuous long opening with four overlapping lids.

These hatches greatly speed loading and have been used almost exclusively on grain cars since the early 1960s. Cars designed for plastic pellets, powders (such as cement), food products, and many chemicals still have round hatches that can be sealed tightly. Hatches on plastic pellet cars are typically 20" (fig. 3-15), with 30" hatches on cars for food products and chemicals.

Early covered hoppers with individual hatches had center-mounted running

The move to continuous trough openings in the early 1960s made it much easier to load grain cars. The hatches are flipped open to the left. *Chessie System*

boards with the hatches near the sides. When center-mounted trough-style hatches came into use, the running boards were moved to both sides and ends and were open in the middle.

Modern cars with individual hatches can be found with either style of running board, depending on whether the hatches are mounted along the roof center line or along the sides.

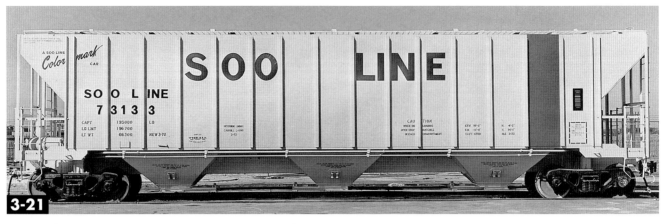

3-21

3-22

3-21 This 4,750-cubic-foot car looks like a PS-2, but it was built by Thrall in 1972. The shape and pattern of the side posts are different, as is the end bracing. *Thrall*

3-22 Another Thrall design resembles a Center Flow car. The shape of the ends, the width of the side sheets, and the roof/side joint of this 5,150-cubic-foot Thrall car are all different from ACF's design. *Jeff Wilson*

3-23 An early high-capacity grain car, built in the mid-1990s, is the 5,400-cubic-foot Johnstown-America Grainporter. These aluminum cars can be spotted by their slab sides. *Jeff Wilson*

3-24 Trinity's 5,161-cubic-foot car is the most popular of the modern 286,000-pound gross rail load grain cars. Note the shape of the ends and the design of the roof that overhangs the sides. *Jeff Wilson*

3-23

3-24

3-25

cars that resembled the ACF design. Figure 3-22 shows a 5,150-cubic-foot Thrall car. Compared with a Center Flow car, there is a notable difference in the shape of the sides at the ends and the shape of the fillets), as well as the shape of the side where it meets the roof.

Another unique modern car, and one of the largest built for grain, is the 5,400-cubic-foot aluminum Grainporter built by Johnstown-America (fig. 3-23). About 1,000 of these flat-sided cars were built from 1994 to 1996.

The most popular modern grain covered hopper is Trinity's 5,161-cubic-foot car, shown in fig. 3-24. This three-bay car has a roof that slightly overhangs the sides and a unique shape to the ends of the sides and the running-board supports. Almost 20,000 of these cars have been built since the late 1990s. Variations include the number of side panels (eight or ten) and the number of running-board supports.

The 5,161-cubic-foot and similar hoppers have sidelined many older 4,427-cubic-foot and other smaller cars, since the move toward 110-ton cars (286,000 pounds gross rail load) in the 1990s. The larger hoppers are especially popular for hauling corn, which isn't as heavy as wheat or soybeans.

Another commonly seen car is the Canadian-style cylindrical covered hopper (fig. 3-25), used for hauling grain and potash. Since the mid-1960s, thousands of these cars have been built by the Canadian companies Hawker Siddeley, Marine Industries, and National Steel Car Co.

Future

Covered hoppers remain the dominant car type, with (in 2003) more than 455,000 in service. Compare this with the next most numerous type of car, the tank car, some 265,000 of which currently ride the rails.

3-25 Canadian railroads have long favored cylindrical covered hoppers for hauling grain and potash. This car, with four outlet bays and round roof hatches, was built by Marine Industries. *Brian C. Nickle*

Builders continue to offer cars in a variety of sizes to match shippers' needs for specific products. For example, ACF currently offers covered hoppers in nine sizes from 3,140 cubic feet to 5,700 cubic feet, along with three Pressureaide cars from 5,000 to 5,750 cubic feet. Counting all variations, Trinity has 22 different covered hoppers in its line.

More and more of the larger grain cars will hit the rails as smaller, older cars reach retirement age, and plenty of two-bay covered hoppers are being built to haul cement, sand, and other dense products.

Unloading gates

Hopper cars are equipped with one of three types of bottom unloading gates: gravity, pneumatic, or combination gravity-pneumatic. Gravity gates (as on cars in figs. 3-9 and 3-21) have a bottom plate that slides away, allowing the load to be dumped straight down between the rails. This is the most common outlet for grain and general-purpose cars. Early covered hoppers (such as figs. 3-3 and 3-5) had pairs of gates at each hopper—one at each side. Center-discharge gates became popular in the early 1960s (the "CD" designation in a PS-2CD car, and the "Center" in Center Flow). The most common today, these have a single gate at each hopper at the center of the car.

Pneumatic-unloading gates are characterized by a horizontal pipe at the bottom of the hopper. When viewed from the side, these hoppers have a V-shape, with the pipe at the bottom of the V (gravity hoppers have a flat area at the bottom). To unload these cars, a vacuum hose is attached to the pipe to draw out the load. Pneumatic-unloading gates are most often found on cars carrying plastic pellets as well as food products (such as flour or sugar), chemicals,

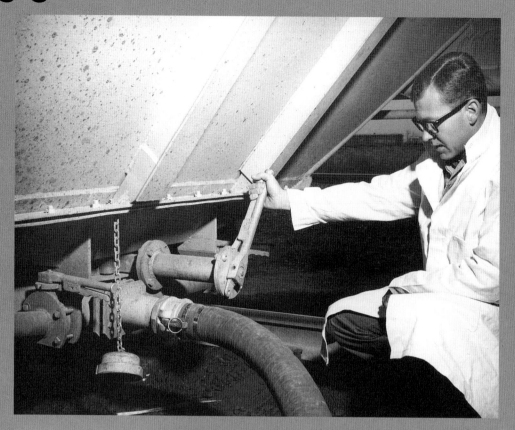

and other commodities that would be easily damaged by outside contamination.

Gravity-pneumatic gates can be unloaded

either way. They have flat bottoms like standard gravity outlets, but also have an unloading pipe across the bottom.

Pneumatic outlets (this is an ACF Pressureaide car) are closed systems, allowing a hose to connect to the outlet pipe. The load is either emptied by vacuum pressure or by pressuring the load to force it out (as on a pressure-differential car). *ACF Industries*

Cars with combination gravity-pneumatic outlets have a standard large center-discharge outlet bay, with a pipe across the bottom. The crank mechanism for moving the gravity gate is visible at right. *Gordon Odegard*

There are many manufacturers of unloading gates, so styles of each can vary greatly from car to car.

The refrigerator car—or "reefer," as it came to be known—was among the earliest specialized cars to appear on railroads. Largely a development of the meat-packing industry in the late 1800s, refrigerator cars allowed fresh meat to be shipped throughout the country from meat-packing centers such as Chicago. The produce industry quickly adopted refrigerator cars as well, allowing people around the country to have fresh fruits and vegetables regardless of season—something not previously possible (fig. 4-1).

4-1 Refrigerator cars have been around since the late 1800s and are used to carry produce, meat, and frozen foods. Mechanical reefers such as this one have on-board diesel engines and compressors to keep loads cool or frozen. *Jeff Wilson*

FOUR

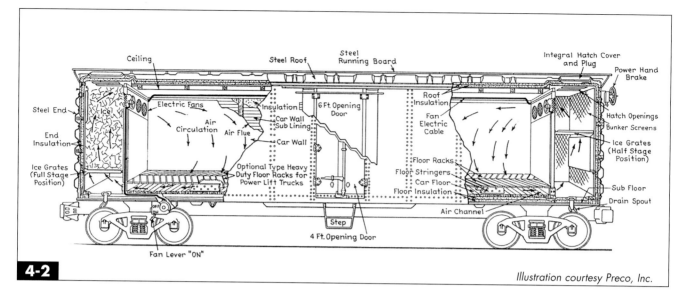

Ceiling — Steel Roof — Steel Running Board — Integral Hatch Cover and Plug — Power Hand Brake

Steel End — Ice — Electric Fans — Air Circulation — Air Flue — Insulation — Car Wall Sub Lining — Car Wall — 6 Ft. Opening Door — Roof Insulation — Fan Electric Cable — Hatch Openings — Bunker Screens

End Insulation — Optional Type Heavy Duty Floor Racks for Power Lift Trucks — Floor Racks — Floor Stringers — Car Floor — Floor Insulation — Ice Grates (Half Stage Position)

Ice Grates (Full Stage Position) — Sub Floor — Drain Spout — Air Channel

Fan Lever "ON" — Step — 4 Ft. Opening Door

4-2

Illustration courtesy Preco, Inc.

Figure 4-2 shows how an ice-bunker refrigerator car works. The design is similar to a boxcar, but with insulated sides, ends, floor, and roof. Cooling is provided by ice, which is placed in bunkers (through roof hatches) at each end of the car. As important as the ice itself is air circulation. It's vital that cold air flow throughout the car and the load, or else part of the load can spoil. Slatted floor racks help cold air penetrate through the entire car. Air-circulating fans came into use in the 1940s.

No United States Railroad Administration (USRA) or American Railroad Association (ARA) standards existed for refrigerator car construction as there were for boxcars and other cars, so reefers were built to many different designs. As with tank cars, railroads were reluctant to build or buy cars for specialized service, so for the most part they left the job of developing them to private owners and leasing companies.

The leader in design, by sheer number of cars operated, was Pacific Fruit Express (PFE), a joint operation of Union Pacific and Southern Pacific. Many other companies would build cars to similar designs. Other sizable car fleets with distinctive designs included Fruit Growers Express (FGE), Santa Fe Refrigerator

Department (SFRD), American Refrigerator Transit (ART), and Union Refrigerator Transit (URT). Some private owners (mainly packing companies) acquired or leased large fleets of cars, including Armour, Swift, and Wilson.

Car sizes and features

By the post-World War I era most new refrigerator cars were 40 feet long, with a 30- to 40-ton capacity. Since the cubic capacity of refrigerator cars was significantly less than a comparable boxcar (due to the thicker insulated sides and the space taken up by the end bunkers), a full load would rarely approach a car's weight limit. Thus, reefers didn't require the 50-ton capacity of most contemporary boxcars. Figure 4-3 shows a typical wood reefer of the 1920s.

Although steel underframes were essentially standard on new refrigerator cars by the 1920s, reefer bodies generally featured all-wood construction, including framing (albeit with steel tension rods), sides, and ends. This was partly because the wood sheathing served as an insulation layer, and some thought that steel sides (or even steel framing) would transmit too much heat through the sides.

As improved insulation materials became available, internal steel framing became popular in

the 1920s, although cars with wood ends and sides would continue to be built through the 1930s. Underframes varied in design from fish-belly to various other types.

Wood roofs, used into the 1910s, gave way to steel. Reefer roofs followed the same designs as boxcars, with the lap-seam roofs common in the 1920s giving way to Hutchins and Viking roofs, Murphy panel roofs, and eventually diagonal-panel roofs by the 1940s. (See chapter 1 for more information on roofs.)

Steel ends began appearing on refrigerator cars in the mid-1920s (fig. 4-4). Dreadnaught ends were common, as with boxcars, but since reefers were usually shorter the patterns varied, with 4/4 and 4/5 patterns common. Also, starting in the 1930s many older wood cars were rebuilt with steel ends. These ends followed the same designs as boxcars, with square corner posts through 1940, and the rounded W-corner post ends thereafter. (See the sidebar on boxcar ends on page 9.)

All-steel refrigerator cars began appearing in 1936, with PFE's R-40-10 cars. By then, steel cars were considered viable, made possible by improvements in insulation materials that negated any extra insulation benefits from the wood sheathing. However, many

4-3 This 40-foot Union Refrigerator Transit RS car is typical of reefers built into the 1920s. It has a steel fishbelly underframe and wood body, including ends and sides. *Hol Wagner collection*

4-4 Refrigerator cars began receiving steel ends around 1930. This PFE car originally had an all-wood body; it was rebuilt with steel ends (Dreadnaught 4/4), fans, convertible bunkers and stage icing in 1946. *R.F. Herold*

4-5 Air-circulating fans on ice cars were powered by generators that in turn were powered by the wheels. *Preco, Inc.*

improved air circulation inside the cars and were pretty much standard on ice-bunker cars built for produce service in the 1940s and later.

Early fans were directly belt driven using a rubber wheel in contact with one of the car's wheels. Mechanical problems led to the use of electric fans powered by a wheel-driven generator.

Other features that appeared in the 1940s included collapsible bunkers, which could be folded out of the way to increase capacity if ice wasn't being used; and stage icing, which used grates to limit space in the bunkers for lading requiring a smaller ice load. Although these features weren't visible from the outside, stenciling

wood-sheathed reefers had long service lives (more so than wood boxcars), resulting in some lasting into the 1960s and even the '70s.

Through this time spotting features on reefers were much the same as with boxcars: type of ends, roof, and sides; side-sill style (straight or notched); roof hatch size and style; door height and width; and trucks.

A major design improvement was the addition of air circulating fans beginning in 1941. Although the fans were internal, cars with fans can be spotted by a disk on the lower-left corner of the side (fig. 4-5). These fans greatly

4-6 Wood remained popular for meat reefers quite late, as shown by this Rath car built in 1947. *Bill Raia collection*

4-7 General American's steel ice reefers had a horizontal strip along the side and improved Dreadnaught ends. *Jay Williams collection*

4-8 This SFRD-class RR-49 reefer, built in 1927, was rebuilt in 1950 with steel sides and ends and a sliding plug door in 1950. *Santa Fe*

on the car sides often indicated both features.

For the most part refrigerator cars were used either for produce or meat service. Packing companies generally owned or leased their cars, and produce shippers relied on companies such as PFE, ART, or FGE for cars.

There were differences between reefer types. For example, meat reefers were equipped with overhead rails to secure meat hooks holding sides of beef. They often had brine tanks instead of ice bunkers, to better hold the salt/crushed ice mix (instead of chunk ice) used to keep the cars at colder temperatures. Although this feature wasn't visible from the outside, stenciling on the car sides indicated the presence of brine tanks instead of bunkers.

Also, meat reefers did not have internal air circulating fans, as the increased air flow would dry out hanging beef. Meat reefers were not set up to run in ventilator service (see the sidebar on page 50), so their roof hatches were either open or closed.

Figure 4-6 shows a typical meat reefer of the post-World War I era. Meat reefers usually wore the colors and logos of their owners or lessors, a colorful practice that continued through the 1960s.

Among the more common steel reefers for meat and other service in the 1950s and later was the URTX car built by General American (fig. 4-7). Since URTX had one of the largest refrigerator car fleets, and leased cars to many railroads and packing companies, these cars could be found across the country. The URTX cars had a horizontal rivet strip along the middle of each side, improved Dreadnaught ends, and diagonal-panel roofs.

Operations for meat reefers differed as well. By and large produce reefers were distributed by their controlling companies (for example, FGE, PFE, and SFRD) to any on-line packing shed in need of a refrigerator car. A PFE car might haul a load of oranges from California to Chicago, then get sent to Texas to be loaded with vegetables.

Meat reefers, on the other hand, were owned or leased by specific companies. Thus, a car leased to Armour would travel exclusively between the company's packing houses and branch houses or other customers. It would not be redirected to a Morrell plant in need of a car.

Most reefers through the ice-bunker era were 40-foot, 40- and 50-ton cars, although a few 50-foot cars were built. These larger cars were usually for specialized service, such as frozen foods.

Most refrigerator cars built through the 1950s had double swinging doors, with either four- or five-foot door openings. The smaller door openings were preferred, since the smaller the opening, the less potential for loss of cold air.

A major visual change began appearing around 1950 with the use of sliding plug doors to replace swinging doors (fig. 4-8). These doors, came in various sizes and designs (six-foot openings were common initially), sealed tightly but allowed easier access

for lift trucks and forklifts, greatly speeding loading and unloading.

Ice-bunker cars began falling in number by the late 1950s, as mechanical refrigerator fleets were growing and railroads were losing produce traffic to trucks. Few ice-bunker cars were built after the mid-1950s (PFE acquired its last ice car in 1957).

By 1973, most icing platforms were gone; the few ice reefers remaining in service had their bunkers removed and were put into top-ice vegetable (TIV) service, where produce loads were covered with a thick layer of crushed ice, but no bunker ice was needed. Other existing reefers simply served as insulated cars. Most ice-bunker cars were off the rails by 1980.

Spotting features of ice-bunker cars include construction material (wood or steel); style of roof and ends; door width and type; roof hatch style; side sill style; and underframe.

Mechanical refrigerator cars

Many experiments in mechanical refrigeration had been conducted through the first half of the 20th century, but it wasn't until the growth of the frozen-food industry in the 1950s that mechanical refrigerator cars began appearing in great numbers. Fruit Growers Express purchased 25 mechanical cars in 1949, with PFE and SFRD following in 1952 (fig. 4-9).

Compared to early mechanical cars, ice-bunker cars were relatively inexpensive to operate and did a very good job of keeping produce and meat cool. Frozen foods, however, required temperatures below zero to stay frozen solid. The initial solution was to use heavily insulated ice-bunker

4-10 This Santa Fe publicity photo shows the parts that go into a mechanical reefer. The car, built in 1963, is 60 feet long with exterior posts, cushion underframe, and a nine-foot plug door. *Santa Fe*

4-11 This UPFE reefer is from the next-to-last group of PFE mechanical cars built, class R-70-20. The 60-foot car has a 10'-6"-wide door. *Jeff Wilson*

4-12 This 65-foot smooth-side FGE mechanical reefer has a 10'-6"door. The car was built in 1972. *Jeff Wilson collection*

4-13 Early insulated boxcars, like this Minneapolis & St. Louis car built in 1957, looked like standard 50-foot boxcars with plug doors. *Jack Pfeifer*

cars with large quantities of salt added to the ice. This kept car temperatures in the single digits but couldn't produce the necessary sub-zero temperatures.

Mechanical reefers use a small diesel engine to drive an alternator, which provides electricity for operating the compressor (fig. 4-9). Fans then distribute the cold air throughout the car. Starting in the 1950s some ice-bunker cars were converted to mechanical refrigeration, but the bulk of mechanical reefers were new cars. Figure 4-10 shows all of the parts used in building a Santa Fe mechanical reefer.

These new mechanical cars were used almost exclusively for frozen goods. Although some early ones were 40-footers, most were 50 to 60 feet long and longer with 70-ton capacity. Figure 4-11 shows a 60-foot exterior-post PFE reefer; fig. 4-12 is a smooth-side Fruit Growers Express car. Other improvements included internal load restraint devices and movable bulkheads as well as the use of cushion underframes. Sliding plug doors of various designs were used. Six-foot door openings were common on early cars, with eight-, nine-, and ten-foot doors on later cars.

Ice-bunker cars continued to be the primary mode of shipping produce through the 1950s and early 1960s, but in the 1960s mechanical reefers with wide-range temperature controls allowed produce to be hauled in mechanical cars. As an example, in 1962 PFE operated about 3,000 mechanical cars and 22,000 ice cars, but by 1969 mechanical cars made up about half of the PFE fleet.

To identify variations among these cars, look at the car length, exterior posts (number, spacing, and style), door style and width, location of vents and screens for refrigeration equipment, style of the car ends, and roof style.

Insulated boxcars

Although insulated boxcars (AAR code RBL) don't have ice bunkers or mechanical refrigeration units, they are classified as refrigerator cars (fig. 4-13). By 1960 vast improvements in insulating materials, namely urethane foam, made insulated boxcars with plug doors very popular.

When loaded with pre-cooled goods, these cars could maintain their internal temperature within a couple of degrees for several

4-14 This Fruit Growers Express bunkerless reefer is among the most common insulated boxcars of the late 1960s through the 1990s. This car was built in 1970. *Jim Hediger*

4-15 This huge modern UPFE reefer has a composite fiberglass body and an end-mounted refrigeration unit. *Jeff Wilson*

4-16 Cryogenic reefers, used for hauling frozen foods, use dry ice instead of mechanical refrigeration. *Jeff Wilson*

carry canned goods and products that require cool temperatures above freezing.

As insulating materials have improved and refrigeration units have become more efficient, the trend in newer reefers has been toward larger cars with increased cubic capacity, allowing them to be filled to their weight limits—something that rarely happened with ice-bunker cars.

Figure 4-15 shows a modern composite body car with an end-mounted refrigeration unit. These huge cars, built by Trinity for the Union Pacific, have a 71-foot inside length (83 feet long overall) and were built beginning in 1998. They feature a composite fiberglass and urethane foam body on a heavy steel frame.

Another common large modern refrigerator car for hauling frozen foods features cryogenic refrigeration (fig. 4-16). Although experimental dry ice cars had been tried many times through the 20th century, these huge cryogenic cars, built since the late 1980s, have made the concept practical. The cars are virtually maintenance-free and can keep their loads well below zero without the need to replenish ice and no refrigeration units to run out of fuel or break down.

days. Their larger capacities also made them more attractive to shippers, and during the 1960s they became standard for carrying canned goods, beer, and other products sensitive to heat. As with reefers these cars continued to grow in size.

Figure 4-14 shows one of the most common styles of RBL cars, built by Fruit Growers Express from 1968 to 1974. Along with FGE, many cars were leased or sold to many other railroads.

Spotting features are the same as with boxcars: number of panels and style of ends, roof, door, and sill.

Modern refrigerator cars

Most of the refrigerator cars operating today are mechanical reefers built in the 1960s and 1970s, along with insulated boxcars. Although some produce and vegetable traffic still travels by rail, reefers today mainly carry frozen foods, while the RBL cars

Ventilator service

Reefers operating in ventilator service had their hatches open to allow air to flow in and through the car. This steel MDT reefer, built in 1947, has 3/4 Dreadnaught ends, Murphy roof, and circulating fans. *New York Central*

Ice-bunker cars did not always have their bunkers filled with ice. If the outside temperature was at or slightly below the desired temperature for the load, the cars would be run in ventilator service, with the ice hatches propped open (ventilator hatch bars could be set at different heights). As the car moved, air would flow in through the lead hatches, through the load, and out the rear hatches. Ventilator service was an economical method to keep cars cool.

Many early refrigerator cars included large side lettering such as "VENTILATOR—REFRIGERATOR" to indicate they could be used for either service. By the 1930s, most cars in produce service could be used as ventilators, so such lettering disappeared.

Ventilator service was used most often for products that required cool, but not cold temperatures, including potatoes and bananas.

Reefers were also often used for canned goods, beer, and other products that didn't require refrigeration but needed protection from heat.

Refrigerator car classifications

The AAR refrigerator car class can provide insight into the type of service a car was designed for. Designations can be found in the *Official Railway Equipment Register* and are often stenciled on the side of the car.

Here are the most common designations:

RS—Ice-bunker reefer

RSM—Ice-bunker reefer with meat rails

RA—Reefer with brine tanks

RAM—Reefer with brine tanks and meat rails

RB, RBL—Bunkerless reefers; RBL cars have adjustable loading devices

RP—Mechanical reefer

RPL—Mechanical reefer with adjustable loading devices

RPM—Mechanical reefer with meat rails

RC—Cryogenic reefer

The hopper car—nearly synonymous with "coal car"—was the staple car for hauling coal from before World War I through the 1970s. Today, bathtub-style gondolas dominate unit coal trains, but plenty of hopper cars still work hauling coal and other bulk commodities (fig. 5-1).

The gondola is a cousin to the hopper. A common early coal hauler as well as the dominant high-capacity modern coal car, gondolas are also used at steel mills, hauling both finished products and scrap.

In addition, many specialized hoppers and gondolas have been built for hauling products such as iron ore, wood chips, and aggregate. We'll start with a look at hopper cars, then move to gondolas.

5-1 Hopper cars and gondolas are among the oldest freight car types. Primarily used for hauling coal, these cars can also carry aggregate and other bulk commodities not affected by the elements. This Coalveyor gondola was built in the late 1970s. *ACF Industries*

Early hopper cars

Hopper cars were among the earliest all-steel cars, entering service in significant numbers at the turn of the 20th century. Hoppers were also among the heaviest early cars, with 50-ton capacity common before World War I.

The hopper was one of the standard designs implemented by the United States Railway Administration (USRA) during World War I. A total of 25,500 USRA 50-ton twin-bay cars were built, with many additional cars built to the USRA or similar designs through the 1920s (see fig. 5-2). These steel cars were 30 feet long with a capacity of 1,880 cubic feet. USRA hoppers are exterior-braced cars, with seven posts on each side.

The USRA cars had long service lives, many lasting through the 1950s. Many were rebuilt over the years. Some retained their original appearance, but with updated brake equipment: AB brakes replaced K brakes, and various types of brake wheels and mechanisms replaced the original vertical brake staffs with horizontal wheels.

A common USRA variation included cars rebuilt with panel sides as fig. 5-3 shows. The panels, applied between the vertical posts, increased the cubic capacity of the cars and made them visually interesting and quite noticeable.

During the teens and 1920s some coal-hauling railroads built larger cars; cars with 70- to 90-ton capacities were fairly common. Some 100-ton (and even larger) cars were also built.

In the 1920s the American Railway Association (ARA) worked to develop standard designs for hoppers. These cars introduced what is known as the offset-side design (fig. 5-4). Instead of visible external vertical posts (as on the USRA cars), the posts were inside and the side sheathing was on the outside. At the top the side angled back in, with triangular braces on the outside. This design—with

5-2

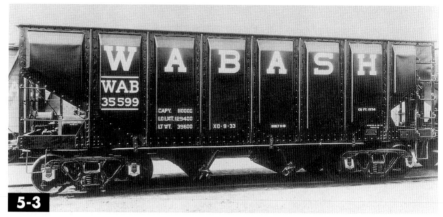

5-3

5-4

bracing on the inside—increased the cubic capacity of the cars.

The first ARA design, submitted in 1926, was for a four-bay 70-ton car (fig. 5-4). The 70-ton car had a 41'-3" inside length and was 10'-6" tall; this was revised in 1929 to a 40'-5" inside length and 10'-8" height. About 14,000 quad hoppers were built to ARA or similar designs through 1930.

In 1930, the initial ARA design for a 50-ton car (34 feet inside length) called for three bays, but few were built. Instead, in 1934 the 70-ton design was changed to a three-bay configuration (fig. 5-5), and the 50-ton car was modi-

5-2 Hoppers built to the USRA design were among the most common coal cars through the 1930s. These 30-foot, 50- and 55-ton cars offered two outlet bays and featured seven exterior vertical posts. *David P. Morgan Library collection*

5-3 Many USRA hoppers were rebuilt with panel sides between posts to expand the capacity. This Wabash car was built in 1919 and rebuilt in 1933. *Wabash*

5-4 This Baltimore & Ohio hopper, a four-bay, 70-ton ARA car, was among the earliest offset-side designs. *Jim Shaughnessy*

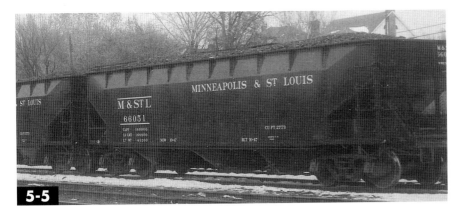

5-5

5-6

fied to have two bays (fig. 5-6).

Both cars would prove to be popular. The 70-ton car had a 40'-8" inside length (the height remained 10'-8") and 10 stiffeners along the top of each side.

The 50- and 55-ton two-bay cars were 34 feet long (33'-0" inside length)—four feet longer than the USRA twin cars—with a standard height of 10'-8". About 127,000 of these 34-foot cars were built through the mid-1950s, when production shifted to 70-ton and larger cars. Many remained in operation into the 1970s.

Spotting features include the stiffeners running along the tops of the sides. The Association of American Railroads (AAR) design called for nine of them, and they were not evenly spaced (see fig. 5-6); however, an alternate design used more even spacing (fig. 5-7). Also, these stiffeners had different designs. Early cars had shaped stampings (sometimes called "hat-shaped") as in fig. 5-7; most later cars had metal angles, as fig. 5-6 shows, but some later cars received hat-shaped stiffeners.

Ends also varied. Most cars had straight ends as figs. 5-6 and 5-7 show, but some cars had ends with angled or oval tops as in fig. 5-8.

5-7

5-8

5-5 The AAR three-bay, 70-ton car was built in large numbers, especially after World War II. This Minneapolis & St. Louis car was built in 1947. *Minneapolis & St. Louis*

5-6 Offset-side cars had interior posts to maximize cubic capacity. The AAR 50- and 55-ton offset-side car was perhaps the most popular coal car of the steam era. This Reading car, built by Bethlehem in 1955, has angled stiffeners at the top of the sides. *Reading Railroad*

5-7 Some AAR cars were built to an alternate standard with a 10'-5" height and even spacing of the stiffeners. This Minneapolis & St. Louis car, built in 1936 by General American, has stamped ("hat-shaped") stiffeners. *Minneapolis & St. Louis*

5-8 Some railroads favored outside-braced cars. This three-bay 70-ton Chesapeake & Ohio car, built in 1949 by Bethlehem Steel, has ends with oval heap shields. *Chesapeake & Ohio*

5-9 This Chicago & Eastern Illinois car follows the AAR standard for a 70-ton, three-bay, outside-braced hopper. It was built by Pressed Steel Car Co. in 1952. *Chicago & Eastern Illinois*

5-10 This Pennsylvania Power & Light car was among the first modern 100-ton hoppers. It's a three-bay, outside-braced car built for unit train service. *David P. Morgan Library collection*

These peaked ends were known as "heap shields." These came in different shapes, with ovals, ovals with notches above the end ladder, and angled ends all employed at various times.

Other variations included side rivet patterns, brake gear, make and style of hopper doors and door locks, and trucks. Another variation was the side sills: Some had straight pieces from the truck bolster to the end, but others had pieces that angled upward.

Yet another variation was in the end panels on the sides. On some cars the taper extended all the way to the end of the car (fig. 5-7); on other cars, the taper ended on the panel (fig. 5-6).

In 1946 the AAR modified both the two- and three-bay designs, making each car larger. The revised two-bay car had an inside length measuring 35'-0", and the three-bay car was stretched to a 41'-8" inside length.

The offset-side hopper was the dominant style of car built into the 1950s (although many outside post cars were also built), but the design had its flaws. The main

problem was that the sides tended to bow out and separate from the posts. Many offset-side cars were rebuilt at least once, and many were rebuilt with outside braces.

Outside-braced cars

Although offset-side cars were the dominant hoppers from the 1920s through the 1950s, many hoppers were built using outside braces during that time (see fig. 5-8). Also, many coal-hauling railroads wanted cars larger than the 50-ton standard of the teens and even the 70-ton cars of the 1920s and '30s.

Large cars, of 90- and 100-ton capacity, were used on the Norfolk & Western and Virginian (which even ran some 120-ton, six-axle coal gondolas) as early as the 1910s. However, cars that large didn't become popular for interchange and general service until the 1960s.

Even with the availability of larger cars, 50-ton cars remained very popular through the 1940s. The reason was that many buyers of coal—such as small-town coal dealers—didn't want or need

shipments larger than 50 or 55 tons. This would change in the 1940s and '50s, as natural gas and fuel oil replaced coal for home heating, and more coal was transloaded to ships or transported to large coal-fired electrical power plants.

Through the 1950s railroads increasingly opted for 70-ton cars, which led to the adoption of an AAR alternate standard for a 70-ton, three-bay, outside-braced car, as fig. 5-9 shows. The standard called for a 40'-8" inside length with 10 side posts, but many railroads and manufacturers built variations of these cars. Spotting features to look for are the number of posts and car length and height.

Modern hoppers

As with other car types, the 1960s brought a growth in car size and capacity for hopper cars. Figure 5-10 shows an early 100-ton hopper: a three-bay, 3,366 cubic-foot car built by Bethlehem in 1964 for unit-train service for Pennsylvania Power & Light Co. (among the earliest unit coal trains). Unit coal trains—solid trains bound for a single customer—increased dramatically in number during the early 1970s.

Through the 1960s and '70s, many companies built 100-ton hopper cars, including Pullman-Standard, Bethlehem, Evans, Greenville, Portec, Trinity, Ortner, and Paccar. Details vary among them; spotting features include the number of bays, car length, num-

War-emergency hoppers

Steel was in short supply during World War II, so the AAR approved a design for a composite hopper car with steel ends, floor, and bracing, but wood sides (you can see the individual planks in the builder's photo of the B&O car). These cars were known as war emergency hoppers, and were quite distinctive in appearance. About 10,000 of these 50-ton cars were built.

These cars were designed to have their wood sides replaced with steel, which many did through the 1950s and '60s as shown by the C&O car. However, some continued running with their original wood sides into the 1960s.

War emergency hoppers had steel frames and ends with wood planks for sides. Bethlehem built this car for B&O in August 1943. *Baltimore & Ohio*

Many war emergency cars were later rebuilt with steel sides, keeping their distinctive side bracing, as with this Chesapeake & Ohio car. *Chesapeake & Ohio*

Ore cars

Ore cars are specialized hopper cars in dedicated duty hauling iron ore. Because iron ore is very heavy and dense, a small car can carry a 70- or 100-ton load. Ore cars are short (about 21 feet) compared to a standard hopper car. Variations include the side shape, end shape, and bracing. Early cars were 70- or 75-ton capacity, with 100-ton cars common in the 1960s and later.

Ore cars are significantly smaller than standard hoppers because of the high density of iron ore. This 70-ton car was built in 1930. *Pressed Steel Car Co.*

Ballast cars

Ballast cars have gates that open to the sides of the rails, and many—like this ACF Hart Selective ballast car—can dump to either side or between the rails. *Andy Sperandeo*

A variation of the standard hopper car is the ballast car. Designed for dumping ballast on the tracks, these cars have doors that open to the side or lengthwise compared to the car.

The photo shows a Hart ballast car (built by ACF), one of the most common ballast car designs. Its bottom gates allow lading to be dumped to either side as well as in the center.

Although designed for maintenance service, these cars can sometimes be found hauling revenue loads of aggregate, sand, or gravel between maintenance duties.

5-11

5-11 This four-bay 100-ton hopper was built in 1976. Spotting features include the end style, angle of the slope sheets, and number and spacing of exterior posts. *David P. Morgan Library collection*

5-12

5-13

5-12 Ortner's distinctive Rapid Discharge hoppers are characterized by their five bays and peaked ends. This 3,800 cubic-foot Santa Fe hopper was manufactured in 1978. *Ortner*

5-13 Hoppers in unit train service with rotary couplers, such as this 100-ton Burlington Northern car, have one end painted a contrasting color. *Jeff Wilson*

5-14 Aluminum is a popular material for modern coal hoppers and gondolas. This 4,300 cubic-foot Johnstown America Auto-Flood hopper has interior bracing and electrically operated doors. *Jeff Wilson*

5-14

ber and style of side posts, and style of the ends and end bracing.

Figure 5-11 shows a four-bay 100-ton car built for the Rio Grande. Hoppers (and later, coal gondolas) built for service in the West were generally slightly larger than cars built to haul Eastern coal, since a given amount of Western coal isn't as heavy as its Eastern counterpart.

Figure 5-12 shows an Ortner Rapid Discharge hopper. These 100-ton cars were popular 1970s and '80s coal haulers; their five

bays and peaked ends make them stand out.

Rotary dumpers came into wide use at electrical utilities through the 1970s, greatly speeding unloading times. Manufacturers began building hopper cars with rotary couplers at one end, allowing the train to remain coupled while loads are dumped. Cars with rotary couplers are marked by painting one end a contrasting color, as fig. 5-13 shows. All cars in a unit train will have their rotary ends facing the same direction (some cars have

rotary couplers—and markings—on both ends). If they're not, then the train is not bound for a plant with a rotary dumper.

Aluminum came into wide use for coal gondolas and hoppers in the 1980s and '90s. Figure 5-14 shows a modern aluminum inside-post hopper, a Johnstown-America Auto-Flood car with electrically operated outlet doors, another feature found on many unit train cars starting in the 1970s.

There are still plenty of hopper cars around, but most unit coal

5-22

5-23

5-24

late 1960s, and many continued in this service through the 1970s. Many of these cars could be found in general service—without their covers—later in their careers.

Welded cars began appearing in the 1960s. Figure 5-21 shows a welded Thrall gondola that follows the basic pattern of that company's cars from the 1960s through the 1970s. The drop side sill is still there but shallower. Note the heavier posts, typical of 100-ton cars. Some gondolas were built with horizontal corrugations to increase the strength of the side panels (fig. 5-22).

Designs have continued to evolve, with the 100-ton welded car now the most common. Straight side sills have been the norm on cars built since the early 1980s (see fig. 5-23).

Spotting features on gondolas include the number and style of posts, type of ends (various styles are used, but Murphy and Dreadnaught are the most common), side sill (straight or fishbelly, with varying amounts of taper), corner ladders or grab irons, brake gear, and trucks.

It can be tough to find interior photos of these freight haulers, but you'll find floors of wood, plate steel, or nailable steel (crosswise pieces resembling planks, with gaps allowing nails to be driven in). Tie-down loops, rods, or straps on the tops of the sides are found on some cars.

Modern coal gondolas

Although a couple of railroads—notably Virginian and Norfolk & Western—had high-capacity coal

gondolas early in the 1900s, it wasn't until the 1970s that big coal gondolas became popular for interchange service.

The shift toward larger coal-fed plants for generating electricity, together with the increased use of rotary dumpers for unloading, increased the popularity of gons over hopper cars for coal service.

Gondolas have the advantage of simpler construction, having no moving hopper doors and locking mechanisms to maintain. Eliminating the hopper outlets and slope sheets also allowed a lot more coal to be carried in a given car of the same length.

Among the first modern unit-train applications of coal cars was in 1960, when the Southern Ry. acquired 750 aluminum coal gondolas from Pullman-Standard (see fig. 5-24). These cars—known as "silversides" on the Southern—were notable in that they marked the first large-scale order for an aluminum car (although many experimental aluminum cars of various types had been built over the years).

They were also the first modern 100-ton capacity coal cars, and the first cars ordered specifically for unit-train coal service. Most lasted in service through the 1980s and into the 1990s.

It was several more years before the idea caught on. Figure 5-25 shows the first of the modern-styled coal gondolas, built in 1969 for Canadian Pacific. These

5-25 Canadian Pacific's unit-train gondolas of 1969 were the first to be built with "bathtubs" that extended below floor level. *Canadian Pacific*

5-26 This 4,240 cubic-foot Coalveyor was the largest of four sizes offered by ACF. This car was built in 1978. *ACF Industries*

5-27 Evans built many 100-ton gondolas for unit train service. Thrall offered similar cars, all characterized by distinctive outside posts that matched the crossbearers. *J. David Ingles*

5-28 Bethlehem's BethGon Coalporter is the most popular modern coal hauler. The 100- and 110-ton cars have ends that resemble hopper cars, but with tubs below floor level. They're made in steel and aluminum versions. *John Harvey*

4,760 cubic-foot cars were just over 58 feet long, with a 48-foot inside length.

The car was the prototype for the Youngstown Bathtub gondola, which had tub-shaped bins on either side of the center sill (thus the term "bathtub gondola") instead of hoppers. The tubs allowed the cars to carry more coal than a standard flat-bottomed gon and also lowered the car's center of gravity.

Other coal gondola designs soon followed. The Coalveyor (fig. 5-26) was an ACF coal gondola built in the late 1970s and early 1980s. The design was also built by other manufacturers as well as the Union Pacific.

Evans and Thrall offered similar high-side gondolas (fig. 5-27). These non-tub cars have heavy vertical posts and cross bracing at each end.

The most popular of the modern coal gons is Johnstown-America's BethGon Coalporter (fig. 5-28). These cars, in production since 1978, are distinguished by their angled end slope sheets, with two lengthwise tubs below

frame level. Early Coalporters were steel; most new cars have aluminum bodies. Trinity also offers a car with a similar design.

Spotting features of coal gons include the number and pattern of side posts, end design, tub design, and body material (aluminum or steel). Most are available in different sizes, with larger cars used in the West. Most cars built into the 1990s are 100-ton cars; newer cars have 110-ton capacities and a 286,000-pound gross rail load.

War-emergency gondolas

This war-emergency gondola has six drop doors and an inside length of 41'-6". It was built in July 1943. *Mt. Vernon Car Manufacturing Co.*

As with hopper cars, the AAR designed war-emergency gondolas as well. Designs included 50-ton high-side cars with either 41'-6" inside length and six or eight drop doors (the Southern car has six drop doors) or 41'-0" cars with 16 drop doors. A 70-ton mill gondola with a 52'-6" inside length was also designed and built.

Wood-chip cars

Modern wood-chip cars are excess height (note the white end panel) with an end door for dumping. Note the mesh screen covering the load. *Jim Hediger*

Another type of specialty gondola is the high-volume wood-chip car, used to transport wood chips from mills to paper manufacturers. Since wood chips are a very light-density item, wood-chip cars have the highest cubic capacity of any gon. Many designs have been made over the years; most are long, excess-height cars.

Purpose-built wood-chip cars first appeared in the 1960s; prior to that, wood chips were carried in older gondolas or hoppers modified with high side extensions to increase the capacity.

Spotting features include the side post pattern, depth and placement of side ribs and braces, and end design. Most of these cars have a door at one end, allowing them to be emptied one at a time by tipping them on end.

FLATCARS

Flatcars have long been used to haul bulky items that won't fit into boxcars and that don't need the sides and ends of gondolas. Common flatcar loads over the years have included tractors and other machinery, pipe, lumber, rail, railcar wheelsets, automobile frames, electrical transformers, wire spools, tanks, and many other items.

Flatcars are often modified to carry specific loads. Specialized flatcars that have been developed from the 1960s through today include piggyback flats (discussed in chapter 7), auto rack cars, coil steel cars (fig. 6-1), and center-beam flats for carrying wood products.

6-1 Along with general service flatcars, long used for hauling bulky items, many specialized types of flatcars have evolved, such as this covered car for hauling coil steel. *Jeff Wilson*

6-2 Although no USRA flatcars were built during World War I, many railroads (such as the Chicago & North Western) later ordered cars based on the USRA design. *Chicago & North Western*

6-3 The 50-ton AAR 1941 flatcar was based on this 52'-6" Union Pacific car. The riveted car has fishbelly sides, wood deck, and 15 stake pockets. This car is has been modified for dedicated service, carrying Kaiser automobile bodies. *Kaiser-Frazer Corp; Jack Mueller collection*

6-3

Flatcars with steel frames and underframes were common by World War I, and the United States Railroad Administration (USRA) approved a design for a 55-ton, 42-foot steel flatcar. Although none were built while railroads were under USRA control, many railroads built or ordered flatcars of this or similar designs after the war (fig. 6-2). These cars were riveted and had fishbelly sides, separate stake pockets riveted in place, and wood decks. Vertical brake staffs with horizontal brake wheels were located at one end.

From the late 1920s into the 1930s, railroads began seeing the versatility of longer flatcars with increased capacity—up to 70 tons. In 1941, the Association of American Railroads (AAR) recommended three flatcar designs, including two 53'-6" cars (one 50-ton, one 70-ton) and a 70-ton, 50-foot car with a cast underframe. The 50-ton car was based on a Union Pacific car built by Pullman-Standard (fig. 6-3). The 53'-6" 70-ton car followed a Pressed Steel Car Co. design for Erie, and the cast underframe car was patterned after Pennsylvania RR's home-built F-30A car.

Flatcars have several key spotting features to watch for. The side sill can be either straight (usually with a prominent center sill) or tapered (fishbelly), with either a one- or two-step taper. Also watch for rivet patterns (no rivets on welded or cast cars) and the number and style of the stake pockets.

One of the most common flatcars built in the 1950s and '60s was the Commonwealth 53'-6" car (the most common length for general service flatcars through the 1960s), based on a one-piece casting made by General Steel Castings (fig. 6-4). These cars were built from the early 1950s through the early 1970s, with few changes during production. Many railroads built their own cars using the GS castings, and GS also sold finished cars under its General Steel Industries division.

Commonwealth cars can be spotted by their lack of rivets, double-tapered side sills, and stake pockets that are integral with the car. Many of these cars were equipped with bulkheads. General Steel offered its own distinctive bulkheads for these cars (fig. 6-4).

As the photos show, most flatcars through this period had a vertical brake staff with horizontal brake wheel at one end. These could be dropped to deck level (fig. 6-5) to make it easier to load and unload the car. Other cars had vertical brakewheels mounted on posts along the side at one end.

Bulkhead flats were common for carrying pulpwood, finished wood products, and pipe. Lengths of 55 and 60 feet were common. Figure 6-6 shows a bulkhead flatcar with a straight side sill.

Along with operating a substantial fleet of piggyback cars, TTX Co. (formerly Trailer Train) has become a leading owner of general-purpose flatcars since the 1960s. TTX owns several types of 60- to 89-foot cars, some of which are converted piggyback cars, and some of which are purpose-built. They are used for many types of loads, including machinery, pipe

6-4

6-4 Commonwealth welded flatcars had stake pockets integral to the casting, flat ends, and sides with a multiple-step taper. This car is equipped with the distinctive bulkheads unique to Commonwealth cars. *David P. Morgan Library collection*

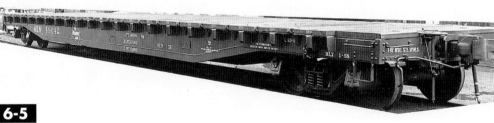

6-5

6-5 Pullman-Standard built this welded PS-4 car for Milwaukee Road in 1958. Note how the brake wheel (next to the coupler) drops down to clear the deck. *Pullman-Standard*

6-6 This welded bulkhead flat, built in 1964, has a straight side sill and a prominent fishbelly center sill. It is 64 feet long between bulkheads. *George F. Melvin*

6-6

65

6-7

6-8

6-7 TTX has converted many former piggyback cars for other uses. One example is this car for hauling pipe, a Pullman-Standard car with S-shaped side channels. *Jeff Wilson*

6-8 Gunderson built this 100-ton bulkhead flatcar for TTX in 1997. *Jeff Wilson*

6-9 This 92-foot long Pennsylvania RR car has a 250-ton capacity and rides on four six-wheel trucks. It is hauling a General Electric steam turbine generator. *General Electric*

6-10 Evans pioneered the idea of dedicated coil-steel cars. This Type 4 coil car, built in 1975, has a pair of angled hoods. *Jim Hediger*

(fig. 6-7), and auto frames. Bulkhead flats are also part of the TTX fleet (fig. 6-8).

Heavy-duty flatcars

Heavy-duty flatcars are a special class of flats. These sometimes have straight decks but often have depressed centers (between the trucks) to allow taller loads (fig. 6-9). They follow many different designs, and many are custom-built by railroads for specific customers. To provide the increased capacity, these cars have six-wheel trucks or multiple four- or six-wheel trucks on span bolsters at each end.

6-9

6-10

These cars are used for exceptionally heavy and large loads (some cars can carry up to 250 tons). The electric industry is a prime user of depressed-center heavy-duty flats, shipping loads such as transformers, generators, turbines, and boilers. These cars often travel as their own trains, requiring restricted speeds and routes carefully planned to ensure adequate clearance.

Coil cars

The coil-steel car is another type of flatcar that evolved to carry a specific product. Thin sheet steel and other metals—used in manufacturing everything from auto-

mobile parts to appliances and aluminum cans—are shipped in coils from manufacturing plants to end users. Coiled metal is easily damaged and needs protection from the elements. Covered gondolas were an early solution to the shipping problem, but gondolas carry a lot of extra tare weight with their ends and sides, which weren't necessary for the load.

Evans came up with a solution

in 1964 when it introduced a 100-ton capacity, cushion-underframe flatcar designed specifically for carrying coiled steel (fig. 6-10). A V-shaped center trough or saddle down the center of the car holds the coils securely, with steel hoods that fit over each half of the car. The idea was a hit with the steel industry, and coil-steel cars have grown in popularity through the 1960s to today. Thrall (now

6-11

6-12

6-13

glass or insulated aluminum, and differences in design now prevent the swapping of covers that was done with early cars. Some modern cars are designed with single car-length covers (fig. 6-11).

Spotting features of these cars include the shape and design of the sides and ends, and the styles of the hoods.

Center-beam flatcars

The center-beam flatcar is a modern solution to the challenge of shipping lumber and lumber products by rail. For the first half of the 20th century the usual method of shipping lumber was standard box-cars—a very laborious approach, as cars were loaded and unloaded board by board.

Flatcars and gondolas (sometimes with bulkheads) were also used, with the load built up board by board. This made loading easier, but the load would then be framed to hold it in place. Excessive force in switching could still shift the loads quite dramatically.

The 1960s saw the all-door box-car, discussed in chapter 1), which protected loads and made loading and unloading faster. However, all-door boxcars were expensive and complex with lots of moving parts to break down and need repair, especially as the cars grew older.

Trinity) has also built a large number of coil cars.

The Evans cars went through several versions, known as Type 1, 2, 3, and 4 cars. The earliest are Type 1s, with a 45'-6" inside length; followed by the slightly longer (48 feet) Type 2s. Both had drop side sills and lacked side running boards. Type 3 cars (starting in 1967) were like Type 2s, but with running boards. Type 4 cars

(as in fig. 6-10), built from 1968 through the end of production in the late 1970s, are the most common, and have straight side sills.

Early cars had interchangeable steel covers, and into the 1990s it was not uncommon to see these cars running with mismatched covers, often with two different styles of covers (rounded or angled) or different road names. Many modern covers are fiber-

The eventual solution came in the form of the center-beam flatcar, which is basically a long bulkhead flat with a center partition or frame. The open design makes loading a car much faster and simpler, and the center partition provides stability for loads, allowing them to be strapped securely in place.

Center beam cars can be found carrying bundled loads of lumber (wrapped or exposed), drywall, hardboard, and many other lumber products.

Canadian National first came up with a design for a center-beam car in the 1960s, licensing the idea to Thrall, although relatively few of them (under 1,000) were built through the 1970s. However, the cars gained in popularity from the mid-1980s to the present.

These cars, built mainly by Thrall and Gunderson (but also by NSC and others), come in two basic styles: the so-called "opera window" (fig. 6-12), which has a solid center wall with oval openings in most panels; and the truss (fig. 6-13). The two common inside lengths for these cars are 60 feet (used for drywall, green lumber, and other heavy products) and, more commonly, 73 feet

6-14

6-15

6-16

6-14 Cables running from the side sills to the top of the car hold loads securely in place. This is an NSC-built truss car. *Jeff Wilson*

6-15 Early auto racks were open. This Whitehead & Kales rack, mounted on an 85-foot flatcar, carried a full load of 15 Corvairs in 1960. *Whitehead & Kales*

6-16 Railroads covered open auto racks with corrugated metal to cut down on damage from vandalism. The flatcar is one of ACF's distinctive cars with visible cross bearers. *Burlington Northern*

(used for most dried lumber and finished products, fig. 6-14).

Along with the length and beam style, spotting features include the number, shape, and arrangement of the oval openings; bulkhead style; number of vertical posts; and type of truss (Howe or Pratt; check the location of the diagonals).

Auto rack cars

Auto racks are so common today that it can be hard to remember that through the 1950s automobiles shipped by rail traveled almost exclusively in boxcars (see chapter 1). However, boxcars were not an efficient way of carrying autos, and by the end of the 1950s railroads had lost most of the long-haul auto carrying business to trucks.

Enter the 85-foot piggyback flatcar. Although designed for carrying truck trailers, the long platform was ideal for holding an auto rack, as automobiles are a comparatively light load for a freight car. The first auto rack cars appeared in 1960, manufactured by American Car and Foundry and Whitehead & Kales (fig. 6-15). Two- and three-level racks were used: Tri-levels carried most standard autos; bi-levels were used for pickup trucks and vans.

The coming of the 89-foot flatcar in the early 1960s provided even more capacity. Racks could be found mounted on any builders' cars (see chapter 7 for differences among 89-foot flats).

Spotting features of open racks include the number, spacing, and style of vertical posts; the location and size of any diagonal bracing;

6-17 This tri-level W&K/Thrall rack is noticeably taller (and has an extra row of metal side panels) than the bi-level car at left. Both have W&K end doors with notches for the decks. *Jeff Wilson*

6-18 Portec/Trinity racks, such as this bi-level, have folding doors of a different style than the W&K racks. *Jeff Wilson*

and the location of lettering panels.

The most common arrangement through the 1990s was for TTX (formerly Trailer Train) to own the flatcars themselves, while individual railroads owned the auto racks. Although TTX has the largest fleet, several railroads operated their own cars with racks. Among them were Santa Fe and Southern Pacific.

Auto racks won the long-distance traffic back from trucks to the rails, and open racks were the standard auto carriers into the mid-1970s. A growing concern by the end of the 1960s was damage to autos by both vandalism (namely rock throwing) and the elements. Railroads and shippers began looking for ways to better protect the autos.

The ultimate solution was the fully enclosed auto rack, but investing in all-new equipment would have been prohibitively expensive, and many open racks were still relatively new. Thus, the first solution was to cover the exposed sides of open auto racks (fig. 6-16). The covers were typically made from corrugated metal, though screen and fiberglass were also tried. Since these conversions were done on a wide scale by a number of railroads, many variations in appearance existed, including corrugation spacing, panel width (based on the type and manufacturer of the open rack), and height of the metal panels.

Throughout the 1970s more and more open cars were covered, and new production shifted to enclosed

6-17

6-18

6-19

6-20

racks. Enclosed racks have been built by Whitehead & Kales (fig. 6-17), which was bought by Thrall in 1982—the most common—and Portec (later built by Trinity), fig. 6-18. Cars with bi-level racks have standard 33" wheels, while cars with tri-level racks have special 28"-diameter wheels to improve the clearance for these tall cars.

The W&K/Thrall racks can be spotted by their clamshell doors, which have notches in them to allow the doors to clear the decks (fig. 6-17). The Portec/Trinity racks have folding doors with vertical separations (fig. 6-18). Another

spotting feature is the lettering panel (or panels), which varies in location by road name.

Some early enclosed racks were built without roofs. This lowering of the overall height allowed them to go on routes with tighter clearances (especially in the East). This became less of a factor in the 1980s as railroads improved clearances on major routes to clear double-stack container cars. The open-top cars then quickly faded from use.

Recent years have brought more innovations in carrying autos, with articulated racks now hitting the rails. These include

6-19 The Auto-Max from Gunderson is a two-unit articulated auto carrier. Note how the sides drop down between the trucks. *Bob Gallegos*

6-20 Thrall's new articulated auto carriers have straight decks like conventional auto racks. *Jeff Wilson*

the Auto-Max, introduced by Greenbrier/Gunderson in 1997 and (as of 2005) used in dedicated trains (fig. 6-19), and the ABL (Articulated Bi-Level) from Thrall (fig. 6-20), which can be found on railroads across the country.

Railroads have been hauling some form of intermodal traffic—trailers and containers that can travel by rail, highway, or ship—since the late 1800s when farm and circus wagons were rolled onto flatcars. The early 1900s saw the birth of intermodal as we now know it, first with railroads hauling less-than-carload (LCL) freight in their own trailers, which they put on flatcars, then with railroads hauling common-carrier trailers, a practice that began in earnest in the 1930s.

Until the early 1950s, railcars used for carrying trailers were usually older 40- to 50-foot flatcars that had been converted by adding trailer jacks, tie-down rails, and bridge plates. This chapter focuses on the next generation of equipment that began appearing in the mid-1950s: flatcars, spine cars, and well cars designed specifically for hauling trailers and/or containers (fig. 7-1).

7-1 Trailers and containers were once carried on modified general-purpose flatcars and gondolas, but the growth in intermodal traffic led to specialized cars such as this double-stack well car for hauling containers. *Jeff Wilson*

SEVEN

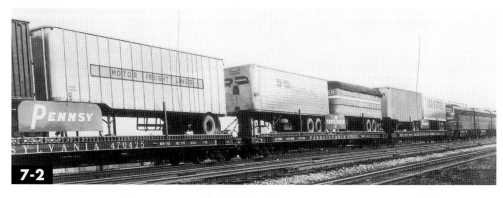

7-2 The first purpose-built piggyback cars were these 75-foot cars built for Pennsylvania RR's TrucTrain service. They became Trailer Train's first cars. *Pennsylvania RR*

7-3 Increasing trailer size led to the 85-foot car in 1958. On this Pullman-Standard car—identifiable by the S-shaped channel sides—the top lip projects outward, the bottom lip inward. The collapsible trailer hitches and bridge plates are for circus wagon loading. *Pullman-Standard*

7-4 Bethlehem's channel-side cars were the most common 89-footers in Trailer Train's fleet. This car is carrying a full load of two 45-foot trailers. *Jeff Wilson*

Knowing the types of equipment made (and when various cars were introduced) will help you more accurately model intermodal operations.

Early piggyback flats

In the early 1950s, piggyback traffic was growing: More than 20 railroads offered some type of service. However, trailer size had increased to 32 and 35 feet, meaning existing 50- and 55-foot flatcars could carry only a single trailer. Since a standard flatcar is rather heavy and overbuilt for hauling a single trailer, that meant railroads were pulling a lot of dead weight.

The time had come for flatcars designed specifically for hauling trailers. The first railroad to acquire them was the Pennsylvania Railroad, which ordered 200 75-foot flatcars from Bethlehem (and built another 300 on its own) in 1955 (fig. 7-2). These cars were intended for Pennsy's TrucTrain service, which hauled trailers in dedicated trains from Chicago to New York and Philadelphia.

Used exclusively for piggyback service, the cars were unique and revolutionary for their time because they had collapsible trailer hitches that locked onto the trailer kingpins. These hitches—American Car and Foundry's (ACF) Model A—eliminated the need for the cumbersome tie-down equipment used on earlier cars. They could accommodate any standard highway trailer without modification.

The cars didn't remain in PRR colors for long, as they became Trailer Train's first cars upon that company's startup in late 1955. The 75-foot cars would be the mainstay of the TT fleet through the late 1950s, when increasing trailer lengths spurred the design of longer flatcars. The Trailer Train concept, advanced by the Pennsy, was to provide a pool of intermodal equipment to member railroads. The idea was a success, and 32 railroads had joined Trailer Train by 1960.

By that time, longer trailer lengths (40-foot trailers in 1957) had resulted in new car designs. The Trailer Train mechanical advisory committee worked with car builders to develop the 85-foot car, which TT began receiving in 1958 (fig. 7-3). By 1960 TT had about 6,100 flatcars in service, including almost 5,000 85-footers.

The 85-footers were built by ACF (the Hitch Hiker), Pullman-Standard (the PS-4PB and low-profile Lo Dek), General American (G-85), and Bethlehem.

89-foot cars

In addition to piggyback service, the long flatcars were also being used with auto racks (shown in chapter 6). In the early 1960s, auto-rack designers discovered that extending flatcar length just four feet (to 89 feet) increased rack capacity by an auto per level.

Trailer Train chose the 89-foot car as its standard, rather than ordering cars of varying lengths for the two services—a move that would prove fortuitous when trailer lengths expanded in the 1970s.

Along with Trailer Train, many railroads bought their own piggyback cars as well. Since TT was the major buyer of piggyback flats, railroads, when buying their own cars, generally bought cars following TT's standard designs.

The most popular of the new long 89-footers was Bethlehem's (TT class F89F), introduced in 1963 (fig. 7-4). These became known as channel-side cars for the shape of their side sills.

The initial offering from ACF looked like the Bethlehem car, but in 1966 the design changed to a distinctive open-sided configuration with exposed cross bearers. Figure 6-16 in chapter 6 shows one of these hard-to-miss cars, a TT class F89G.

Pullman-Standard's car looked like Bethlehem's, but with an S-shaped side instead of the C shape (figure 7-3 shows the 85-foot version of this car). These were TT class F89E. You can identify these cars by the lower lip on the side turning inward instead of outward as on the Bethlehem cars.

Most of these early cars were set up with hitches for carrying trailers, but a growing number of containers traveling by rail needed space as well.

The solution was the all-purpose flush-deck car—so called because the deck is flush with the top of the side—shown in fig. 7-5. The first ones, built by ACF, were delivered in 1967, and Bethlehem and PS followed shortly with similar cars. All-purpose cars have collapsible hitches and adjustable container pedestals, allowing them to haul either trailers or containers. The container pedestals fold into the car deck, and they slide in channels on the deck, allowing the car to haul any combination of container lengths.

These flatcars formed the backbone of the piggyback fleet well into the 1980s. Early piggyback cars were equipped with pairs of collapsible hitches—one at the end and one at the middle—to facilitate end or "circus" loading. As lift-on/lift-off facilities became more common in the 1970s and later, many cars were modified with pairs of hitches (often fixed) at the ends, which allowed two 45-foot trailers to ride back-to-back.

An interesting modification to flatcars appeared in the Long Runner car, made by connecting a pair of 89-foot cars with a drawbar (fig. 7-6). This allows the two-unit pair to carry three 53-foot trailers, with the middle trailer straddling the two cars. Some of these cars also have hitches arranged to allow the car to carry four 45-foot trailers if needed. Trailer Train (which became TTX Co. in 1991), began converting cars for this service in 1987.

Spine cars

The 89-foot flatcar remained the mainstay of piggyback service through the 1970s. However, by that time the number of end-loading (or "circus-style") ramps was rapidly decreasing, replaced by larger terminals with overhead cranes or side-loading forklifts that greatly reduced the loading and unloading time for trailers.

The flatcar deck, a critical part of circus unloading, wasn't needed for lift-off service—a platform was needed only under the trailer wheels. Flatcars were heavy, and, if a good deal of the steel could be removed, railroads would realize

7-5 All-purpose flush-deck cars have collapsible hitches and adjustable container pedestals built into the deck. The slots allow the pedestals to slide to fit any container length. *Jeff Wilson*

7-6 Long Runner cars were made by connecting two 89-foot cars with a drawbar. At left is a PS channel-side car; at right is a flush-deck car. *Jeff Wilson*

7-7 Santa Fe's home-built Ten-Pack Fuel Foilers were the first widely successful spine cars. *Santa Fe*

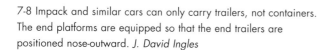

7-8 Impack and similar cars can only carry trailers, not containers. The end platforms are equipped so that the end trailers are positioned nose-outward. *J. David Ingles*

7-9 Container-only (NTTX) spine cars are simple skeleton cars that can be identified by their lack of trailer hitches. *Jeff Wilson*

7-10 This unit of a 53-foot all-purpose spine is loaded to capacity, hauling a 53-foot J.B. Hunt container on chassis. *Jeff Wilson*

7-11 Platforms of Twin-28 spines can haul single long trailers or containers or a pair of back-to-back 28-foot trailers. *Jeff Wilson*

substantial fuel savings from the reduced weight of the railcars.

Thus the spine car was developed. Spine cars are just that: a heavy center beam, or spine, with platforms to support trailer wheels (which could be much lighter than a flatcar deck). Spine cars could also be designed so the trailers sit lower than on a flatcar, lowering the center of gravity and improving the ride and tracking.

The Santa Fe was a pioneer in the development of spine cars. Although several experimental cars had been tried over the years, the Santa Fe developed a winner with its Fuel Foiler articulated spine car

in 1978 (fig. 7-7). The cars were exclusive to the Santa Fe and never traveled off line because they didn't meet Association of American Railroads (AAR) interchange standards for cushioning.

The Itel Corp. bought the patent rights to the Fuel Foiler design in 1981 and modified it to meet AAR interchange rules. The company began selling the cars, which it dubbed Impacks (short for InterModal Package) in sets (fig. 7-8). Five-unit sets were the most common, but sets from three to ten units were also built.

Along with TTX, which runs the cars with UTTX and TTLX report-

ing marks, several railroads also bought these or similar designs built by ACF (Versa-Deck) and Thrall (ARC-5). All of these cars were designed strictly for trailers.

The next spine car to hit the rails was called just that: the spine car. Delivered in 1987, the five-unit cars built for Trailer Train (NTTX reporting marks) carry containers only (fig. 7-9). Each platform can carry a 40- to 48-foot container, and the middle and end platforms can each carry a pair of 20-foot containers. The 350 cars delivered were the only ones built because well cars soon became the dominant means of carrying containers.

7-12

7-13

7-12 Front Runner cars are single-unit lightweight platforms with single axles at each end. This car was built by Paccar in 1984. *Jeff Wilson*

7-13 Southern Pacific's first double-stack cars used substantial bulkheads to hold the top containers in place. *Bob MacDonald*

Trailer Train began working with manufacturers on a car that could be used for either piggyback trailers or containers—a cross between the spine and Impack-style cars. The result was the all-purpose spine car, one of the most successful intermodal cars to hit the rails (fig. 7-10). The cars, first delivered in 1988, are versatile, as they can carry either trailers or containers as needed. They are much lighter than well cars, and their low profile made them ideal for routes that couldn't handle the tall double-stack cars.

Built by Bethlehem, Gunderson, Thrall, and Trinity, each platform of the first AP spines (built through 1993) can carry a trailer or container up to 48 feet long, and the end platforms can each carry a pair of 20-foot containers. These cars are simply labeled "all-purpose spine car."

In 1993, manufacturers began making lengthened versions of the cars, which can handle containers or trailers up to 53 feet long. As fig. 7-10 shows, these cars have "53" lettering on the sides of the platforms.

The newest versions of the cars are the Twin 28 spine cars. Each platform on these cars can carry a single trailer up to 57 feet long or a pair of 28-foot trailers (fig. 7-11).

Two other cars that fit into the spine or skeleton category are the 4-Runner and Front Runner. The 4-Runner was first to enter service, in 1981. The 4-Runner was a set of four drawbar-connected single-platform units, each of which had a single axle at each end. Tracking problems made these cars less than successful; just over 100 were placed in service.

After experiments with that design, a scaled-down single-unit car, the Front Runner, was introduced in 1983 (fig. 7-12). The Front Runner is a low-riding single-unit platform with a single axle at each end. The cars, built by four manufacturers, can carry one trailer from 40 to 48 feet. More than 3,000 had been built by 1990.

Double-stack well cars

In the 1970s, railroads began looking for more efficient ways of carrying containers than on flat-

car decks. Sea-Land worked with ACF Industries and the Southern Pacific to develop the first double-stack well car, which made its debut in 1977.

The initial single-unit cars could carry either standard ISO (International Organization for Standardization) 40-foot containers or Sea-Land's 35-foot containers, with the top container held by bulkheads (railroads didn't trust standard inter-box connectors, or IBCs, to do the job). The car remained in service for two years. ACF then delivered a three-unit car to the SP, and SP then ordered 42 five-unit sets of the cars, which became known simply as Double-Stacks. They entered service in 1981 (fig. 7-13).

The new cars were successful for many reasons. First, a lot of dead tare weight was eliminated. A five-unit articulated car has just six trucks, compared to ten trucks of the standard flatcars it is replacing. Also, train length is significantly reduced, as is slack action. Eliminating all those couplers results in smoother train

7-14

7-15

7-16

7-17

handling and less shock to loads.

The first car to hit the market in significant numbers was Thrall's five-unit Lo-Pac 2000, bought by American President Lines and Maersk in 1985 (fig. 7-14). These didn't have bulkheads, relying instead on standard IBCs to hold the upper containers in place.

Gunderson's first entry in the well car market, in 1985, was the Twin-Stack (fig. 7-15). These five-unit articulated cars are distinguished by their bulkheads. These were followed by a car without bulkheads, the flat-sided Maxi-Stack I, in 1988 (fig. 7-16). Another early well car design was Trinity's Backpacker, shown in fig. 7-17.

Well sizes increase

These early cars were designed with 40-foot wells for carrying 40-foot ISO containers (or pairs of 20-foot containers). However, in the late 1980s, container sizes began to grow, and soon 45- and 48-foot containers became popular. As longer containers were used, weight capacity had to be

addressed: Most early well cars used 100-ton trucks at the articulated joints, with standard 70-ton trucks at the ends. This meant that a pair of fully loaded 20-foot containers could max out the weight for a unit, resulting in an unused top position. To solve the problem, manufacturers lengthened their well cars and using 125-ton trucks at the articulated joints.

Thrall brought out the Lo-Pac II in 1986, which had the same design as the earlier car, but with 40-foot end units and 48-foot intermediate wells. By 1989 the Lo-Pac II had all 48-foot wells.

Gunderson improved its car with the Maxi-Stack II, which had 40-foot wells in the end units and 45-foot intermediate units. Few were built, as production shifted to the Maxi-Stack III (fig. 7-18), which came out in 1989. The Maxi III, with 48-foot, 125-ton capacity wells throughout, became the most popular articulated well car of the 1990s.

Trinity also each came out with longer versions of its Backpacker,

7-14 Thrall's Lo-Pac 2000 can be identified by its exterior braces and squared-off ends. Early cars such as this one had 40-foot wells. *Jeff Wilson*

7-15 Gunderson's first well car was the Twin-Stack, which had 40-foot wells and bulkheads. *Jeff Wilson*

7-16 Gunderson's Maxi-Stack I is basically a Twin-Stack without bulkheads. It can be identified by its deep, flat slab sides. *Jeff Wilson*

7-17 The Trinity Backpacker has angled sides. The end units on this car have 40-foot wells, with intermediate wells at 48 feet. *Jeff Wilson*

and Canadian maker National Steel Car (NSC) developed a car with 48-foot wells.

In the meantime, stand-alone cars became popular in the early 1990s. The main reason was capacity: Even after going to the 125-ton articulated car, it was still possible to surpass the weight limit of a well with three fully loaded containers.

The stand-alone car solved that problem because it can carry any combination of containers. Gunderson's Husky Stack, which first appeared in 1990, was the first popular design to catch on (fig. 7-19). The car was basically a single-well version of the Maxi-Stack III. This was followed in 1993 by the All-Purpose Husky Stack, which has trailer hitches at each end (fig. 7-20) to increase the flexibility of the car. Thrall and NSC followed Gunderson's lead with their own stand-alone cars based on their articulated cars.

The longest of the double-stack cars is Gunderson's Husky Stack 2+2, built in the mid-1990s, which has a 56-foot well. The car was designed to carry four 28-foot containers (two down and two up, hence 2+2).

A variation on the stand-alone car is the drawbar-connected sets of stand-alone cars, with three- and four-unit sets the most common (fig. 7-21). Except for their drawbars, the cars are the same as stand-alone cars; the connected

7-18

7-19

7-20

7-18 The most popular articulated well car of the 1990s was Gunderson's Maxi-Stack III. It has 48-foot wells throughout. The car has flat upper sides that angle in at the bottom, and a unique angled cutout near the ends. *Jeff Wilson*

7-19 Stand-alone well cars became popular in the 1990s. This is a Gunderson Husky Stack. *Jeff Wilson*

7-20 Manufacturers increased the flexibility of many of their well cars by adding trailer hitches. This is an All-Purpose Husky Stack. *Jeff Wilson*

set is assigned a single car number.

As domestic containers followed trailer length to 53 feet in the 1990s, manufacturers again looked for bigger cars. Although longer containers could be carried in the top positions of shorter cars, more capacity was needed for the bottom positions.

Double-stack cars with 53-foot wells were the answer. The stretch in length meant new designs, generally with deeper side walls. Manufacturers, including Gunder-son (fig. 7-22), National Steel Car (fig. 7-21), and Thrall (fig. 7-23), developed new articulated, stand-alone, and drawbar-connected cars based on their old ones.

Spotting features of well cars includes the side shape, pattern of bracing and side posts, end shape, and length. The length is easy to spot, as the well length is marked on the side of each unit to make the cars easy to identify for loading.

7-21

7-22

7-21 This is the end unit of a drawbar-connected National Steel Car 53-foot well car—you can see the drawbar at left. NSC's cars can be spotted by their exterior posts and the curved cutouts near the wheels at the ends. *Jeff Wilson*

7-22 Gunderson's 53-foot cars resemble its earlier 48-foot cars, but with deeper sides. This is a three-unit articulated car. *Jeff Wilson*

7-23 Thrall's 53-foot articulateds have the same characteristics as the company's earlier cars, with vertical exterior posts and squared-off ends. This is a three-unit car. *Jeff Wilson*

7-23

CAR COMPONENTS

Many components are common to all freight cars. These include trucks, wheels, couplers, and brake equipment.

Trucks are a key spotting feature of freight cars (fig. 8-1). They have evolved substantially from the pressed-steel archbar design of the pre-World War I era through early cast solid-bearing trucks to roller-bearing trucks of today. Knowing the differences between the various types of trucks will help you in identifying and modeling freight cars.

Brake components aren't as visible as trucks or couplers, but their appearance can help identify an era of a car. Understanding how a train's air brakes work will also help you in detailing models.

We'll look at the development, spotting features, and usage of trucks, couplers, and brakes on freight cars.

8-1 At first glance they might look alike, but freight car trucks are not all the same. They have evolved a great deal over the years, from early 20th century archbar designs to modern roller-bearing trucks like this one. *Jeff Wilson*

EIGHT

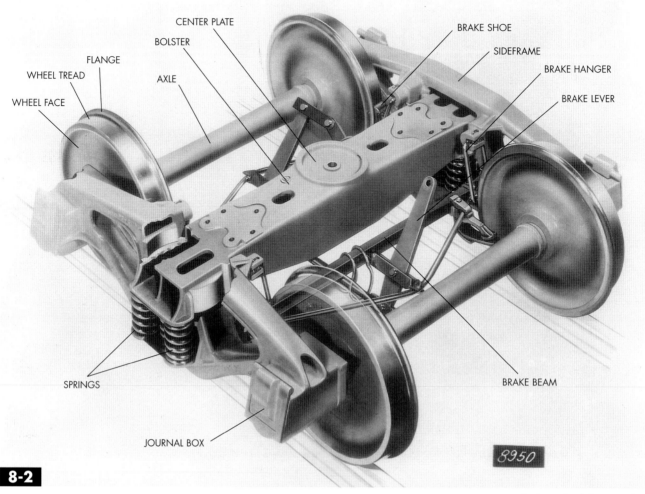

CENTER PLATE
BOLSTER
FLANGE
WHEEL TREAD
AXLE
WHEEL FACE
BRAKE SHOE
SIDEFRAME
BRAKE HANGER
BRAKE LEVER
SPRINGS
BRAKE BEAM
JOURNAL BOX

8-2

8950

Buckeye Steel Castings Co.

Trucks

It's easy to overlook trucks when studying freight car details. At first glance one truck might look like any other. However, a closer look reveals many differences, from major ones—such as roller- and solid-bearing trucks—to small details. Understanding the types of prototype trucks and wheels will help you choose the proper ones for your models, making them more realistic.

Freight car trucks and wheels have evolved substantially, and railroads have used hundreds of different truck designs over the years. We'll look at the most commonly used trucks from the World War I era through today.

Truck anatomy

Figure 8-2 shows the parts of a typical freight car truck. The car

8-3

8-3 Journal boxes hold cotton waste impregnated with lubricating oil. The oil lubricates the axle end and bearing. *Erie RR*

rides on the bolster, held in place by a kingpin that rests in the truck's center plate, the circular pocket on top of the bolster.

The bolster isn't anchored solidly to the sideframe. Instead, it rests atop a series of springs (four or more, called the spring package) in each sideframe. The

size and number of springs vary based on the capacity of the truck: larger springs—and more of them—allow heavier loads. The springs cushion the ride by allowing the bolster to float up and down in the sideframes.

The sideframes, in turn, place their load on the ends of the axles. Early trucks, such as the one in fig. 8-2, are known as solid-bearing trucks (often incorrectly called friction bearings). In these the journal box (fig. 8-3) surrounds the bearing and axle end. The journal box is packed with a fibrous cotton material—called waste—soaked in lubricating oil. The axle and bearing surfaces are lubricated by wicking oil from the impregnated waste.

Later trucks use sealed roller bearings. These roll with much less friction and require no lubri-

8-4

8-5

8-6

8-4 Archbar trucks were made of pressed steel components bolted together. *Jeff Wilson*

8-5 Andrews trucks have cast sideframes, but separate journal boxes. A steel bar connects the frame to the bottom of the journal box. *Rail Data Services Collection*

8-6 The Bettendorf T-section truck was the first with journal boxes cast as part of the sideframe. Note the T-shaped cross section of the sideframe. *David P. Morgan Library collection*

cation. We'll look at these trucks later in this chapter.

Trucks have several brake components. Most visible are the brake beam and brake shoes, which can be seen through the sideframes.

Trucks are classified by weight. The weight rating isn't the load that a single truck can carry, but the weight of the car itself. Hence, 50-ton trucks are designed to be used under 50-ton capacity freight cars, and so on.

Archbar, Andrews

The most common trucks used in the early 1900s were archbar trucks (fig. 8-4). These were made of pressed-steel components that were bolted together. Although they worked well, archbar trucks required lots of maintenance. Their bolts needed frequent tightening, as they tended to work

loose with the shocks and jolts of operation.

Although some archbar trucks were built into the 1920s, they had largely been superseded by more advanced designs by the midteens. Archbar trucks were eventually banned completely from interchange service in 1941.

By World War I, state-of-the-art trucks had cast sideframes, which eliminated the problems of the bolts and connectors of the archbar truck. The most popular of these early cast trucks was the Andrews (fig. 8-5). Andrews sideframes still used separate journal boxes and could be identified by the steel bar connecting the sideframe and the bottom of the journal box. Andrews trucks were in production from around 1910 through the 1930s. One of their big selling features was that journal boxes from archbar trucks

could be reused in new Andrews trucks. Andrews trucks could no longer be used in interchange service after 1956.

Bettendorf, AAR trucks

The next generation of freight car trucks eliminated the separate journal boxes, instead casting them as integral parts of the sideframe. The Bettendorf Co. was the first to do this (as early as 1903), using a cast sideframe with a T-shaped cross section (see fig. 8-6). The Bettendorf design was popular through the teens.

Significantly stronger trucks with U-shaped cross sections eventually superseded T-section trucks. These trucks, which have become most identified with the modern steam and early diesel eras, have become generically—and incorrectly—as Bettendorf trucks (see fig. 8-7).

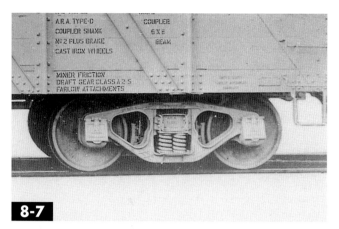

8-7

8-8

8-9

8-7 An improvement to the early cast truck was the change to a U cross section sideframe, shown here on a 1923-built car. *Milwaukee Road*

8-8 Dalman trucks had a unique sideframe and multi-level spring package design. *David P. Morgan Library collection*

8-9 The Barber S-2 was a commonly used truck of the late steam and early diesel eras. *Jerry A. Pinkepank*

The cast-steel U-section truck was eventually adopted as an American Railway Association (ARA, later called the American Association of Railroads or AAR) standard: the Type Y truck. Because the Bettendorf Company developed the concept and built thousands of these trucks, the style has become widely known as a Bettendorf truck. However, Bettendorf widely licensed ele-

ments of the design, so trucks of this type were manufactured by many builders.

Each of these trucks follows the AAR standard, but many have varying details, including side-frame shape, spring size and styles, bolster design, and journal-box lids.

Along with improved strength, manufacturers worked to improve the riding characteristics of trucks by cutting down on excess lateral and vertical movement.

An early (1920s) attempt at improving riding quality was the Dalman truck. This truck had eight springs in each sideframe (compared to five on most other trucks), with springs on different levels. As fig. 8-8 shows, this, along with a unique sideframe, gave Dalman trucks a distinctive appearance.

The two most popular types of improved trucks came along a bit

later: the Barber S-2 (fig. 8-9) and the ASF A-3 Ride Control (fig. 8-10), introduced during World War II. Both were advertised to ride more smoothly, cut down on wheel and spring wear, and be easier on track and roadbed. The A-3 caught on rapidly and became the most popular truck used through the end of the solid-bearing era. The two trucks are similar, but are shaped differently in the bolster end and spring areas.

Many other stabilized trucks were also introduced, including the National B-1. Figure 8-11 shows this truck, which had a unique spring package with stabilizing wedges.

A note on truck manufacturers and designs: Freight-car trucks were built by many manufacturers from the steam era through the 1960s. Major producers included American Steel Foundries (ASF),

8-10

8-10 The ASF Ride Control truck was the most popular solid-bearing truck from the end of World War II to the end of the solid-bearing era. *Lee Langum*

8-11 The National B-1 truck had a distinctive sideframe, spring package, and bolster design. *David P. Morgan Library collection*

8-12 This cutaway view shows how roller bearings function over the axle ends. *Hyatt*

8-11

8-12

Bettendorf Co., Buckeye, National, Symington-Gould, Standard Car Truck Co., and others.

Although most companies had their own truck designs, customers could order trucks of almost any design from any other member of the Four-Wheel Truck Association. Thus a railroad could order an A-3 Ride Control truck from Buckeye as well as ASF. Also, any given design was available in many variations, including different spring packages and journals (and thus different tonnage ratings), standard or double-truss design, and other details.

The best way to identify solid-bearing trucks is by reading the information cast into the sideframe. Information generally includes the manufacturer, truck type, spring package, other foundry information, and sometimes the railroad for which the

truck was built. If in doubt, compare details on prototype photos to available truck models to determine the closest match.

Roller-bearing trucks

The main problem with solid-bearing trucks was that the journal boxes required frequent lubrication. This was labor intensive, and the result of a dry bearing was an overheated journal, which could result in a fire or broken axle. The eventual solution was to develop trucks with roller-bearing journals (fig. 8-12).

Roller bearings greatly reduced friction and drag, and didn't require lubrication. Roller-bearing trucks had been around since the turn of the 20th century, and began to see frequent use in the 1930s on passenger equipment. However, because of their additional cost, roller-bearing trucks

didn't come into wide use on freight equipment until the late 1950s and 1960s. These trucks are identified by their roller-bearing end caps on the axle ends (figs. 8-12 and 8-13).

New cars built after 1966 were required to have roller-bearing trucks, and solid-bearing trucks were banned from interchange service in the 1990s.

The two most popular modern trucks are the ASF Ride Control, made by ASF-Keystone, and the Barber S-2, made by Standard Car Truck Co. (fig. 8-14), both of which date back to earlier solid-bearing designs. Other common modern trucks include the ASF Ridemaster and National C-1. Each is made with various spring packages and other options in 70- to 125-ton versions.

As with solid-bearing trucks, the easiest way to identify roller-

8-13 Roller-bearing trucks, such as this 70-ton ASF Ride Control, have end caps that rotate. The end caps have different designs depending upon the manufacturer of the roller bearings. *Jeff Wilson*

8-14 The Barber S-2 is one of the most common modern trucks in service. This is a 100-ton truck on a tank car. *Scott Hartley*

8-15 The ribs on the back mark this as a cast-iron wheel. Cast-iron wheels weren't used on new equipment after 1957, and were banned from interchange use in 1970. *Jeff Wilson*

bearing trucks is on the sideframes, as the manufacturer's name and truck type are stamped on the side. If you can't read the lettering, use the shape of the sideframe in matching it to a model.

Wheels

Wheels on prototype cars have a number of differences, but for modelers the most important detail is probably the size. The 33"-diameter wheel is standard on freight equipment of 70-ton capacity and under. For 100-ton trucks, 36" wheels are used, and for 125-ton trucks, 38" wheels.

An exception is that smaller wheels (28" diameter) are used on triple-deck auto-rack cars. This allows these 70-ton cars to ride lower so they can negotiate tighter clearances.

Many model wheelsets have ribs cast on the back of the wheel (see fig. 8-15). This was a characteristic of many—but not all—prototype cast-iron wheels (known as "chilled" wheels for the heat treatment of the treads). The ribs were designed to better dissipate the heat generated during braking, which could weaken the wheel.

Chilled wheels faded from use in the 1950s and were forbidden on new cars after 1957. They were banned from interchange use in 1970. Modern wheels are cast or wrought steel and don't have the ribs. Also, many steam-era cars didn't have chilled wheels, as steel wheels began increasing in popularity starting in the mid-1920s.

Steel wheels on freight cars are either single-wear (1W), or two-wear (2W). This information is

usually stenciled on the car end. Single-wear wheels (which have 1¼" rims) are designed to be scrapped after the tread profile wears to a certain point. Two-wear wheels have thicker (2") rims that are designed to be turned (recut and reshaped) during the car's life to return the wheel to its proper contour.

From a railroad's economic perspective, 1W wheels are lighter and less expensive. On heavy-duty cars where the wheels will need turning at least once during a car's lifetime, 2W wheels pay for themselves because turning is less costly than buying new wheels.

Couplers

The AAR knuckle coupler has been a part of railroading since the turn of the 20th century.

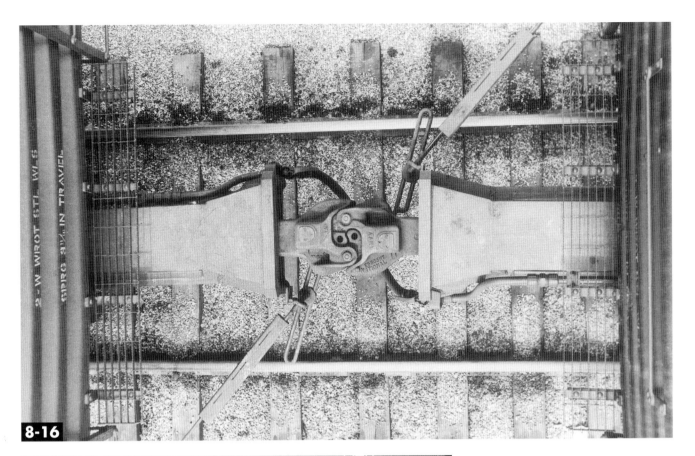

8-16

8-17

Couplers work by the moveable knuckle, which opens outward to mate with the coupler on the adjoining car (see fig. 8-16).

In order to couple cars, the knuckle on one or both cars is opened. Backing one car into another will automatically close the knuckles and couple the cars.

To uncouple cars, a crew member opens a knuckle by pulling the uncoupling lever.

Couplers have evolved in style over the past 100 years, but have retained the same basic appearance. An exception has been the shelf-type coupler (fig. 8-17). These couplers, used since 1978 on tank cars carrying hazardous commodities, are designed to stay together in case of derailments, thus preventing couplers from separating and puncturing the end of an adjacent tank car. An earlier single-shelf coupler, the Type F interlocking coupler, had been used since 1970 on tank cars carrying hazardous materials.

Uncoupling levers come in many shapes and sizes—see photos throughout this book for examples. Each car has an uncoupling lever on each end; they are positioned on the knuckle side of the coupler (so that as you're looking at the side of the car, the uncoupling lever will be at right).

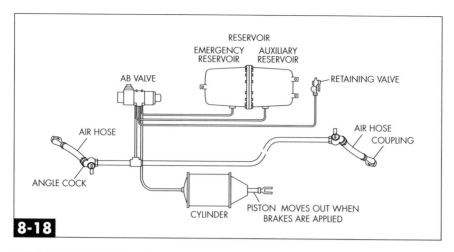

8-18

8-19 The AB brake components on this covered hopper are in clear view. *Erie RR*

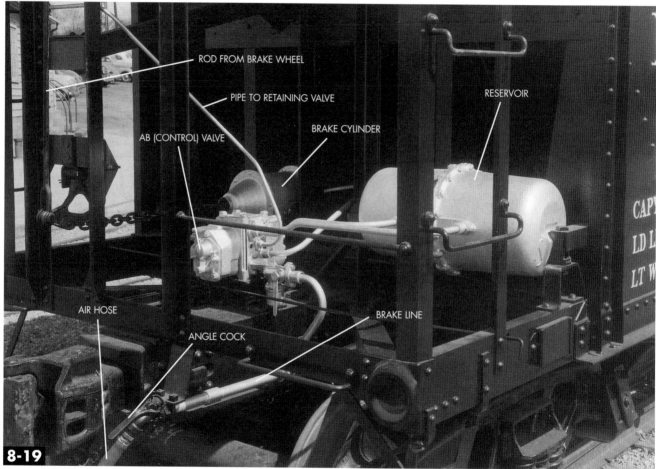

8-19

Brakes

The brake system is an integral part of every freight car, and understanding its components and how they work can help you make more accurate models. Brake gear is largely hidden on many house cars (such as boxcars and reefers), but it is visible on many other cars, such as tank cars.

Figure 8-18 shows an overview of an AB brake system, which—

although it has been modernized over the years with the ABD, ABDW, and ABDX systems—has been standard on new equipment since 1933. Figure 8-19 shows the various AB components in view on a covered hopper car.

The air hoses at each end of a freight car, when connected, form a continuous pipeline to the locomotive. This is called the train line. Air pumps or compressors in

the locomotive pressurize the train line (90 pounds of pressure for most modern freight trains).

The control valve on each car is the heart of the system. The control valve routes air from the train line into the reservoir, keeping the reservoir fully charged.

To apply the brakes, the engineer releases air from the train line. The control valve senses the drop in pressure and routes air

TRIPLE VALVE — RESERVOIR — CYLINDER

8-20

BRAKE WHEEL
HOUSING
RETAINING VALVE
A.T.S.F.
10135
BRAKE PLATFORM
TACK BOARD
IW WROT STEEL WHEELS
POLING POCKET
UNCOUPLING LEVER
AIR HOSE

8-21

T.C. 546

8-22

8-20 The combined K brake components are quite visible on this 1923-built gondola. *Milwaukee Road*

8-21 Ajax was the most common type of hand brake. Ajax brake wheels were fairly intricate, and the Ajax name was cast on the housing. *Santa Fe*

8-22 Miner brake wheels had solid centers and six spokes. Note the indentations around the outside of the wheel at the spokes. *J. Parker Lamb*

from the reservoir into the cylinder. The piston in the cylinder moves outward, moving linkage which forces the brake shoes against the wheels. The amount of air released regulates the amount of pressure applied to the wheels.

When the engineer releases the brakes, the compressor again charges the air line. The control valve senses this change in pressure, releases the air from the cylinder, and begins routing air back into the reservoir, recharging the system. This action takes place on every car of the train.

The reservoir has two halves: service and emergency. For a normal (service) brake application, air comes from the service half of the reservoir. When an emergency application is made (all of the air released from the train line), the control valve routes all of the air from the reservoir to the cylinder.

Another important component is the retaining valve, or retainer. Setting this causes some air to be retained in the cylinder regardless of brake application or release.

8-23 Equipco brake wheels had an intricate spiral pattern. *ACF Incorporated*

8-24 Universal brake wheels had solid cupped centers, with simple spiral-pattern spokes. *Hagley Museum and Library*

8-25 AAR standard wheels resembled the Universal design, but with straight spokes. *Norfolk & Western*

8-23

8-24

8-25

Retainers were often set on cars before descending steep grades. The usual location for the retaining valve is next to the brake wheel on the end of the car.

The layout of brake components varies widely among cars (as fig. 8-19 shows), but the components remain the same.

K brakes

The most common type of air brakes used from World War I though the 1920s was the K brake. Figure 8-20 shows a gondola with KC brake components (so called because they had the valve, reservoir, and cylinder combined).

K brakes operated in a similar manner to the AB brake shown in fig. 8-18, but the reservoir did not have a separate emergency section, and the valve controlling the system (known as the "triple valve") didn't have as many functions as the later AB valve. Also, K brakes were slower in responding than AB brakes—a serious drawback as trains became longer and railroad cars grew heavier.

The K system was not allowed on new equipment after 1932, and K brakes were banned on cars in interchange service after 1953. Many cars originally equipped with K brakes were later rebuilt with AB brakes—check prototype photos if you're modeling a specific era.

Hand brakes

The brake wheel is among the most noticeable brake components. The brake wheel on early (into the 1930s) cars was usually mounted horizontally atop a vertical brake staff (fig. 8-20). Turning the wheel pulled a chain connected to the piston in the brake cylinder, applying the brake; turning the wheel the other way released the brake.

Starting in the 1930s, power hand brakes came into use (fig. 8-21). These were generally mounted vertically on the car, on top of a gear box. Turning the wheel pulled up a rod, which, via a clevis at the bottom of the rod, pulled a rod connected to the cylinder shaft.

From the 1930s through the 1950s, car manufacturers used a variety of styles of brake wheels and housings from several manufacturers. The most commonly used types included those made by Ajax (fig. 8-21), Miner (fig. 8-22), Equipco (fig. 8-23), and Universal (fig. 8-24).

A problem was that brake wheels were not interchangeable, making repairs difficult. In the late 1950s and into the 1960s, an AAR standard design for a brake wheel was developed, which could be used on brake housings from any manufacturer (see fig. 8-25).

Jeff Wilson collection

Freight car lettering

What's required and what it means

1) **Road name and herald**. This lettering isn't required, and its use varies greatly among railroads and eras. Many railroads also added slogans, including passenger train promos.

2) **Reporting marks (required)**. Each railroad or private owner is assigned a unique set of identifying initials (large railroads or corporations may have several different reporting marks). Cars with reporting marks ending in X are privately owned.

3) **Number (required)**. The car's number is unique to that set of reporting marks.

4) **Capacity**. The car's designed capacity in pounds (to the nearest 100). Since 1985 this is no longer required on new cars; many older cars have this line painted out.

5) **Load limit**. The maximum weight allowed for the load itself.

6) **Light weight**. The car's weight when empty. If the word "new" appears, the weight was taken when built (and the date is the built date). Cars are periodically reweighed, generally after repairs are made. When a new light weight is stenciled, the shop initials and date are added.

7) **AAR mechanical code classification**. In this case, XML, which indicates a boxcar equipped with loading devices.

8) **Built date**. The date the car left the factory. On newer cars this appears in the consolidated stencil.

9) **Dimensional data**. The internal and external measurements of the car.

10) **Consolidated stencils**. These began appearing in 1972. Early consolidated stencils were single panels; later, multiple panels were used. On these is stenciled information regarding brake and axle maintenance.

11) **ACI (Automatic Car Identification) plate**. ACI was an automated car identification system that used trackside scanners to read colored panels on cars. The system was introduced in 1967; all cars in interchange service were required to have ACI plates by 1970. The system didn't work well (grime and dirt made the panels unreadable) and the requirement for ACI plates was eliminated in 1977. Cars built after that date won't have ACI plates, but plates were often left on older cars. A solution to this problem was the electronic identification tag, shown in the photo on page 90.

12) **Wheel inspection dot.** These marks began appearing in March 1978 when a type of wheel was found to be defective, and all cars were required to be inspected. Cars without the banned wheels received a black square with yellow dot; cars with the wheels received a white dot, and these wheels had to be replaced by December 1978. Cars built or repainted in 1979 and later won't have this mark.

13) **Special equipment.** If a car is equipped with special equipment (this car has DF-2 loading devices), it will usually be stenciled on the car.

14) **Route and tack boards.** These wood plates are located on car sides and ends so that notes can be tacked to them. The small boards are known as route boards, and these are for information on car routing. The large tack boards are for other instructions, for example, notes on how to unload a shipment.

Automatic Equipment Identification (AEI) tags were required on cars as of 1994. These use passive radio signals to transmit data to railside scanners, avoiding the grime problem that plagued the earlier ACI system. You'll find tags on each car side, toward the right end of the car. *Jeff Wilson photo*

Car Builders Cyclopedia and Official Railway Equipment register

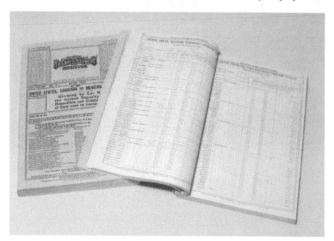

The *Official Railway Equipment Register* lists all the freight equipment in service in North America. *Jeff Wilson photo*

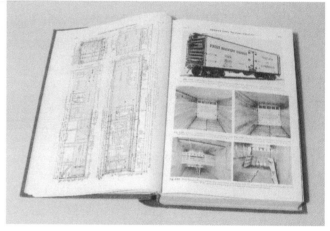

The *Car Builders Cyclopedia* contains drawings, photos, and other information on all types of freight cars. *Jeff Wilson photo*

Two of the most important references for freight car spotting and modeling are the *Car Builders Cyclopedia*, often called simply "the 'Cyc," and the *Official Railway Equipment Register*, or ORER.

The *Cyclopedia* has been published on an irregular schedule (every few years) since the 1800s, and in the 1960s, it was combined with the *Locomotive Cyclopedia* as the *Car and Locomotive Cyclopedia*. The book includes drawings and photos of all types of cars, and includes ads, explanations, and drawings of ancillary equipment (brakes, trucks, wheels, roofs, ends, etc.). Having one for the era you model will help you model and understand freight cars much better.

The ORER is a railroad-by-railroad listing of all freight equipment in service in North America.

Information provided for each car or car series includes AAR mechanical code; interior and exterior length, height, and width; door size; cubic capacity; bunker capacity (for reefers); and weight capacity—all valuable information when trying to identify a car in a photo. Other information includes summaries of types of equipment in service; construction material (wood or steel); and special equipment (such as drop ends on gons or cushion underframes). Other areas of the ORER define plate clearances and illustrate and list AAR car codes. You'll find an ORER from the era you model to be a valuable reference.

You can find copies of both publications at dealers specializing in railroad publications and collectibles, as well as on eBay.

Freight car timeline

1917 USRA (United States Railroad Administration) assumes control of U.S. railroads

1918 ARA (American Railway Association) is formed

1920 USRA control ends

1928 Steel center sills required on cars for interchange

1933 AB brakes required on all new cars

1934 AAR (Association of American Railroads) is formed

1941 Archbar trucks banned from interchange

1945 Steel running boards required on new cars

1953 KC brakes banned from interchange

1956 Andrews trucks banned from interchange

1957 Iron wheels no longer allowed on new equipment

1966 Roller-bearing trucks required on all new/rebuilt 100-ton cars

1966 Running boards no longer on new equipment

1966 Brake wheels mounted low on new equipment

1968 Roller-bearing trucks required on all new cars

1970 Iron wheels banned from interchange

1970 Roller-bearing trucks required on all rebuilt cars

1972 Consolidated stencils first used

1979 Running boards to be removed from house cars

1994 AEI tags required

1995 Solid-bearing trucks banned from interchange

Freight car builders

ACF Industries – Currently building cars. Formerly American Car & Foundry (until 1954).

Berwick Foundry & Forge – No longer building cars.

Bethlehem Steel Car Co. – Carmaking facility sold to Johnstown America Corp.

Evans Products Co. – Bought U.S. Railway Equipment Co. in 1960s; no longer building cars.

FMC Corp. – Plant purchased by Greenbrier Companies in early 1980s, which renamed it Gunderson.

General American Car Co. – No longer building cars. Car designs licensed to Trinity.

Greenville Steel Car Co. – Acquired by Trinity in 1986.

Gunderson – Currently building cars. A division of Greenbrier Companies.

Johnstown America Corp. – Currently building cars. Successor to Bethlehem Steel Co.'s Freight Car Division.

Magor Freight Car – Later a division of Fruehauf; no longer building cars.

Marine Industries Ltd. – (Canadian) No longer building cars.

Mt. Vernon Car Manufacturing Co. – No longer building cars.

National Steel Car Ltd. – (Canadian) Currently building cars.

North American Car Co. – Designs sold to Trinity and Thrall in early 1980s.

Ortner Freight Car Co. – Acquired by Trinity in 1984.

Pacific Car & Foundry – Later Paccar. No longer building cars.

Pennsylvania Tank Car Co. – No longer building cars.

Portec Inc. – No longer building cars.

Pressed Steel Car Co. – No longer building cars.

Pullman-Standard – Created by merger of Pullman Co.'s freight car building division and Standard Steel Car in the mid-1930s. Assets acquired by Trinity in 1984.

Southern Iron & Equipment Co. (SIECO) – Acquired by Evans in early 1970s.

Standard Tank Car Co. – Bought by GATC in late 1920s.

Thrall Car Manufacturing Co. – Acquired by Trinity in 2001.

Trenton Works – (Canadian) Purchased by Greenbriar in mid-1990s.

Trinity Industries Inc. – Currently building cars. Acquired General American (1983), Pullman Standard (1984), Ortner Freight Car Co. (1984), Greenville Steel Car (1986), Thrall Car Manufacturing (2001).

Union Tank Car Co. – Purchased Phoenix-Graver (formerly Graver Tank & Manufacturing Co.) in 1957. Currently building cars.

Youngstown Steel Door Co. – No longer building cars.

List of available models

Descriptions include the names of the prototypes the models are based on if applicable. Space prohibits listing all cars and all variations that have been produced. Space also precludes a detailed assessment of each model: Some are very close to their prototypes, others have details that are not accurate. Only plastic mass-produced cars and kits are listed; resin or wood craftsman kits are not included.

Some of the cars listed may not have been in production for some time—several years in some cases—but are included as a reference. Many hobby shops and dealers often have cars in stock that haven't been produced recently, and internet sites such as eBay are also good places to track down rare or out-of-production models.

Key:

DD – double-door	X-post – exterior post	t – ton
4D – four-door	XH – excess height	All boxcars are single-door unless
ED – end-door	ft – foot	otherwise noted.
PD – plug door	cf – cubic feet	

Prototype/description	Model mfr.	Number series	Prototype/description	Model mfr.	Number series
HO scale			PS-1 40-ft	Accurail	3400
			PS-1 40-ft	Kadee	4000
Boxcars			PS-1 50-ft	InterMountain	45900
USRA 40-ft single-sheathed	Tichy	4026	PS-1 50-ft	Kadee	6000
USRA 40-ft steel-side rebuild	Tichy	4028	PS-1 50-ft DD	Kadee	6700
USRA 40-ft double-sheathed	Accurail	4600	PS-1 50-ft DD	InterMountain	45600
40-ft single-sheathed 6-panel	Accurail	7100	AAR 50-ft	Accurail	5700
50-ft single-sheathed ED	Roundhouse	2100	AAR 50-ft DD	Accurail	5900
50-ft single-sheathed DD, ED	Roundhouse	2130	50-ft PD SS	Accurail	5800
Mather 40-ft single-sheathed	Proto 2000	30800	50-ft combination-door SS	Accurail	5300
PRR X29 40-ft	Red Caboose	7000	Evans 53-ft DD PD	Atlas	1750
PRR X31 40-ft round-roof	Bowser	55300	PS 40-ft high-cube	Hi-Tech	7000
PRR X31 40-ft DD round-roof	Bowser	55340	ACF 50-ft 5,080-cf X-post	Accurail	5600
PRR X32 50-ft round-roof	Bowser	55420	ACF 50-ft SS	Atlas	1330
PRR X32 50-ft DD round-roof	Bowser	55400	FMC 50-ft X-post	Roundhouse	1950
PRR X33 50-ft DD ED round-roof	Bowser	55460	FMC 50-ft X-post DD plug/		
AAR 1937 40-ft	InterMountain	45700	sliding doors	Roundhouse	1930
AAR 1937 40-ft	Red Caboose	8000	PC&F 50-ft, 14-ft	Athearn	4380
AAR 40-ft DD	Red Caboose	8500	PS 50-ft 5,277-cf	InterMountain	47500
AAR 1937 modified 40-ft	InterMountain	45800	PS 50-ft 5,277-cf	Roundhouse	1900
AAR ACF 40-ft	Red Caboose	8600	PS 50-ft 5,344-cf	Athearn	5810
AAR 40-ft, late	Accurail	3500	PS 50-ft waffle-side	Walthers	
AAR 40-ft	C&BT	10100	SIECO 50-ft	Athearn	4200
AAR 40-ft	Roundhouse	10600	Berwick 60-ft DD waffle-side	Athearn	4000
AAR 40-ft DD	Accurail	3600	Gunderson 60-ft X-post XH	Athearn	4100
AAR 50-ft	Proto 2000	21500	Gunderson 60-ft SS XH	Athearn	4130
AAR 50-ft DD auto	Proto 2000	30350	Gunderson 60-foot XH	Walthers	932-7100
AAR 50-ft DD ED auto	Proto 2000	30300			

Prototype/description	Model mfr.	Number series
Thrall all-door	Walthers	932-7000
PS 86-ft high-cube DD auto parts	Walthers	932-3500
Greenville 86-ft XH DD auto parts	Athearn	1970
PS 86-ft XH 4D auto parts	Walthers	932-3530
Thrall 86-ft XH 4D auto parts	Athearn	1980
PS 60-ft SD auto parts	Walthers	932-3550
PS 60-ft SD	InterMountain	46900
PS 60-ft DD auto parts	Walthers	932-3580
ACF 60-ft SD auto parts	Atlas	1650
ACF 60-ft DD auto parts	Atlas	1670

Covered hoppers

Prototype/description	Model mfr.	Number series
ACF 2-bay early cement	Atlas	1800
ACF 2-bay early cement	Eastern	2000
ACF 2-bay early cement	Kato	380000
Enterprise 2-bay cement	Eastern	2020
Greenville 2-bay modern cement	Walthers	932-5400
NSC 64-ft 4-bay plastic pellet	Walthers	932-7150
PS-2 2-bay cement	Kadee	
PS-2 3,219-cf 3-bay	Con-Cor	
PS-2 4,427-cf 3-bay low-side	Walthers	932-5700
PS-2 4,427-cf 3-bay high-side	Proto 2000	30100
PS-2 4,740-cf 3-bay	Athearn	7150
PS-2 4,750-cf 3-bay	InterMountain	45300
ACF Center Flow 2-bay cement (post-1971)	InterMountain	46500
ACF Center Flow 3,500-cf cylindrical 3-bay	Atlas	1930
ACF Center Flow 3,960-cf cylindrical 6-bay	Atlas	1950
ACF Center Flow 4,600-cf 3-bay (post-1971)	Accurail	2000
ACF Center Flow 4,650-cf 3-bay (pre-1971)	Atlas	1450
ACF Center Flow 4,650-cf 3-bay (post-1971)	InterMountain	47000
ACF Center Flow 5,250-cf 4-bay (pre-1971)	Athearn	1900
ACF Pressureaide 4-bay	Atlas	1500
FMC 4,700-cf 3-bay	Roundhouse	35200
NSC 4,550-cf cylindrical 4-bay	InterMountain	45100
Trinity 5,161-cf	Athearn	4250
Trinity 5,161-cf	LBF	5100

Prototype/description	Model mfr.	Number series
Airslide 40-ft 1-bay early	Con-Cor	9700
Airslide 40-ft	Eastern	2600
Airslide 40-ft	Walthers	932-4600
Airslide 50-ft. 2-bay	Walthers	932-3680

Flat cars

Prototype/description	Model mfr.	Number series
USRA 42-ft	Red Caboose	2200
ACF 40-ft	Tichy	4021
PRR F30 50-ft	Bowser	55950
AAR 50t, 53-ft	Proto 2000	21900
SIECO 50-ft bulkhead pulpwood	Walthers	932-5780
GSC Commonwealth 53-ft	Tichy	1000
GSC Commonwealth 53-ft	Walthers	3750
TTX 60-ft	InterMountain	46400
72-ft center beam, truss	Walthers	932-4100
72-ft center beam, opera window	Walthers	932-4104
Evans Type 4 coil cars	Walthers	932-3820
89-ft bi-level open auto rack	Accurail	9200
89-ft tri-level open auto rack	Accurail	9300
W&K 89-ft encl. tri-level auto rack	Walthers	932-4850
Auto-Max articulated auto rack	Athearn	4400

Gondolas

Prototype/description	Model mfr.	Number series
USRA steel 46-ft	Walthers	932-7450
USRA composite drop-bottom	InterMountain	46600
USRA Composite drop-bottom	Red Caboose	5100
40-ft steel GS	Roundhouse	1360
40-ft steel GS	Bowser	55900
Steel drop-bottom	Red Caboose	50000
52-ft 70t drop-end mill	Proto 2000	23700
54-ft riveted steel mill	Con-Cor	9000
65-ft welded steel mill	Walthers	932-3270
AAR 65-ft steel mill	Eastern	3010
AAR war-emergency mill	Tichy	1040
ACF Coalveyor	Atlas	1000
Bathtub 100t	InterMountain	47100
Bathtub 100t	Roundhouse	1660
BethGon Coalporter	LBF	1400
BethGon Coalporter	Walthers	932-5300
Johnstown AeroFlo	LBF	1500
Thrall 100t coal	Roundhouse	1640
Trinity Aluminator	LBF	1600

Hoppers

Prototype/description	Model mfr.	Number series
Greenville 7,000-cf wood chip	Walthers	932-5680
Greenville 100t 2-bay aggregate	Walthers	932-7400
Ortner 100t aggregate	Walthers	932-7050
USRA 55t 2-bay	Accurail	2600
USRA 50t 2-bay	Tichy	4027
USRA 50t 2-bay panel-side rebuild	Accurail	2800
USRA 50t 2-bay panel-side rebuild	Tichy	4029
PRR H21a 50t 4-bay	Bowser	54050
AAR 50t 2-bay offset-side	Atlas	1880
AAR 50t 2-bay offset-side	Athearn	5400
AAR 50t 2-bay offset-side, oval heap shields	Atlas	1890
ARA 70t 4-bay offset-side	Athearn	1750
AAR 70t 3-bay offset-side	Accurail	7500
AAR 70t 3-bay offset-side	Roundhouse	1600
AAR 70t 3-bay offset-side	Stewart	10300
AAR 70t 3-bay X-post	Stewart	10000
AAR 50t war emergency	Athearn	6100
AAR 50t war emergency	Proto 2000	23800
55t fishbelly	Stewart	10100
Ballast car, offset-side	Roundhouse	1580
Ballast car, X-post	Roundhouse	1560
40-ft 3-bay X-post	Roundhouse	1480
PRR H39 12-panel 3-bay	Stewart	10200
N&W H11 100t 3-bay	Bowser	55100
Greenville 100t coal	Con-Cor	9300
Trinity RD4 coal	Walthers	932-7800
Ortner Rapid Discharge 100t 5-bay	Roundhouse	1720
PRR G39 70t ore	Stewart	10600
70-t ore car, "Minnesota"	Walthers	932-4400
Ore car, tapered side	Roundhouse	1400
Ore car, rectangular side	Roundhouse	1420

Intermodal cars

Prototype/description	Model mfr.	Number series
Bethlehem 75-ft flat	Walthers	932-3950
PS 85-ft flat	Athearn	
Bethlehem 89-ft flat	Walthers	932-4950
All-purpose 89-ft flush-deck flat	Accurail	8900
Gunderson Twin-Stack 5-unit well	A-Line	27103
Gunderson 48-ft Husky Stack well	A-Line	27200
Gunderson 48-ft Husky Stack well	Athearn	7260
All-purpose 89-ft flush-deck flat	Accurail	8900
Gunderson 48-ft Husky Stack AP well	Walthers	932-4300
Gunderson 48-ft Maxi-Stack III 5-unit well	Athearn	5911
Gunderson 48-ft Maxi-Stack III 5-unit well	Con-Cor	195500
Gunderson 48-ft Husky Stack AP well	Con-Cor	198200
NSC 53-ft stand-alone well	Walthers	932-3945
NSC 53-ft 3-unit drawbar well	Walthers	932-3940
Thrall 5-unit well	InterMountain	47300
Impack trailer-only spine car	Athearn	5550
AP spine car, 48-ft, 5-unit	Walthers	932-3932

Refrigerator cars

Prototype/description	Model mfr.	Number series
General American 36-ft wood ice	Atlas	6100
Mather 37-ft wood ice	Red Caboose	31000
40-ft wood ice	Accurail	4800
40-ft wood ice	Red Caboose	4400
PFE R-30-12 40-ft wood ice	Red Caboose	4000
PFE R-30-12-9 40-ft wood ice	Red Caboose	4100
PFE R-40-4 or R-30-9 40-ft wood ice	Tichy	4024
PFE R-40-10 40-ft steel ice	InterMountain	46700
PFE R-40-23 40-ft steel ice	InterMountain	45500
PFE R-40-23 40-ft steel ice	Athearn	1600
URTX 40-ft steel ice	Walthers	932-2570
ATSF steel rebuilt ice-bunker	C&BT	7000
ATSF steel ice	InterMountain	46100
ATSF modern steel PD ice	C&BT	7500
FGE SS RBL	Walthers	932-4750
North American 50-foot SS RBL	Walthers	932-3450
North American 50-foot X-post RBL	Walthers	932-3600
PFE R-50-6	Athearn	1610
PFE R-70-12 50-ft mechanical	Athearn	1630
PFE R-70-16 57-ft mechanical	Con-Cor	9800
PFE R-70-20 57-ft mechanical	Athearn	5470

Tank cars

Prototype/description	Model mfr.	Number series
ACF Type 21 8,000-gal	Proto 2000	21800
ACF Type 21 10,000-gal	Proto 2000	23100
ACF Type 27 8,000-gal	InterMountain	46300
ACF Type 27 10,000-gal	InterMountain	46200
10,000-gal welded	Red Caboose	3000

Prototype/description	Model mfr.	Number series		Prototype/description	Model mfr.	Number series
11,000-gal early LPG	Atlas	1060		PS 50-ft waffle-side	Roundhouse	81700
Trinity 19,000-gal corn syrup	InterMountain	47800		86-ft DD auto parts	Con-Cor	555650
Funnel-Flow 30-ft, 12,000-gal	Walthers	932-5100		86-ft 4D auto parts	Con-Cor	555600
Funnel-Flow 40-ft, 16,000-gal	Walthers	932-7200		ACF 60-ft auto parts	Atlas	37200
Funnel-Flow 54-ft, 23,000-gal	Walthers	932-7250		ACF 60-ft DD auto parts	Atlas	36800
65-ft, 33,000-gal, LPG/anhydrous	Walthers	932-7300				
14,000-gal Kaolin	Atlas			**Covered hoppers**		
17,360-gal	Atlas	1550		Airslide, 40-ft (early version)	Atlas	38600
23,500-gal	Atlas	1620		Airslide, 50-ft	Delaware Vy.	2300
30-ft frameless non-pressure	Roundhouse	3300		3,000-cf 2-bay X-post	Red Caboose	15000
50-ft frameless non-pressure	Roundhouse	1370		PS-2 2-bay	Atlas	3150
Gen. Am. 50-ft TankTrain unit car	Roundhouse	1390		PS-2 3,219-cf 3-bay	Bachmann	73800
				PS-2 4,427-cf 3-bay	Walthers	932-8650
# N scale				PS-2 3-bay	Con-Cor	1950
## Boxcars				PS-2 4,740-cf 3-bay	Red Caboose	15400
USRA 40-ft single-sheathed wood	Atlas	41700		PS-2 4,750-cf 3-bay	InterMountain	65300
USRA 40-ft single-sheathed				PS-2 4,750-cf 3-bay	Red Caboose	15600
modernized	Micro-Trains	28100		FMC 4,700-cf 3-bay	Red Caboose	15200
40-ft double-sheathed wood	Micro-Trains	39000		ACF X-post 2-bay early cement	Kato	1860200
50-ft single-sheathed DD	Walthers	8350		ACF Center Flow 2-bay cement	InterMountain	66500
X29 40-ft	Red Caboose	17000		ACF Center Flow 2,970-cf		
AAR 1937 40-ft	InterMountain	65700		2-bay cement	Micro-Trains	92100
AAR 1937 modified 40-ft	InterMountain	66800		ACF Center Flow cylindrical 3-bay	Delaware Vy.	3000
AAR 1944 40-ft	deLuxe	14000		ACF Center Flow 4,650-cf 3-bay	InterMountain	67000
AAR 40-ft 12-panel	InterMountain	66000		ACF Center Flow 4,650-cf 3-bay		
AAR 50-ft	InterMountain	65600		(post-1971)	Micro-Trains	94100
PS-1 40-ft	Micro-Trains	20600		ACF Center Flow 4-bay pellet	Bachmann	70500
PS-1 50-ft	Micro-Trains	31200		ACF Pressureaide	Atlas	40100
PS-1 50-ft	Roundhouse	81800		NSC 4,550-cf cylindrical	InterMountain	65100
PS-1 50-ft PD	Roundhouse	81900		Trinity 5,161-cf 3-bay	LBF	5100
40-ft PD	Micro-Trains	21400				
50-ft PD	Micro-Trains	38300		**Flat cars**		
50-ft DD PD	Micro-Trains	75100		USRA 42-ft fishbelly	Red Caboose	16000
Thrall all-door	Red Caboose	17400		50-ft steel fishbelly	Micro-Trains	45000
Evans 53-ft DD PD	Atlas	31000		62-ft bulkhead	Micro-Trains	54100
ACF Precision Design 50-ft X-post	Atlas	45200		AAR 53-foot	deLuxe	190400
50-ft X-post	Micro-Trains	25600		GSC Commonwealth 53-ft	Walthers	8200
Berwick 50-ft X-post	Roundhouse	83100		Six-axle depressed-center		
FMC 50-ft X-post	Roundhouse	8250		heavy-duty	Micro-Trains	109000
FMC 50-ft PD X-post	Roundhouse	8360		Thrall 61-ft center beam	Micro-Trains	53000
FMC 50-ft DD plug/sliding	Roundhouse	82300		Gunderson 61-ft center beam		
PC&F 62-ft PD X-post	Red Caboose	17200		opera windows	Micro-Trains	53500
PS 50-ft X-post	Roundhouse	8130		Thrall 61-ft center beam, I-beam	Micro-Trains	53700

Prototype/description	Model mfr.	Number series
73-ft center beam, truss	Red Caboose	16500
73-ft center beam, opera windows	Red Caboose	16600
Evans 100t coil car Type 4	Red Caboose	17600
100t coil car	Walthers	932-8250
89-ft bi-level open auto rack	Micro-Trains	112500
89-ft tri-level open auto rack	Micro-Trains	112000
89-ft tri-level enclosed auto rack	Micro-Trains	111000
Thrall articulated auto rack	Atlas	40900

Gondolas

Prototype/description	Model mfr.	Number series
USRA composite drop-bottom	InterMountain	66600
40-ft GS drop-bottom	Dimi Trains	1106
50-ft steel	Micro-Trains	105000
50-ft steel drop-end	Micro-Trains	46300
Thrall 100t 50-ft mill	Roundhouse	8400
Gunderson wood chip, deep-rib	deLuxe	100000
Gunderson wood chip, shallow-rib	deLuxe	160000
Wood chip, smooth-side	deLuxe	170000
Thrall high-side 100t coal	Roundhouse	8100
ACF Coalveyor 100t	Atlas	43800
BethGon Coalporter	deLuxe	120000
BethGon Coalporter	LBF	5400
Trinity Aluminator	LBF	5700
Johnstown AeroFlo 100t	LBF	5800

Hoppers

Prototype/description	Model mfr.	Number series
Ortner 3-bay aggregate	Micro-Trains	12500
55t fishbelly 2-bay	Atlas	41000
AAR 55t 2-bay offset-side	Micro-Trains	55000
USRA 50t 2-bay	Micro-Trains	56000
50t 2-bay peaked end	Con-Cor	175200
50t 2-bay composite-side	Micro-Trains	57000
ARA 70t 4-bay offset-side	Bachmann	73300
AAR 70t 3-bay offset-side	Roundhouse	8620
AAR 70t 3-bay X-post	Roundhouse	8600
90t 3-bay X-post	Atlas	32600
100t 3-bay X-post	Micro-Trains	108000
Ortner Rapid Discharge 100t 5-bay	Red Caboose	15800
70-ton ore cars	Atlas	32000

Intermodal cars

Prototype/description	Model mfr.	Number series
89-ft all-purpose flat	Micro-Trains	71000
58-ft converted piggyback flat	Micro-Trains	64000
Thrall 48-ft 5-unit well	Walthers	8100
Thrall 48-ft stand-alone well	Walthers	8050
Gunderson Twin-Stack 5-unit well	deLuxe	150000
Gunderson 48-ft Husky Stack well	Con-Cor	603100

Refrigerator cars

Prototype/description	Model mfr.	Number series
36-ft wood ice	Micro-Trains	58500
36-ft wood ice	Roundhouse	8680
40-ft wood ice	Micro-Trains	49000
40-ft wood ice	Atlas	41400
PFE R-40-10 steel ice	Micro-Trains	59000
PFE R-40-23 steel ice	InterMountain	65500
PFE R-40-23 steel ice	Red Caboose	18000
40-ft steel ice	Model Power	3700
40-ft steel ice PD	Bachmann	105100
40-ft steel ice PD	Red Caboose	18400
40-ft PD ice R-40-26	Micro-Trains	
ATSF 40-ft steel ice	InterMountain	66100
50-ft steel ice PD	Model Power	4000
50-ft mechanical PD	Atlas	36500
52-ft mechanical PD	Micro-Trains	69100
57-ft mechanical PD	Bachmann	148200
57-ft mechanical PD	Red Caboose	18600
FGE PD RBL	Atlas	33600
FMC 50-ft PD RBL	Roundhouse	8360
North American 50-ft PD RBL	Walthers	8950
North American 50-ft X-post PD RBL	Walthers	8800
76-ft cryogenic PD	Walthers	932-8000

Tank cars

Prototype/description	Model mfr.	Number series
ACF Type 27 8,000-gal	InterMountain	66300
ACF Type 27 12,000-gal	Micro-Trains	65000
11,000-gal LPG	Atlas	43300
ACF 23,500-gal frameless	Atlas	30700
ACF 17,360-gal insulated	Atlas	43500
Trinity 17,600-gal corn syrup	Atlas	40200
Kaolin tank car	Atlas	34800
33,000-gal LPG	Atlas	37100
40-ft Funnel Flow	Con-Cor	160100
46-ft Funnel Flow	Con-Cor	160200
56-ft Funnel Flow	Con-Cor	160300
50-ft frameless	Roundhouse	8440
56-ft	Micro-Trains	110000
60-ft	Con-Cor	400556300

CONTENTS

Key

Objectives are numbered consecutively within each topic as laid out in the Mathematics Framework, pages 6–11,

Year 9 Objectives C1 and H9 are also addressed in Year 8, Chapters 13 and 21 respectively.

U = Using and applying mathematics to solve problems

N = Numbers and the number system

C = Calculation

A = Algebra

S = Shape, space and measure

H = Handling data

INTRODUCTION

The Letts *KS3 Maths Classbook* is designed to give complete coverage of all Key Objectives for Years 7, 8 and 9 as set out in the Framework for Teaching Mathematics.

The classbook has been written in 33 chapters, and is set out in an order which closely follows the Framework yearly teaching programmes. Chapters 1 to 11 cover the various core topics for Year 7 in Number and the Number System; Calculations; Algebra; Shape, space and measure; and Handling data. This pattern is followed for Year 8 in Chapters 12 to 22, and for Year 9 in Chapters 23 to 33.

The final core topic, Using and Applying Mathematics, is embedded within many activities within this book. The chapters where these Objectives feature heavily are indicated on the contents pages.

How to use this book

Each chapter begins with an outline of the key points to be covered. This is followed by a number of topic sections, each providing explanations, worked examples and exercises for completion. Each chapter concludes with a summary plus a Review Exercise to ensure understanding and consolidate the key points.

Calculators

Throughout the book the need for a calculator is indicated by the following symbols:

 indicates that a calculator is prohibited;

 indicates that a calculator is allowed.

Star questions

In the end of Chapter reviews, certain questions are marked with a star: ✱

This symbol indicates that the question is deliberately more challenging.

Self-check

Throughout the book, key questions have been marked with a tick: ✓ Wherever this symbol appears, it means that the answer is given at the back of this book. Once such a question has been attempted, check the answer before completing the rest of the exercise.

I would like to thank Vicky and Helen at Letts, and Sarah and Gail at Hart McLeod, for all their hard work in editing and checking the material for this revised edition of the *Classbook*. Thanks too, to the children at Christ's Hospital, who have inspired many of the questions in the exercises. Finally, special thanks are due to my wife, Rosemarie, without whose support this book would not have been even remotely possible.

1 Working with whole numbers

1.1 Place value

Our number system works in base 10. Each figure in a number has a place value – units, tens, hundreds etc. The place values change by a factor of 10 as you move from one column to the next.

Question   Sarfraz looks at the number 3842.
He wants to read the number out loud. What should he say?

Solution

1000	100	10	1
3	8	4	2

> These are the place values. The units are on the right-hand end. Multiply by 10 each time you move one column to the left.

The 3 means three thousand.
The 8 means eight hundred.
The 4 means four tens or forty.
The 2 means two units.

Sarfraz should say 'three thousand, eight hundred and forty-two'.

Question   Write in figures 'twelve thousand, four hundred and thirty-two'.

Solution   Begin by drawing up a set of place value headings:

10 000	1000	100	10	1

> The figures (or digits) are grouped in blocks of three. Do not use commas.

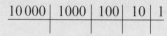

Twelve thousand, ...

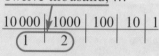

... 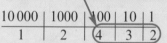 four hundred and thirty-two.

The final answer is written 12 432

EXERCISE 1.1

Write in figures:

1. Four thousand, two hundred and sixty-six
2. Thirteen thousand, five hundred and ninety-three ✓
3. Eleven thousand, four hundred and five
4. Twenty thousand, nine hundred and seven
5. Thirty-three thousand, one hundred and eight
6. Nine thousand and eighty
7. Five thousand and forty-nine
8. Thirteen thousand, two hundred
9. Twenty thousand and three ✓
10. Seven hundred thousand and fifty-six.

Write in words:

11. 6394
12. 7032
13. 12 342
14. 63 207 ✓
15. 90 265
16. 14 205
17. 7073
18. 10 005
19. 67 256
20. 32 067 ✓

1.2 Addition and subtraction of whole numbers

You have probably had plenty of practice at adding or subtracting whole numbers, using 'carry' or 'exchange' where necessary.

When adding and subtracting make sure that the place values line up, as in these examples.

Question   Add three hundred and sixty-five to seven thousand, nine hundred and eleven. Give your answer in words.

Solution   The numbers are 365 and 7911.

1000	100	10	1
	3	6	5
7	9	1	1

Write one number underneath the other.
Make sure the place values line up.

1000	100	10	1
	3	6	5
7	9	1	1
₁ 2	2	7	6

Add the units, then the 10s, then the 100s and so on.
Here 3 + 9 = 12 so the 1 is carried across to the next column…

1000	100	10	1
	3	6	5
7	9	1	1
8₁	2	7	6

... and here is the final result.

The answer is eight thousand, two hundred and seventy-six.

Question Take 2391 away from 4672.

Solution There are two different methods for dealing with the 'exchange'. Use whichever one you have seen before.

Method 1

1000	100	10	1
4	6	7	2
2	3	9	1
			1

Start by subtracting in the units column...

1000	100	10	1
4	⁵6̷	¹7	2
2	3	9	1
			1

... then move to the 10s. An 'exchange' is needed here -- there are two different ways of doing it.

1000	100	10	1
4	⁵6̷	¹7	2
2	3	9	1
2	2	8	1

Finish by subtracting the 10s, then the 100s, then the 1000s.

Method 2

1000	100	10	1
4	6	7	2
2	3	9	1
			1

1000	100	10	1
4	6	¹7	2
2	⁴3̷	9	1
			1

1000	100	10	1
4	6	¹7	2
2	⁴3̷	9	1
2	2	8	1

So 4672 − 2391 = 2281

EXERCISE 1.2

Work out these additions and subtractions.

1. 2592 + 1377
2. 147 + 174
3. 39 733 + 56 882 ✓
4. 2877 + 506
5. 5644 + 6729
6. 1277 − 1146
7. 4672 − 1950
8. 12 577 − 9769 ✓
9. 329 − 77

Work out these additions and subtractions. In each case, write the answer in words.

(10) 471 + 229

(11) 6529 + 3382

(12) 176 – 92

(13) 3396 – 1839

(14) 12 376 + 9428 ✓

(15) 2786 – 292

(16) 468 774 + 399 235

(17) 23 967 – 4750 ✓

(18) 2785 – 1493

(19) 85 113 + 24 278

(20) 64 307 – 4982

1.3 Multiplying and dividing by 10 or 100

If you multiply a whole number by 10 then all the digits move one place to the left. If you multiply by 100 the digits move two places to the left. In division the digits move to the right instead.

Question   Work out 3753 × 100.

Solution   The digits all move two places to the left, like this:

100 000	10 000	1000	100	10	1
			3	7	5	3
3	7	5	3	0	0

Two extra zeroes come in here as the digits have all moved two places left.

3753 × 100 = <u>375 300</u>

Question   Divide 23 600 by 10.

Solution   The digits move one place to the right:

23 600 ÷ 10 = <u>2360</u>

EXERCISE 1.3

Work out these multiplications and divisions.

(1) 452 × 100

(2) 2506 × 10

(3) 13 866 × 100

(4) 455 × 10

(5) 6370 × 100 ✓

(6) 23 900 ÷ 10 ✓

(7) 9060 ÷ 10

(8) 450 000 ÷ 100

(9) 12 000 ÷ 10

Work out these multiplications and divisions. In each case, write the answer in words.

10 93 000 000 ÷ 100

14 25 000 ÷ 100

18 14 000 ÷ 100

11 1600 × 10

15 830 × 100 ✓

19 450 000 ÷ 100

12 500 × 10

16 640 000 ÷ 100 ✓

20 20 000 × 10

13 1800 ÷ 10

17 2000 × 100

1.4 Multiplication up to 10 by 10

You have probably learnt some of the basic 'times tables' – especially the 2× and 5× tables.

The tables up to 10× are shown in this multiplication square:

	1	2	3	4	5	6	7	8	9	10
1	1	2	3	4	5	6	7	8	9	10
2	2	4	6	8	10	12	14	16	18	20
3	3	6	9	12	15	18	21	24	27	30
4	4	8	12	16	20	24	28	32	36	40
5	5	10	15	20	25	30	35	40	45	50
6	6	12	18	24	30	36	42	48	54	60
7	7	14	21	28	35	42	49	56	63	70
8	8	16	24	32	40	48	56	64	72	80
9	9	18	27	36	45	54	63	72	81	90
10	10	20	30	40	50	60	70	80	90	100

Question Find the value of 3×7.

Solution Looking along the '3' row and down the '7' column:

	1	2	3	4	5	6	7	8	9	10
1	1	2	3	4	5	6	7	8	9	10
2	2	4	6	8	10	12	14	16	18	20
3	3	6	9	12	15	18	21	24	27	30

So $3 \times 7 = \underline{21}$.

EXERCISE 1.4

Learn the tables in the multiplication square. Then cover up the square, and find the values of these:

1 4 × 8 ✓   **5** 5 × 5   **9** 7 × 7

2 6 × 5   **6** 3 × 4   **10** 9 × 4

3 3 × 3   **7** 6 × 5   **11** 6 × 3

4 7 × 2   **8** 3 × 8 ✓   **11** 9 × 7

1.5 Factors and multiples

Multiples may be found by looking along a multiplication square. For example, the multiples of 2 are 2, 4, 6, 8, 10 and so on.

The multiplication square on the previous page only gives the first ten multiples. Times tables do, of course, carry on after this, without limit.

| **Question** | Write down the first five multiples of 7. |
| **Solution** | Using the square, the multiples are <u>7, 14, 21, 28, 35</u>. |

| **Question** | Is 44 a multiple of 8? |
| **Solution** | Look along the '8' row: |

| 8 | 8 | 16 | 24 | 32 | 40 | 48 | 56 | 64 | 72 | 80 |

44 is not here.

44 is not in this list.
Therefore <u>44 is not a multiple of 8.</u>

| **Question** | Is 72 a multiple of 6? |
| **Solution** | Look along the '6' row: |

72 is beyond the end of these numbers.

| 6 | 6 | 12 | 18 | 24 | 30 | 36 | 42 | 48 | 54 | 60 |

Continuing past 60 in jumps of 6 we get more multiples of 6:
60, 66, 72, 78 …

∴ <u>72 is a multiple of 6.</u>

The symbol ∴ means therefore.

A number is a **factor** of a second number if it divides exactly into it with no remainder. The second number is a **multiple** of the first one.

Question	Is 4 a factor of 20?
Solution	Turn the question round: is 20 a multiple of 4?
	Looking along the multiplication square in the '4' row we can see that 20 is a multiple of 4.
	∴ 4 is a factor of 20.

Question	Find all the factors of 20.
Solution	From the multiplication square, $2 \times 10 = 20$ and $4 \times 5 = 20$.
	You can also make 20 using $1 \times 20 = 20$.
	∴ The factors of 20 are 1, 2, 4, 5, 10 and 20.

Remember to include 1 and the number itself (20) in the list of factors.

EXERCISE 1.5

1 Write down:

a) The first three multiples of 5

b) The first five multiples of 3

c) The first four multiples of 9 ✓

d) The first three multiples of 8

e) The first six multiples of 7

f) Is 72 a multiple of 9?

g) Is 87 a multiple of 7?

h) Is 42 a multiple of 3?

i) Is 38 a multiple of 6? ✓

j) Is 75 a multiple of 5?

k) Is 6 a factor of 18?

l) Is 3 a factor of 23?

m) Is 5 a factor of 52?

n) Is 7 a factor of 42? ✓

o) Is 8 a factor of 52?

2 Find all the factors of:

a) 12   b) 15   c) 16 ✓   d) 18   e) 30

1.6 Prime numbers

The number 7 is a **prime** number because it has only two factors: itself and 1.
$1 \times 7 = 7$ so 7 has factors of 1 and 7.

The number 8 is not a prime number because it has more than two factors:

$1 \times 8 = 8$ and $2 \times 4 = 8$ so 8 has factors of 1, 2, 4 and 8.
8 is called a **composite** number because it has more than two factors.

The number 1 has only one factor, $1 \times 1 = 1$, so it is neither a prime number nor a composite number.

Here are some facts about prime numbers:
- The first few primes are 2, 3, 5, 7, 11, 13, 17.
- Apart from 2, all prime numbers are **odd**.
- The prime numbers do not appear inside the multiplication square, except under the $1 \times$ heading.
- There are infinitely many prime numbers, but mathematicians have not yet discovered an easy way of detecting the very large ones.

Question	Find all the prime numbers between 30 and 40.
Solution	Since all the primes (apart from the first one) are odd, we need to consider the numbers 31, 33, 35, 37, 39.

33 is a multiple of 3, because $3 \times 11 = 33$.
35 is a multiple of 5, because $5 \times 7 = 35$.
39 is a multiple of 3, because $3 \times 13 = 39$.
It is not possible to find factors of 31 or 37.

∴ Prime numbers between 30 and 40 are <u>31 and 37</u>.

EXERCISE 1.6

1. Find the next prime number after 17.
2. Find all the prime numbers between 20 and 30.
3. Decide whether 15 is prime or composite.
4. Decide whether 41 is prime or composite.

5 Decide whether 73 is prime or composite. ✓

6 Find the next prime number after 53. ✓

7 Find all the prime numbers between 40 and 50. ✓

8 Decide whether 27 is prime or composite. ✓

9 Decide whether 79 is prime or composite.

10 Decide whether 81 is prime or composite.

SUMMARY

- In this chapter you have revised place value, including writing numbers in figures and in words. You have practised adding and subtracting whole numbers without a calculator, ensuring that place values (e.g. the units) line up.

- You have also revised basic multiplication facts up to 10 x 10, and how to multiply and divide by 10 or 100 without a calculator. These are important skills, which may be tested (without a calculator) as part of either a Key Stage 3 or GCSE examination.

- You have learnt how to find factors and multiples of numbers, and how to recognise prime numbers.

REVIEW EXERCISE 1

1 Write in figures:
   a Twelve thousand, four hundred and one
   b Sixty-five thousand, seven hundred and four
   c Sixty-three thousand and ninety
   d Four hundred and two thousand, six hundred and eleven
   e Five thousand and forty.

2 Write in words:
   a 22 301   b 450 207   c 50 056   d 103 246   e 7209

3 Work out these additions and subtractions:
   a 45 203 + 2948   b 8699 + 7546   c 14 203 − 9731
   d 1577 − 899   e 9622 + 1379   f 12 788 − 9949
   g 23 577 + 72 845   h 12 003 − 9844   i 1035 + 44 396

4 Work out these multiplications and divisions:
   a 6000 × 100   b 800 × 10   c 5000 × 100   d 4000 ÷ 100

9

      e $6000 \div 10$ **f** $226\,000 \times 100$ **g** $226\,000 \div 100$

5 Write down the answers to these multiplications:

    a 9×2 **b** 6×9 **c** 8×8 **d** 3×7

    e 4×8 **f** 7×5 **g** 4×4 **h** 5×7

    i 6×8 **j** 8×5 **k** 7×4 **l** 9×9

6 Is 32 a multiple of 6?   **7** Is 7 a factor of 54?

8 Is 39 a prime number?   **9** Find all the factors of 14.

10 Is 84 a multiple of 7?   **11** Is 9 a factor of 57?

12 Is 69 a prime number?   **13** Find all the factors of 32.

14 ✳ $16\,000 \div 200$

15 ✳ The number of people attending each of four football matches are 26 409, 31 322, 17 488 and 29 277. Find the total number of people who attended.

16 ✳ The caterers at an open-air concert provided meals for 7500 people, but 11 277 people turned up. All the meals were sold. How many of the concert-goers were unable to buy a meal?

17 ✳ The three volumes of a set of guide books contain 686, 722 and 692 pages.
    a How many pages are there in total?
    b If the volumes are reprinted so that they are all the same length, how many pages will each volume contain?

18 ✳ A machine sorts plastic bricks into bags of 200. There are 46 000 bricks altogether. How many bags can be filled?

19 ✳ The Hundred Years War started in 1337 and finished in 1453. For how many years did it last?

20 ✳ An airline owns 20 aircraft, and each aircraft can carry 243 passengers. How many passengers can all the aircraft carry in total?

2 Long multiplication and long division

OUTLINE

In this chapter you will learn how to:
- multiply larger numbers using long multiplication
- divide two numbers using tables in reverse
- divide two numbers using long division.

You will also practise multiplication and division using tables.

A calculator will not be required for this chapter, except perhaps for checking.

2.1 Long multiplication

To multiply a 3-digit number by a 2-digit number without a calculator, long multiplication is used. The larger number is written in the first line, with the smaller number underneath. Multiplications then follow, one line at a time.

Question   Multiply 269 by 32.

Solution

$$
\begin{array}{ccc}
2 & 6 & 9 \\
\times\ 3 & & 2 \\
\hline
\end{array}
$$

Copy out the question, with the larger number, 269, above the smaller one, 32.

$$
\begin{array}{ccc}
2 & 6 & 9 \\
\times\ 3 & & ② \\
\hline
\mathbf{5} & \mathbf{3} & \mathbf{8}
\end{array}
$$

Multiply by the units digit, 2. The answer to 269 times 2 is 538.

$$
\begin{array}{ccc}
2 & 6 & 9 \\
\times\ ③ & & 2 \\
\hline
5 & 3 & 8 \\
& & \mathbf{0}
\end{array}
$$

Now for the 30, represented by this 3. Enter a zero (0) underneath the 538.

$$
\begin{array}{cccc}
& 2 & 6 & 9 \\
\times & 3 & & 2 \\
\hline
& 5 & 3 & 8 \\
\mathbf{8} & \mathbf{0} & \mathbf{7} & \mathbf{0}
\end{array}
$$

… then multiply 269 by 3. The answer, 807, is written alongside the zero.

$$
\begin{array}{r}
2\quad 6\quad 9 \\
\times\qquad 3\quad 2 \\
\hline
5\quad 3\quad 8 \\
8\quad 0\quad 7\quad 0 \\
\hline
\mathbf{8\quad 6\quad 0\quad 8}
\end{array}
$$

Finally, add up 538 and 8070 to obtain the grand total of 8608.

So $269 \times 32 = \underline{8608}$

Check: 269×32 is about $300 \times 30 = 9000$ so 8608 looks about right.

The same method can be used for longer problems, with more lines of working. The next question shows all the stages completed.

Question   Multiply 1876 by 274.

Solution

The 1876 has been multiplied by 4, then by 70, and finally by 200.

$$
\begin{array}{r}
1\quad 8\quad 7\quad 6 \\
\times\qquad 2\quad 7\quad 4 \\
\hline
7\quad 5\quad 0\quad 4 \\
1\quad 3\quad 1\quad 3\quad 2\quad 0 \\
3\quad 7\quad 5\quad 2\quad 0\quad 0 \\
\hline
\mathbf{5\quad 1\quad 4\quad 0\quad 2\quad 4}
\end{array}
$$

This triangular pattern of 0s always occurs in this type of problem.

So $1876 \times 274 = \underline{514\,024}$

Check: 1876×274 is about $2000 \times 300 = 600\,000$ so 514 024 looks about right.

EXERCISE 2.1

1. 175×19
2. 324×47 ✓
3. 822×13
4. 453×33
5. 775×26
6. 47×74
7. 309×23

8. 512×62 ✓
9. 936×79
10. 308×81
11. 327×121
12. 985×39
13. 505×120
14. 51×729

15. 405×90
16. 3522×23
17. 4977×49 ✓
18. 532×619
19. 225×225 ✓
20. 57×924

2.2 Long division

Some simple division problems may be solved by using multiplication tables in reverse. Harder problems are solved using long division. The two numbers are written in the same line, separated by a bracket. Working is done underneath, and the answer appears on the top.

Question   Divide 6071 by 13.

Solution

$$1 \quad 3 \enclose{longdiv}{6 \quad 0 \quad 7 \quad 1}$$

> Set out the division, taking care to space out the figures; place value is very important! Do not cramp up your work.

13, 26, 39, 52, 65, 78, 91, 104, 117

> Make a list of the multiples of 13, going up from 1×13 to 9×13 – this saves time later.

$$\begin{array}{c} \quad\;\; 4 \\ 1 \quad 3 \enclose{longdiv}{6 \quad 0 \quad 7 \quad 1} \\ 5 \quad 2 \end{array}$$

> 13 into 6 won't go, so try 13 into 60. The best you can do is $4 \times 13 = 52$.

$$\begin{array}{c} \quad\;\; 4 \\ 1 \quad 3 \enclose{longdiv}{6 \quad 0 \quad 7 \quad 1} \\ 5 \quad 2 \downarrow \\ \hline 8 \quad 7 \end{array}$$

> Subtract 52 from 60 to get 8. Bring down the next figure, 7, to get 87.

$$\begin{array}{c} \quad\;\; 4 \quad 6 \\ 1 \quad 3 \enclose{longdiv}{6 \quad 0 \quad 7 \quad 1} \\ 5 \quad 2 \\ \hline 8 \quad 7 \\ 7 \quad 8 \end{array}$$

> Try 13 into 87. The best you can do is $6 \times 13 = 78$.

$$\begin{array}{c} \quad\;\; 4 \quad 6 \\ 1 \quad 3 \enclose{longdiv}{6 \quad 0 \quad 7 \quad 1} \\ 5 \quad 2 \\ \hline 8 \quad 7 \\ 7 \quad 8 \downarrow \\ \hline 9 \quad 1 \end{array}$$

> Subtract 78 from 87, and bring down the next figure, 1, to get 91.

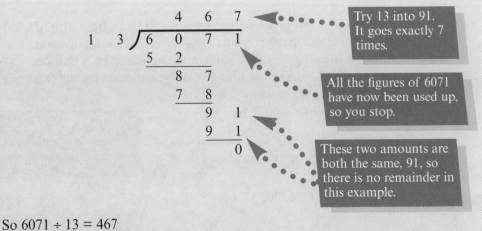

$$
\begin{array}{r}
4\quad 6\quad 7 \\
1\ \ 3\ \overline{)\ 6\quad 0\quad 7\quad 1} \\
5\quad 2\ \ \ \ \ \ \ \ \ \ \\
\overline{\ \ \ 8\quad 7\ \ \ \ \ \ } \\
7\quad 8\ \ \ \ \ \\
\overline{\ \ \ \ \ 9\quad 1} \\
9\quad 1 \\
\overline{\ \ \ \ \ 0}
\end{array}
$$

Try 13 into 91. It goes exactly 7 times.

All the figures of 6071 have now been used up, so you stop.

These two amounts are both the same, 91, so there is no remainder in this example.

So 6071 ÷ 13 = 467

Check: 6071 ÷ 13 is about 6000 ÷ 10 = 600 so 467 looks about right.

The same method can be used for longer problems, with more lines of working.

The next question shows all the stages completed. This time there is a remainder.

Question Divide 91 481 by 17.

Solution

$$
\begin{array}{r}
5\quad 3\quad 8\quad 1 \\
1\ \ 7\ \overline{)\ 9\quad 1\quad 4\quad 8\quad 1} \\
8\quad 5\ \ \ \ \ \ \ \ \ \ \ \ \ \\
\overline{\ \ \ 6\quad 4\ \ \ \ \ \ \ \ } \\
5\quad 1\ \ \ \ \ \ \\
\overline{\ \ \ \ \ 1\quad 3\quad 8\ \ \ } \\
1\quad 3\quad 6\ \ \\
\overline{\ \ \ \ \ \ \ \ \ \ 2\quad 1} \\
1\quad 7 \\
\overline{\ \ \ \ \ \ \ \ \ \ 4}
\end{array}
$$

This can be written as $5381\frac{4}{17}$ if you want to give the remainder as a fraction.

So: 91 481 ÷ 17 = 5381 remainder 4.

Check: 91 481 ÷ 17 is about 90 000 ÷ 20 = 4500 so 5381 looks about right.

EXERCISE 2.2

1 Work out the answers to these long divisions. State the value of any remainder.

a) $33\,278 \div 14$

b) $110\,964 \div 21$ ✓

c) $4931 \div 19$

d) $71\,855 \div 22$

e) $101\,664 \div 32$

f) $119\,940 \div 28$

g) $33\,891 \div 43$

h) $764\,332 \div 31$

i) $22\,275 \div 81$ ✓

2 Work out the answers to these long divisions. Give the remainder as a fraction.

a) $9266 \div 41$

b) $11\,062 \div 29$

c) $7861 \div 53$

d) $20\,020 \div 82$

e) $29\,703 \div 77$

f) $53\,487 \div 31$

g) $22\,999 \div 24$

h) $23\,396 \div 62$

i) $98\,901 \div 99$ ✓

SUMMARY

- In this chapter you have learnt to multiply a 3-digit number by a 2-digit number without using a calculator. You have also learnt how to divide one number by another using long division, giving the remainder either as a whole number or as a fraction.

- Long multiplication and long division without a calculator are skills which may be tested in the Key Stage 3 exam and at GCSE.

REVIEW EXERCISE 2

1 Write down the answers to the following multiplication and division problems:

a 7×5

b 4×10

c 9×2

d 8×9

e 8×4

f $48 \div 4$

g $18 \div 3$

h $22 \div 2$

i $24 \div 3$

j $49 \div 7$

k 11×4

l 7×7

m $35 \div 5$

n $84 \div 7$

o 4×9

p $121 \div 11$

q 12×12

r $64 \div 8$

s $48 \div 6$

t 11×12

2 Use long multiplication to work out these:

a 127×15

b 34×160

c 418×24

d 318×53

e 1251×42

f 713×731

3 Use long division to work out these:

a $945 \div 21$

b $9683 \div 23$

c $23\,901 \div 31$

d $30\,233 \div 49$

e $8701 \div 27$

f $84\,121 \div 19$

4 In an international soccer tournament there are twenty-four teams, and each team has a squad of sixteen players. How many players are there in the tournament?

5 Thirteen coaches leave an airport, with forty-seven passengers on board each coach. Another coach carries 32 passengers. Find the total number of passengers on all fourteen coaches.

6 ✳ A school tuck shop buys 144 pencils at 19p each, and 64 pens at 93p each.
   a Find the cost of all the pencils.
   b Find the cost of all the pens.
   c Find the total cost of all the pencils and pens together.

7 ✳ On a visit to my local pet shop I buy seven tins of dog meat at 49p for each tin, three toys at 67p each toy, and a bottle of flea shampoo costing £1.67.
   a Calculate the total amount spent on all these items.
   b Calculate the change I should receive from a £10 note.

8 ✳ Work out the exact value of $1 \times 2 \times 3 \times 4 \times 5 \times 6 \times 7 \times 8 \times 9 \times 10 \times 11 \times 12$.

9 ✳ At Silvertub School there are 27 classes. This year there are 521 pupils, and the Head Teacher wants to arrange the classes so that they are all as near to the same size as possible. How many pupils should the Head place in each class?

10 ✳ At Greyhall School there are 31 classes, all containing the same number of pupils. There are 744 pupils altogether. Find the number of pupils in each class.

11 ✳ a Make a list of the first twenty multiples of 17 (i.e. 17, 34, 51 etc.)
   b Make a list of the first twenty multiples of 19.
   c Find a number which both 17 and 19 divide into exactly.

3 Working with decimals

OUTLINE

In this chapter you will revise:
- place value in decimal notation
- adding and subtracting decimals
- ordering decimals.

You will also learn how to:
- multiply and divide decimals by whole numbers.

A calculator should not be used in this chapter.

3.1 Revision of decimal notation

Fractions expressed in tenths can also be written using **decimal notation**.
For example, one-tenth is the same as 0.1.
Similarly, seven-tenths is the same as 0.7.
The number after the decimal point tells you how many tenths there are.

Question Write these numbers as decimals:

a) three-tenths   b) nine-tenths   c) six and seven-tenths.

Solution a) Three-tenths = 0.3

b) Nine-tenths = 0.9

b) Six and seven-tenths = 6.7

Question Write these decimals as fractions:

a) 0.9   b) 2.1   c) 3.7

Solution a) $0.9 = \frac{9}{10}$ b) $2.1 = 2\frac{1}{10}$ c) $3.7 = 3\frac{7}{10}$

If there are two places of decimals then the two places represent
tenths and hundredths respectively.

Question Write four and thirteen-hundredths:

a) as a fraction, using figures   b) as a decimal.

Solution a) $4\frac{13}{100}$ b) 4.13

EXERCISE 3.1

1 Write these as decimals:

a) Seven-tenths

b) Six and one-tenth

c) One and nine-tenths ✓

d) Four and seven-tenths

e) Two and three-tenths

f) Ten and seven-tenths.

2 Write these as decimals:

a) $2\frac{9}{10}$ ✓

b) $1\frac{1}{10}$

c) $6\frac{7}{10}$

d) $4\frac{3}{10}$ ✓

e) $5\frac{7}{10}$

f) $12\frac{9}{10}$

3 Write these as decimals:

a) Eleven-hundredths

b) One and seven-hundredths

c) Six and thirty-nine-hundredths ✓

d) Twenty and forty-nine-hundredths.

4 Write these as decimals:

a) $5\frac{67}{100}$ ✓

b) $8\frac{91}{100}$

c) $3\frac{19}{100}$

d) $5\frac{7}{100}$

3.2 Ordering decimals

Sometimes you need to arrange a list of decimals in order of size.
Compare the figures in the higher place value positions first (those on
the left), then work across towards the right.

Question	Arrange in increasing order of size: 2.512, 2.205, 2.56, 2.7, 2.562

Solution Writing the numbers so the place values line up:

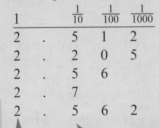

1		$\frac{1}{10}$	$\frac{1}{100}$	$\frac{1}{1000}$
2	.	5	1	2
2	.	2	0	5
2	.	5	6	
2	.	7		
2	.	5	6	2

These figures in the units column are all equal …

… so you look at the figures in the $\frac{1}{10}$ column next …

… and so on across the place values.

The sorted list becomes:

```
2  .  2  0  5
2  .  5  1  2
2  .  5  6
2  .  5  6  2
2  .  7
```

In increasing order of size the decimals are: 2.205, 2.512, 2.56, 2.562, 2.7

EXERCISE 3.2

1 Arrange each of these lists of decimals in order of size, smallest first.

a) 5.202, 5.221, 5.51, 5.251, 5.502

b) 3.21, 3.003, 3.209, 3.3, 3.01 ✓

c) 0.725, 0.527, 0.75, 0.57, 0.572

d) 1.55, 1.402, 1.541, 1.45, 1.425

e) 10.66, 10.655, 10.665, 10.656, 10.555

2 Arrange each of these lists of decimals in order of size, largest first.

a) 0.365, 0.42, 0.37, 0.415, 0.4 ✓

b) 0.084, 0.07, 0.091, 0.019, 0.08

c) 12.5, 12.44, 12.477, 12.407, 12.4

d) 1.55, 1.485, 1.5, 1.49, 1.51

e) 0.772, 0.727, 0.277, 0.707

3.3 Adding and subtracting decimals

Decimals are added and subtracted in the same way as whole numbers. Make sure that you line up the decimal points in all the numbers.

Question   Add 16.3 and 7.2.

Solution   Write out an addition, lining up the decimal points:

$$
\begin{array}{r r r c r}
10 & 1 & & \tfrac{1}{10} \\
\hline
1 & 6 & . & 3 \\
+ & 7 & . & 2 \\
\hline
\end{array}
$$

Then add up just as if these were whole numbers:

10	1		$\frac{1}{10}$
1	6	.	3
+	7	.	2
2	3	.	5

$16.3 + 7.2 = \underline{23.5}$

Sometimes you need to insert an extra zero to make sure that the numbers line up at the decimal point.

Question   Work out 32.5 − 19.14.

Solution   Write 32.5 as 32.50 so that both numbers have two decimal places.

10	1		$\frac{1}{10}$	$\frac{1}{100}$
3	2	.	5	0
− 1	9	.	1	4
1	3	.	3	6

$32.5 − 19.14 = \underline{13.36}$

Question   Alex has £34.77. He spends £16.83. How much money does he have left?

Solution

10	1		$\frac{1}{10}$	$\frac{1}{100}$
3	4	.	7	7
− 1	6	.	8	3
1	7	.	9	4

Remember to include the £ sign when you write the final answer to a question about money.

He has £17.94 left

EXERCISE 3.3

Work out these additions and subtractions. Do not use a calculator:

1 14.1 + 3.8

2 25.6 + 19.7

3 1.3 + 0.8

4 44.2 + 18.6 ✓

5 12.8 − 9.3 ✓

6 45.2 − 17.3

7 16.1 − 9.2

8 142.8 − 29.1

9 12.63 + 9.48

10 67.2 + 13.89

11 14.81 − 1.49

12 66.27 − 14.98

13 63.6 − 9.41 ✓

14 14.82 + 18.42 ✓

15 77.06 − 67.6

16 Add together £10.99 and £13.99.

17 Add together £11.61 and £6.40.

18 Take £2.44 from £5.28.

19 Jim has £46.25. He spends £13.76. How much money does he have left?

20 Tessa has £55.30. She buys a hat, and then finds she has £38.31 left. How much did she pay for the hat? ✓

3.4 Multiplying and dividing decimals by whole numbers

Sometimes you will need to multiply or divide a decimal by a simple whole number. Make sure the place value columns are neatly lined up throughout your working. Then just position the decimal point in the answer so that it is directly underneath the decimal point in the original number.

Question   Work out 21.6 × 3

Solution

$$
\begin{array}{r}
2\quad 1\,.\;6 \\
\times \qquad 3 \\
\hline
\end{array}
$$

Set the problem up like an ordinary whole number long multiplication. Position the decimal point in the original number.

$$
\begin{array}{r}
2\quad 1\,.\;6 \\
\times \qquad 3 \\
\hline
6\quad 4\quad 8
\end{array}
$$

Carry out the multiplication, ignoring the decimal point

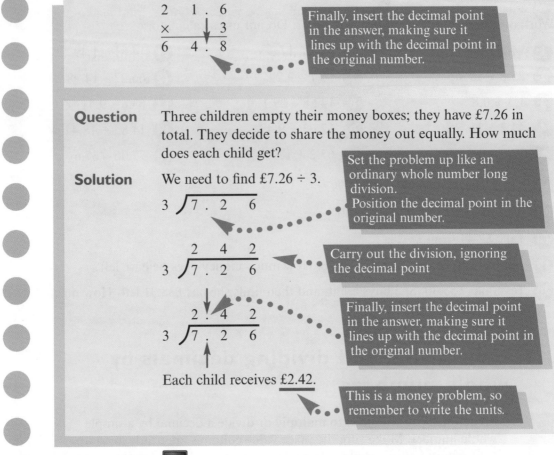

```
  2   1 . 6
×       ↓ 3
  6   4 . 8
```

Finally, insert the decimal point in the answer, making sure it lines up with the decimal point in the original number.

Question Three children empty their money boxes; they have £7.26 in total. They decide to share the money out equally. How much does each child get?

Solution We need to find £7.26 ÷ 3.

```
3 ) 7 . 2   6
```

Set the problem up like an ordinary whole number long division.
Position the decimal point in the original number.

```
      2   4   2
3 ) 7 . 2   6
```

Carry out the division, ignoring the decimal point

```
      2 . 4   2
3 ) 7 . 2   6
```

Finally, insert the decimal point in the answer, making sure it lines up with the decimal point in the original number.

Each child receives £2.42.

This is a money problem, so remember to write the units.

EXERCISE 3.4

Carry out these multiplications. Remember to set your working out using neat columns of figures.

1 45.2 × 3 ✓   **4** 18.25 × 3   **7** 42.71 × 5

2 17.4 × 4   **5** 48.22 × 2   **8** 8.25 × 6

3 66.2 × 7   **6** 12.3 × 9   **9** 10.4 × 8

Carry out these divisions. Remember to set your working out using neat columns of figures.

10 22.8 ÷ 3   **13** 145.5 ÷ 5   **16** 5.52 ÷ 4

11 10.5 ÷ 5 ✓   **14** 35.28 ÷ 8   **17** 80.5 ÷ 7

12 14.4 ÷ 6   **15** 734.4 ÷ 9   **18** 50.36 ÷ 4

19 Susan works in a shop for 7 hours and is paid £4.83 per hour. Find her total pay for the day.

20 Tom cycles three times around his favourite circuit, travelling a total distance of 25.8 kilometres. Find the length of one circuit. ✓

SUMMARY

- In this chapter you have revised writing and ordering decimals using one or two decimal places. The first decimal place tells you the number of tenths, the second the number of hundredths.

- You have also revised addition and subtraction of decimals, taking care to line up the two numbers at the decimal points. Arithmetic with two decimal places often occurs in questions about money.

- You have learnt how to multiply and divide decimals by simple whole numbers, by lining up the decimal point in the answer with that given in the original number.

REVIEW EXERCISE 3

1 Write as decimals:

a three and one-tenth

b four and sixty-one-hundredths

c five and four-hundredths.

2 Write as decimals:

a $1\frac{1}{10}$ b $1\frac{1}{100}$ c $1\frac{11}{100}$ d $4\frac{17}{100}$ e $2\frac{71}{100}$

3 Arrange these four numbers in order of size, smallest first.

0.799, 0.77, 0.701, 0.797

4 Arrange these six numbers in order of size, largest first.

3.566, 3.503, 3.53, 3.536, 3.635, 3.6

5 Work out these additions and subtractions:

a 16.3 + 8.9   b 71.6 − 52.4   c 12.35 + 7.28   d 96.11 − 47.83

e 12.1 − 9.09   f 63.8 − 38.6   g 12.9 + 1.09

6 Work out these multiplications and divisions:

a 55.2 × 7   b 37.25 × 8   c 1.78 × 3   d 68.4 ÷ 3

e 7.05 ÷ 3   f 39.2 ÷ 7   g 44.22 ÷ 6   h 95.22 × 7

7 ✳ The tables below show some results from a school athletics day:

100 Metres	
Joel	15.23 secs
Marcel	14.77 secs
Norman	15.08 secs
Tony	14.91 secs
Vinay	15.03 secs

Triple Jump	
Courtney	6.251 metres
Damini	6.521 metres
Mercedes	6.35 metres
Stacey	6.509 metres
Virginia	6.348 metres

a Who came first in the 100 metres?

b Who came third in the triple jump?

c Who came next after Vinay in the 100 metres?

d Who won the triple jump?

e Homan was injured and so could not take part in the 100 metres. He can usually run this event in 15.15 seconds. In what position do you think Homan would have finished if he had been fit enough to take part?

8 ✳ Melissa is driving a taxi. When she sets off on a journey the distance meter on the instrument panel looks like this:

1 8 6 2 4 3

This means that the taxi has travelled 18 624.3 kilometres.

At the end of her journey the meter looks like this:

1 8 6 5 9 5

How far did Melissa travel during this journey?

9 ✳ Martin goes shopping with a £50 note. He spends £13.21 on clothes, £15.48 on food and £13.87 on stationery.

a How much does Martin spend altogether?

b How much money does Martin have after the shopping trip?

10 ✳ Three friends share out their winnings after a day at the races. One receives £7.27, another receives £4.87 and the third one receives £3.66.

a How much did the three friends win in total?

b How much would each have received if the winnings had been shared equally?

4 Working with fractions

In this chapter you will revise:
- recognising fractions of a whole
- working with equivalent fractions.

You will also learn how to:
- cancel down a fraction into its simplest form.

4.1 Fractions of a whole

A fraction contains two whole numbers, one over the other.
The bottom number is the **denominator** – it tells you how many equal parts the whole amount is divided into.
The top number is the **numerator** – it tells you how many of these parts to count.

Question What fraction of this circle is coloured?

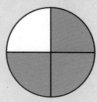

Solution There are 4 equal parts. 3 of them are coloured.

Therefore $\frac{3}{4}$ of the circle is coloured.

Question What fraction of this rectangle is coloured?

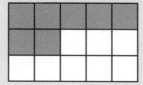

Solution There are 15 equal parts. 7 of them are coloured.

Therefore $\frac{7}{15}$ of the rectangle is coloured.

EXERCISE 4.1

Write down fractions to describe the coloured portion in each of these diagrams:

1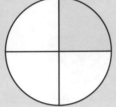

2

3 ✓

4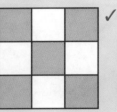

5

6

7

8

9

10 ✓

4.2 Equivalent fractions

Look at these diagrams:

 $\frac{3}{4}$ $\frac{6}{8}$

The coloured portion is exactly the same in both, so $\frac{3}{4}$ is the same as $\frac{6}{8}$.

Fractions like $\frac{3}{4}$ and $\frac{6}{8}$ are called **equivalent fractions**.

You can use simple arithmetic to find equivalent fractions, as in the following two examples.

Question Find two other fractions which are equivalent to $\frac{3}{5}$.

Solution Start with $\frac{3}{5}$ and multiply both numbers by 2:

$\frac{3 \times 2}{5 \times 2} = \frac{6}{10}$

Start with $\frac{3}{5}$ and multiply both numbers by 3:

$\frac{3 \times 3}{5 \times 3} = \frac{9}{15}$

$\frac{3}{5}$ is equivalent to $\frac{6}{10}$ and $\frac{9}{15}$.

There are also many others.

Question Find the missing number if $\frac{5}{8} = \frac{20}{\text{❋}}$.

Solution 5 has been multiplied by 4 to make 20.

Doing the same on the bottom, $8 \times 4 = 32$.
The missing number is 32.

EXERCISE 4.2

1 Find two other fractions which are equivalent to $\frac{1}{3}$.

2 Find two other fractions which are equivalent to $\frac{3}{7}$.

3 Find three other fractions which are equivalent to $\frac{4}{9}$. ✓

4 Find the missing number if $\frac{3}{4} = \frac{30}{\text{❋}}$.

5 Find the missing number if $\frac{7}{8} = \frac{\text{❋}}{24}$.

6 Find the missing number if $\frac{2}{11} = \frac{8}{\text{❋}}$. ✓

7 Find the odd one out from this list: $\frac{2}{3}, \frac{5}{8}, \frac{6}{9}, \frac{10}{15}$.

8 Find the two equivalent fractions in this list: $\frac{2}{3}, \frac{3}{4}, \frac{4}{5}, \frac{5}{8}, \frac{6}{8}$.

9 Joe says, '$\frac{1}{3}$ is the same as $\frac{3}{10}$.' Is he right or wrong?

10 Sarita says, '$\frac{3}{4}$ is the same as $\frac{75}{100}$.' Is she right or wrong?

4.3 Cancelling a fraction into its simplest terms

Look at the diagrams below:

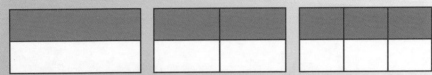

They illustrate that the fractions $\frac{1}{2}$, $\frac{2}{4}$ and $\frac{3}{6}$ are really all the same, they are **equivalent fractions**.

The fraction $\frac{1}{2}$ is said to be in its **lowest terms** because it cannot be written using simpler numbers.
The fractions $\frac{2}{4}$ and $\frac{3}{6}$ can be **cancelled down** to give an answer of $\frac{1}{2}$.

Question Write these fractions in their lowest terms:

a) $\frac{6}{10}$ b) $\frac{15}{55}$ c) $\frac{36}{84}$

Solution a) $\dfrac{\overset{3}{\cancel{6}}}{\underset{5}{\cancel{10}}} = \dfrac{3}{5}$

The 6 and the 10 can each be divided by 2.

b) $\dfrac{\overset{3}{\cancel{15}}}{\underset{11}{\cancel{55}}} = \dfrac{3}{11}$

The 15 and the 55 can each be divided by 5.

c) $\dfrac{\overset{18}{\cancel{36}}}{\underset{42}{\cancel{84}}} = \dfrac{\overset{9}{\cancel{18}}}{\underset{21}{\cancel{42}}}$

$= \dfrac{\overset{3}{\cancel{9}}}{\underset{7}{\cancel{21}}}$

$= \dfrac{3}{7}$

The 36 and the 84 can each be divided by 2, then by 2 again, then by 3.

EXERCISE 4.3

Write these fractions in their simplest terms. Show each step of the cancelling process.

1 $\frac{4}{10}$	**3** $\frac{20}{70}$	**5** $\frac{4}{12}$	**7** $\frac{16}{24}$	**9** $\frac{30}{45}$	**11** $\frac{18}{27}$
2 $\frac{6}{9}$ ✓	**4** $\frac{18}{30}$	**6** $\frac{11}{33}$	**8** $\frac{15}{25}$	**10** $\frac{16}{80}$ ✓	**12** $\frac{42}{70}$

SUMMARY

• In this chapter you have revised fractions of a whole, and equivalent fractions.

• You have also learnt how to cancel a fraction down into its simplest terms, sometimes known as writing it in its lowest terms.

REVIEW EXERCISE 4

I Write down the fraction that is coloured in each of these diagrams:

a 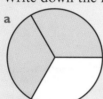   b 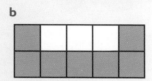   c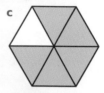

d 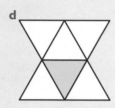   e 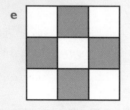   f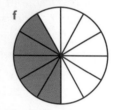

2 Copy these diagrams and shade the given fraction:

a 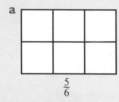   b 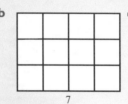   c 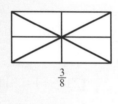   d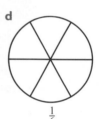

$\frac{5}{6}$ $\frac{7}{12}$ $\frac{3}{8}$ $\frac{1}{6}$

3 Simplify these fractions:

   a $\frac{21}{24}$ b $\frac{35}{45}$ c $\frac{18}{30}$ d $\frac{27}{63}$

4 Find the missing number in each list of equivalent fractions:

   a $\frac{3}{8}, \frac{6}{16}, \frac{9}{24}, \frac{12}{*}, \frac{30}{80}$ b $\frac{2}{5}, \frac{4}{10}, \frac{6}{15}, \frac{*}{25}$

5 Find the odd one out in each of these lists:

   a $\frac{1}{4}, \frac{2}{8}, \frac{3}{12}, \frac{5}{16}, \frac{10}{40}, \frac{12}{48}$ b $\frac{2}{3}, \frac{7}{10}, \frac{14}{20}, \frac{35}{50}$

6 Cancel these fractions down so they are in their lowest terms:

   a $\frac{5}{15}$ b $\frac{13}{26}$ c $\frac{60}{80}$ d $\frac{12}{20}$ e $\frac{44}{77}$ f $\frac{24}{42}$ g $\frac{105}{140}$ h $\frac{144}{360}$

7 ✳ Here is a list of fractions:

   $\frac{3}{4}, \frac{1}{2}, \frac{2}{3}, \frac{5}{6}, \frac{3}{8}, \frac{7}{10}, \frac{2}{5}, \frac{3}{10}, \frac{1}{4}$

   a Write each fraction so that it has a denominator of 120.

   b Use your answers from **a** to help you arrange the fractions in order of
      size, smallest first.

5 Fractions, decimals and percentages

In this chapter you will revise:
- finding a fraction of a given amount ● finding a percentage of a given amount.

You will also learn how to:
- convert fractions into percentages
- convert percentages into fractions
- recognise the equivalence between fractions, decimals and percentages
- solve problems using fractions, decimals and percentages.

5.1 Finding a fraction of a given amount

Question Find three-quarters of 1244.

Solution

Divide by 4 to find **one**-quarter …

$1244 \div 4 = 311$

$311 \times 3 = 933$

… then multiply by 3 to find **three**-quarters.

So $\frac{3}{4}$ of 1244 is 933.

EXERCISE 5.1

Find:

1. One-fifth of 75
2. Three-eighths of 352 ✓
3. $\frac{2}{7}$ of 133
4. $\frac{5}{12}$ of 192
5. Two-thirds of 5841
6. Five-ninths of 126
7. $\frac{4}{9}$ of 5607

8. $\frac{2}{13}$ of 52
9. Three-quarters of 124 ✓
10. Three-tenths of 3560
11. $\frac{2}{11}$ of 1936
12. $\frac{5}{7}$ of 427 ✓
13. Seven-tenths of 1250

14. Four-fifths of 905
15. $\frac{1}{12}$ of 1320
16. $\frac{3}{16}$ of 256
17. Two-sevenths of 161
18. Five-eighths of 232
19. $\frac{7}{8}$ of 296
20. $\frac{8}{9}$ of 216.

5.2 Percentages

'Per cent' means 'out of 100'. The symbol for 'per cent' is %.
100% represents a complete whole.

Question What percentage of this circle is coloured?

Solution There are four equal parts.

$100\% \div 4 = 25\%$
One part is coloured.

So 25% is coloured.

Example What percentage is coloured in this diagram?

Solution There are five equal parts.

$100\% \div 5 = 20\%$

Two parts are coloured.
$2 \times 20\% = 40\%$

So 40% is shaded.

EXERCISE 5.2

Find the percentage that has been shaded in each of these diagrams:

1

2 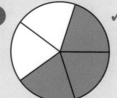 ✓

3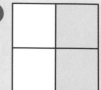

4

5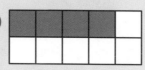

6

31

5.3 Finding a percentage of a given amount

To find **1%** of a quantity, divide by **100**.
Other percentages can then be found easily.

Question Find 27% of £160.

Solution 1% of 160 is 160 ÷ 100 = 1.6

27% is 27 × 1.6 = 43.2

> Divide by 100 to find 1% …

> … then multiply by 27 to find 27%.

So 27% of £160 is £43.20

Some percentage questions can be shortcut by using simple fractions.

$$10\% = \tfrac{1}{10} \qquad 25\% = \tfrac{1}{4} \qquad 50\% = \tfrac{1}{2} \qquad 75\% = \tfrac{3}{4}$$

Question Last Sunday there were 124 people in the congregation for the morning service at St Mary's Church. The vicar is expecting an increase of 25% next week. How many people does he expect?

Solution 25% is the same as $\tfrac{1}{4}$.

> Find $\tfrac{1}{4}$ of 124 …

124 ÷ 4 = 31.

124 + 31 = 155.

> .. then add it on.

The vicar expects 155 people next week.

EXERCISE 5.3

1. Find 18% of 3500. ✓
2. Find 3% of 600.
3. Find 75% of 240.
4. Find 8% of 220.
5. Find 50% of 60.
6. Find 60% of 80.
7. Find 21% of $2000. ✓

8. Find 18% of £150.
9. Find 10% of £12 500.
10. Find 6% of 45 000 people.
11. Increase 240 by 35%. ✓
12. Increase $600 by 13%.
13. Decrease 800 by 25%.

14. Find 6% of 1800.
15. Decrease £3000 by 4%.
16. Find 12.5% of £400.
17. Increase 580 by 25%.
18. Decrease 360 by 70%. ✓
19. Find 12% of 80.
20. Find 80% of 12.

5.4 Changing fractions into percentages

To change a fraction to a percentage, multiply it by **100%**.

Question	Write $\frac{4}{5}$ as a percentage.
Solution	We need to find $\frac{4}{5} \times 100\%$.
	$\frac{1}{5}$ of 100% is 20%.
	$\therefore \frac{4}{5}$ of 100% is $4 \times 20\% = 80\%$.
	So $\frac{4}{5} = \underline{80\%}$.

Question	Write $\frac{5}{7}$ as a percentage.
Solution	We need to find $\frac{5}{7} \times 100\%$.
	By calculator, $\frac{5}{7} \times 100\% = 71.42857\ldots\%$
	So $\frac{5}{7} = \underline{71.4\%}$ (to one decimal place).

EXERCISE 5.4

Change these fractions into percentages. If any are not exact then give the answer correct to one decimal place.

1. $\frac{3}{8}$
2. $\frac{2}{3}$
3. $\frac{9}{10}$
4. $\frac{3}{20}$
5. $\frac{7}{20}$

6. $\frac{5}{8}$ ✓
7. $\frac{3}{40}$
8. $\frac{4}{11}$ ✓
9. $\frac{1}{20}$
10. $\frac{5}{7}$ ✓

11. $\frac{9}{11}$
12. $\frac{7}{9}$
13. $\frac{7}{25}$
14. $\frac{5}{12}$
15. $\frac{2}{15}$

16. $\frac{11}{50}$
17. $\frac{7}{50}$ ✓
18. $\frac{19}{25}$
19. $\frac{24}{25}$
20. $\frac{14}{15}$

5.5 Changing percentages into fractions

To change a percentage into a fraction, divide it by **100%** and cancel the fraction down into its simplest terms if possible.

Question	Write 24% as a fraction.
Solution	24% is the same as $\frac{24}{100} = \frac{12}{50} = \frac{6}{25}$
	So 24% = $\underline{\frac{6}{25}}$

Remember to cancel down the fraction as far as possible.

An alternative method is to enter the fraction as 24 ⌐ 100 using the fraction key $\boxed{a^b\!/_c}$ on your calculator. The calculator will then automatically cancel the fraction for you. If the percentage is not a whole number you may need to multiply the top and bottom of the fraction before cancelling, as in this next worked example.

Question Write $37\frac{1}{2}\%$ as a fraction.

> Multiply top and bottom by 2.

Solution $\dfrac{37\frac{1}{2}}{100} = \dfrac{75}{200} = \dfrac{15}{40} = \dfrac{3}{8}$

So $37\frac{1}{2}\%$ is the same as $\dfrac{3}{8}$.

EXERCISE 5.5

Change these percentages into fractions. You may use the cancelling method shown in the example, or your calculator's fraction key, to give the fraction in its simplest form.

1 32% ✓	**6** 18%	**11** 5%	**16** 86%
2 4%	**7** $2\frac{1}{2}\%$ ✓	**12** $17\frac{1}{2}\%$	**17** 26%
3 44%	**8** 61%	**13** 50%	**18** 19%
4 16%	**9** 99%	**14** 15% ✓	**19** $16\frac{2}{3}\%$ ✓
5 14%	**10** 80%	**15** 55%	**20** 12.5%

5.6 Fractions, decimals and percentages

Fractions, decimals and percentages can be thought of as three different ways of writing the same quantity. For example, $\frac{1}{4}$, 0.25 and 25% are all equivalent, i.e. they all have the same value.

To turn a decimal into a percentage is easy – you just multiply it by 100%, in other words, move the decimal point two places. So 0.35 is 35%, 0.69 is 69% and so on.

Question   Fill in the missing gaps in these statements:

a) $\frac{3}{4} = 0.75 = \square\%$

b) $\frac{4}{5} = \bullet = 80\%$

c) $\frac{11}{20} = \bullet = \square\%$

Solution   a) $0.75 \times 100\% = 75\%$ so $\square = \underline{75}$

b) $80\% = 0.80 =$ so $\bullet = \underline{0.8}$

b) $\frac{11}{20} \times 100 = 55$, so $\bullet = \underline{0.55}$ and $\square = \underline{55}$

EXERCISE 5.6

Find the value of the missing symbol in each of these sets of equivalent amounts:

1 $\frac{3}{5}$ $= 0.6$ $= \square\%$

2 $\frac{9}{10}$ $= \bullet$ $= 90\%$ ✓

3 $\frac{1}{20}$ $= \bullet$ $= \square\%$

4 ❖ $= 0.44 = \square\%$

5 ❖ $= 0.36 = \square\%$

6 ❖ $= 0.72 = \square\%$

7 ❖ $= 0.3$ $= \square\%$

8 $\frac{17}{20}$ $= \bullet$ $= \square\%$

9 ❖ $= \bullet$ $= 65\%$ ✓

10 ❖ $= \bullet$ $= 2\%$

SUMMARY

- In this chapter you have revised how to find fractions and percentages of a given amount, and how to solve problems about percentage increase or decrease.

- You have learnt how to change a fraction into a percentage by multiplying by 100%, and how to change a percentage into a fraction by dividing by 100%.

- You have also learnt to recognise the equivalence of fractions, decimals and percentages.

- Percentage problems are often set in the context of money; further practice of percentage problems will be found in the following Review section. Remember that answers to money problems should be written using two decimal places.

REVIEW EXERCISE 5

I Find:

a Three-fifths of 750   b Seven-eighths of 1024   c $\frac{4}{15}$ of 81 million

d $\frac{4}{15}$ of 180   e Nine-tenths of 120   f Five-elevenths of 121

g $\frac{3}{10}$ of 360   h $\frac{6}{7}$ of 98.

2 Calculate:

a 12% of $250 **b** $17\frac{1}{2}$% of £450 **c** 25% of £640

d 3% of 2500 people **e** 82% of 5000 m **f** $33\frac{1}{2}$% of 900 litres.

3 Increase £250 by 12%.   **4** Increase 650 kg by 4%.

5 Decrease $45 by 9%.   **6** Increase 300 cm by 90%.

7 Decrease 7000 m by 15%.   **8** Decrease 56 000 by 4%.

9 Find the smallest and the largest quantity in each list:

a two-fifths, 20%, one-third, 35%

b 50%, four-ninths, 43%, nine-twentieths

c five-sevenths, 71%, two-thirds, 65%.

10 Last year I spent £260 on rail fares, and this year I expect to spend 6% more. Calculate how much I expect to spend on rail fares this year.

11 One mile is 1760 yards. How many yards are there in three-quarters of a mile?

12 A certain type of radio is supposed to be sold for £35. Three shops offer different sale prices:

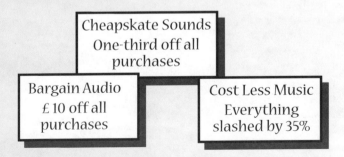

Cheapskate Sounds
One-third off all purchases

Bargain Audio
£10 off all purchases

Cost Less Music
Everything slashed by 35%

Find the actual cost of the radio at each of the three shops. State which is offering the best deal.

13 One ton is 2240 pounds. How many pounds are there in two and three-eighths tons?

14 Annabel scored 38 out of 40 in a mathematics test and 11 out of 16 in an English test. In which subject did she achieve the higher percentage?

15 One acre is 4840 square yards. How many square yards are there in two-elevenths of an acre?

16 Of the items stocked in a shop, 12% are made in Britain.
The shop stocks 350 items altogether. How many of these are made in
Britain?

17 ✳ There are 630 pupils at Westbury School. Two-sevenths of them wear
glasses and 10% wear contact lenses. How many pupils wear neither?

18 ✳ Of the 120 people at a theatre performance, 24 are senior citizens.
What percentage of the audience is this? What fraction is it?

19 ✳ Half of the children at my school are boys, and 10% of them are 16
or over. There are 135 boys under 16. How many children altogether are
there at my school?

20 ✳ A holiday apartment costs £896 to hire, but a 10% discount is offered
for early booking. A deposit of one-quarter of the total bill has to be
sent at the time of booking.
Calculate the size of deposit required when an early booking is
made.

21 ✳ On a double-decker bus there are 9 passengers on the upper deck and
15 passengers on the lower deck.
What percentage of the passengers are on the upper deck?

22 ✳ A ship is carrying 540 passengers. Half of them are English and
one-third are American; the rest are Australian.
a How many Australian passengers are there?
b What fraction of all the passengers are Australian?

23 ✳ I have just had my car serviced. The bill is in two parts. Part 1 of the
bill is for £165.00 plus VAT (a tax) at $17\frac{1}{2}$%; Part 2 of the bill is for
£140.00 but does not attract VAT. Find the total amount that I have to
pay for my car service.

24 ✳ A certain plant grows by 5% of its height each day. At midday on
Monday it was 400 mm high.
a How tall was it at midday on Tuesday?
b How tall was it at midday on Wednesday?

6 Introducing algebra

OUTLINE

In this chapter you will learn how to:
- use letters to represent numbers
- construct and use simple formulae
- use brackets in arithmetic and algebra
- substitute numbers into algebraic formulae.

A calculator will be required for some of the substitution questions.

6.1 Letters for numbers

In this section you will be using letters to represent numbers. You will then be adding, subtracting, multiplying or dividing whole numbers, and using symbols to record the result.

If x represents some unknown number, for example, then

2 more than x is written as $x + 2$

3 less than x is written as $x - 3$

5 times x is written as $5x$

x divided by 4 is written as $\frac{x}{4}$

Question	I think of a number, then take away 7. If x is the number I think of, write down an expression for the result.
Solution	Using the above rules, the result is clearly $\underline{x - 7}$.

Question	I think of a number. First I double this number, then I add 3. If x is the number I think of, write down an expression for the result.
Solution	The doubling is done first... ... so the x becomes $2x$. Then 3 is added... ... so the $2x$ becomes $\underline{2x + 3}$.

Note that when there are two operations, the order is important. The following shows the same worked example, but with the order of the operations reversed.

Question	I think of a number. First I add 3, then I double this number. If x is the number I think of, write down an expression for the result.

Solution	3 is added first...

... so the x becomes $x + 3$.
Then this is doubled...
... so the $x + 3$ becomes $\underline{2(x + 3)}$.

> Note how brackets must be used to show that the whole of $(x + 3)$ is to be doubled.

EXERCISE 6.1

1 Write down an expression for the result in each of the following. Use x to represent the original number.
   a) Add 7.   b) Multiply by 4.   c) Multiply by 4, then add 7. ✓   d) Divide by 6.
   e) Multiply by 3, then subtract 2.

2 Write down an expression for the result in each of the following. Use y to represent the original number.
   a) Add 5, then multiply by 3.   b) Subtract 4, then multiply by 5. ✓
   c) Multiply by 6, then add 10.   d) Divide by 2, then add 2.
   e) Add 100, then double.

6.2 Constructing and using formulae

Some algebra questions are written as 'number machines'. You start at the INPUT, and follow the instructions in the boxes, in order, until you emerge at the OUTPUT.

Question	Look at this number machine:

If x is the input, write a formula for the output.

Solution	Work your way through the diagram:

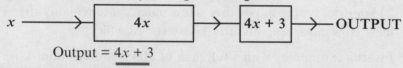

Output = $\underline{4x + 3}$

Other algebra questions are set as real world problems. First work out what to do if the information had been given in number form, then apply the same rules to the letters.

Question I start the day with a tub containing 125 Smarties. Each hour I eat 6 Smarties.

a) How many do I have left after 4 hours?
b) How many after n hours?

Solution In 4 hours I eat $6 \times 4 = 24$ Smarties.
I have $125 - 24 = \underline{101}$ left.

In n hours I will eat $6n$ Smarties.
I have $\underline{125 - 6n}$ left.

EXERCISE 6.2

1 Write algebraic formulae for these number machines. Let the input number be x.

a) Input; multiply by 3; add 6; output
b) Input; multiply by 2; subtract 5; output ✓
c) Input; add 1; multiply by 3; output
d) Input; subtract 2; multiply by 7; output
e) Input; square; add 1; output
f) Input; square; double; add 3; output
g) Input; subtract 3; square; output

2 Write algebraic formulae to answer these questions.

a) I have £3 in my bank account, and I save £2 every month. How much money do I have after 3 months? How much do I have after x months?

b) A reservoir is 60 feet deep at the beginning of August, but the level then goes down a foot every day. How deep is it after one week? How deep is it after n days?

c) Baby Georgina weighed 9 pounds at birth, and then gained 2 pounds each month. What did she weigh when she was six months old? What was her weight after x months? ✓

d) A floppy disk can store 1440 kilobytes of data. I want to store some files of size 20 kilobytes on the floppy disk. How much space remains after I have stored 12 files? How much remains after I have stored n files?

e) I start a car journey with a full tank of 70 litres. Each hour I use up 8 litres. How much fuel remains after 3 hours? How much remains after x hours?

f) At the beginning of the school year the stationery room has 1200 green exercise books. If 90 books are issued each month how many are left after n months?

g) I am buying some new furniture on interest-free credit. I begin by owing the shop £1500, but each month this figure is reduced by £50. How much do I still owe after 8 months? How much after *t* months? ✓

h) Theatre tickets cost £3 for an adult and £2 for a child. Find the total cost for 6 adults and 3 children. Find the total cost for *x* adults and *y* children.

i) A taxi firm operates cars, which can carry four passengers, and minibuses which can carry nine passengers. Find the number of passengers who can be carried by two cars and five minibuses. How many passengers can be carried by *a* cars and *b* minibuses?

6.3 Introducing brackets

You should already be aware that dividing and muliplying take priority over adding and subtracting when you do ordinary arithmetic.

Question   Work out the value of $3 + 5 \times 2$.

Solution $3 + (5 \times 2)$

$= 3 + 10$

$= \underline{13}$

> There are two processes: + and ×. The × has to be done first, even though it occurs later in the expression.

If you want the processes to be done in the opposite order, then brackets should be used. (Some TV game shows appear not to know this!)

If you have to work out the value of a numerical expression containing **brackets** use the following steps:

- the part written **inside** the brackets should be worked out first
- Division and Multiplication come next
- finally Addition and Subtraction.

These rules are sometimes remembered by the 'word' BODMAS – which will be used in the next section.

Question   Work out the value of $(3 + 5) \times 2$.

Solution $\underset{\textstyle\frown}{(3 + 5)} \times 2$

> This time there are **brackets**, so work that part out first.

$= 8 \times 2$

$= \underline{16}$

Sometimes there can be more than one set of brackets. The principle is the same – find the value of the insides of the brackets first.

Question   Work out the value of $(3 + 8) \times 2 + 18 \div (7 - 4)$.

Solution $(3 + 8) \times 2 + 18 \div (7 - 4)$

> There are two sets of **brackets**, so clear them first.
> $3 + 8 = 11$ and $7 - 4 = 3$.

$= 11 \times 2 + 18 \div 3$

> Now do the $\times$ and $\div$ stages, leaving the $+$ until the very end.

$= 22 + 6$

$= \underline{28}$

EXERCISE 6.3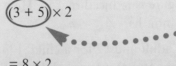

Find the values of each of these. Do them one step at a time, and do not use a calculator.

1. $3 \times 4 + 2$ ✓
2. $3 + 4 \times 2$ ✓
3. $4 + (5 - 3)$
4. $(4 + 9) - 3$
5. $6 + 9 \div 3$

6. $3 \times (12 + 3)$
7. $2 \times (6 - 3) + 1$
8. $(15 - 3) \div 4$
9. $6 + 2 \times (6 + 2)$
10. $4 \times 5 + 6 \times 7$

11. $4 \times (5 + 6) \times 7$
12. $(13 - 2) \times (3 + 4)$ ✓
13. $13 - 2 \times 3 + 4$
14. $25 \times (5 - 1) - 99$
15. $(10 + 1) \times (10 - 1)$

Work out the values of each of these. You will find a calculator helpful.

16. $2.4 + 5 \times (3.6 + 6.3)$ ✓
17. $2.2 + 3.3 \times 4.4 - 5.5$
18. $9.6 \div (2.1 - 0.7) + 3.5 \times 3$
19. $2.2 \times 3.3 + 4.4 \times 5.5$
20. $(7.1 + 4.5) \div (0.8 + 1.7)$

6.4 Substitution

You will often need to substitute numbers in place of letters in an algebraic formula. You might need to use BODMAS:

Brackets ◄••••••••• Brackets should be dealt with first …

Order ◄••••••••• … then Order (squares, cubes etc.)

Division ◄•••••••

Multiplication ◄•••• Multiplying and Dividing next (in any order) …

Addition ◄•••••• … and finally Adding and Subtracting (again in any order).

Subtraction ◄•••••

Question If $a = 5$ and $b = 4$ work out the value of $3a + b^2$.

Solution $3a + b^2 = 3 \times 5 + (4)^2$ ◄•••••• Brackets and Order done first …

$= 3 \times 5 + 16$ ◄•••• … then the Multiplication …

$= 15 + 16$ ◄••• … and lastly the Addition.

$= 31$

Question If $c = 1$, $d = 4$ and $e = 2$ work out the value of $2(4c + 3e)^2 - 3d$.

Solution $2(4c + 3e)^2 - 3d = 2(4 \times 1 + 3 \times 2)^2 - 3 \times 4$

$= 2(4 + 6)^2 - 3 \times 4$ ◄•••••• Bracket first: $4 + 6 = 10$

Squaring next: $10^2 = 100$ •••••► $= 2(10)^2 - 3 \times 4$

$= 2 \times 100 - 3 \times 4$ ◄•••••• Then Multiply …

$= 200 - 12$ ◄•••••• … and finish with the Subtraction.

$= 188$

EXERCISE 6.4

1 If $a = 6$, $b = 2$ and $c = 3$ then work out the value of:
a) $3a - 4b$ b) $6b + a^2$ c) $3(2a + c) + 4b$ ✓   d) $10(a + c + 4)$
e) $5a + 4b - c^2$ f) $4a - 3b + 2c \div 3$ ✓   g) $(a + 2b + c)^2$ h) $3(a + b) - 2(b + c)$

2 If $p = 7$, $q = 2$ and $r = 3$ work out the value of:
a) $p + q + r$ b) $2p + 3q + 4r$ c) $p^2 + q^2 + r^2$ ✓   d) $(p + q + r)^2$
e) $2p - 3q + 4r^2$ f) $p^2 + q \div 2 + 5r$

3 If $x = 8$, $y = 4$ and $z = 3$ work out the value of:
a) $4(x + y)$ b) $2x - 3y + 4z$ c) $x - y^2$ d) $2(x - y) - z^2$ ✓
e) $(2x - y) \div z$ f) $x \div y + z$

SUMMARY

- In this chapter you have learnt how to use letters to stand for numbers; you have used algebraic formulae to describe 'number machines' (simple flow charts) and practised turning written information into algebra.

- You have also learnt how to use brackets, and you have begun to substitute numbers into algebraic formulae.

Remember to use BODMAS when there are several different stages involved. You may safely use a calculator for harder problems, all modern scientific calculators have the BODMAS principle programmed into the chip.

REVIEW EXERCISE 6

1 Write down an expression for the result in each of the following. Let the original number be x.
   a Add 11.   b Subtract 5.   c Multiply by 6.   d Divide by 3.
   e Multiply by 5, then add 4.   f Add 4, then multiply by 5.
   g Subtract 3, then multiply by 12.   h Add 6, then multiply by 2.
   i Add 5, then add 6.   j Subtract 2, then add 3.

2 Write down algebraic formulae for the following number machines:
   a Input; multiply by 4; subtract 5; output
   b Input; subtract 5; multiply by 4; output
   c Input; subtract 2; square; output
   d Input; add 5; subtract 7; output

3 Write down algebraic expressions for each of the following:

a I have to write some thank-you letters after my birthday. Each letter takes 5 minutes.

   i How long does it take to write 6 letters?

   ii How long does it take to write n letters?

b My piggy bank contains £5.00 in two pence coins. I buy some sweets, which cost two pence each.

   i How much money will I have left if I buy 12 sweets? (answer in pence)

   ii How much will I have left if I buy n sweets? (answer in pence)

   iii What problem occurs if n is bigger than 250?

4 Without using a calculator, work out the value of:

  a $4 \times 5 + 6 \times 7$ b $6 + 10 \div 2$ c $(3 + 7) \times 3$ d $3 + 7 \times 3$

5 If $a = 5$, $b = 6$ and $c = 7$, work out the value of:

  a $3a + 4b$ b $5a + 2 \times (b + c)$ c $a^2 + b^2 - c^2$ d $(a + b) \times (b + c)$

6 ✳ The number x is used as input with this set of instructions: Input; add 1; cube; add 1; output. Write down a formula for the output.

7 ✳ My money-box contains x 1p coins, y 2p coins and z 5p coins.

a Write down a formula for the total number of coins, n.

b Write down a formula for the total value of the coins, v.

8 ✳ A water tub contains 45 gallons of rainwater. A three-gallon watering can is filled n times from the tub. Write down a formula for the amount of water remaining in the tub. Explain briefly any restrictions on the value of the number n.

9 ✳ Use your calculator to work out the value of:

$$\sqrt{\left(\frac{3.4 \times 1.8}{2.7 + 1.4}\right)}$$

10 ✳ Look at this number machine:

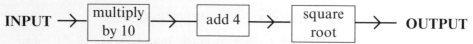

a What is the output when the number 6 is input?

b What is the output when the number x is input?

7 Graphs of straight lines

In this chapter you will revise:
- x and y coordinates in the first quadrant
- negative coordinates.

You will then learn how to:
- draw up tables of values for linear functions
- plot graphs of linear functions.

7.1 x and y coordinates revised

The **x-axis** is a straight line which runs from left to right.
The **y-axis** is a straight line which runs from bottom to top.
The x-axis and the y-axis cross at the **origin**, O.
Points are described by two numbers: x, then y.
For example, (2, 3) means $x = 2$ and $y = 3$.

Question The grid shows some points on an x–y coordinate system.
A is at (2, 3).

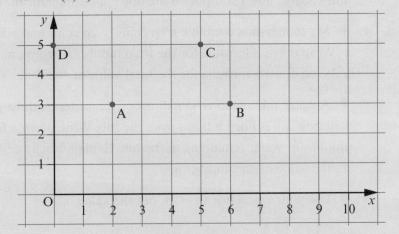

a) Write down the coordinates of B, C and D.

b) Mark the point E so that it is halfway between A and B.

c) Write down the coordinates of E.

Solution a) B is at (6, 3), C is at (5, 5) and D is at (0, 5).

b)

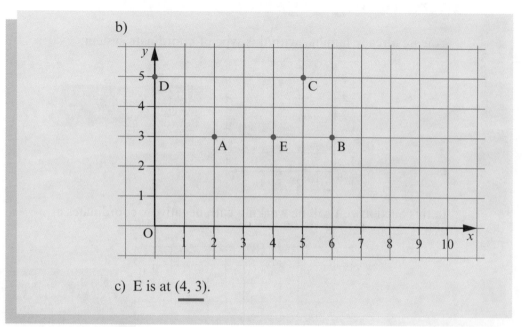

c) E is at (4, 3).

EXERCISE 7.1

1 Plot the points A (1, 1), B (4, 1), C (4, 4) and D (1, 4). What shape is formed by the four points? ✓

2 Plot the points P (1, 1), Q (7, 1), R (7, 3) and S (1, 3). What shape is formed by the four points? The point M is exactly halfway between P and R. Plot the point M, and write down its coordinates.

3 Plot the points U (1, 3), V (3, 5) and W (5, 3). Add point X to your diagram so that the four points form a square. Write down the coordinates of X.

4 The four points A, B, C, D all lie in a straight line. They are A (2, 3), B (3, 4), C (⬛) and D (5, 6). The coordinates of C have accidentally been smudged.

a) Plot the points A, B and D. ✓ b) Suggest coordinates for point C. ✓

5 Draw a pair of coordinate axes in which x and y can each range from 0 to 10. A scale of 1 centimetre to 1 unit will work well for this question.
Plot each of these four shapes on your coordinate axes:

a) Join (2, 4) to (3, 2), then to (7, 2), then to (8, 4), then back to (2, 4).
b) Join (4, 4) to (4, 9).
c) Join (2, 5) to (4, 5), then to (4, 9), then back to (2, 5).
d) Join (4, 5) to (7, 5), then to (4, 8), then back to (4, 5).

When you have finished you should have a picture. What do you think it is?

7.2 Introducing negative coordinates

You are already familiar with this type of coordinate system:

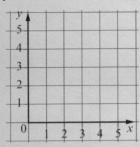

This is called the **first quadrant**.

In this Section you will be working with negative *x*-coordinates as well.

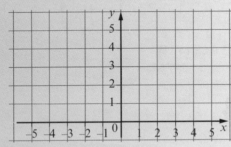

This new region on the left is called the **second quadrant**.

Question   Draw coordinate axes in which *x* can run from –10 to 10 and *y* from 0 to 10.

a) Plot these points and join them up to form a rectangle: (6, 2), (–8, 2), (–8, 8), (6, 8).

b) Write down the coordinates of the centre of the rectangle.

Solution

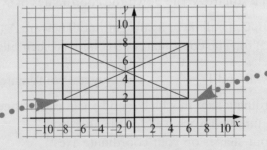

When plotting (6, 2) remember to go 6 across first, then 2 up.

The centre of the rectangle is at (–1, 5).

When plotting (–8, 2) you plot –8 in the across (*x*) direction first, then 2 in the up (*y*) direction.

EXERCISE 7.2

For each question, draw up a fresh set of coordinate grids on squared paper. You should let x run from –10 to 10 and y from 0 to 10. A scale of 1 unit to 1 grid square should work well.

1 Connect up the points (3, 3), (–7, 3), (–5, 8) and (5, 8), then join back to (3, 3) again to form a closed shape. What name does this shape have?

2 Connect up the points (–5, 1), (1, 1), (1, 7) and (–5, 7), then join back to (–5, 1) again. What shape have you made? ✓

3 Connect up the points (9, 2), (–7, 2), (–5, 6), (7, 6) then back to (9, 2) again. What name is given to the shape you have made? ✓

4 Follow these instructions to make a drawing of Tom a cat:
a) Join (3, 6) to (4, 9), then to (2, 8).
b) Join (–5, 6) to (–6, 9), then to (–4, 8).
c) Join (0, 3) to (–2, 3), then to (–1, 2), then back to (0, 3).
d) Join (–3, 6) to (–3, 5), then to (–2, 5), then (–2, 6), then back to (–3, 6).
e) Join (0, 5) to (1, 5), then to (1, 6), then (0, 6), then back to (0, 5).
f) Join (–1, 1) to (3, 2), then to (3, 6), then (2, 8), then (–4, 8), then (–5, 6), then (–5, 2), then back to (–1, 1).

5 Follow these instructions to spell a favourite word:
a) Join (–10, 2) to (–10, 6), then to (–9, 4), then (–8, 6) then (–8, 2).
b) Join (–7, 2) to (–6, 6), then to (–5, 2). Join $(-6\frac{1}{2}, 4)$ to $(-5\frac{1}{2}, 4)$.
c) Join (–3, 2) to (–3, 6). Join (–4, 6) to (–2, 6).
d) Join (–1, 6) to (–1, 2). Join (–1, 4) to (1, 4). Join (1, 2) to (1, 6).
e) Join (4, 6) to (2, 6), then to (2, 4), then (4, 4), then (4, 2), then (2, 2).
f) Join (6, 3) to (7, 2), then to (8, 6).

7.3 Coordinates in all four quadrants

The system with negative numbers on the axes can be extended further still:

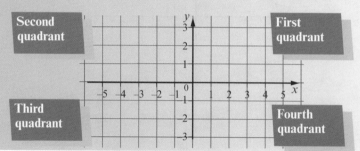

There are now many different ways in which minus signs can appear, so you need to be careful when reading or plotting points.

Question   Write down the coordinates of the points A, B, C, D, E in the diagram below.

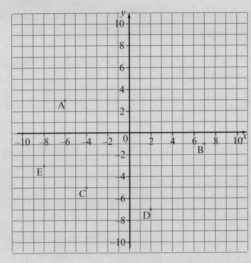

Solution   A is at (–6, 3).   B is at (7, –1).   C is at (–4, –5).

D is at (2, –7).   E is at (–8, –3).

EXERCISE 7.3

1 Write down the coordinates of P, Q, R, S, T and U in the diagram below. ✓

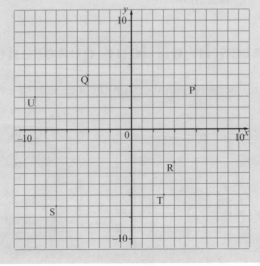

2 Look at this diagram.

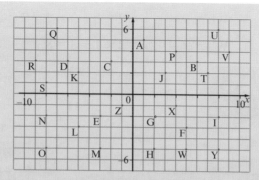

Use this diagram as a codebreaker to decode the following message:

(–8, –2) (–8, –5) (5, –5) // (8, –5) (–8, –5) (8, 6) // (–2, 3) (1, 5) (–8, –2) //
(8, 6) (–8, 1) (–3, –2) // (1, 5) (–5, –3) (–5, –3) // (5, –3) (–8, –5) (8, 6) (–9, 3) //
(–7, 6) (8, 6) (1, 5) (–6, 3) (–9, 3) (1, 5) (–8, –2) (7, 2) (–8, 1) //!

3 Draw a set of coordinate axes in which x and y can run from –10 to 10. Then construct these four shapes on your grid:

a) Join (5, 1) to (8, 4), then to (5, 7), then (2, 4), then back to (5, 1). Label this A.

b) Join (2, –3) to (5, –2), then to (8, –3), then (5, –4), then back to (2, –3). Label this B.

c) Join (–3, –3) to (–7, –1), then to (–6, –3), then to (–7, –5), then back to (–3, –3). Label this C.

d) Join (–7, 1) to (–5, 3), then to (–5, 7), then (–7, 5), then back to (–7, 1). Label this D.

e) Write down the name for each of the quadrilaterals A, B, C, D.

7.4 Graphs of linear functions

A **linear function** has the form $y = ax + b$, for example $y = 2x + 3$.
Linear functions are so called because their graphs are straight lines.
The number a in front of the x tells you how steep the graph will be.
It is called the **gradient**.
To draw the graph of a linear function, work out the coordinates of
three points, then join them up with a straight line.

Question   Draw the graph of $y = 2x + 3$ for values of x from –2 to 4.

Solution

x	–2	1	4
y			

First, choose three x-values at different parts of the range, e.g. –2, 1 and 4.

When $x = -2$, $y = 2 \times -2 + 3 = -4 + 3 = -1$

When $x = 1$, $y = 2 \times 1 + 3 = 2 + 3 = 5$

When $x = 4$, $y = 2 \times 4 + 3 = 8 + 3 = 11$

Now write the y-coordinates in the table.

x	–2	1	4
y	–1	5	11

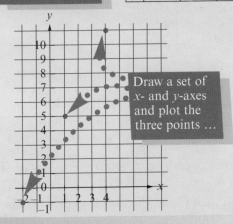

Draw a set of x- and y-axes and plot the three points …

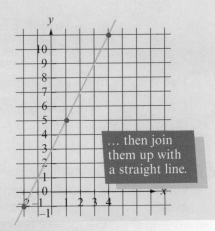

… then join them up with a straight line.

The straight line should pass through all three points, and continue slightly beyond them.
Remember to label the x- and y-axes.

Question   Draw the graph of $y = -\frac{1}{2}x + 6$ for values of x from –4 to 10.

Solution   Consider the points where $x = -4$, 0 and 10.

x	–4	0	10
y			

x	–4	0	10
y	8	6	1

When $x = -4$, $y = -\frac{1}{2} \times -4 + 6 = 2 + 6 = 8$

When $x = 0$, $y = -\frac{1}{2} \times 0 + 6 = 0 + 6 = 6$

When $x = 10$, $y = -\frac{1}{2} \times 10 + 6 = -5 + 6 = 1$

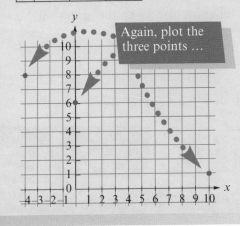

Again, plot the three points …

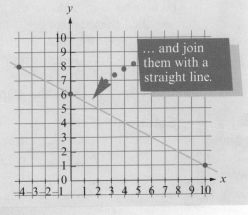

… and join them with a straight line.

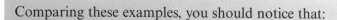

Comparing these examples, you should notice that:

$y = 2x + 3$ has a **positive gradient** of 2. It goes **up** as you move to the right.

$y = -\frac{1}{2}x + 6$ has a **negative gradient** of $-\frac{1}{2}$. It goes **down** as you move to the right.

EXERCISE 7.4

In each question, calculate the coordinates of three points on the line. Then draw a pair of coordinate axes, and plot the line over the given range of values of x.

1. $y = x + 1$ for values of x from -5 to 5
2. $y = 3x + 2$ for values of x from -5 to 5 ✓
3. $y = 4x - 1$ for values of x from 0 to 5
4. $y = \frac{1}{2}x + 3$ for values of x from 0 to 20
5. $y = \frac{1}{4}x + 12$ for values of x from -12 to 12
6. $y = 6 - x$ for values of x from 0 to 6
7. $y = 10 - 2x$ for values of x from -2 to 6
8. $y = -3x + 1$ for values of x from -1 to 3 ✓
9. $y = -\frac{1}{2}x + 12$ for values of x from -10 to 10
10. $y = 4x$ for values of x from 0 to 5

SUMMARY

- In this chapter you have revised x- and y- coordinates, and extended their use into all four quadrants. Remember that the across (x) number is plotted first, then the up (y) number. Minus signs indicate moving left (x) or down (y) instead.

- You have learnt how to plot the graphs of straight lines, by making a table of points first. Although only two points are necessary to define a straight line, it is safer to plot at least three.

REVIEW EXERCISE 7

1 Sanjay draws this rectangle on a coordinate grid.

a Write down the coordinates of the four corners of Sanjay's rectangle

b Joanne draws a rectangle by moving Sanjay's rectangle 3 units to the left.

Write down the coordinates of the four corners of Joanne's rectangle.

c Wil draws a rectangle by moving Sanjay's rectangle 3 units down and 4 units to the left.

Write down the coordinates of the four corners of Wil's rectangle.

2 On a sheet of A4 squared paper draw up a set of coordinate axes so that x can run from –18 to 15 and y from –15 to 20. A scale of 1 unit to one 5 mm square is recommended.

On your grid plot the following points. Join each point to the next one, in order, to reveal an animal.

(11, 3), (13, 0), (13, –3), (13, –7), (13, –9), (14, –12), (11, –13), (5, –13), (–1, –13), (–6, –13), (–10, –13), (–13, –12), (–16, –10), (–16, –9), (–16, –8), (–15, –8), (–14, –9), (–13, –10), (–10, –11), (–3, –12), (–2, –11), (–1, –10), (0, –10), (0, –8), (–1, 0), (–4, 2), (–6, 4), (–7, 7), (–7, 9), (–8, 10), (–9, 9), (–10, 10), (–11, 11), (–10, 12), (–10, 14), (–8, 15), (–8, 16), (–7, 18), (–6, 17), (–5, 16), (–2, 15), (0, 11), (1, 10), (4, 9), (5, 9), (7, 8), (9, 6), (11, 3).

3 The table shows some values for the function $y = 2x - 3$.

x	–3	0	2	5
y		–3		7

a Copy the table, and fill in the missing values.

b Plot the graph of $y = 2x - 3$ on a coordinate grid in which x can run from –3 to 5.

4 The table shows some values for the function $y = -3x + 5$.

x	-1	0	2	4
y	8		-1	

   a Copy the table, and fill in the missing values.

   b Plot the graph of $y = -3x + 5$ on a coordinate grid in which x can run from -1 to 4.

5 Draw the graph of $y = \frac{1}{2}x - 1$ for values of x from -6 to 6.

6 Draw the graph of $y = 2 - x$ for values of x from -10 to 10.

7 Draw the graph of $y = 2x - 1$ for values of x from -5 to 5.

8 Write down the gradient of each of these lines:

   a $y = 3x + 7$ **b** $y = 3x - 7$ **c** $y = 2x + 1$ **d** $y = -5x + 2$

9 ✳ Draw a pair of coordinate axes in which x and y can each run from -10 to 10.

   a Plot three points on the line $y = 3x - 2$ and join them up to obtain the graph of the line.

   b On the same diagram, draw the graph of $y = 2x + 4$.

   c Write down the coordinates of the point where these two lines cross.

8 Lines and angles

OUTLINE

In this chapter you will revise:
- parallel and perpendicular lines ● acute, obtuse and reflex angles
- measuring and drawing angles to the nearest degree.

You will also learn how to solve problems using:
- the sum of angles at a point ● the sum of angles on a line
- the sum of angles in a triangle.

A protractor will be required for the measuring and drawing exercises.

8.1 Parallel and perpendicular lines

Two straight lines which remain the same distance apart from each other are called **parallel**.

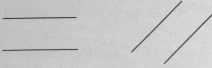

Two straight lines which cross at a right angle are called **perpendicular**.

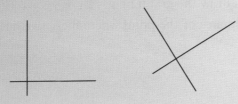

Question The diagram contains six lines, labelled L1, L2, L3, L4, L5 and L6.

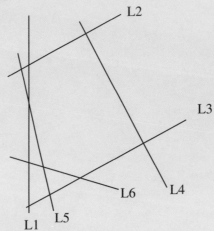

a) Write down the names of two lines which are parallel.
b) Write down any pairs of lines which are perpendicular.

Solution a) L2 and L3 are parallel.
b) L2 and L4 are perpendicular; so are L3 and L4.

EXERCISE 8.1

1 Write down the names of any pairs of lines which are parallel. ✓

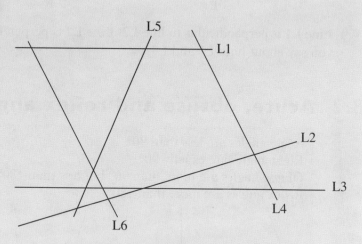

2 Write down the names of any pairs of lines which are perpendicular. ✓

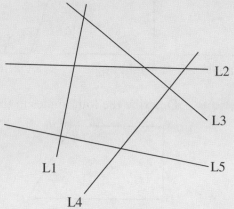

3 Make a copy of this drawing. Then add a line through A which is parallel to the line BC.

•A

B ———————————— C

4 Make a copy of this drawing. Then add a line through D which is perpendicular to the line EF.

• D

E ——————————————————— F

5 Line L1 is perpendicular to line L2. Line L2 is perpendicular to line L3. What can you say about lines L1 and L3? ✓

8.2 Acute, obtuse and reflex angles

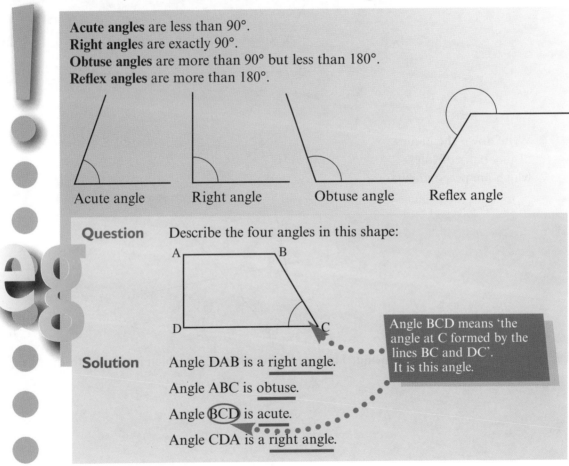

Acute angles are less than 90°.
Right angles are exactly 90°.
Obtuse angles are more than 90° but less than 180°.
Reflex angles are more than 180°.

| Acute angle | Right angle | Obtuse angle | Reflex angle |

Question Describe the four angles in this shape:

Solution Angle DAB is a right angle.

Angle ABC is obtuse.

Angle BCD is acute.

Angle CDA is a right angle.

Angle BCD means 'the angle at C formed by the lines BC and DC'. It is this angle.

EXERCISE 8.2

Say whether each of these angles is an acute, right, obtuse or reflex angle.

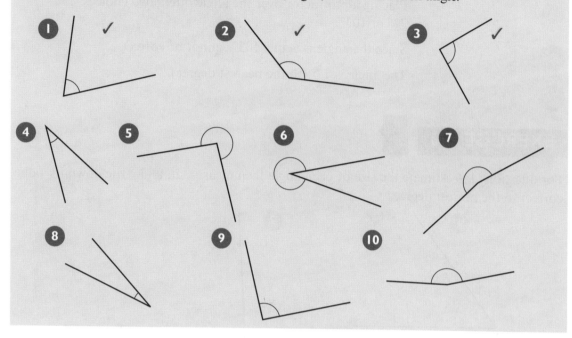

8.3 Drawing and measuring angles

Semicircular protractors have two scales marked on them.
One scale runs from 0° to 180° and the other runs from 180° to 0°.
Estimate the size of the angle first – by judging whether it is acute
or obtuse. This helps to ensure that you use the correct scale.

Question Measure this angle to the
nearest degree:

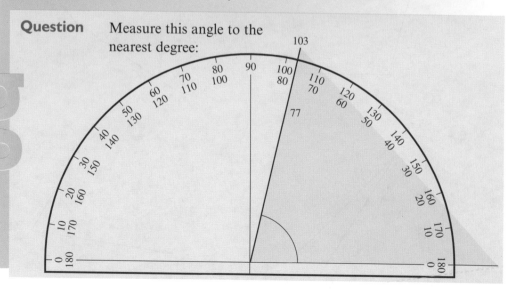

Solution   By eye, the angle is clearly acute.

Placing a protractor over the angle offers two choices:
77° or 103°.

Since the angle is acute, 103° cannot be correct.

The angle is 77° (to the nearest degree).

EXERCISE 8.3

For questions 1–6 estimate the size of each angle then measure it, and write down its value correct to the nearest degree.

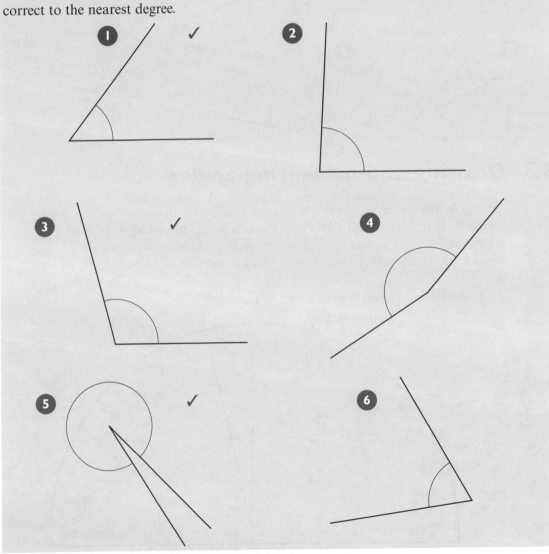

7 Use a protractor to draw these angles. Try to make your diagrams accurate to the nearest degree.

a) 22° d) 17° g) 225° j) 90°

b) 45° e) 80° h) 190° k) 350°

c) 170° f) 127° i) 66° l) 115°

8.4 Angles at a point

When angles meet at a point they all add up to 360°.

Question   Find the missing angle x.

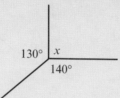

Solution   Since the angles meet at a point they all add up to 360°.

Therefore $130 + 140 + x = 360$

$$270 + x = 360$$

$$x = 360 - 270$$

$$= 90°$$

EXERCISE 8.4

Find the missing angles in each of these diagrams. Show your working clearly.

1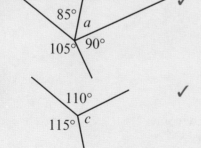

85°
a
105° 90°

2
b 127°
100° 80°

3
110°
115° c

4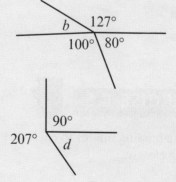

90°
207° d

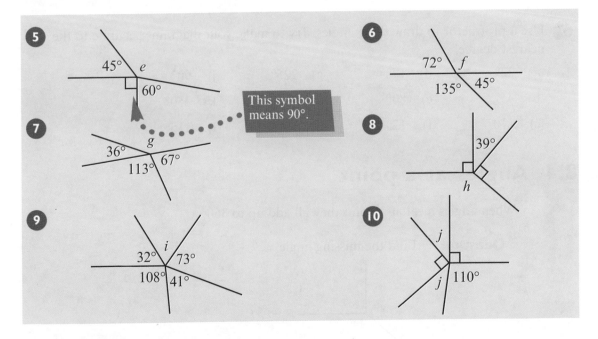

5 45° *e* 60°

This symbol means 90°.

6 72° *f* 135° 45°

7 36° *g* 113° 67°

8 39° *h*

9 32° *i* 73° 108° 41°

10 *j* *j* 110°

8.5 Angles on a line

When angles lie on a line they all add up to 180°.

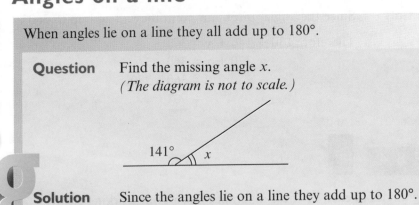

Question Find the missing angle *x*.
(*The diagram is not to scale.*)

141° *x*

Solution Since the angles lie on a line they add up to 180°.
$141 + x = 180$
$x = 180 - 141$
so $x = 39°$

EXERCISE 8.5

Find the missing angles in each of these diagrams. Show your
working clearly.

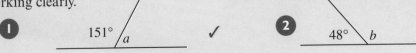

1 151° *a* ✓

2 48° *b*

3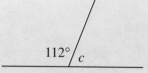
112° c

4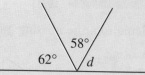
58°
62° d

5 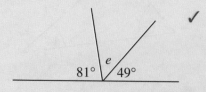 ✓
e
81° 49°

6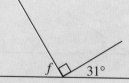
f 31°

7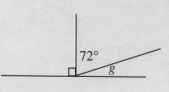
72°
g

8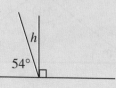
h
54°

9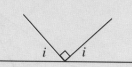
i i

10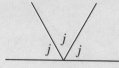
j
j j

8.6 Angles in a triangle

The three angles in a triangle add up to 180°.

Question Find the missing angle, marked x.
(The diagram is not to scale.)

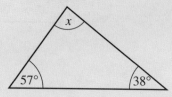

x

57°   38°

Solution x, 57° and 38° add up to 180°.
$$x + 57 + 38 = 180$$
$$x + 95 = 180$$
$$x = 180 - 95$$
$$x = \underline{85°}$$

EXERCISE 8.6

Find, by calculation, the missing angles marked with letters.

1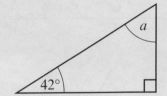

2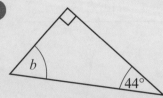

3

4

5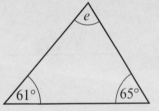

6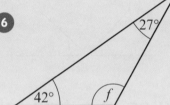

7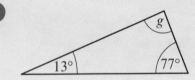

8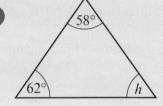

REVIEW EXERCISE 8

I a Give the three-letter name of each of the angles *a* to *f* and say
whether it is an acute, right or obtuse angle.

  b Are any of the lines parallel?

  c Are any of the lines perpendicular?

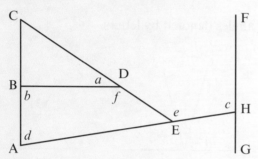

2 Measure the sizes of each of the three
angles in triangle ABC. Check that
they add up to 180°.

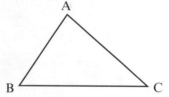

3 Measure the sizes of each of the
four angles in the quadrilateral
ABCD. Check that they add up
to 360°.

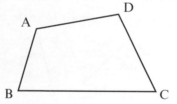

4 Find the size of the missing angles denoted by letters.
(The diagrams are not drawn to scale.)

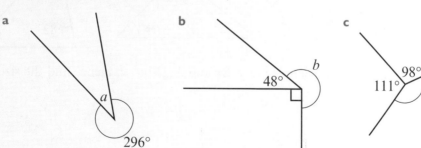

65

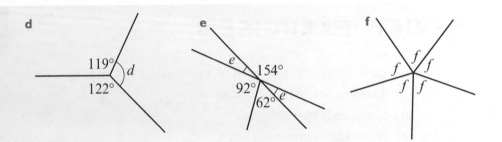

5 Find the size of the missing angles denoted by letters.
(The diagrams are not drawn to scale.)

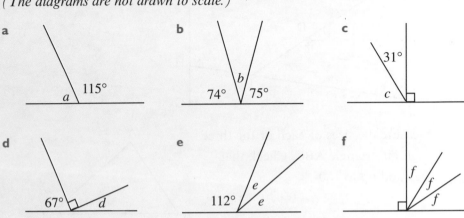

6 Find the size of the missing angles denoted by letters.
(The diagrams are not drawn to scale.)

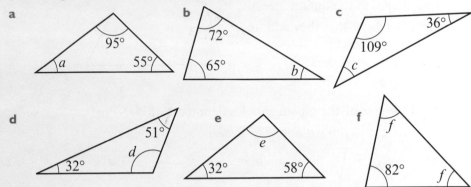

7 ✳ The angles in a triangle are x, $2x$ and $3x$. Find x. Hence find the size of each angle.

9 Metric units

In this chapter you will learn how to:
- work with basic metric units for length, mass, capacity and time
- choose appropriate metric units
- read measurements from scales.

9.1 Basic metric units

You are already familiar with these metric units for length, mass and capacity:

Length   10 millimetres (mm) = 1 centimetre (cm)
100 centimetres = 1 metre (m)
1000 metres = 1 kilometre (km)

Mass   1000 grams (g) = 1 kilogram (kg)
1000 kilograms = 1 tonne (t)

Capacity   1 cubic centimetre (cm^3) is the same as 1 millilitre (ml)
1000 cubic centimetres = 1000 millilitres = 1 litre (l)

You have also met these units of time:

Time   60 seconds (s) = 1 minute (min)
60 minutes = 1 hour (h)
24 hours = 1 day
365 days = 1 calendar year

Question	Write 123 mm in centimetres and millimetres.
Solution	123 mm = 120 mm + 3 mm
	= 12 cm + 3 mm
	123 mm = 12 cm and 3 mm

Question	Write 55 hours in days and hours.
Solution	2 days is 2×24 = 48 hours.
	55 hours = 48 hours + 7 hours
	= 2 days + 7 hours
	55 hours = 2 days and 7 hours

Question	Write 7 kg 250 g in grams.
Solution	7 kg = 7000 g
	So 7 kg 250 g = 7000 g + 250 g
	= 7250 g

EXERCISE 9.1

1. Write 155 mm in centimetres and millimetres. ✓

2. Write 31 h in days and hours.

3. Write 1350 g in kilograms and grams.

4. Write 288 cm in metres and centimetres.

5. Write 320 sec in minutes and seconds.

6. Write three years and forty-five days in days.

7. Write 2500 millilitres in litres. ✓

8. Add together 4.2 metres, 125 centimetres and 48 millimetres.
   Give your answer in mm.

9. Add together 5.65 kilograms and 250 grams. Give your answer in kg.

10. From a container holding 5 litres, 650 millilitres is poured out.
    How many litres are left?

9.2 Choosing and using metric units

Question	What metric unit would you use to measure the mass of an egg?
Solution	An egg weighs about 70 g, or 0.070 kg. It is better to avoid the use of long decimals, so a suitable unit is grams.

Question	Suggest, in metric units, the height of an oak tree.
Solution	An oak tree might be 20 metres high.

EXERCISE 9.2

1 Write down a suitable metric unit for measuring each of the given objects (e.g. grams).

a) The length of an athletics track

b) The mass of a sparrow

c) The diameter of a tennis ball ✓

d) The amount of paint in a large can

e) The total running time of a pop CD

f) The mass of a railway carriage

g) The volume of a coffee cup

h) The width of a pencil

i) The mass of a turkey

j) The length of a motorway ✓

2 Suggest a metric measurement for each object (e.g. 20 metres).

a) The height of a table above the floor

b) The mass of a blue whale

c) The mass of a new-born baby

d) The thickness of a slice of bread

e) The amount of liquid in a milk shake

f) The mass of a coin ✓

g) The diameter of a hamburger

h) The capacity of a rucksack

i) The length of a carrot

j) The volume of a thermos flask

9.3 Reading measurements from scales

Question   Read the measurement
indicated on this scale:

Solution   The value is between 3 and 4.
There are ten intervals, so each unit is 0.1.
The marked value is midway between 3.7 and 3.8.

The scale indicates 3.75

EXERCISE 9.3

Read the values given on each of these scales, giving your answer to a sensible degree of accuracy.

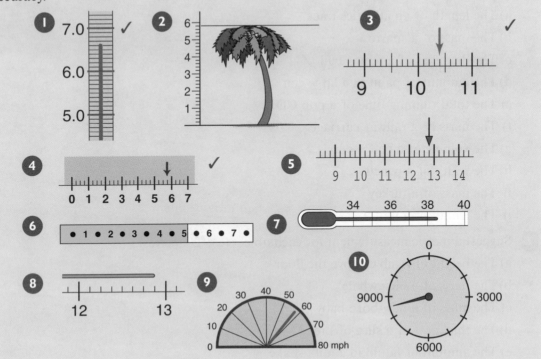

* In this chapter you have practised converting quantities from one metric unit to another. Remember that there are 100 centimetres in a metre but 1000 grams in a kilogram.

* You have chosen suitable metric units for measurement, and practised reading amounts shown on scales. Look for opportunities to practise in the world around you – the supermarket, or car dashboard, for example.

REVIEW EXERCISE 9

1 Write 25 mm in centimetres and millimetres.
2 Write 1200 g in kilograms and grams.
3 Write 170 min in hours and minutes.
4 Write 480 cm in metres and centimetres.
5 Write two and a half hours in minutes.
6 Write 5 min 30 s in seconds.

7 Write 6 kg 300 g in grams.

8 Write 10 m 4 cm in centimetres.

9 Write 5 days and 6 hours in hours.

10 Write 11 litres 50 millilitres in millilitres.

11 Write down a suitable metric unit for measuring each of these quantities.

  a The width of a classroom.

  b The thickness of a magazine.

  c The mass of a key ring.

  d The capacity of a car's petrol tank.

  e The time it takes to bake a pizza.

12 Estimate the following measurements in metric units.

  a The length of a swimming pool.

  b The volume of water in a full washing-up bowl.

  c The mass of a large Christmas cake.

  d The time it takes to walk 4 km.

  e The thickness of a computer floppy disk.

Read the values on each of these scales, giving your answer to a sensible level of accuracy.

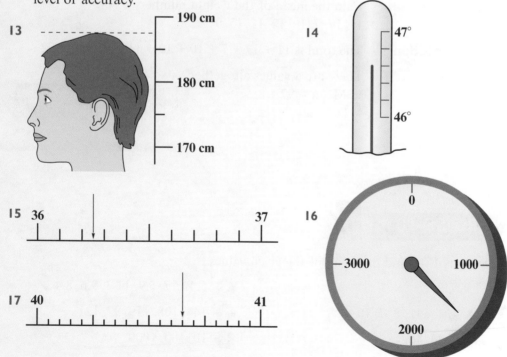

71

10 Averages and spread

10.1 Finding the mean

The mean is one way of describing the average of a set of data. It is the quantity that most people have in mind when they talk about the 'average', although there are other sorts of average, such as the median and the mode.

The **mean** is the ordinary average of a set of numbers:
Mean = (the total of all the values in a data set) ÷ (the number of values)

Question	Find the mean of these eight numbers: 11 17 7 10 12 11 15 9
Solution	The total is $11 + 17 + 7 + 10 + 12 + 11 + 15 + 9 = 92$

There are 8 values altogether.
∴ Mean = 92 ÷ 8
= 11.5 ◄••••••••••

> The mean does not have to be a whole number, even if all the values in the data set are whole numbers.

EXERCISE 10.1

In questions **1–16** find the mean of the given values.

① 8, 3, 5, 2, 2

② 7, 8, 4, 11, 12, 8, 7, 10 ✓

③ 54, 27, 33, 46, 48

④ 5.4, 7.7, 5.9, 11.3, 9.6, 8.4 ✓

⑤ 144, 108, 119, 97, 121

⑥ 10, 100, 1000

7   7, 8, 9, 10, 11, 12, 13

8   2.4, 5.6, 7.2, 6.7

9   2, 3, 5, 7, 11, 13, 17, 19

10   1, 2, 0, 0, 2, 1, 2, 1

11   63, 11, 4, 21, 105

12   −1, 2, 0, −2, 1, 3 ✓

13   2, 2, 2, 6, 6, 6

14   1103, 1245, 1381

15   3000, 4000, 7000, 10 000

16   0.05, 0.12, 0.005, 0.012

17   Five items in a clothes shop are priced at £10.99, £12.50, £25.10, £17.45 and £2.50. Find the mean price of the five items.

18   Four movies last for 121 minutes, 135 minutes, 141 minutes and 167 minutes. Find the mean length of the movies.

19   Eight punnets of strawberries are counted, and found to contain 16, 19, 18, 21, 15, 16, 20 and 17 fruits respectively. Find the mean number of strawberries per punnet.

20   Ten confectionery bars are weighed on a digital balance. The weights, to the nearest gram, are recorded as 63, 66, 68, 65, 66, 68, 67, 70, 66 and 69 grams. Find the mean weight.

The label carries the message 'Average weight 65 grams'. Do you think the manufacturer is justified in making this claim? ✓

10.2   Median and mode

The mean is not the only way of finding the average of a set of values. Two other common measures are the median and the mode.

The **median** is the middle value, once the values have been arranged in order of size.
The **mode** is the value which occurs most often.

Question   Find the median and mode of this set of values:
10 9 7 9 9 8 4 8 7 6 11

Solution   First, arrange the values in order of size:
4 6 7 7 8 8 9 9 9 10 11
↑

The median is 8. ◀ ┈┈┈┈ There are five numbers above it and five below.

The mode is 9. ◀ ┈┈┈┈ 9 occurs more often than any other value in the list.

73

Question Find the median and mode of these values:
6 7 7 9 10 11 13 13 14 19

Solution This time there are two middle numbers:
6 7 7 9 10 11 13 13 14 19

The median is 10.5

This always happens when you have an even number of values – in this case 10. Simply take the mean of the two middle values.

There are also two modes.
The modes are 7 and 13 (bimodal)

Bimodal means 'having two modes'. Sometimes there are more than two modes, and sometimes there is no mode at all.

EXERCISE 10.2

In questions **1–10** find the median and the mode.

1 1, 3, 3, 5, 5, 6, 7, 7, 7 ✓

2 2, 2, 7, 9, 11

3 4, 11, 12, 14, 16, 16

4 5, 7, 7, 8, 11, 15, 15

5 1, 2, 4, 5, 7, 9, 11, 12, 17

6 1, 2, 1, 2, 2, 1, 2, 1, 0, 3

7 9, 3, 6, 5, 14, 3, 12, 7 ✓

8 1.9, 2.6, 2.2, 2.8, 2.6, 2.1, 2.5

9 56, 63, 45, 32

10 2, 7, 4, 8, 7, 7, 2, 4, 9, 11, 4, 2

10.3 The range

Mean, median and mode are three different ways of finding a typical, or 'average', member of a data set, but they do not tell you any information about the way in which the data are spread out. The amount of spread can be measured, in a very simple way, by using the range.

The **range** is the difference between the extreme values.
Range = (the greatest value) – (the least value)

Question Find the range of this set of values:
11 17 7 10 12 11 15 9

Solution The greatest value is 17, the least is 7.

∴ Range = 17 − 7

= 10 ◄••••

> Don't just say 'from 7 to 17' – you must carry out the subtraction.

EXERCISE 10.3

Using the data sets from questions **1–10** of Exercise 10.2, find the range in each case.

10.4 Tally charts and frequency diagrams

Question Class 2B carried out a traffic survey. Fifty cars were chosen at random as they approached the traffic lights outside the school, and the number of occupants recorded. Here are the results:

```
1 3 1 2 1     2 1 4 3 3     2 1 2 2 3
1 2 2 4 3     1 2 1 2 4     4 1 1 1 2
2 2 1 2 3     2 2 1 3 5     4 5 2 1 2
4 3 2 1 2
```

Draw up a frequency table, and display the results in a diagram. State the value of the mode.

Solution We begin by preparing a tally chart:

Number of occupants	Tally	Frequency
1					
2			
3			
4		
5		

> The numbers 1, 3, 1, 2, 1 are tallied like this.

This is the finished tally chart:

Number of occupants	Tally	Frequency
1	ⵏ ⵏ ⵏ	15
2	ⵏ ⵏ ⵏ IIII	19
3	ⵏ III	8
4	ⵏ I	6
5	II	2

The data can be displayed in a bar chart or a vertical line graph:

Tallies are tied up in bundles of 5.

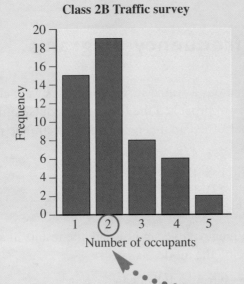

Class 2B Traffic survey

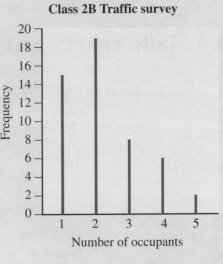

Class 2B Traffic survey

The graph peaks at 2, so this is the mode.

The mode is 2.

EXERCISE 10.4

① For each set of data, construct a tally chart, and illustrate the data with a frequency diagram.

a) 7 8 9 7 7   4 7 8 7 5   5 7 7 6 7   8 7 7 5 7

b) 1 4 5 6 2   2 2 1 4 3   1 4 5 6 6   2 2 1 3 5
     3 1 3 2 6   2 6 6 2 1   3 2 4 6 6   5 6 4 6 6

c) 0 0 1 4 1   0 1 0 1 0   0 1 1 3 2   2 3 2 3 3
    1 0 2 2 0   0 2 2 1 0

d) 16 10 11 15 15   20 16 15 11 10   16 11 16 15 16   17 14 17 16 18
    15 15 17 13 17   17 16 14 18 14   15 14 18 15 17   16 16 16 16 16

2 The diagram below illustrates the scores of 80 Year 7 pupils in a mathematics test:

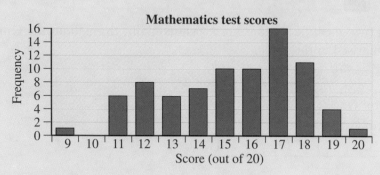

a) Write down the value of the mode.
b) Find the range of the scores.

3 The diagram shows the scores obtained when an ordinary six-sided die is thrown repeatedly.

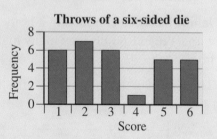

a) Calculate the total number of throws.
b) Write down the value of the mode. ✓

10.5 Comparing two distributions

Question Here are the pulse rates of 10 boys and 12 girls:

Boys: 54 71 66 58 61 62 66 73 66 62

Girls: 61 69 76 62 64 60 69 68 77 75 75 78

Calculate the mean and the range for each group. Comment briefly on how the two groups compare.

Solution For the boys, 54 + 71 + ... + 62 = 639

Mean = 639 ÷ 10 = 63.9   Range = 73 − 54 = 19

For the girls, 61 + 69 + ... + 78 = 834

Mean = 834 ÷ 12 = 69.5   Range = 78 − 60 = 18

Comment The boys seem to have a much lower mean value than the girls, i.e. their average pulses are slower. The ranges are almost identical however, indicating that the variation is similar within each group.

EXERCISE 10.5

1 The temperatures at two scientific stations are measured daily, throughout the year. The results are summarised in this table:

	Station A	Station B
Maximum temperature °C	18°	24°
Minimum temperature °C	3°	–6°
Median temperature °C	10°	11°

Comment briefly on how the two stations compare. ✓

2 Janine has been conducting a homework survey. She asked a random sample of Year 7 and Year 11 pupils how many nights they spend doing more than 30 minutes of homework.

The results of Janine's survey are shown in these diagrams.

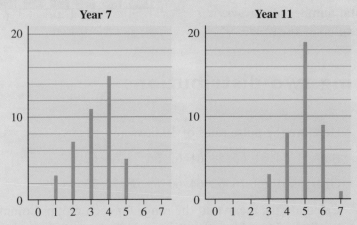

a) Suggest suitable labels for the *x*- and *y*-axes on these diagrams.
b) Find the mode and range for the Year 7 pupils.
c) Find the mode and range for the Year 11 pupils.
d) Comment briefly on how the two sets of data compare.

3 The weights, in kilograms, of thirteen girls were recorded as follows:
     55 43 45 52 41 38 47 44 43 41 51 42 45

The weights, in kilograms, of fourteen boys were similarly recorded:

55 43 58 61 44 66 54 61 49 55 58 57 52 59

a) Find the mean and range of the girls' weights.

b) Find the mean and range of the boys' weights.

c) Comment briefly on the two sets of data.

4 The salaries of twenty accountants are to be compared. Ten of them are fully qualified, while the other ten are still trainees. The salaries, in £, are summarised in this table:

	Fully Qualified	Trainee
Least value	37 200	21 700
Median	41 100	25 250
Mean	43 200	24 700
Greatest value	45 500	29 350

Comment briefly on any similarities or differences between the two groups. ✓

5 Greenview School's Head Teacher is analysing recent results of the school's soccer team. The number of goals scored in home and away matches are given in the tables below.

Home matches   6 0 1 3 3   4 3 4 4 5   1 3 4 1 3   1 2 5
Away matches   2 2 0 1 2   0 0 2 1 3   2 1 2 0 2   0 2 2

a) Draw up two tally charts to show the frequencies of the number of goals scored in home matches and away matches.

b) Illustrate both distributions with vertical line graphs.

c) Comment briefly on the two distributions.

SUMMARY

- In this chapter you have learnt how to find the mean of a data set. Remember that the mean is the usual 'average' in everyday use; it does not have to be a whole number. Two other 'averages' are the mode (most frequent) and median (middle value). Remember to arrange the values in order of size before finding the median.

- You have also learnt how to find the range, and used it to measure the amount of spread.

- It is often useful to make a tally chart, from which a frequency diagram can be drawn. The mode will correspond to the highest point of the frequency diagram, which can be drawn either as a bar chart (thick columns, not touching) or a vertical line graph (thin lines).

- When comparing two data sets you should look at the average (mean, median or mode) and also the spread (measured by the range).

REVIEW EXERCISE 10

1 Find the mean and range of each data set:

  a 6, 2, 6, 10, 5

  b 101, 118, 107, 121, 114

  c 6.5, 5.8, 7.2, 7.0, 6.8, 6.1, 8.0, 7.7

  d 5, 11, 8, 8, 7, 3, 12, 9, 10, 11

  e 2.2, 3.5, 4.8, 7.6, 8.0

  f 3, 1, 4, 1, 6

  g 4, –1, –5, 1, –1, 5

  h 90, 88, 96, 90, 84, 92

2 Find the median and the mode of each data set:

  a 2, 9, 3, 2, 5, 3, 8, 3, 6

  b 5, 9, 4, 12, 6, 5, 8, 4

  c 1, 3, 2, 3, 1, 1, 3, 2, 1, 3

  d 61, 27, 43, 41, 29, 55, 48

  e 8, 3, 7, 8, 3, 2, 5, 8, 1, 8

  f 97, 98, 99, 100, 101

  g 1, 5, 10, 20, 1000

  h 74, 77, 81, 77, 75, 81, 75, 84, 77, 81

3 Draw up a tally chart to show the frequency of each letter of the alphabet in this extract of text:

  On a clear night, away from city lights, try looking up and estimating the number of stars visible to the unaided eye. The answer is several thousand.

  a State the modal letter.

  b Explain why you cannot find a mean for this set of data.

4 The diagram shows the results of a survey about brothers and sisters:

Number of brothers or sisters	Year 7 pupils Frequency	Year 11 pupils Frequency
0	6	3
1	21	11
2	25	26
3	8	14
4	0	4
5	0	1
6 or more	0	0
Total	60	59

  a Draw two vertical line graphs to show the two sets of data.

  b Comment briefly on any differences between the results for Year 7 pupils and Year 11 pupils.

5 The graph shows information about some cars at a used car sale.

 a Calculate the total number of cars.

 b State the value of the mode.

 c Calculate the mean number of previous owners of a used car.

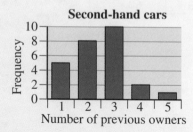

6 Vinay counts the number of letters in each word of a sample of text from the eighteenth century, and another sample from the twentieth century. Here are his results:

	Eighteenth-century text	Twentieth-century text
Least length	2	2
Greatest length	17	11
Mean length	4.25	4.28

Vinay says 'If you look at the greatest lengths then it is clear that eighteenth-century writers used much longer words than we do nowadays.'

Explain carefully whether you agree with Vinay's conclusion.

7 ✳ The table shows part of a brochure for a winter holiday:

Departure	Hotel Galli	Hotel Amerikan	Hotel Capriolo	Hotel Cassana
Dec 20	485	479	419	439
Dec 27	545	549	499	649
Jan 03	455	329	299	489
Jan 10	455	335	309	385
Jan 17	465	349	319	389
Jan 24	485	369	329	405

 a Find the mean price for the four hotels in the week departing Jan 10.

 b Find the mean price of a week at the Hotel Capriolo.

 c Find the ranges of the prices in the four hotels during these six weeks.

8 ✳ The table shows the examination results of three students in four subjects.

Student	Mathematics	English	French	Science
Damian	43	58	84	48
Lois	77	55	66	51
Richard	79	11	68	60

a Find the mean score for each student.

b Find the mean score for each subject.

c Calculate the range of the marks.

d Richard was ill on the day of one of these examinations.

Say which one you think it was.

9 ✳ Three jazz CDs have 7 tracks, 4 tracks and 13 tracks, while five folk CDs have 13 tracks, 11 tracks, 12 tracks, 15 tracks and 11 tracks.

a Find the mean number of tracks on the three jazz CDs.

b Find the mean number of tracks on the five folk CDs.

c Find the mean number of tracks on all eight CDs.

10 ✳ Each week I buy one national lottery ticket, and I choose the same six numbers each time. Five of the numbers are 5, 6, 11, 14 and 17, but I have forgotten the sixth number. I can remember, however, that the mean of my six numbers is 15.
Calculate the value of the sixth number.

11 ✳ Class 4E are comparing the amount of pocket money they each receive. The ten boys have a mean of 80 pence per week, the least being 50 pence and the greatest £1.25. For the fifteen girls the mean is £1.00, with the least being 85 pence and the greatest £1.40.

a John says 'the mean for the class is 90 pence'. Explain how you think John obtained this figure, and say briefly why it is wrong.

b Calculate the correct mean amount of pocket money for Class 4E.

c Find the range for the class.

12 ✳ Catherine says 'If you look at 1, 2, 2, 4, 5 then the mean is 2.8 but the mode is only 2. This demonstrates that the mean is always greater than the mode'.
Explain carefully whether you think Catherine's statement is correct.

13 ✳ Here is a reminder of the number of days in each month during a leap year of 366 days:

Month	Jan	Feb	Mar	Apr	May	Jun	Jul	Aug	Sep	Oct	Nov	Dec
Days	31	29	31	30	31	30	31	31	30	31	30	31

a Write down the modal length of a month in a leap year.

b Find the median length of a month in a leap year.

c Find the mean number of days of a month in a leap year.

d Are any of these answers different in a normal year of 365 days?

11 Introducing probability

OUTLINE

In this chapter you will learn how to:
- recognise situations in which the outcome is uncertain
- use basic vocabulary such as 'fair', 'likely' and 'certain'
- solve simple problems using a probability scale from 0 to 1.

11.1 Uncertainty

Probability is a way of examining events when the outcome is **uncertain**.

For example, when an ordinary die is thrown, then the outcome is uncertain, because the score could be 1, 2, 3, 4, 5 or 6.

When 2 is multiplied by 5, however, the outcome is certain – it can only be 10.

EXERCISE 11.1

For each of these situations say whether the given outcome is certain or uncertain.

1. The number obtained by adding 7 and 10.
2. The number obtained by spinning a spinner labelled 1, 2, 3.
3. The result of tossing a coin. ✓
4. The number of tenths equivalent to the decimal 0.5.
5. The number of goals scored in next year's Cup Final.
6. The number of cards in a normal pack.
7. The number of plants which will germinate (grow) from a batch of 10 seeds.
8. The reply which my friend will give when I ask 'Think of a number between 1 and 10'.
9. The size of the angle in one corner of a rectangle. ✓
10. The number of faces on a cube.

11.2 The language of probability

If something **must** happen then the outcome is **certain**.
If something **might** happen then the outcome is **possible**.
If something **cannot** happen then the outcome is **impossible**.

Question   Two ordinary dice are thrown, and the scores are added together to make a single total. Describe the likelihood that this total is:

a) at least 2
b) 10
c) 14.

Solution   a) The lowest total is 1 + 1 = 2, so all the totals are at least 2.
This outcome is certain.

b) A total of 10 could happen (e.g. 6 + 4), but it does not have to be 10.
This outcome is possible.

c) The highest total that could happen is 6 + 6 = 12.
A total of 14 is impossible.

If something has just as much chance of happening as not happening we say it has an **even chance**.
If something has more chance of happening than not, we say it is **likely**.
If something has less chance of happening than not, we say it is **unlikely**.

Question   A bag contains 20 counters. There are 10 red, 6 blue and 4 green. The bag is shaken and then one counter is removed. Describe the probability that it is:

a) blue   b) red   c) not green.

Solution   a) Only a few of the counters are blue.
This outcome is unlikely.

b) Exactly half of the counters are red, so a counter is just as likely to be red as it is to not be red.
This outcome has an even chance.

c) Most of the counters are not green.
This outcome is likely.

If an experiment is set up so that the different outcomes all have an equal chance of happening then we say the experiment is **fair**.

Question   This spinner is used to select a number 1, 2 or 3.
Is it fair?

Solution   The three sectors are all of equal size, so the spinner is fair.

EXERCISE 11.2

1 Ten counters numbered 1, 2, 3,... 10 are placed in a bag. One counter is chosen at random. Say whether the following outcomes are likely, unlikely or have an even chance:
a) the number is 1   b) the number is 5 or less   c) the number is not 3.

2 Use the words impossible, unlikely, even chance, likely or certain to describe the probability that:
a) my teacher remembers to come to school next Monday
b) a 7 is obtained when an ordinary dice is thrown
c) someone I know will win the National Lottery jackpot this weekend
d) a piece of toast lands butter side up, when dropped.

3 Arthur has two dice, a red one and a blue one. He throws each dice sixty times, and counts the number of times that each score from 1 to 6 is obtained.
Here are the results:

Score on red die	1	2	3	4	5	6
Number of times	10	11	10	10	9	10

Score on blue die	1	2	3	4	5	6
Number of times	12	11	12	11	10	4

a) Does it look as if the red die is fair?
b) Does it look as if the blue die is fair?

11.3 The probability scale from 0 to 1

Probabilities are measured on a scale from 0 to 1.
A probability of 0 means an outcome is impossible.
A probability of 1 means an outcome is certain.

If an experiment has several **equally likely outcomes** then the probability can be calculated as follows:

$$\text{probability} = \frac{\text{number of ways of achieving the required result}}{\text{total number of all possible outcomes}}$$

Question　A letter is chosen at random from the letters of the word MOUSE. Calculate the probability that it is a vowel, and indicate the result on a probability scale from 0 to 1.

Solution　There are five letters, M, O, U, S, E – all equally likely.
There are three vowels, O, U, E.
so Probability(vowel) = $\frac{3}{5}$

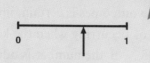

It is usually better to leave answers as fractions rather than decimals.

EXERCISE 11.3

Solve these probability questions, and illustrate each one on a probability scale from 0 to 1.

1 A whole number between 1 and 10 (inclusive) is chosen at random. Find the probability that it is 8. ✓

2 A whole number between 1 and 10 (inclusive) is chosen at random. Find the probability that it is 8, 9 or 10. ✓

3 A letter from the word FORTUNE is chosen at random. Find the probability that it is a vowel.

4 A letter from the word RANDOM is chosen at random. Find the probability that it is not a vowel.

5 Anwar, Bethany and Carlos write their names on three slips of paper, and put them in a bag. A name is chosen at random. Find the probability that it is Bethany.

6 A month of the year is chosen at random. Find the probability that it begins with the letter J. ✓

7 A fair six-sided die is thrown. Find the probability that the score is 2.

8 A fair six-sided die is thrown. Find the probability that the score is at least 2.

SUMMARY

● In this chapter you have recognised that the result (or outcome) of a probability experiment is uncertain. You have begun to use the basic vocabulary of probability.

● You have also calculated simple probabilities, and displayed them on a scale from 0 (impossible) to 1 (certain).

REVIEW EXERCISE 11

1 A computer has been programmed so that a random whole number between 1 and 100 will appear on the screen when a key is pressed. Say whether you think each of these outcomes is certain, impossible, likely, unlikely or has an even chance of occurring when the key is pressed
   a the number is smaller than 85   b the number is odd
   c the number is 13   d the number is a multiple of 20.

2 Christine chooses a two-digit number at random from this list:
   25 26 35 36 45 46 55 56
   Say whether you think each of these outcomes is certain, impossible, likely, unlikely or has an even chance of occurring:
   a the number is a multiple of five
   b the number is prime
   c the two digits add up to eleven.

3 ✳ Debbie has a blank six-sided die. She wants to colour the faces so that:
   ● the probability of getting a purple face is more than an even chance;
   ● a yellow face is just as likely as a green face.
   Describe how you think Debbie colours in the six faces of the die.

4 ✳ Rana has a bag which contains 6 red balls and 2 green balls. She adds some more balls to the bag so that when a ball is chosen at random there is an even chance that it is red.
   a What is the smallest number of balls Rana could have added to the bag?
   b Does it matter what colour they are?

End of year review exercises

EXERCISE Y7.1

Do this exercise as mental arithmetic – do not write down any working.

1   Write seventy thousand, two hundred and forty-one in figures.
2   Write 34 060 in words.
3   Add together 46, 39 and 54.
4   Work out 540 – 99.
5   Find 352 × 10.
6   Find 5600 × 100.
7   Find 43 000 ÷ 10.
8   Find 108 000 ÷ 100.
9   Write down the value of 7 × 8.
10 Write down the first five multiples of 9.
11 Is 45 a multiple of 7?
12 Write down all the factors of 20.
13 Is 6 a factor of 44?
14 Write down one example of a prime number between 20 and 30.
15 Is 47 a prime number?
16 Write two and nine-tenths as a decimal.
17 Write $6\frac{49}{100}$ as a decimal.
18 Write 2.7 as a fraction.
19 Write the fraction $\frac{24}{40}$ in its simplest form.
20 Work out:
    a 8.5 × 3   b 16.48 ÷ 4.

EXERCISE Y7.2

Do this exercise as mental arithmetic – do not write down any working.

1   Work out 14.6 + 8.5.
2   Work out 21.4 – 9.9.
3   Amy spends £14.50 on a CD and £3.65 on a book. How much does she spend in total?

4   What fraction of this diagram has been shaded? What percentage is this?

5   Mark scores 43 out of 50 in a French test. What percentage is this?

6   Write 44% as a fraction, cancelling your answer down into its simplest form.

7   Find the values of the missing symbols: ✳/20 = 0.65 = ◆%.

8   Alison thinks of a number, x. She multiplies it by 3, then adds 2. Write a formula for her answer.

9   I start with £20 in my bank account, and I save £5 a month. Write a formula for the amount I have after n months.

10   Work out the value of $4 \times (7 - 4) + 2$.

11   Two of the angles in a triangle are 71° and 22°. Find the third angle, and say whether it is acute or obtuse.

12   What metric unit would you use to measure the mass of a pen?

13   What metric unit would you use to measure the height of a classroom block?

14   Write 6 kg 45 grams in grams.

15   What reading is shown on this scale?

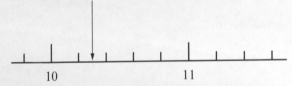

16   Find the mean of 5, 10 and 12.

17   A letter is chosen at random from the letters of the word COMPUTER. Find the probability that it is a C.

18   A letter is chosen at random from the letters of the word FERRET. Find the probability that it is an R.

19   Find three-quarters of 160.

20   Find 30% of 130.

EXERCISE Y7.3

You should show all necessary working in this exercise.

1 Multiply 226 by 13.

2 Work out 4255 ÷ 23.

3 Six children measured the height of a postage stamp:

Paul	Hannah	Jo	Carlo	Indira	Lowell
2.6 cm	2.511 cm	2.55 cm	25.22 mm	2.531 cm	2.507 cm

Rewrite the table to show the measurements in order of size, smallest first, making sure that they are all in centimetres.

4 Make a copy of this diagram, and shade $\frac{3}{4}$ of it.

5 Find two equivalent fractions in this list: $\frac{2}{3}$ $\frac{3}{4}$ $\frac{5}{8}$ $\frac{6}{9}$ $\frac{9}{10}$.

6 Find **a** 15% of 80 **b** 31% of 5600.

7 If $x = 2.5$ and $y = 4.8$, find the values of **a** $3x + 4y$ **b** $(x + 2y)^2$
   c $(4x - y) \div 2$

8 Dionne has been drawing spots on a coordinate grid:

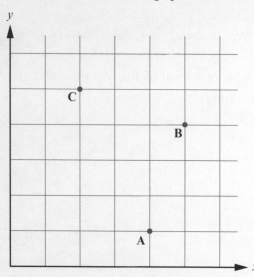

She has marked A at (4, 1) and B at (5, 4).

a Write down the coordinates of C.

b Dionne wants to add a point D so that A, B, C and D form a square. Write down the coordinates of D.

9 Draw a set of coordinate axes so that x and y can run from –10 to 10. Then plot A(8, 8), B(–5, 8), C(–8, –8) and D(8, –8). Join the points up in order, then join D back to A to complete a quadrilateral. What type of quadrilateral is it?

10 Draw a set of coordinate axes on which x and y can each run from –5 to 10. Plot the graph of $y = 2x - 1$.

11 Twelve children were asked how many letters they received last week. Their replies were:

0 3 6 2 3 2 3 1 2 3 0 3

a Write the numbers in order of size, smallest first.

b Find the mean, median and mode of the data.

c Find the range.

12 Jatin counts the number of spelling mistakes on each page of a newspaper. The results are:

0 2 1 2 0 4 2 3 3 1 2 3 2 3 4 3 1 0 3 4

a How many pages are there in the newspaper?

b What is the mode of the number of spelling mistakes?

c What is the mean?

13 Alice has to cycle 10 km to school. She cycles 3.4 km and then stops for a rest.

a How much further does she have to cycle?

b Sarfraz says, 'Alice stopped roughly half-way through her journey.' Petra says, 'Alice stopped roughly one-third of the way through her journey.' Which one of them is right?

14 51 is a prime number. True or false?

12 Working with whole numbers

OUTLINE

In this chapter you will learn how to:
- work with negative numbers, without a calculator
- express a positive whole number in terms of its prime factors
- find highest common factors
- find lowest common multiples.

12.1 Adding and subtracting with negative numbers

You have probably seen a number line set out like this:

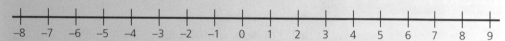

The larger numbers are to the right, smaller ones to the left.
We write 7 > 5 to mean '7 is greater than 5'.
Similarly –8 < –5 means '–8 is less than –5'.

Question   Arrange these in order of size: 6.22, –7.5, –5.3

Solution   Consider their positions on the number line:

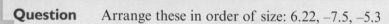

So –7.5 < –5.3 < 6.22

When you: **add** a **positive** number – the result is a number further to the **right**;

add a **negative** number – the result is a number further to the **left**.

For subtraction, these rules are reversed:
When you: **subtract** a **positive** number the result is a number further to the **left**;

subtract a **negative** number the result is a number further to the **right**.

Question Work out: –6 + 4; 7 + (–2); 12 – 9; 6 – 11; 5 – (–14); –4 – (–10).

Solution Using the number line and the rules above,

$-6 + 4 = \underline{-2}$

$7 + (-2) = \underline{5}$

$12 - 9 = \underline{3}$

$6 - 11 = \underline{-5}$

$5 - (-14) = \underline{19}$

$-4 - (-10) = \underline{6}$

This is 'five take away negative fourteen'. It is the same as 'five take away minus fourteen'.

This is 'negative four take away negative ten'. It is the same as 'minus four take away minus ten'.

EXERCISE 12.1

① Arrange these numbers in order of size, smallest first:

a) –4, 6, –3   b) 10, –3, –7   c) –3.5, 3.5, 1.4

d) 14.66, –7.5, –7.33, 14.05 ✓   e) 0.05, –0.32, –0.310, 0.6

② Work out these:

a) –7 + 3   b) –5 – 6 ✓   c) 6 + (–3)

d) –2 + (–5) ✓   e) 5 – 7   f) 4 – (–7)

g) – 7 – (–8)   h) 2.4 – 3.6   i) –5.5 + 7.5

j) 12.4 – (–3.6) ✓   k –1.4 + (–1.5)   l) –2.8 – 2.8

m) 6.37 – 2.5 – (–1.5)

③ On the moon the daytime temperature reaches 105°C, but at night falls to –155°C. Find the difference between day and night temperatures on the moon.

④ During Christmas week last year I recorded the temperature as 3°C on Monday, –4°C on Tuesday and –2°C on Wednesday.

a) Which day was the warmest?

b) Which day was the coldest?

c) Which was the warmer out of Tuesday and Wednesday, and by how much?

12.2 Multiplying and dividing with negative numbers

You are already familiar with the rules for adding or subtracting negative numbers. You may find it helpful to use a directed number line.

Sometimes brackets are included around a negative number.

These examples remind you of how the various rules apply.

Written with brackets	Written without brackets
2 + (–3) = –1	2 + –3 = –1
(–3) + (–2) = –5	–3 + –2 = –5
(–2) + 5 = 3	–2 + 5 = 3
2 – 8 = –6	2 – 8 = –6
2 – (–8) = 10	2 – –8 = 10
–3 – (–1) = –2	–3 – –1 = –2

The rules for multiplication and division are a little different.

When two negative numbers are multiplied (or divided) the answer is positive. This result is sometimes remembered as 'two minuses make a plus', but be careful to use this rule correctly.

Here are some examples showing how the rules for multiplication and division apply.

Multiplication	Division
$3 \times 5 = 15$	$20 \div 4 = 5$
$3 \times (–5) = –15$	$20 \div (–4) = –5$
$(–3) \times 5 = –15$	$(–20) \div 4 = –5$
$(–3) \times (–5) = 15$	$(–20) \div (–4) = 5$

Take care with problems involving more than one stage.

Multiplications and divisions should be done **before** any addition or subtraction.

Question Work out $2 \times –3 – 16 \div (–4)$

Solution $2 \times –3 – 16 \div (–4)$

First, work out $2 \times –3 = –6$ and $16 \div (–4) = –4$

$= –6 – –4$

$= –2$

Then finish with the subtraction

EXERCISE 12.2

Work out the value of each expression.

1 $4 \times (-6)$

2 $6 \times (-3)$ ✓

3 $-3 \times (-2)$

4 $2 \div (-1)$

5 $-18 \div 6$

6 $-10 \div (-5)$

7 $-8 \div 2$

8 $-3 \times (-15)$ ✓

9 $5 - (-5)$

10 $5 + (-5)$

11 $6 - -2$

12 $-3 - 4$

13 $4 + -8$

14 $-10 \div -1$

15 3×-6

16 -4×-5

17 -2×8

18 $12 \div -6$

19 $-18 \div 3$

20 $-36 \div -3$

21 $8 \times 3 - 2 \times 4$ ✓

22 $8 \times (-3) + 4 \times (-5)$

23 $-6 \times 10 + 7 \times 11$

24 $4 + 3 \times 5 - 18$

25 $2.5 \times 4 - 1.6 \times 10$

12.3 Writing a number as a product of prime factors

Sometimes we need to express a number as a product of **prime factors**.
Remember that the first few primes are: 2, 3, 5, 7, 11, 13, 17, 19, ...

Question Write 30 as a product of prime factors.

Solution $30 = 2 \times 15$

$= 2 \times 3 \times 5$

As 30 is even we write $30 = 2 \times 15$ first.
Now we break up the 15 into 3×5.
Stop here because 2, 3 and 5 are all prime.

Question Write 120 as a product of prime factors.

Solution $120 = 2 \times 60$

$= 2 \times 2 \times 30$

$= 2 \times 2 \times 2 \times 15$

$= 2 \times 2 \times 2 \times 3 \times 5$

$= 2^3 \times 3 \times 5$

The factor 2 occurs three times, i.e. as $2 \times 2 \times 2$.
Notice how this is written for short as 2^3, or 'two cubed'.

Question A number has been written as a product of prime factors; it is $2 \times 3^2 \times 5 \times 11$.

Write this number in ordinary form.

Solution
$$2 \times 3^2 \times 5 \times 11 = 2 \times 9 \times 5 \times 11$$
$$= 18 \times 5 \times 11$$
$$= 90 \times 11$$
$$= 990$$

EXERCISE 12.3

Write the given number as a product of prime factors.

1	42	**6**	90	**11**	49	**16**	60
2	66 ✓	**7**	55	**12**	48	**17**	44
3	12	**8**	50	**13**	54	**18**	144 ✓
4	36 ✓	**9**	28	**14**	24	**19**	36
5	72	**10**	35	**15**	76	**20**	360

12.4 Highest common factor

The highest common factor (HCF) of two numbers is the biggest number that divides into them both without leaving any remainder.
For example, the HCF of 20 and 30 is 10.
Highest common factors are not always very obvious. This section shows you a way of finding the HCF using prime factors.

Question Find the highest common factor of 35 and 55.

Solution First, write the numbers as products of prime factors.

$$35 = 5 \times 7$$
$$55 = 5 \times 11$$

The factor of 5 is common to both, but 7 only occurs in the first one and 11 only in the second.

Therefore the HCF of 35 and 55 is 5.

Question Find the HCF of 48 and 180.

Solution $48 = 2^4 \times 3$
$180 = 2^2 \times 3^2 \times 5$

Look at the powers of 2:
$48 = 2^4 \times 3$
$180 = 2^2 \times 3^2 \times 5$

> There are 4 factors of 2 in 48 but only 2 factors of 2 in 180. Pick the lower of these: 2

Now look at the powers of 3:
$48 = 2^4 \times 3$
$180 = 2^2 \times 3^2 \times 5$

> There is 1 factor of 3 in 48 and 2 factor of 3 in 180. Pick the lower of these: 1

Finally, look at the powers of 5:
$48 = 2^4 \times 3$
$180 = 2^2 \times 3^2 \times 5$

> There is 0 factor of 5 in 48 and 1 factor of 5 in 180. Pick the lower of these: 0

Putting all this together,

$\text{HCF} (48, 180) = 2^2 \times 3^1 \times 5^0$

$= 4 \times 3$

> HCF (48, 180) is a short way of writing 'the highest common factor of 48 and 180'.

$= \underline{12}$

EXERCISE 12.4

Find the highest common factor of each of these pairs of numbers.

1 12 and 20   **6** 92 and 98   **11** 240 and 280   **16** 144 and 120 ✓

2 16 and 26   **7** 36 and 42   **12** 14 and 34   **17** 75 and 125

3 18 and 45 ✓   **8** 140 and 210 ✓   **13** 92 and 104   **18** 90 and 110

4 25 and 40   **9** 42 and 56   **14** 52 and 91   **19** 4 and 60

5 36 and 48   **10** 77 and 110   **15** 70 and 98   **20** 48 and 55

12.5 Lowest common multiple

The lowest common multiple of two numbers is the smallest number that both of them will divide into without leaving any remainder.
The LCM of 20 and 30 is 60.
Lowest common multiples are not always very obvious. Once again, there is a method based on prime factors.

Question Find the lowest common multiple of 35 and 55.

Solution First, write the numbers as products of prime factors.
$35 = 5 \times 7$
$55 = 5 \times 11$

The factor of 5 is common to both, and also 7 occurs in the first one and 11 in the second.

The LCM must include all of these, so

$LCM\ (35, 55) = 5 \times 7 \times 11$
$\underline{= 385}$

Question Find the LCM of 48 and 180.

Solution $48 = 2^4 \times 3$
$180 = 2^2 \times 3^2 \times 5$

Look at the powers of 2:
$48 = 2^4 \times 3$
$180 = 2^2 \times 3^2 \times 5$

> There are 4 factors of 2 in 48 but only 2 factors of 2 in 180. Pick the higher of these: 4

Now look at the powers of 3:
$48 = 2^4 \times 3$
$180 = 2^2 \times 3^2 \times 5$

> There is 1 factor of 3 in 48 and 2 factors of 3 in 180. Pick the higher of these: 2

Finally, look at the powers of 5:
$48 = 2^4 \times 3$
$180 = 2^2 \times 3^2 \times 5$

> There is 0 factor of 5 in 48 and 1 factor of 5 in 180. Pick the higher of these: 1

Putting all this together,

$LCM\ (48, 180) = 2^4 \times 3^2 \times 5^1$

$= 16 \times 9 \times 5$

> LCM (48, 180) is a short way of writing 'the lowest common multiple of 48 and 180'.

$\underline{= 720}$

EXERCISE 12.5

1 Find the lowest common multiple of each of these pairs of numbers.

a) 12 and 20   c) 18 and 45   e) 36 and 48   g) 14 and 22

b) 16 and 26 ✓   d) 25 and 40   f) 6 and 20   h) 36 and 60

i) 44 and 55   l) 18 and 20   o) 33 and 55 ✓   r) 48 and 55

j) 16 and 36   m) 14 and 30   p) 33 and 6

k) 28 and 42   n) 27 and 36   q) 4 and 60

2 Virginia has two friends who sometimes come round to her house to play. Sarah comes round once every 4 days, and Jasmine comes round once every five days. How often are both friends at Virginia's house together?

3 Gerald has two friends who sometimes come around to his house to watch TV. Deryn comes around once every 9 days and Tony comes around once every 15 days. How often are both friends at Gerald's house together?

SUMMARY

- In this chapter you have used non-calculator methods to work out the values of expressions containing negative whole numbers. Remember to do all the multiplications and divisions **before** the additions and subtractions.

- You have learnt how to write a number as a product of its prime factors, and you have used the prime factorisation method to help you find the HCF and LCM of a pair of numbers.

REVIEW EXERCISE 12

1 Without using a calculator, work out the value of these:

   a $-5 + 12$ **b** $-12 + 5$ **c** $17 - (-3)$ **d** $-6 + (-5)$ **e** $21 + (-5)$

   f $-7 - (-7)$ **g** $0 - (-4)$ **h** $5 - (-6)$ **i** $-7 + (-8)$ **j** $(-2) \times (-5)$

   k 4×-3 **l** $2 \times -3 + 5 \times -6$ **m** $(-4) \div (-2)$ **n** $2.4 \times (-10)$

   o $2 + (-5) - (-4)$ **p** $2 \times (-5) \times (-4)$

2 The table shows some information about the weather during a particular 24-hour period in five French ski resorts:

Resort	Tignes	Val Thorens	Les Arcs	Valmorel	Pra Loup
Temperature (maximum) °C	12°	11°	11°	14°	15°
Temperature (minimum) °C	–5°	–9°	–4°	–3°	–1°
Sunshine (hours)	4.2	3.9	4.4	4.1	8.4

  a In one of these resorts the maximum temperature was 15° higher than the minimum temperature. Which resort?

  b Find the difference between the maximum and minimum temperatures in Valmorel.

c Find:

   i the highest temperature in the table

   ii the lowest temperature in the table

   iii the difference between the highest and the lowest temperatures.

d One of these resorts is the highest ski resort in Europe, and so it tends to experience colder temperatures than the others. Which one do you think it might be?

Another resort is much further south than the rest, and so it tends to have more sunshine. Which one do you think it might be?

e Find the average number of hours of sunshine for the five resorts.

3 Write each of these numbers as a product of primes:

  a 45   b 80   c 88   d 18   e 55   f 256   g 98   h 180

  i 106   j 240

4 Multiply out these numbers to give an answer as an ordinary number.

  a $2^2 \times 11$ b 2×3^2 c $3^2 \times 5$ d $2 \times 3 \times 5^2$ e 3×5^2

  f 3×7^2 g $2^2 \times 3^4$ h $2 \times 3 \times 7^2$ i $2^4 \times 3^2 \times 5$

5 Use the method of prime factorisation to help you find these highest common factors and lowest common multiples.

  a HCF of 12 and 40   b HCF of 28 and 35   c HCF of 49 and 70

  d HCF of 36 and 54   e LCM of 16 and 24   f LCM of 28 and 35

  g LCM of 49 and 70   h LCM of 36 and 54

6 ✳ A lighthouse keeper is looking at three flashing buoys, which are marked on his map as P, Q and R. The lamp at P flashes once every 30 seconds, while Q flashes once every 48 seconds and R flashes once every 80 seconds.

  a Find the lowest common multiple of 30, 48 and 80.

  b All three lamps flash together at exactly midnight. What time will it be when they next all flash together?

7 ✳ Seven ships, A, B, C, D, E, F, G are all in harbour together on 1 July. 01. Ship A returns every day, ship B returns every 2 days, ship B returns every 3 days, and so on, with ship G returning every 7 days. What will be the date when they are next all in harbour together?

13 Working with decimals

In this chapter you will revise:
- place value in decimal notation
- addition and subtraction of numbers written as decimals.

You will then learn how to:
- multiply and divide decimals by whole numbers
- multiply two decimals without a calculator
- divide one decimal by another without a calculator
- solve problems using decimals.

13.1 Adding and subtracting with decimals

When a number is written in decimals each figure to the left of the decimal point has a place value, units, tens, hundreds etc.
The figures to the right of the decimal point have place values too, tenths, hundredths, thousandths etc.

Question Doris looks at the number 62.359.

Doris wants to read the number out loud. What should she say?

Solution

1000	100	10	1		$\frac{1}{10}$	$\frac{1}{100}$	$\frac{1}{1000}$
		6	2	.	3	5	9

These are the place values.

The 6 means six tens or sixty.
The 2 means two units.
The 3 means three-tenths.
The 5 means five-hundredths.
The 9 means nine-thousandths.

Note: you **never** say sixty-two point three hundred and fifty-nine. Just name the figures after the decimal point.

Doris should say 'sixty-two point three five nine.'

Question Add together 153.27 and 76.6.

Solution Begin by drawing up a set of place value headings:

100	10	1		$\frac{1}{10}$	$\frac{1}{100}$
1	5	3	.	2	7
	7	6	.	6	0

In this example it is helpful to insert an extra zero.

Line the numbers up at the decimal point.

100	10	1		$\frac{1}{10}$	$\frac{1}{100}$
1	5	3	.	2	7
	7	6	.	6	0
2	2	9	.	8	7

So 153.27 + 76.6 = <u>229.87</u>

Decimals are subtracted in the same way.

Line the two numbers up at the decimal point, insert extra zeroes at the right-hand end if necessary, then subtract as normal. Remember to put a decimal point in the answer.

EXERCISE 13.1

1 Write in figures:
   a) Sixteen point seven four two   b) One hundred and five point two
   c) Ten point nought nought six. ✓

2 Write in words:
   a) 69.25 ✓   b) 184.06   c) 21.060

3 Work out these additions and subtractions:
   a) 21.44 + 19.8   b) 366.7 + 29.53   c) 409.46 + 27.8   d) 355.202 + 28.49
   e) 142.26 − 78.63 ✓   f) 166.27 − 84.5   g) 245.2 − 62.17   h) 143.4 − 76.88
   i) 29.295 + 83.4   j) 735.68 − 153.75   k) 10.04 − 0.2   l) 399.99 + 24.2 ✓
   m) 16.3 + 7.277   n) 0.35 − 0.07

13.2 Multiplying and dividing a decimal by a whole number

Multiplying or dividing a decimal by a simple whole number is easily done without a calculator.

Question   Multiply 17.452 by 20.

Solution   First, set up the place values:

100	10	1		$\frac{1}{10}$	$\frac{1}{100}$	$\frac{1}{1000}$
	1	7	.	4	5	2

Next multiply by 2:

100	10	1		$\frac{1}{10}$	$\frac{1}{100}$	$\frac{1}{1000}$
	3	4 .		9	0	4

Then multiply by 10:

100	10	1		$\frac{1}{10}$	$\frac{1}{100}$	$\frac{1}{1000}$
3	4	9 .		0	4	

> To multiply by 10 move all the digits one column to the left.

So $17.452 \times 20 = \underline{349.04}$

Question   Divide 14.8 by 4

Solution

$$\begin{array}{r} 3\ 7 \\ 4\overline{)1\ 4\ 8} \end{array}$$

> Using ordinary whole number division, divide 148 by 4 to get 37.

$$\begin{array}{r} 3\ .7 \\ 4\overline{)1\ 4\ .8} \end{array}$$

> Now restore the decimal point.

Therefore $14.8 \div 4 = \underline{3.7}$

EXERCISE 13.2

Work out these without using a calculator.

1 75.34×2

2 231.02×3

3 $144.68 \div 2$

4 $636.256 \div 2$

5 24.225×20 ✓

6 17.55×200

7 $45.035 \div 5$ ✓

8 63.224×200

9 $196.28 \div 20$

These questions are a little harder. Work them out as before, but you may wish to use a calculator for checking.

10 12.7×40

11 $58.8 \div 7$

12 1.22×8

13 $36.5 \div 5$

13 $15.96 \div 12$

15 84.7×6

16 44.3×11

17 $8.91 \div 9$

18 $20.8 \div 16$

13.3 Multiplying one decimal by another

To multiply two decimals together without a calculator you follow
these three steps:
- remove the decimal points
- multiply the numbers using ordinary long multiplication
- put the decimal point back in at the end.

If you count how many figures there are after the decimal points in
the question, there should be the same total in the answer.

Question   Work out 1.34×0.4

Solution   Consider 134×4 ◀•••• First, remove the decimal points.

Using ordinary multiplication,

$$\begin{array}{r} 1\ 3\ 4 \\ \times\ \ \ 4 \\ \hline 5\ 3\ 6 \end{array}$$

◀•••••• Next, do an ordinary multiplication.

Finally, count the decimals.
1.34×0.4 makes 3 figures after the decimal points.

In the original question there are 3 figures after the decimal
points.
Therefore there must be 3 in the answer as well.

Answer: $1.34 \times 0.4 = \underline{0.536}$

You probably think of multiplication as a way of making something bigger.
If you **multiply by a decimal between 0 and 1**, however, then the
number actually **gets smaller**.
In the example above, multiplying by the number 0.4 has **reduced** 1.34
down to 0.536.

Question   Work out 10.4×3.5

Solution   Consider 104×35. ◀•••• First, remove the decimal points.

Using long multiplication,

$$\begin{array}{r} 1\ 0\ 4 \\ \times 3\ 5 \\ \hline 5\ 2\ 0 \\ 3\ 1\ 2\ 0 \\ \hline 3\ 6\ 4\ 0 \end{array}$$

◀•••• Next, do an ordinary multiplication.

Finally, count the decimals.
10.4×3.5 makes 2 figures after the decimal points.

In the original question there are 2 figures after the decimal
points.

Therefore there must be 2 in the answer as well.
$10.4 \times 3.5 = 36.40$

Answer: $10.4 \times 3.5 = \underline{36.4}$

> Note that the final 0 is now not necessary so it can be dropped. You must not do this until the very end, otherwise the decimal point might end up in the wrong place!!

Sometimes the answer to the long multiplication does not contain enough figures when you come to put the decimal point back in. If this happens then simply insert some extra zeroes in front.
This tends to happen when you are multiplying two small numbers, as in the next example.

Question Work out 0.012×0.043.

Solution Consider 12×43.

Using long multiplication,

$$
\begin{array}{r}
1\ 2 \\
\times 4\ 3 \\
\hline
3\ 6 \\
4\ 8\ 0 \\
\hline
5\ 1\ 6 \\
\end{array}
$$

> Count the decimals.
> 0.012×0.043 makes 6 figures after the decimal points.

> To get the six figures you think of 516 as 000 516

In the original question there are 6 figures after the decimal points.
Therefore there must be 6 in the answer as well.

Answer: $0.012 \times 0.043 = \underline{0.000\ 516}$

EXERCISE 13.3

1. 2.55×0.4 ✓
2. 1.76×1.2
3. 3.5×2.4
4. 16.2×1.8
5. 13.6×0.03
6. 6.04×1.7
7. 19.2×3.6
8. 0.144×2.1
9. 66.2×4.8
10. 125×0.035 ✓
11. 0.03×0.055
12. 0.025×0.4
13. 12.8×0.74
13. 1355×1.9
15. 47.2×0.45
16. 0.85×0.95
17. 1.8×665
18. 1.5^2 (reminder: this means 1.5 times 1.5) ✓
19. 0.4^2
20. 3.01^2

13.4 Dividing one decimal by another

Sometimes you need to divide one decimal by another, without a calculator. To do this:
- multiply both numbers by 10, or 100, or 1000, until the number you are dividing by has become a whole number
- then use ordinary long division.

Question   Work out $298.41 \div 2.1$

Solution   First, multiply both numbers by 10.
The problem becomes: $2984.1 \div 21$
Using ordinary long division,

```
        1 4 2 . 1
  2 1 / 2 9 8 4 . 1
        2 1
        ‾‾‾
          8 8
          8 4
          ‾‾‾
            4 4
            4 2
            ‾‾‾
              2 1
              2 1
              ‾‾‾
```

> There is no need to multiply or divide the final answer in any way – the answer to $2984.1 \div 21$ is exactly the same as $298.41 \div 2.1$

Answer: $298.41 \div 2.1 = \underline{142.1}$

Remember that any decimal number may be followed by as many zeroes as you like.
Sometimes it is necessary to include some of these extra zeroes, when the division does not go exactly.

Question   Work out $36.524 \div 0.17$ giving your answer correct to 3 decimal places.

Solution   First, multiply both numbers by 100.
The problem becomes: $3652.4 \div 17$
Using ordinary long division,

```
        2 1 4 . 8
  1 7 / 3 6 5 2 . 4 0 0 0
        3 4
        ‾‾‾
          2 5
          1 7
          ‾‾‾
            8 2
            6 8
            ‾‾‾
            1 4 4
            1 3 6
            ‾‾‾‾‾
                8
```

> This is as far as the problem goes at first.
> To continue to more decimal places, write in these extra zeroes.

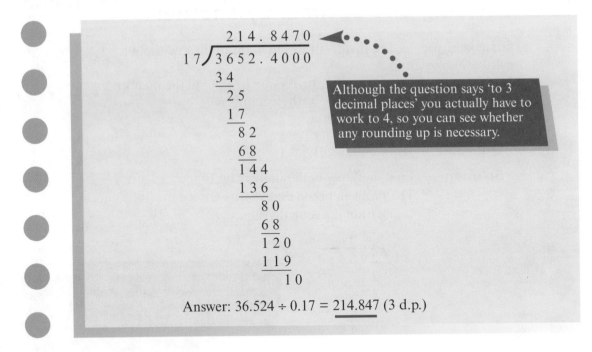

$$
\begin{array}{r}
214.8470 \\
17\overline{)3652.4000} \\
\end{array}
$$

Although the question says 'to 3 decimal places' you actually have to work to 4, so you can see whether any rounding up is necessary.

Answer: $36.524 \div 0.17 = \underline{214.847}$ (3 d.p.)

EXERCISE 13.4

Work out the answers to these division problems, without using a calculator.
Each one should give an exact answer.

1 $4.55 \div 0.7$ ✓   **5** $450.8 \div 2.3$ **9** $0.12 \div 0.3$ **13** $21.28 \div 1.6$

2 $27.45 \div 0.9$ **6** $876.6 \div 1.5$ **10** $0.136 \div 0.08$ **14** $7.983 \div 0.009$ ✓

3 $158.4 \div 1.2$ **7** $2.304 \div 0.16$ ✓   **11** $6.375 \div 0.15$ **15** $3.5266 \div 0.22$

4 $58.94 \div 1.4$ **8** $4.599 \div 0.45$ **12** $0.1624 \div 0.04$ **16** $69.48 \div 7.2$

SUMMARY

- In this chapter you have revised decimal notation and simple addition and subtraction of decimals.
- You have learnt how to multiply and divide one decimal by another, without a calculator. Remember to count the number of digits after the decimal point in a multiplication problem; the answer will contain the same number of decimal digits, although some of them may be zeroes. For division, simply multiply both numbers by 10, 100 etc. first, so that the second number becomes a whole number.

REVIEW EXERCISE 13

1 Without using a calculator, work out these additions and subtractions:

   a $25.28 + 47.63$ **b** $104.74 + 63.27$ **c** $48.29 - 9.05$ **d** $29.25 + 111.8$

   e $23.46 - 1.99$ **f** $123.28 - 97.65$ **g** 1.33×0.8 **h** $0.012 \div 0.8$

   i 2.5×3.5 **j** $38.25 \div 1.7$ **k** 0.538×0.07 **l** 3.84×1.2 **m** $33.51 \div 1.5$

   n $12.194 \div 0.07$ **o** 44.2×1.6 **p** 12.77×3.4 **q** $0.713 \div 4.6$

   r $126.04 \div 9.2$ **s** 98.7×0.066 **t** $56.22 \div 2.3$ (answer correct to 2 d.p.)

2 Solve these problems, without using a calculator.

   a Peter has 26 floppy disks for his computer. Each one can hold 1.44 megabytes of data. How much data can the disks hold in total?

   b ✳ Over six weeks Susan saves £1.26, £4.25, £1.55, £2.48, £1.33 and 50 pence. Find the total amount that she saves.

   c ✳ A camera costs £64. I have £10 towards this already, and I am able to save £4.50 each week. How many weeks will it take until I can afford the camera?

   d ✳ Three rods measure 1.65 m, 2.21 m and 3.4 m. Find the total length if all three rods are laid out end to end.

   e ✳ Terri has £25.66 in her bank account. She writes out three cheques, for £10.43, £16.25 and £21.44. The bank honours these three cheques, but then writes to Terri telling her that her account is overdrawn. They charge her £15 for writing the letter. Find the size of Terri's overdraft, including the charge for the letter.

   f ✳ Desmond visits the United States of America. He has $20.00 in his pocket, but then he buys a burger for $2.45 and a postcard for 35 cents. He finds a quarter and a dime. How much money has he got now? ($1 is 100 cents, a quarter is 25 cents and a dime is 10 cents.)

14 Percentages, ratios and the unitary method

In this chapter you will revise:
- equivalence of fractions, decimals and percentages
- finding percentages of an amount.

You will then learn how to:
- find percentage increase/decrease using multiplying factors
- work with simple ratios • solve word problems using the unitary method.

14.1 Fractions and percentages

To write one number as a fraction of another, simply set up the fraction and cancel if possible.

Question   Express 42 as a fraction of 78.

Solution $\frac{42}{78} = \frac{21}{39} = \frac{7}{13}$

> You can also check this using the fraction key on your calculator. Key in
>
>    4   2 $a^b/_c$ 7   8   =
>
> and the cancelled result should be displayed.

Question   Express 55 cm as a fraction of 3.6 m.

Solution   3.6 m = 360 cm

$\frac{55}{360} = \frac{11}{72}$

> You must convert both lengths into the same units first.

Question   Express 63 as a percentage of 180.

Solution $\frac{63}{180} = \frac{7}{20}$

Then $\frac{7}{20} \times \frac{100\%}{1} = \underline{35\%}$

EXERCISE 14.1

1 Express the first quantity as a fraction of the second.
Cancel down where possible.

a) 70, 95   b) 44, 77   c) 38, 48 ✓   d) 39, 91   e) 35, 95   f) 84 cm, 1.64 m
g) 350 g, 2.25 kg   h) 25 min, 2 h   i) 65 mm, 19 cm   j) 65 ml, 13 cl ✓

2 Express the first quantity as a percentage of the second.

a) 48, 60 ✓   b) 19, 25   c) 3, 20   d) 18, 45   e) 56, 80   f) 7, 40
g) 74 cm, 2 m ✓   h) 18 min, 1 h   i) 850 m, 5 km   j) 750 g, $2\frac{1}{2}$ kg

14.2 Fractions and decimals

To change a fraction into a decimal simply carry out the division,
using a calculator if necessary.

Question   Express $\frac{5}{8}$ as a decimal.

Solution   Using a calculator to work out $5 \div 8$,
$\frac{5}{8} = \underline{0.625}$

Question   Express $3\frac{5}{7}$ as a decimal, correct to 4 decimal places.

Solution $5 \div 7 = 0.714\,285...$

So $3\frac{5}{7} = \underline{3.7143}$ correct to 4 d.p.

To change a decimal into a fraction set up a fraction out of 10, 100,
1000 etc., then cancel.

Question   Change 4.72 into a fraction, using mixed fraction notation.

Solution $0.72 = \frac{72}{100} = \frac{36}{50} = \frac{18}{25}$

∴ $4.72 = 4\frac{18}{25}$

Question   Write 3.725 in the form $\frac{a}{b}$ where a and b are whole numbers.

Solution $0.725 = \frac{725}{1000} = \frac{145}{200} = \frac{29}{40}$

$3.725 = 3\frac{29}{40}$ ◀ ⋯⋯ This is a **mixed fraction**.

$= \frac{3 \times 40 + 29}{40}$

$= \frac{120 + 29}{40}$ ◀ ⋯⋯ This is the same answer, converted into a **top-heavy fraction**.

$= \frac{149}{40}$

EXERCISE 14.2

1 Change these fractions into decimals, correct to 4 decimal places where necessary.

a) $\frac{3}{8}$ ✓ b) $2\frac{7}{10}$ c) $5\frac{1}{4}$ d) $\frac{3}{11}$ e) $2\frac{1}{3}$ f) $\frac{4}{9}$ g) $\frac{5}{12}$ h) $3\frac{1}{7}$ i) $\frac{7}{16}$

j) $4\frac{9}{14}$ ✓

2 Write these decimals as fractions, giving your answers as mixed fractions where necessary.

a) 0.88 ✓ b) 0.124 c) 0.225 d) 4.15 e) 3.64 ✓ f) 0.036 g) 2.95

h) 0.66 i) 1.85 j) 0.316

14.3 Decimals and percentages

To change a decimal into a percentage, multiply by 100%. This moves the decimal point 2 places right.

Question	Express 0.225 as a percentage.
Solution	$0.225 \times 100\% = \underline{22.5\%}$

To change a percentage into a decimal, divide by 100%. This moves the decimal point 2 places left.

Question	Express 37.8% as a decimal.
Solution	$37.8\% \div 100\% = \underline{0.378}$

Question	Express $12\frac{1}{2}\%$ as a decimal.
Solution	$12\frac{1}{2}\% = 12.5\%$
	$12.5\% \div 100\% = \underline{0.125}$

EXERCISE 14.3

1 Change these decimals into percentages:
a) 0.38 b) 0.7 ✓ c) 0.315 d) 0.205 e) 1.43 f) 6.2 ✓ g) 1.707
h) 0.080 i) 0.1 j) 4.4

2 Change these percentages into decimals:
a) 65% b) $33\frac{1}{3}\%$ ✓ c) 2.5% d) 18% e) 150% f) 77% g) 6%
h) $7\frac{1}{2}\%$ ✓ i) 105% j) 88%

14. 4 Finding a percentage of an amount

To find a percentage of an amount, just divide the percentage by 100 to get a decimal. Then multiply that decimal onto the given amount.

Question	Find 15% of £240.
Solution	15 ÷ 100 = 0.15, so 15% is equivalent to 0.15
	By calculator, 240 × 0.15 = 36
	Therefore 15% of £240 = £36

EXERCISE 14.4

1 Find 30% of £60. ✓

2 Find 25% of £600.

3 Find 60% of $250.

4 Find 83 % of £40 000.

5 Find 65% of 440.

6 Find 2% of 1600.

7 A French exam is marked out of 60 marks. Sophie scores 85%. How many marks is this?

8 A university has 12 000 students but during a 'flu epidemic 36% of them are ill. How many students is this?

9 360 children took a mathematics test, and 70% of them passed. ✓
a) How many children passed?
b) How many did not pass?

10 An instant supermarket meal weighs 450 grams, and has a fat content of 6%. How much fat does the meal contain?

14.5 Using multiplying factors

To increase an amount by a certain percentage, a **multiplying factor** can be used.
For a 3% increase the factor is 1.03, for a 12% increase it is 1.12 and so on.
For a 3% decrease the factor is 0.97, for a 12% decrease it is 0.88 and so on.

Question	Increase £425 by 3%.
Solution	The multiplying factor is 1.03.
	£425 × 1.03 = £437.75

Question Decrease 1600 litres by 9%.

Solution The multiplying factor is 0.91.
1600 litres × 0.91 = <u>1456 litres</u>

Question A shop increases all its prices by 12%. The price of a jacket after the increase is £61.60. Find its price before the increase.

Solution Let the price before the increase be £x.
The multiplying factor for a 12% increase is 1.12.
$$1.12 \times x = 61.60$$
$$x = 61.60 \div 1.12$$
$$= 55$$

The original price was <u>£55</u>.

Warning!
If you decrease £61.60 by 12% you get an incorrect answer (£54.21)
This is because 12% of the new price is £7.39, but 12% of the original price is £6.60.

EXERCISE 14.5

1. Use a multiplying factor to make the required increase or decrease.
   a) Increase 25 000 by 13%.   b) Increase 350 by 6%. ✓
   c) Decrease 7500 by 18%.   d) Increase $140 by 65%.
   e) Decrease £975 by 4%. ✓

2. Last season the average number of people who watched Swindon Town play soccer each week was 26 300. Town have now been promoted, and the manager expects to see a 15% increase in attendance.
   a) Write down the multiplying factor for a 15% increase.
   b) Find the average weekly attendance this season, assuming the manager's prediction to be right. (Give your answer to the nearest hundred.)

3. Last summer I went on holiday to France. The ferry fare was £39. This year the ferry company has reduced all its fares by 11%.
   a) Write down the multiplying factor for an 11% decrease.
   b) Find the ferry fare this year.

4. A computer is advertised for a price of £699 plus VAT. The present rate of VAT is $17\frac{1}{2}$%.
   a) Write down the multiplying factor for a $17\frac{1}{2}$% increase.
   b) Find the total cost of the computer including VAT.

5 My bill in a restaurant was £20.72 including a service charge of 12%. ✓
a) Write down the multiplying factor for a 12% increase.
b) Use this factor to find the cost before the service charge was added.

6 A packet of cereal says: 16% extra – FREE. The packet contains 435 g. Find the amount of cereal that the packet would contain without the extra 16%.

14.6 Using ratios

Questions involving **ratios** can often be treated in a similar way to fractions.
It is important to add up the parts of a ratio first, so the total can be used to identify the fractions represented by the component parts.
For example, in a ratio of 3 : 4 the total is 7, so the two parts are equivalent to fractions of $\frac{3}{7}$ and $\frac{4}{7}$.

Question Two chemicals are mixed in the ratio 3 : 4. Find the amount of each chemical, if 350 g of the mixture is to be made.

Solution 3 + 4 = 7
350 ÷ 7 = 50
3 × 50 = 150
4 × 50 = 200

> Here we are finding that each share is 50 g so 3 shares is 150 g and 4 shares is 200 g.

The amounts are 150 g and 200 g.

Question In Year 5 at Greenview school 14 children catch the bus to school, 21 walk and 49 come by car.
a) Write this information as a ratio in its simplest form.
b) Assuming that this ratio applies throughout the school, find the total number who come by car. There are 324 children at the school altogether.

Solution a) The ratio is 14 : 21 : 49 which can be written as
2 : 3 : 7

> All three numbers can be divided by 7 to cancel the ratio down.

b) 2 + 3 + 7 = 12. The children who come by car comprise $\frac{7}{12}$ of the school.

324 ÷ 12 = 27

> Find $\frac{1}{12}$

27 × 7 = 189

> Find $\frac{7}{12}$

189 children come by car.

EXERCISE 14.6

1 Cancel down each ratio into its simplest form.
a) $20:35$ b) $18:24$ ✓   c) $15:12$ d) $60:84$ e) $350:550$
f) $125:225$ g) $40:60:75$ h) $100:65:55$ ✓   i) $18:36:42$
j) $35:90:65$ k) $35\,\text{cm}:2.4\,\text{m}$ l) $450\,\text{g}:3.5\,\text{kg}$

2 A sheet of Christmas gift-wrap paper is 1.2 m long. It is cut into two pieces, the longer one being 75 cm in length. Find the ratio of the lengths of the two pieces, giving your answer in its simplest form.

3 During a school week I have 6 periods of mathematics, 10 periods of science and 24 periods of other subjects. ✓
a) Write this information as a ratio, in its simplest form.
b) I plan to do five hours of revision next Sunday. The amount of time spent on each subject is to be in the same ratio as the number of periods I get each week. How much time should I spend on mathematics revision?

14.7 The unitary method

The **unitary method** is a way of solving word problems on proportion.
The idea is to break a problem up into a number of smaller steps.
At each step you decide whether to **multiply** or **divide**.

Question	A bag of food is sufficient to feed 6 guinea pigs for 8 days. How long will it last if there are 2 guinea pigs to feed instead?

Solution

The bag will last 6 guinea pigs for 8 days.

> As we change 6 guinea pigs to 1 guinea pig the food will last longer, so MULTIPLY by 6.

The bag will last 1 guinea pig for 8×6 days.

The bag will last 1 guinea pig for 48 days.

> As we change 1 guinea pig to 2 guinea pigs the food will last for less time, so DIVIDE by 2.

The bag will last 2 guinea pig for $48 \div 2$ days.

The bag will last 2 guinea pigs for 24 days.

Question	When a team of 12 examiners mark 9000 A-level scripts it takes them 24 days.

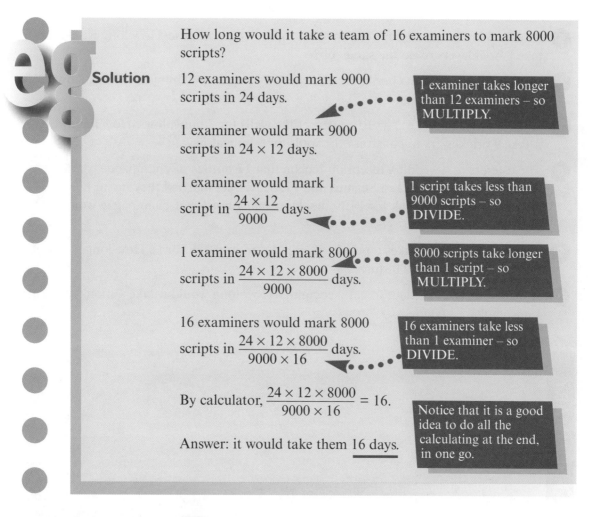

Solution

How long would it take a team of 16 examiners to mark 8000 scripts?

12 examiners would mark 9000 scripts in 24 days.

> 1 examiner takes longer than 12 examiners – so MULTIPLY.

1 examiner would mark 9000 scripts in 24 × 12 days.

1 examiner would mark 1 script in $\dfrac{24 \times 12}{9000}$ days.

> 1 script takes less than 9000 scripts – so DIVIDE.

1 examiner would mark 8000 scripts in $\dfrac{24 \times 12 \times 8000}{9000}$ days.

> 8000 scripts take longer than 1 script – so MULTIPLY.

16 examiners would mark 8000 scripts in $\dfrac{24 \times 12 \times 8000}{9000 \times 16}$ days.

> 16 examiners take less than 1 examiner – so DIVIDE.

By calculator, $\dfrac{24 \times 12 \times 8000}{9000 \times 16} = 16$.

Answer: it would take them 16 days.

> Notice that it is a good idea to do all the calculating at the end, in one go.

EXERCISE 14.7

Each of these questions should be set out using the unitary method, as shown in the examples.

1 It takes Rosemarie 28 minutes to put sticky labels inside 84 mathematics text books. How long will it take her to put sticky labels inside 120 text books?

2 When Stacey goes hill walking it takes her 75 minutes to walk 5 kilometres. How long would it take her to walk 8 kilometres? ✓

3 Postman Nick takes 3 hours to deliver the post to 280 houses. How long would it take him to deliver the post to 350 houses?

4 A certain amount of fuel is enough to last 12 taxis for 5 days. How long would the same amount of fuel last 15 taxis?

5 It takes 6 bricklayers 4 days to construct the walls for a house. How long would it take 8 bricklayers to do the same job?

6 David is proofreading a book. He can check 50 pages in 40 minutes. How many pages can he check in 2 hours?

7 It takes 5 bricklayers 6 days to construct the walls for 2 bungalows. How long would it take 9 bricklayers to construct the walls for 6 bungalows?

8 The caterers at a wedding reception reckon that 12 bottles of champagne would last 20 guests for 1 hour. When Seamus and Francesca get married they invite 120 guests, and expect them to drink for $1\frac{1}{2}$ hours. How many bottles of champagne would be needed?

9 At a local laundry it takes 6 people 40 minutes to iron 120 shirts. How long would it take 4 people to iron 300 shirts? ✓

10 It takes 7 monkeys 7 days to eat 7 coconuts. How long would it take 1 monkey to eat 1 coconut?

SUMMARY

- In this chapter you have revised the equivalence of fractions, decimals and percentages.

- You have solved problems on ratio and percentage, using a multiplying factor to deal with percentage increase and decrease.

- You have also learnt how to use the unitary method to solve word problems on proportion. Remember to set the steps out one line at a time, and save all the calculating until the end.

REVIEW EXERCISE 14

1 Write the first quantity as a fraction of the second, and also as a percentage of the second. Simplify your answers where possible.

   a 24, 60   **b** 132, 240   **c** 5000, 8000   **d** 63, 105

   e 30 s, $2\frac{1}{2}$ min   **f** 230 ml, 4 l   **g** 78 cm, 1.2 m   **h** 81 min, $1\frac{1}{2}$ h

2 Change these fractions into decimals, correct to 3 decimal places where necessary:

   a $\frac{17}{20}$ **b** $\frac{5}{8}$ **c** $\frac{5}{7}$ **d** $4\frac{7}{10}$ **e** $\frac{8}{9}$ **f** $3\frac{1}{3}$ **g** $\frac{37}{50}$ **h** $2\frac{7}{100}$

3 Change these decimals into fractions, and also into percentages:

   a 0.06   **b** 0.65   **c** 0.28   **d** 0.44   **e** 0.025   **f** 0.125   **g** 2.6

4 Change these percentages into decimals:
   a 25%   **b** 9%   **c** $22\frac{1}{2}$%   **d** 204%

5 Lois and Richard buy some tickets in a school raffle. Lois buys 13 tickets and Richard buys 7 tickets. They agree to share any prize between them, in the ratio of the number of tickets they bought. When the raffle is drawn Lois wins a prize of £15. Calculate the amount that each receives when they share this prize.

6 In Bluebell Wood there are 20 silver birch trees, 8 maple trees and 12 oak trees.
   a Write down the ratio of silver birch : maple : oak trees in Bluebell Wood, giving your answer in its simplest form.
   b In Shelley Wood there are 200 trees in total. Assuming that they are all silver birch, maple, or oak, and in the same ratio as in Bluebell Wood, find the number of trees of each kind in Shelley Wood.

7 The number of bacteria in a certain colony grows by 30% every day. On Day 1 there are 6000 bacteria. Find out how many there will be on:
   a Day 2   **b** Day 3   **c** Day 7

8 As part of a computer upgrade I decide to buy a new hard disk drive. The same unit is available from two suppliers, who advertise as follows:

BARGAIN PC SUPPLIES
Superturbo 1.4 Gb hard disk
only £149 + VAT

None Better Peripherals
Superturbo 1.4 Gb hard disk
only £177 including VAT

Work out whether Bargain PC Supplies or None Better Peripherals is giving the cheaper overall cost, assuming a VAT rate of $17\frac{1}{2}$%.

9 A sweet shop sells coloured sweets in mixed bags. The sweets are red, green and yellow in the ratio 4 : 5 : 11.
   a What percentage of the sweets are red?
   b How many of each colour would you expect to find in a bag containing 80 sweets?

10 Express the ratio 26 : 65 : 91 in its simplest form.

Answer these questions using the unitary method. Set your working out clearly.

11 A carpet fitter thinks that 1 roll of underlay is enough to fit 12 average size rooms.

 a How many rooms could he fit from 8 rolls?

 b How many rolls would he need to fit 45 average size rooms?

12 On a school trip it costs $13.20 for 6 children to visit a submarine museum. How much would it cost for 17 children?

13 In a biology experiment it is noticed that a certain type of bean shoot grows by 35 mm in 5 days. How much would it be expected to grow in 7 days?

14 On a high altitude expedition to the Himalayas a group of 8 mountaineers decide to take bottled oxygen to breathe while they are sleeping. They take enough oxygen to last for 12 nights, but in the end two of them are unable to make the trip through illness. How many nights would the oxygen last the remaining mountaineers?

15 ✳ A square measures 15 cm by 15 cm, and a second square measures 20 cm by 20 cm.

 a Find the ratio of their perimeters.

 b Find the ratio of their areas.

16 ✳ A camera costs $126.50 including sales tax of 15%. Calculate its cost before the sales tax is added.

17 ✳ My photocopier is set to produce copies which are 41% larger than the originals. A copy comes out of the machine; it contains a diagram which is 98 mm wide. How wide (to the nearest millimetre) was the original diagram?

18 ✳ The school office reckons that 20 reams of paper will last 10 sixth form students for 4 terms.

 a How many reams of paper will be needed by 16 sixth formers for 6 terms?

 b How long will 27 reams of paper last for a class of 18 sixth formers?

15 Algebra

In this chapter you will learn how to:
- simplify formulae
- multiply out and simplify brackets
- substitute whole numbers into simple formulae.

15.1 Simplifying formulae

$a + a$ is written as $2a$
$3 \times b$ is written as $3b$
$2c + 3c$ is simplified to $5c$
$2d + 3e$ cannot be simplified

Question   Simplify these expressions:

a) $4a + a$ b) $5 \times b + 2 \times c$
c) $3 \times d - 2 \times e + 4 \times d$ d) $9 \times f \times f$

Solution   a) $4a + a = \underline{5a}$ b) $5 \times b + 2 \times c = \underline{5b + 2c}$

c) $3 \times d - 2 \times e + 4 \times d$ d) $9 \times f \times f = \underline{9f^2}$
   $= 3d - 2e + 4d$
   $= \underline{7d - 2e}$

EXERCISE 15.1

Simplify these algebraic expressions:

1 a) $a + a + a$ b) $3b + 2b - b$ c) $c + c + 3c$

2 a) $8d - 3d$ b) $4 \times e + 5 \times e$ c) $9 \times f - 3 \times f$

3 a) $5j - 2k - 2j$ b) $3l - 2l + 6l$ c) $m + 2n + 3m + 4n$ ✓

4 a) $5 \times p \times p$ b) $4 \times q + 3 \times r \times r - 3 \times q$ c) $3 \times x \times x - 2 \times x + x \times x$

5 a) $9s + 7t + 5s - 3t$ b) $15u - 8u - 6u$ c) $6x - 15x + 21x$

6 a) $7 \times y \times y \times y$ ✓   b) $5 \times z + 6 \times a + 7 \times z$ c) $4 \times b \times b + 5 \times b \times b + 7 \times b$ ✓

15.2 Multiplying out brackets

Sometimes you will need to multiply out brackets in algebra problems. You will often see the instruction 'Simplify…' in such a problem.

Question Simplify $2(x + 3y)$.

Solution $2(x + 3y)$

$= 2x + 6y$

> The 2 outside the bracket tells you that the contents of the bracket must be multiplied by 2. x becomes $2x$, and $3y$ beomes $6y$.

Sometimes there might be two sets of brackets to multiply out. Look for opportunities to collect matching terms together afterwards.

Question Simplify $2(x + 3) + 5(2x + 1)$.

Solution $2(x + 3) + 5(2x + 1)$

$= 2x + 6 + 5(2x + 1)$

$2x + 6 + 10x + 5$

$= 12x + 11$

> First multiply out each set of brackets in turn.

> Then collect together matching terms.

Special care needs to be taken when a question involves minus signs.

Question Simplify $6(x + 2) + 3(2x - 3)$.

Solution $6(x + 2) + 3(2x - 3)$

$= 6x + 12 + 6x - 9$

$= 12x + 3$

> When collecting together matching terms:
> $6x + 6x$ gives $12x$
> $+ 12$ and $- 9$ gives $+3$.

EXERCISE 15.2

1 Multiply out the brackets in each of the following:
a) $2(x + 4y)$ ✓ b) $3(x + 2y)$ c) $5(2x + y)$ d) $7(a + 5)$ e) $10(2b + 3)$
f) $15(2c + 1)$ g) $6(3d + 4)$ h) $20(3e + 2)$ i) $8(f + 7)$ j) $12(2x + 5y)$
k) $5(8y + 3)$ l) $11(3x + 7)$ m) $6(5x - 2)$ n) $7(12 - 7x)$ o) $15(2x - 5y)$

2 Multiply out the brackets and simplify each of the following:
a) $4(x + 1) + 5(x + 2)$ ✓ b) $4(2x + 1) + 5(3x + 2)$ c) $3(x + 2) + 2(x + 3)$
d) $3(4x + 2) + 2(3x + 1)$ e) $3(4x + 7) + 2(3x + 2)$ f) $12(y + 5) + 10(2y + 7)$
g) $4(5x + 2) + 3(8x + 3)$ h) $3(7x + 2) + 7(5x + 3)$ i) $5(9x + 1) + 9(5x + 1)$
j) $8(4x + 5y) + 3(5x + 3y)$

3 Simplify:
a) $4(x + 1) + 3(x - 2)$ b) $2(3x + 2) + 5(2x - 1)$ c) $5(2x + 5y) + 6(2x - y)$ ✓
d) $3(4x - 5) + 7(2x + 3)$ e) $12(4x + 7y) + 15(3x - 5y)$

15.3 Substituting into formulae

You will often need to substitute numbers for letters in algebraic formulae. Remember to carry out calculations in accordance with BODMAS, which you met on page 41. Of course, your calculator has BODMAS logic built in to its memory.

Question   Given that $A = 4bc$, find the value of A when $b = 2$ and $c = 3$.

Solution   Using these values we have

$A = 4 \times b \times c$
$\quad = 4 \times 2 \times 3$
$\quad = 8 \times 3$
$\quad = 24$

Question   If $C = x + 3(y + 2z)$, find the value of C
when $x = 5$, $y = 2$ and $z = 3$.

Solution   Using these values we have
$C = x + 3 \times (y + 2 \times z)$
$\quad = 5 + 3 \times (2 + 2 \times 3)$ ◄ ⋯ BODMAS requires us to find the value of the bracket first.

$\quad = 5 + 3 \times (2 + 6)$
$\quad = 5 + 3 \times 8$
$\quad = 5 + 24$ ◄ ⋯⋯⋯ Now do the × (M) before the + (A)
$\quad = 29$

EXERCISE 15.3

1 $A = ab + 8$. Find A if $a = 7$ and $b = 2$. ✓

2 $V = u + at$. Find V if $u = 4$, $a = 5$ and $t = 10$.

3 $L = m(10 + n)$. Find L if $m = 100$ and $n = 3$.

4 $T = 5a + 2bc$. Find T when $a = 7$, $b = 2$ and $c = -3$.

5 $Q = a^2 + b^2 + c^2$. Find Q when $a = 3$, $b = 4$ and $c = 5$. ✓

6 $y = 3x^2 + 5x + 4$. Find y when $x = 3$.

7 $A = (p + q) \times (r + s)$. Find A when $p = 7$, $q = 3$, $r = 5$ and $s = 6$.

8 $S = Pt(1 + \frac{r}{100})$. Find S when $P = 1500$, $t = 3$ and $r = 6$.

9 $y = x^2 - 4x + 5$. Find y when $x = 7$.

10 $y = x^2 - 3x + 7$. Find y when $x = -3$.

SUMMARY

- In this chapter you have practised simplifying formulae by collecting like terms, and you have learnt how to multiply out and simplify algebraic expressions involving brackets.

- You have also had further practice of substituting positive and negative whole numbers into algebraic formulae. Remember to use BODMAS when there are several different processes involved.

REVIEW EXERCISE 15

1 Simplify the following expressions:

a $5 \times p \times 3 \times p$ **b** $5x + 11x - 15x$ **c** $a + 2b + 3a - 4b$

d $7y - 13y + 6y$ **e** $5c + 6d + 7cd$ **f** $10x - 5y - 14x + 2y$

g $2e^2 + 3f - e^2$ **h** $15a - 13b - 14a + 14b$ **i** $7x + 3(2x + 5) + 3$

j $5(2x + 3) + 2(x + 3) + 5$ **k** $2(3x + 4) + 3(x - 5)$

l $3x + 2(2x + 5) - 4x + 3(x + 1)$

2 $F = ma$. Find F when $m = 12$ and $a = 3$.

3 $s = ut + 5t^2$. Find s when $u = 4$ and $t = 3$.

4 $w = 3f + 4g - 5h$. Find w when $f = 30$, $g = -3$ and $h = 12$.

5 $y = 5n^2 + 7n + 3$. Find y when $n = -2$.

6 ✳ Simplify $4a + 5a^2 + 6a$.

7 ✳ Simplify $5p + 4q - 3p - 2pq + 6q$.

8 ✳ $p = \frac{1}{u} + \frac{1}{v}$, $f = \frac{1}{p}$.

Find p when $u = 10$ and $v = 20$.

Find f when $u = 10$ and $v = 20$.

9 ✳ $\frac{1}{r} = \frac{1}{s} + \frac{1}{t}$. Find r when $s = 4$ and $t = 5$.

16 Gradient and intercept of a straight line

In this chapter you will revise:
- plotting the graphs of straight lines.

You will then learn how to:
- find the equation of a straight line, by looking at its gradient and intercept.

16.1 Plotting straight lines

To plot the graph of a straight line, such as $y = 3x + 2$, just work out the positions of at least three points on the line. Then join them using a ruler. This line will slope at an angle to the x- and y-axes.

Lines such as $x = 3$ (where there is no y term at all) will be vertical (parallel to the y-axis).

Lines such as $y = 4$ (where there is no x term at all) will be horizontal (parallel to the x-axis).

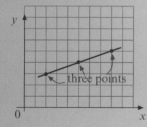 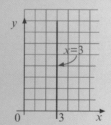 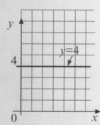

Question   Plot the graph of $y = 2x + 4$, for values of x from 0 to 10.

Solution

x	0	5	10
y			

> Choose values of x near the beginning, middle and end of the given interval.

When $x = 0$, $y = 2 \times 0 + 4 = 4$
When $x = 5$, $y = 2 \times 5 + 4 = 14$
When $x = 10$, $y = 2 \times 10 + 4 = 24$.

x	0	5	10
y	4	14	24

> These values show you that x must range from 0 to 10, and y from 4 to 24.

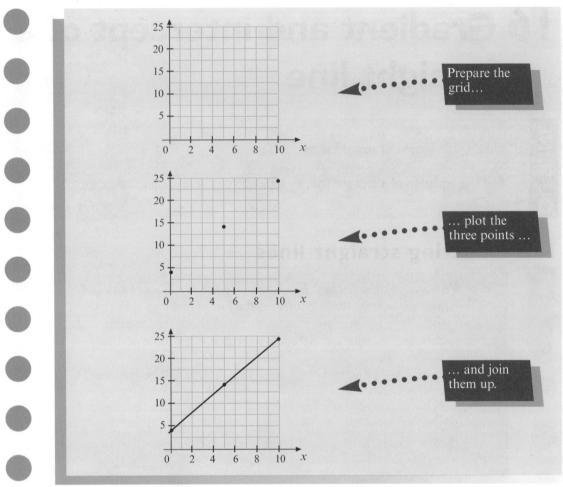

Prepare the grid…

… plot the three points …

… and join them up.

EXERCISE 16.1

Draw the graphs of each of these lines, over the given range of values of x.

1 $y = 3x + 1$, for values of x from 0 to 10. ✓

2 $y = x + 5$, for values of x from 0 to 10.

3 $y = 2x - 1$, for values of x from 0 to 5.

4 $y = 3x - 4$, for values of x from 0 to 8.

5 $y = x + 7$, for values of x from −5 to 5.

6 $y = 10 - x$, for values of x from 0 to 10.

7 $y = 4$, for values of x from 0 to 10.

8 $y = 1 + 2x$, for values of x from 0 to 6.

16.2 Working in reverse

For the line $y = mx + c$
the number m is called the **gradient** and c is called the **intercept**.
The gradient tells you how steep the line is.
The intercept tells you where the line crosses the y-axis.

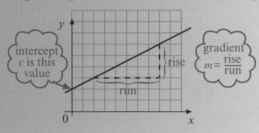

Question   Work out the equation of the straight line plotted below.

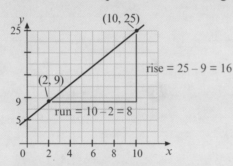

Solution   Let the line be $y = mx + c$
The gradient is $16 \div 8 = 2$, so $m = 2$.
The intercept is 5, so $c = 5$.
Therefore the required equation is $y = 2x + 5$.

EXERCISE 16.2

For each of the graphs below, find the equation of the straight line.

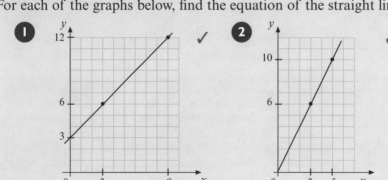

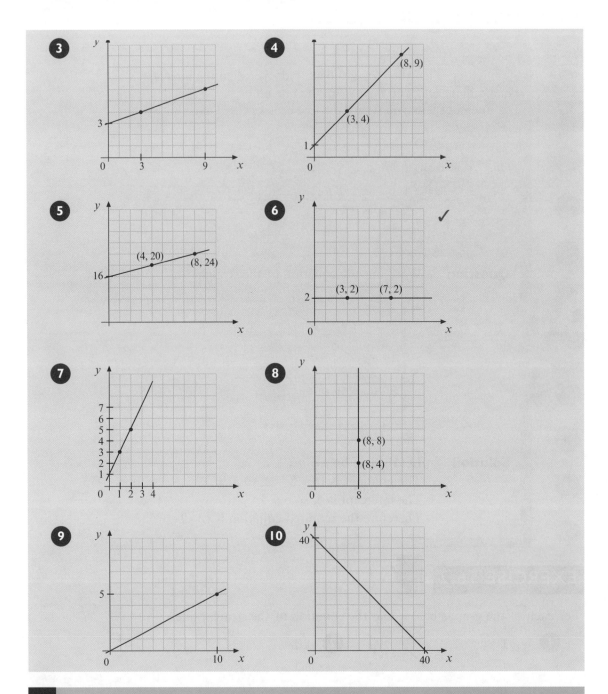

SUMMARY

- In this chapter you have revised plotting the graph of a straight line, given a formula connecting y and x.

- You have found the gradient and the intercept of a graph, and used these to deduce its equation. This is a vital skill in helping to understand the links between the algebra and geometry sections of your Key Stage 3 course.

REVIEW EXERCISE 16

I Plot the following graphs on squared paper. You should draw up a table containing at least three points first.

   a $y = 2x + 7$, for values of x from 0 to 10.

   b $y = 8 - x$, for values of x from 0 to 8.

   c $y = 5$, for values of x from 0 to 10.

   d $y = \frac{1}{2}x + 8$, for values of x from 0 to 12.

   e $y = 2x + 20$, for values of x from 0 to 10.

2 For each of the graphs below, find the gradient and intercept, and hence write down the equation of the graph.

   a 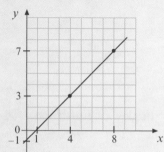   **b**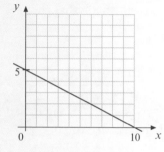

   c 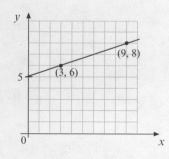   **d**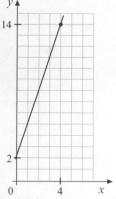

3 ✳ Draw up a set of coordinate axes in which x can run from 0 to 20 and y from 0 to 10. Use the same scale on both axes.

   Plot each of these three lines on the same diagram:

   a $y = 2x$ **b** $y = 10 - \frac{1}{2}x$ **c** $y = 2$.

   You should find that the three lines intersect to form a triangle.

   d Write down the coordinates of the three corners (vertices) of the triangle.

   e What type of triangle is this?

17 Lines and angles

In this chapter you will learn how to:
- identify and use alternate (Z) angles
- identify and use corresponding (F) angles
- understand simple geometric proofs.

You will also practise solving problems using alternate and corresponding angles together.

17.1 Alternate angles

The diagram shows two **parallel lines** and a third line, called a **transversal**, cutting across them.

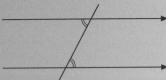

The two marked angles are called **alternate angles**, or (informally) **Z-angles**. **Alternate angles are equal.**

To see that this is true, consider a letter Z, and rotate it through 180° about its centre:

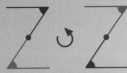

Since the two letter Z's are identical, the two marked angles must be equal in size.

Question	Find the values of the angles marked a, b, c. Give a brief reason in each case.

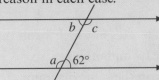

Solution	$a = 180 - 62°$
	$= 118°$ (angles on a straight line add up to 180°)
	$b = \underline{62°}$ (alternate to marked 62° angle)
	$c = \underline{118°}$ (alternate to angle a)

EXERCISE 17.1

1 Write down the letters of the angles which are alternate to:

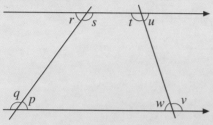

a) p　b) s　c) t　d) w.

Find the angle represented by the letters in these diagrams. Give a brief reason in each case.

2 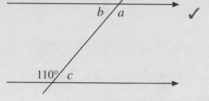 ✓

3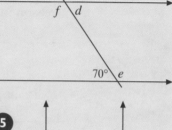

4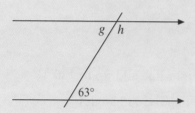

5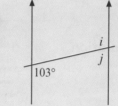

17.2 Corresponding angles

The diagram shows two **parallel lines** and a third line, called a **transversal**, cutting across them.

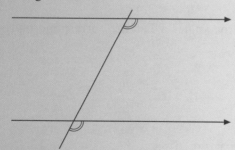

The two marked angles are called **corresponding angles**, or (informally) **F-angles**.
Corresponding angles are equal.

To see that this is true, consider a letter F, and translate (slide) it as shown in the diagram below:

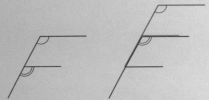

Since the two letter F's are identical, it follows that the two marked angles must be equal in size.

Question   Find the values of the angles marked *a*, *b*, *c*. Give a brief reason in each case.

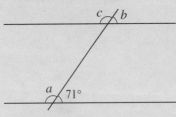

Solution $a = 180 - 71°$

            $= \underline{109°}$ (angles on a straight line add up to 180°)

    $b = \underline{71°}$ (corresponding to marked 71° angle)

    $c = \underline{109°}$ (corresponding to angle *a*)

EXERCISE 17.2

❶ Write down the letters of the angles which are corresponding to:

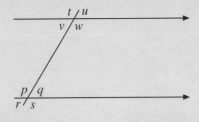

a) *p*   b) *s*   c) *t*   d) *w*.

2 Find the angle represented by the letters in these diagrams. Give a brief reason in each case.

a) 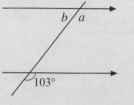 ✓

b)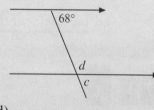

c)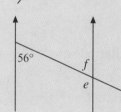

d)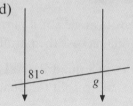

17.3 Geometric proofs

You can prove some results in geometry, by using simpler (i.e. more basic) results. This sounds straightforward, but it does require some inventiveness! You should try to develop your proof in very small steps, so that it is easy for someone else to follow and check it.

Question   Prove that the angles in a triangle add up to 180°.

Solution   Let the three angles be denoted by letters a, b, c.

Now draw a line through the top vertex, parallel to the base line.

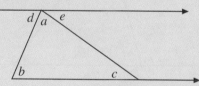

$a + d + e = 180°$ (angles on a straight line)

but $d = b$ (alternate angles)

$\therefore a + b + e = 180°$

also $e = c$ (alternate angles)

$\therefore a + b + c = 180°$

i.e. the angles in the triangle add up to 180°.

EXERCISE 17.3

1 Prove that the opposite angles of a parallelogram are equal.
(Hint: draw a diagonal across the parallelogram, then use alternate angles.)

2 Prove that the angles in a quadrilateral add up to 360°.
(Hint: draw a diagonal, to split the quadrilateral into two triangles.)

3 Deduce the result for the sum of the angles in a pentagon, and prove it.

OUTLINE

● In this chapter you have learnt how to recognise alternate (Z) and corresponding (F) angles, and you have begun to use them to prove geometric results. Remember to give brief reasons whenever you are making deductions using properties of these angles.

REVIEW EXERCISE 17

1 Look at the pairs of named angles in this diagram and say whether they are alternate, corresponding or neither.

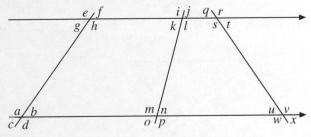

a d and u **b** b and g **c** i and o **d** p and m **e** m and l

f u and q **g** r and x **h** v and s.

2 Find the values of the angles represented by the letters. Give a brief reason in each case.

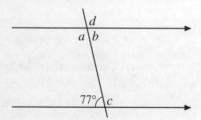

3 Find the values of the angles represented by the letters. Give a brief reason in each case.

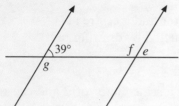

4 a Without looking back to page 133, write out a proof that the angles in a triangle add up to 180°.

   b Now carry out the following activity. Draw a triangle on a sheet of paper or card, and colour the three angles in three different colours, such as red, green and blue. Cut (or rip) the three angles off the triangle, and fit them all together at a point. What do you notice?

   c Do you think that **a** and **b** are both acceptable proofs that the angles in a triangle add up to 180°?

5 ✳ The diagram shows a regular pentagon and its diagonals.

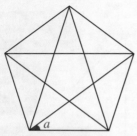

   a Make a copy of this diagram in your exercise book.

   b Shade in all of the angles which are equal in value to the angle marked *a*.

   c Can you work out the value of angle *a*?

18 Enlargement

OUTLINE

In this chapter you will learn how to:
- enlarge a shape using a whole number scale factor
- find the scale factor and centre of enlargement, given the object and image.

18.1 Enlargement

To **enlarge** a shape you need a **scale factor** and a **centre of enlargement**. The enlargement is constructed by drawing rays outward from the centre of enlargement.

Question Enlarge this flag, using a scale factor of 2 and centre of enlargement (0, 0).

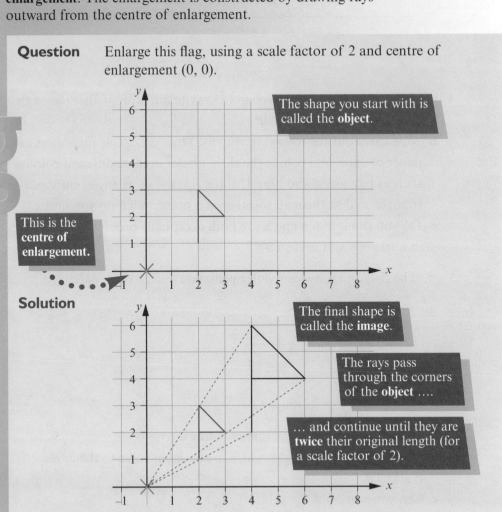

The shape you start with is called the **object**.

This is the **centre of enlargement**.

Solution

The final shape is called the **image**.

The rays pass through the corners of the **object** ....

... and continue until they are **twice** their original length (for a scale factor of 2).

The centre of enlargement does not always have to be at the origin.

Question Enlarge this flag, using a scale factor of 2 and centre of enlargement (0, 1).

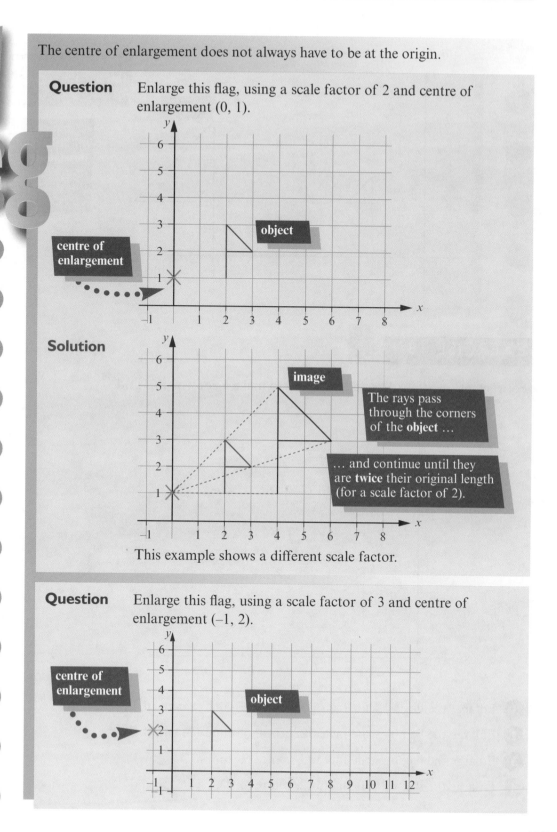

Solution

The rays pass through the corners of the **object** …

… and continue until they are **twice** their original length (for a scale factor of 2).

This example shows a different scale factor.

Question Enlarge this flag, using a scale factor of 3 and centre of enlargement (−1, 2).

137

Solution

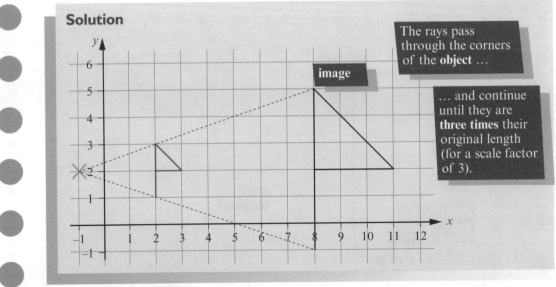

The rays pass through the corners of the **object** ...

... and continue until they are **three times** their original length (for a scale factor of 3).

EXERCISE 18.1

For each of questions **1–4** you will need to make a copy of this grid:

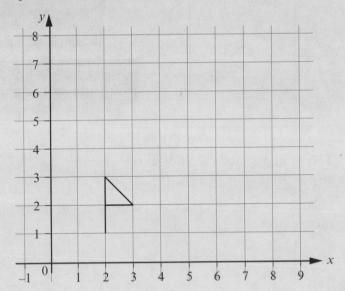

1 Enlarge the flag by scale factor 3, centre of enlargement (0, 0).

2 Enlarge the flag by scale factor 2, centre of enlargement (0, 2).

3 Enlarge the flag by scale factor 3, centre (1, 0).

4 Enlarge the flag by scale factor 2, centre (3, 1).

For each of questions **5–7** you will need to make a copy of this grid:

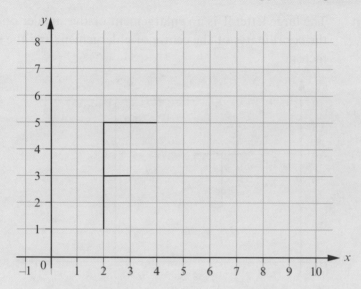

5 Enlarge the letter F by scale factor 2, centre of enlargement (1, 2).

6 Enlarge the letter F by scale factor 2, centre of enlargement (–1, 2).

7 Enlarge the letter F by scale factor 2, centre (5, 2).

8 Draw coordinate axes so that x and y can each range from –2 to 10.
   a) Construct rectangle ABCD where A is (9, 7), B (9, 9), C (6, 9) and D (6, 7).
   b) Enlarge the rectangle by scale factor 3, centre (10, 10).

9 Draw coordinate axes so that x and y can each range from –2 to 10.
   a) Construct a kite by joining the points (–1, 8), (2, 10), (4, 8), (2, 6) then back to (–1, 8).
   b) Enlarge the kite by scale factor 2, centre (–1, 10).

10 Draw coordinate axes so that x and y can each range from –2 to 10.
   a) Construct a triangle by joining the points (2, 2), (4, 5) and (1, 5).
   b) Enlarge the triangle by scale factor 3, centre (1, 3).

18.2 Finding the centre and the scale factor

To find the centre and scale factor, trace the rays backwards from the image through the object. The rays all come together, or **converge**, at the centre of enlargement.

Question   The large letter T is an enlargement of the smaller one. Find the coordinates of the centre of enlargement and the scale factor.

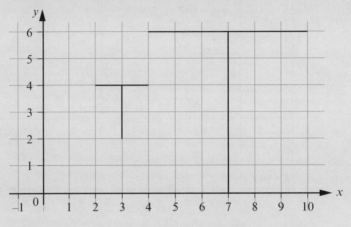

Solution

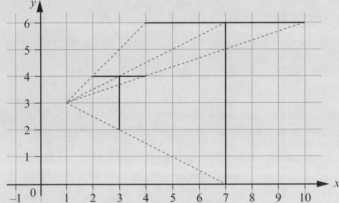

The centre of enlargement is (1, 3)

By comparing the height of the object (2 squares) and image (6 squares) the scale factor can be found:

Scale factor = 6 ÷ 2 = 3

EXERCISE 18.2

Copy each of these diagrams on to squared paper. The larger shape is an enlargement of the smaller one. Add suitable rays to your diagrams, and hence find the coordinates of the centre of enlargement and the scale factor in each case.

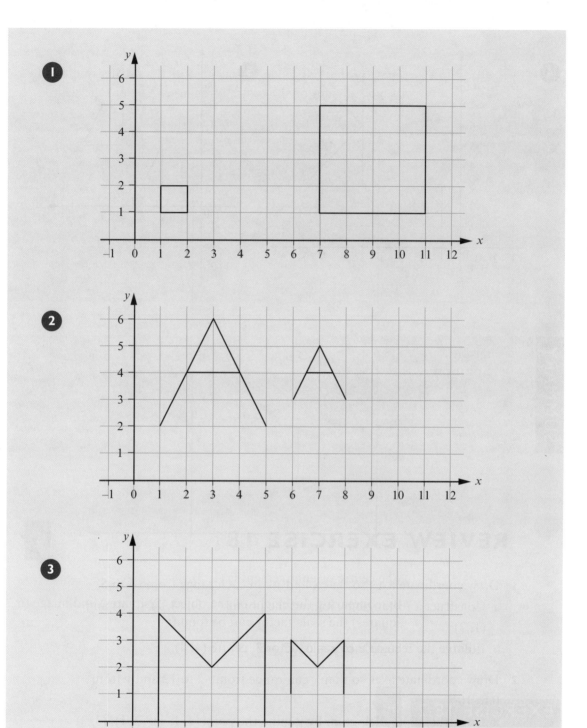

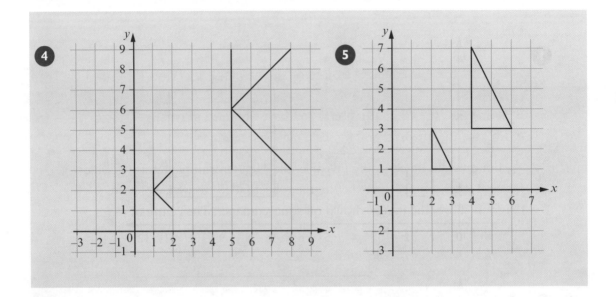

- In this chapter you have learnt how to enlarge a shape from a given centre of enlargement, using a whole number enlargement factor.

- You have also worked backwards from a given object and image, to find the centre and the scale factor of the enlargement.

REVIEW EXERCISE 18

1   Draw coordinate axes so that x and y can each range from –5 to 5.
   a   Construct a rectangle by joining the points (3, 1), (4, 2), (2, 4) and (1, 3).
   b   Enlarge the rectangle by scale factor 3, centre (4, 4).

2   Draw coordinate axes so that x can range from –2 to 12 and y from 0 to 10.
   a   Construct a parallelogram by joining the points (–1, 1), (2, 1), (3, 3) and (0, 3).
   b   Enlarge the parallelogram by scale factor 3, centre (–1, 0).

3 Draw coordinate axes so that *x* can range from 0 to 10 and y from
   –2 to 12.

   a Construct a quadrilateral by joining the points (1, 0), (1, 2), (3, 4) and
   (5, 4).

   b Name the type of quadrilateral you have obtained in part **a**.

   c Enlarge the quadrilateral by scale factor 3, centre (–1, 0).

4 ✳ Jim drew an object using invisible ink. He then enlarged it using scale
   factor 4 (and ordinary ink) before the object faded from view. The
   diagram shows the image, drawn on squared paper. The centre of
   enlargement is at (0, 1).

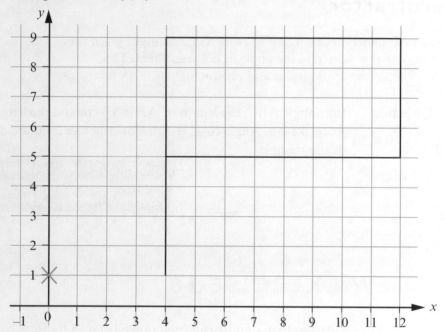

Make a copy of this diagram, and add the position of the object (using
ordinary ink).

19 Geometric constructions

OUTLINE

In this chapter you will learn how to:
- use a ruler and protractor to construct triangles
- use a ruler and compasses to construct triangles
- construct perpendicular bisectors using compasses
- construct angle bisectors using compasses.

19.1 Constructing a triangle using ruler and protractor

You may sometimes be asked to construct a triangle, given the lengths of two sides and the angle in between them. This construction requires a ruler and protractor.

Question   In triangle ABC, the length of AB is 5.6 cm and the length of AC is 4.8 cm. Angle BAC is 50°. Construct an accurate drawing of the triangle.

Solution

Leave enough room above AB so you can complete the diagram. Measure AB so it is 5.6 cm.

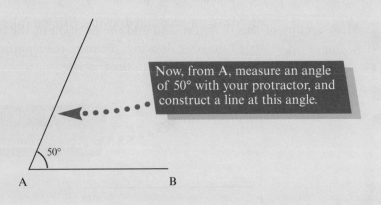

Now, from A, measure an angle of 50° with your protractor, and construct a line at this angle.

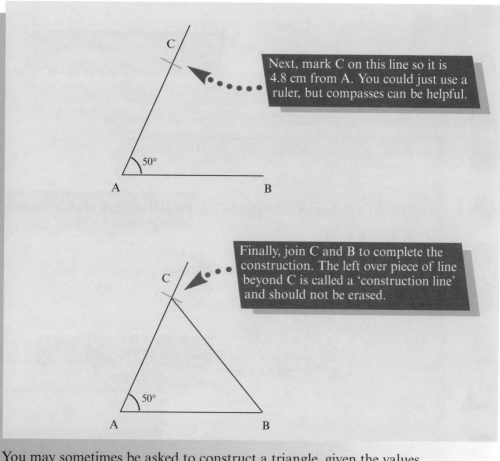

Next, mark C on this line so it is 4.8 cm from A. You could just use a ruler, but compasses can be helpful.

Finally, join C and B to complete the construction. The left over piece of line beyond C is called a 'construction line' and should not be erased.

You may sometimes be asked to construct a triangle, given the values of two angles and the length of the side in between them. Again, this construction requires a ruler and protractor.

Question   In triangle PQR, the length of PQ is 6.5 cm. Angle RPQ is 65° and angle RQP is 48°.

a) Make an accurate drawing, using a ruler and protractor.

b) From your drawing, measure the lengths of the two remaining sides in the triangle.

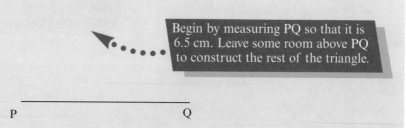

Begin by measuring PQ so that it is 6.5 cm. Leave some room above PQ to construct the rest of the triangle.

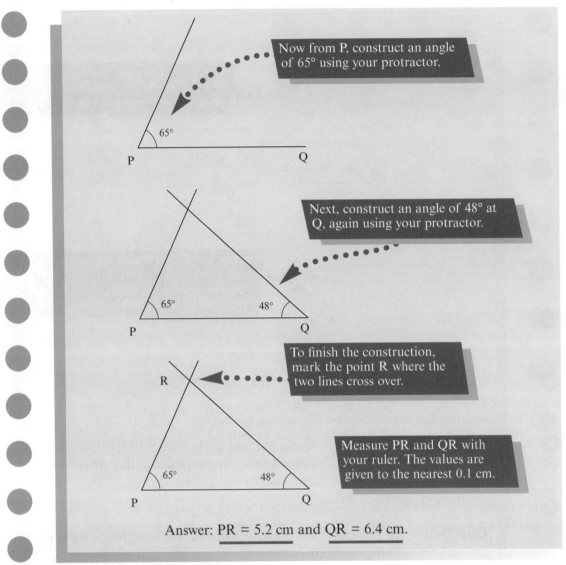

Now from P, construct an angle of 65° using your protractor.

65°

P   Q

Next, construct an angle of 48° at Q, again using your protractor.

65°   48°

P   Q

To finish the construction, mark the point R where the two lines cross over.

R

Measure PR and QR with your ruler. The values are given to the nearest 0.1 cm.

65°   48°

P   Q

Answer: PR = 5.2 cm and QR = 6.4 cm.

EXERCISE 19.1

1. These six diagrams show sketches (not to scale) of triangles. Construct accurate drawings of them, using a ruler and protractor.

a)

4.8 cm

48°

5.7 cm

b)

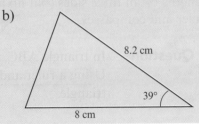

8.2 cm

39°

8 cm

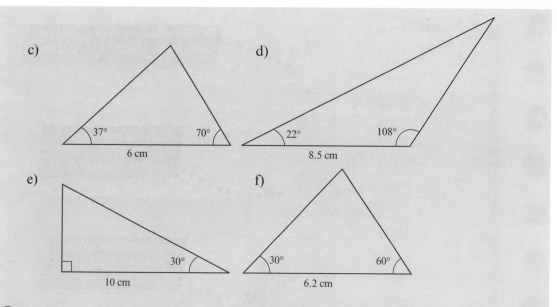

c) 37° 70° 6 cm

d) 22° 108° 8.5 cm

e) 30° 10 cm

f) 30° 60° 6.2 cm

2 In triangle ABC, angle ABC = 80°, AB = 10 cm and BC = 12 cm.
a) Make an accurate drawing of the triangle.
b) Measure the length of AC to the nearest 0.1 cm.

3 In triangle PQR, QR = 9 cm, angle PQR = 51°, angle PRQ = 58°.
c) Make an accurate drawing of the triangle.
d) Measure the lengths of PQ and PR, giving each one to the nearest 0.1 cm.

4 In triangle ABC, AB = 12.2 cm, BC = 8.7 cm and angle ABC = 95°. Make an accurate drawing of the triangle, and use it to find values of the other two angles in the triangle.

5 In an isosceles triangle, the two base angles are each 55° and the base is 12 cm long. Make an accurate drawing of the triangle, and use it to find the lengths of the other two sides of the triangle.

19.2 Constructing a triangle using ruler and compasses

You may sometimes be asked to construct a triangle, given the lengths of all three sides (but no angles). This construction requires a ruler and compasses.

Question   In triangle ABC, AB = 3 cm, BC = 3.5 cm and AC = 2.5 cm. Using a ruler and compasses, make an accurate drawing of the triangle.

Solution

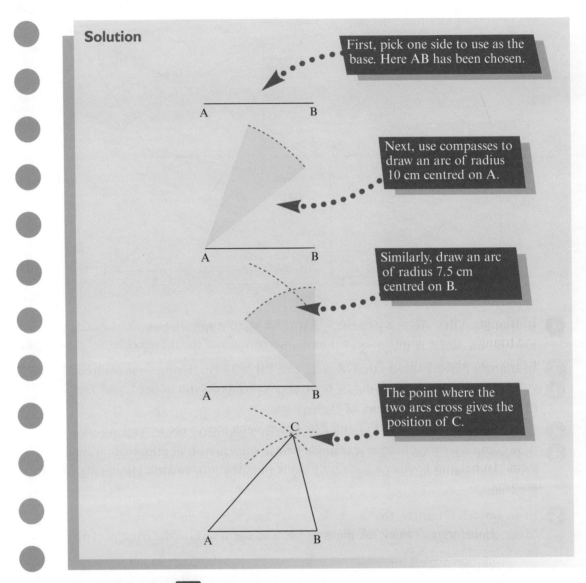

First, pick one side to use as the base. Here AB has been chosen.

Next, use compasses to draw an arc of radius 10 cm centred on A.

Similarly, draw an arc of radius 7.5 cm centred on B.

The point where the two arcs cross gives the position of C.

EXERCISE 19.2

1 These six diagrams show sketches (not to scale) of triangles. Construct accurate drawings of them, using a ruler and compasses.

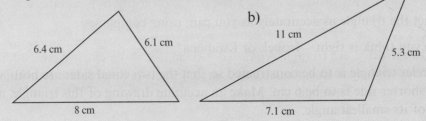

a)

6.4 cm   6.1 cm

8 cm

b)

11 cm

5.3 cm

7.1 cm

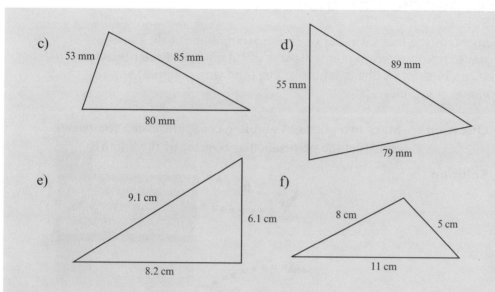

c) 53 mm, 85 mm, 80 mm

d) 55 mm, 89 mm, 79 mm

e) 9.1 cm, 6.1 cm, 8.2 cm

f) 8 cm, 5 cm, 11 cm

2 In triangle ABC, AB = 8 cm, BC = 9 cm, AC = 10 cm. Make an accurate drawing of the triangle, using compasses, and measure the sizes of the three angles.

3 In triangle PQR, PQ = 5 cm, QR = 12 cm, PR = 13 cm. Using your compasses, construct an accurate drawing of the triangle. What do you notice about the largest angle in the triangle?

4 Isobel and Kwabena have found a question in a geometry book. The question says 'Use compasses to construct a triangle whose sides are of lengths 4 cm, 6 cm and 8 cm.' Isobel and Kwabena have both done the question, and are talking about their answers.

> *Isobel says: 'I think it's an obtuse-angled triangle.'*

> *Kwabena says: 'I think it's an acute-angled triangle.'*

Construct the triangle as accurately as you can, using compasses.

Who do you think is right – Isobel, or Kwabena?

5 An isosceles triangle is to be constructed so that the two equal sides are both 8 cm, and the shorter side is to be 6 cm. Make an accurate drawing of this triangle, and find the size of its smallest angle.

19.3 Perpendicular bisector

Sometimes you may be asked to draw a straight line at the same distance from two given points. This is called a **perpendicular bisector**, and can be drawn using compasses. The following example shows you how it is done.

Question Mark two points, A and B, 6 cm apart. Using compasses, construct the perpendicular bisector of the line AB.

Solution

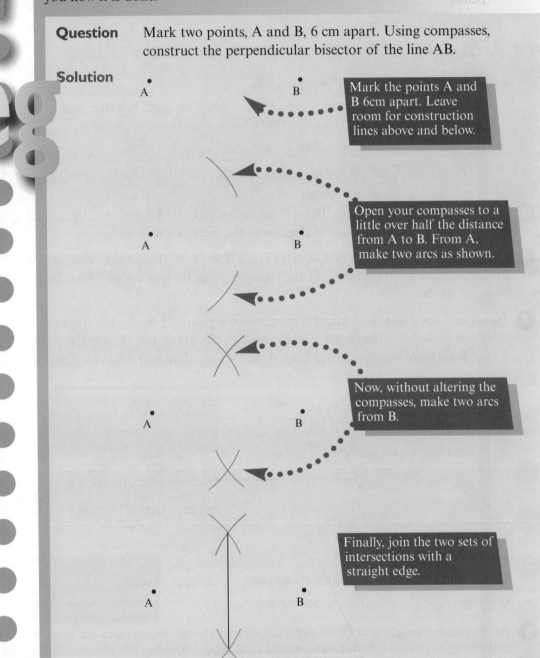

Mark the points A and B 6cm apart. Leave room for construction lines above and below.

Open your compasses to a little over half the distance from A to B. From A, make two arcs as shown.

Now, without altering the compasses, make two arcs from B.

Finally, join the two sets of intersections with a straight edge.

EXERCISE 19.3

1 Draw two points A and B, so that B is 10 cm to the right of A. Using compasses, construct the perpendicular bisector of the line AB.

2 Draw two points P and Q, so that P is 8 cm below Q. Using compasses, construct the perpendicular bisector of the line PQ.

19.4 Angle bisector

Sometimes you may be asked to draw a straight line which splits a given angle into two equal parts. This is called an **angle bisector**, and can be drawn using compasses. The following example shows you how it is done.

Question Using compasses, construct the angle bisector of the angle given below.

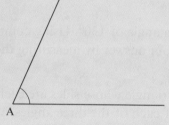

Solution

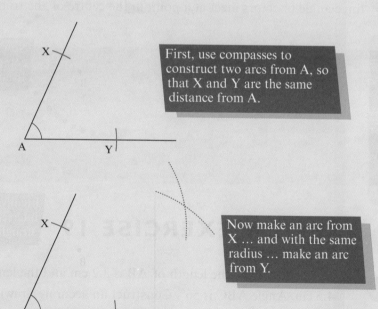

First, use compasses to construct two arcs from A, so that X and Y are the same distance from A.

Now make an arc from X ... and with the same radius ... make an arc from Y.

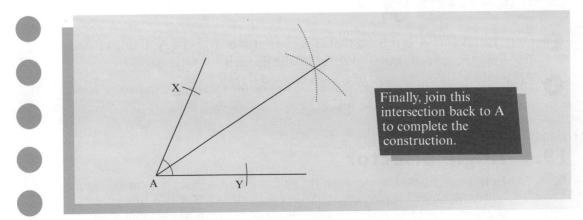

Finally, join this intersection back to A to complete the construction.

EXERCISE 19.4

1 Use your protractor to draw an angle of 70°. Using compasses, construct the angle bisector of this angle. Check your answer by measuring the final angles with your protractor.

2 Use your protractor to draw an angle of 130°. Using compasses, construct the angle bisector of this angle. Check your answer by measuring the final angles with your protractor.

3 Using compasses, construct a triangle whose sides are each 12 cm long. Now construct the angle bisectors of each of the three angles. You should find that all three angle bisectors meet at a point in the centre of the triangle.

SUMMARY

- In this chapter you have learnt how to construct triangles using geometrical instruments including protractors and compasses.

- You have also learnt how to construct perpendicular bisectors and angle bisectors.

- Compass construction questions feature in Key Stage 3 and GCSE examination papers. The examiner will expect you to leave your construction lines clearly visible, especially if you have used compasses.

REVIEW EXERCISE 19

1 In triangle ABC, the length of AB is 3.2 cm and the length of BC is 4.5 cm. Angle ABC is 56°. Construct an accurate drawing of the triangle, and use it to measure the length of the side AC.

2 In triangle PQR, the length of PQ is 5.6 cm and the length of PR is 6.5 cm. Angle QPR is 130°. Construct an accurate drawing of the triangle, and use it to measure the length of the side QR.

3 In triangle LMN, LM = 4.2 cm, LN = 5.2 cm and MN = 6.2 cm. Make an accurate drawing of the triangle, and measure the size of the smallest angle in the triangle.

4 In triangle EFG, EF = 6.5 cm, FG = 5.5 cm and EG = 8.2 cm. Make an accurate drawing of the triangle, and measure the size of the largest angle in the triangle.

5 Draw two points A and B so that AB = 9 cm.
  a Using compasses, construct the perpendicular bisector of AB.
  b Hence construct a rhombus whose diagonals are of length 9 cm and 6 cm.

6 With a straight edge only, draw an acute angle of the size of your choice. Now use compasses to construct the angle bisector. Finally, use your protractor to check that the angle has been bisected correctly.

7 ✳ Using a ruler and compasses, but no protractor, construct an isosceles right-angled triangle with short sides of length 5 cm. Make sure all your construction lines are clearly visible.

8 ✳ Martina decides to make a triangle with sides of 4 cm, 5 cm and 10 cm. She does not succeed.
  a Using compasses, try to construct Martina's triangle.
  b Explain carefully why the construction is not possible.

9 ✳ Two ice cream sellers, A and B, work on a small island. When holidaymakers wish to buy an ice cream, they walk to the nearer of the two sellers.
  a Make a drawing of an island, and mark the two sellers A and B. The island can be whatever shape you like, and the sellers A and B can be wherever you like too!
  b Using compasses and a straight edge, divide the island up into two regions, corresponding to the 'catchment area' for each of the two ice cream sellers. You may wish to colour the regions in two different colours.

10 ✳ Repeat question **9**, but now using three ice cream sellers, A, B and C.

20 Area and volume

OUTLINE

In this chapter you will learn how to:
- find areas of triangles
- find areas of quadrilaterals
- find areas of compound shapes
- find volumes and surface areas of cuboids
- solve problems involving areas and volumes.

20.1 Areas of triangles

For a triangle with base b and perpendicular height h the area A can be found by using this result:

$$A = \frac{b \times h}{2}$$

Question   Find the area of this triangle.

(The diagram is not to scale. All lengths are in centimetres.)

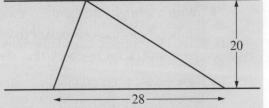

Solution $b = 28$ and $h = 20$

$$A = \frac{b \times h}{2}$$

$$= \frac{28 \times 20}{2}$$

$$= \frac{560}{2}$$

$$= \underline{280 \text{ cm}^2}$$

Notice that $\dfrac{28 \times 20}{2} = \dfrac{560}{2} = 280$ and ...

$\dfrac{28 \times 20}{2} = 14 \times 20 = 280$ and ...

$\dfrac{28 \times 20}{2} = 28 \times 10 = 280$ and ...

all give the same result.

The same formula can be used even when the triangle is obtuse-angled.

Question   Find the area of this triangle.

(The diagram is not to scale. All lengths are in millimetres.)

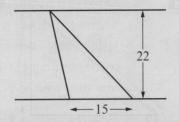

Solution $b = 15$ and $h = 22$

$$A = \frac{b \times h}{2}$$

Explain your working clearly.

$$= \frac{15 \times 22}{2}$$

$$= \frac{330}{2}$$

$$= \underline{165 \text{ mm}^2}$$

EXERCISE 20.1

1 Find the areas of these triangles, correct to 3 significant figures where appropriate:

a) Base 12 cm, perpendicular height 26 cm ✓
b) Base 16 cm, perpendicular height 19 cm
c) Base 40 mm, perpendicular height 49 mm
d) Base 32 cm, perpendicular height 21 cm
e) Base 6 m, perpendicular height 11 m
f) Base 11 cm, perpendicular height 13 cm ✓
g) Base 12.5 cm, perpendicular height 8.5 cm
h) Base 4.8 m, perpendicular height 8.7 m
i) Base 165 mm, perpendicular height 223 mm
j) Base 340 mm, perpendicular height 420 mm.

Find the areas of the triangles in these diagrams. In some cases you have been given more information than you actually need. *(The diagrams are not drawn to scale. Take all measurements as centimetres.)*

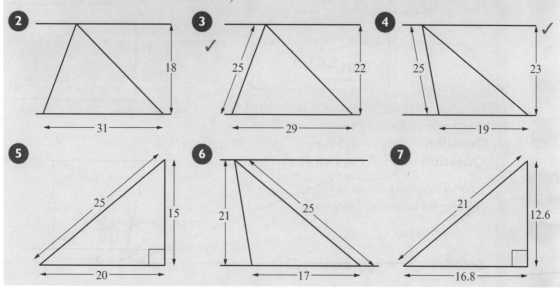

20.2 Areas of quadrilaterals

The area of a square, rectangle, parallelogram, rhombus or trapezium can be found by using one of the following standard results:

Quadrilateral	Area formula	Example
Square	Area $= a \times a$ $= a^2$	Area $= 8 \times 8$ $= 64 \text{ cm}^2$ 8 cm 8 cm
Rectangle	Area $= a \times b$ $= ab$	Area $= 8 \times 5$ $= 40 \text{ cm}^2$ 5 cm 8 cm
Parallelogram	Area $= b \times h$ $= bh$	Area $= 8 \times 5$ $= 40 \text{ cm}^2$ 5 cm 8 cm
Rhombus	Area $= \frac{1}{2} \times a \times b$ $= \frac{ab}{2}$	Area $= \frac{1}{2} \times 10 \times 14$ $= \frac{140}{2}$ $= 70 \text{ m}^2$ 5 m 7 m 7 m 5 m
Trapezium	Area $= \frac{1}{2} \times (a + b) \times h$ $= \frac{h(a + b)}{2}$	Area $= \frac{1}{2} \times (10 + 14) \times 8$ $= \frac{1}{2} \times 24 \times 8$ $= 12 \times 8 = 96 \text{ m}^2$ 10 m 8 m 14 m

Question   Name this type of quadrilateral, and find its area.

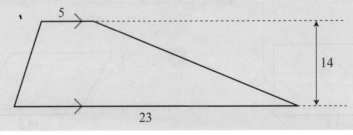

Solution   This is a <u>trapezium</u>, with $a = 5$, $b = 23$ and $h = 14$.

$$\text{Area} = \frac{h(a + b)}{2}$$

$$= \frac{14 \times (5 + 23)}{2}$$

$$= \frac{14 \times 28}{2}$$

$$= 7 \times 28$$

$$= \underline{196} \text{ square units}$$

EXERCISE 20.2

Name each of these quadrilaterals, and find its area. *(All lengths are in centimetres.)*

1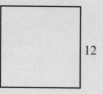
12
12

2 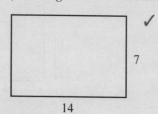 ✓
7
14

3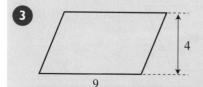
4
9

4 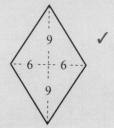 ✓
9 6 6 9

5 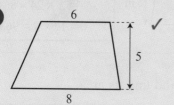 ✓
6
5
8

6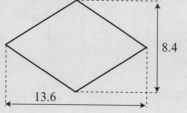
8.4
13.6

7
4.2
7.8

8 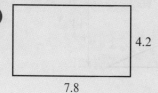 ✓
6.5
15.5

20.3 Areas of compound shapes

The areas of more complicated shapes can be found by breaking them up into smaller parts. Each separate area is found, then they are all added together.

Question   Find the area of the letter F. *(All lengths are in centimetres. The diagram is not to scale.)*

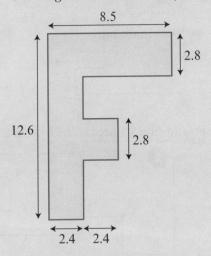

Solution

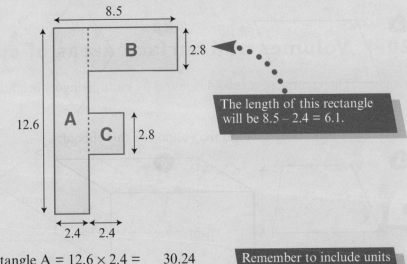

The length of this rectangle will be $8.5 - 2.4 = 6.1$.

Area of rectangle A = $12.6 \times 2.4 =$ 30.24
Area of rectangle B = $2.8 \times 6.1 =$ 17.08
Area of rectangle C = $2.8 \times 2.4 =$ 6.72

Remember to include units in your final answer.

Total   54.04

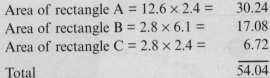

The area of the letter F is 54.0 cm² (correct to 3 s.f.).

EXERCISE 20.3

For each of these compound shapes make a neat sketch and add dotted lines to break it up into simpler pieces. Find the area of each piece, and the total area for each compound shape. (*All the lengths are in centimetres.*)

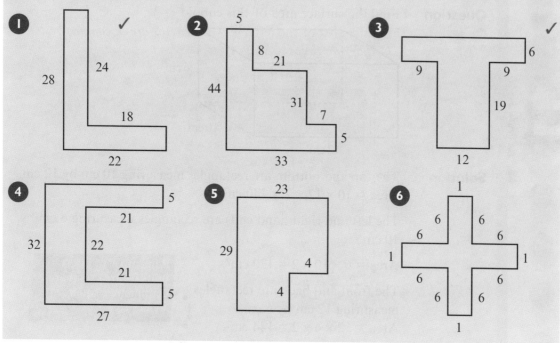

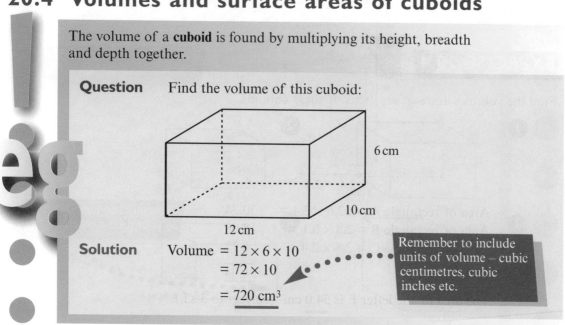

20.4 Volumes and surface areas of cuboids

The volume of a **cuboid** is found by multiplying its height, breadth and depth together.

Question Find the volume of this cuboid:

6 cm

10 cm

12 cm

Solution Volume = $12 \times 6 \times 10$

= 72×10

= 720 cm^3

Remember to include units of volume – cubic centimetres, cubic inches etc.

The **surface area** of a cuboid is found by working out the area of each face separately, then adding them all together. You can do this quite quickly, since the six faces comprise three matching pairs.

Question   Find the surface area of this cuboid.

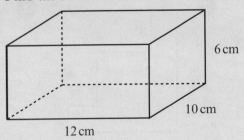

Solution   The top and bottom are rectangles measuring 10 cm by 12 cm.
Area = $10 \times 12 \times 2 = 240$ cm².

The left and right hand ends are rectangles measuring 6 cm by 10 cm.

Area = $6 \times 10 \times 2 = 120$ cm².

The front and back are rectangles measuring 12 cm by 6 cm.
Area = $12 \times 6 \times 2 = 144$ cm².

> Remember to insert units of area – square centimetres, square inches etc.

Adding these three results,
total surface area = $240 + 120 + 144 = \underline{504 \text{ cm}^2}$.

EXERCISE 20.4

Find the volumes and surface areas of these cuboids.

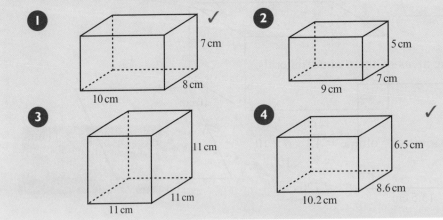

5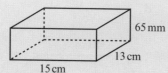

65 mm

13 cm

15 cm

6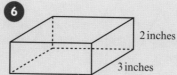

2 inches

3 inches

6 inches

SUMMARY

- In this chapter you have calculated areas of triangles and quadrilaterals using standard formulae. You have found areas of compound shapes by breaking them up into smaller pieces.

- You have also found the volume of a cuboid, by multiplying its three dimensions together, and you have found its surface area by repeated application of the result for the area of a rectangle.

REVIEW EXERCISE 20

1 Find the areas of these triangles. *All the lengths are in centimetres.*

a
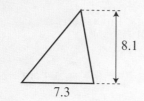

8.1

7.3

b
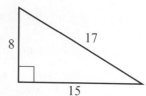

8   17

15

c
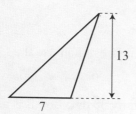

13

7

d
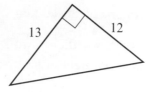

13   12

2 Find the areas of these quadrilaterals.

a
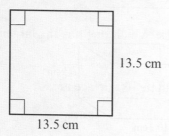

13.5 cm

13.5 cm

b
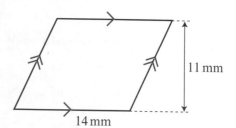

11 mm

14 mm

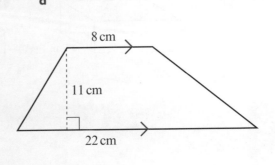

c

48 mm

18 mm

d

8 cm

11 cm

22 cm

3 A cuboid measures 21 cm by 19 cm by 14 cm. Find its volume, correct to 2 significant figures.

4 A cuboid measures 20 cm by 50 mm by 70 mm. Find its volume in cubic centimetres.

5 ✳ Two of the dimensions of a cuboid are 21 cm and 25 cm. Its volume is 15 225 cm³. Find the third dimension.

6 ✳ A cube has a volume of 6859 cm³. Find its dimensions.

7 ✳ A cuboid measures 26 cm by 130 cm by 2.3 m.
Find:
a the total area of all 6 faces

b the volume of the cuboid.

[Hint: decide whether to work in centimetres or metres, then use the same units throughout.]

8 ✳ Box A is a cuboid, measuring 20 cm by 24 cm by 30 cm. Box B is also a cuboid, but it measures 15 cm by 16 cm by 60 cm.
a Calculate the volume of both boxes. Which one has the larger volume?

b Calculate the surface area of both boxes. Which one has the larger area?

9 ✳ A cube has a volume of 729 cm³. Calculate its surface area.

21 Graphs and charts

OUTLINE

In this chapter you will learn how to:
- recognise discrete and continuous data
- construct pie charts for categorical data
- construct vertical line graphs
- use frequency tables to construct histograms and frequency polygons
- construct and interpret scatter diagrams.

21.1 Discrete and continuous data

Quantities like length, time or weight are **continuous**. They are usually obtained by measurement, and can only be recorded to a limited level of accuracy (e.g. 3 significant figures).

Quantities like the number of people on a bus, or the number of marbles in a bag are **discrete**. They are usually obtained by counting, and can be recorded exactly.

Question   Decide whether each of these is discrete or continuous:

a) the number of pages in a book;
b) the temperature of a cup of tea;
c) the area of a sheet of paper.

Solution   a) The number of pages can be counted exactly: it is <u>discrete</u>.
b) The temperature can only be measured approximately: it is <u>continuous</u>.
c) The area can only be measured approximately: it is <u>continuous</u>.

EXERCISE 21.1

Say whether each of these is discrete or continuous.

1 The number of words on a page of a newspaper. ✓

2 The length of a CD track, in minutes.

3 The time taken for a girl to run 100 m.

4 The number of files stored on a computer floppy disk.

5 The length of a roll of adhesive tape.

6 The marks scored in a 25-question multiple-choice test.

7 The area of a wall, in square metres. ✓

8 The number of 1-litre pots of paint required to paint a wall. ✓

9 The amount of money in my bank account on a given day.

10 The weight of a tomato.

21.2 Introducing pie charts

A pie chart is used to display categorical (descriptive) data, i.e. the sizes of various classes, or categories. The frequencies are scaled until they add up to 360, then drawn using a protractor. Alternatively you can scale them to percentages, then use a pie chart scale.

Question   In a car park it is found that there are 11 red, 8 blue, 6 white, 3 green and 2 black cars. Display this information in a pie chart.

Solution   First we draw up a frequency table:

Colour	Frequency	Pie Chart Angle
Red	11	
Blue	8	
White	6	
Green	3	
Black	2	

The frequencies add up to $11 + 8 + 6 + 3 + 2 = 30$

$360 \div 30 = 12$, so all the frequencies are multiplied by 12.

Colour	Frequency	Pie Chart Angle
Red	11	$11 \times 12 = 132$ 132°
Blue	8	$8 \times 12 = 96$ 96°
White	6	72°
Green	3	36°
Black	2	24°

The resulting pie chart may now be drawn:

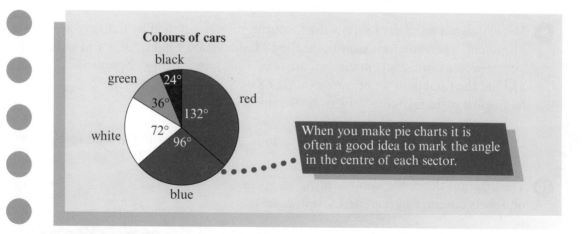

Colours of cars

black 24°
green 36°
red 132°
white 72°
96°
blue

When you make pie charts it is often a good idea to mark the angle in the centre of each sector.

EXERCISE 21.2

1. Martina is going to draw a pie chart to display the colours of 20 pencils. Three of them are red. What angle should she make the red sector of the pie chart?

2. Luc is drawing a pie chart to show the types of weather on different days during the year. 40% of the days are wet. What angle should he draw for this slice of the pie chart?

3. Sixty shoppers were asked to name their favourite type of fizzy drink. Twenty-four named cola, 18 lemonade, 13 orange, and 5 other drinks. Display this information in a pie chart.

4. A school's mathematics department has an annual budget of £6000. £3000 is spent on books, £1600 on photocopying, £900 on classroom equipment and £250 on staff training. Display this information in a pie chart (don't forget to include a category for 'other'). ✓

5. I emptied my money-box and found that it contained exactly 90 coins. Thirty of them were 2p coins, seven 1p, twenty-one 10p, twenty-six 5p and the rest were foreign. Draw a pie chart to illustrate this information.

6. Tim is a concert violinist. He reckons that he practises for 5 hours a day, teaches for 3 hours a day, and sleeps for 8 hours a day. Half the remaining time is spent eating, and the remainder doing other things. Draw a pie chart to illustrate this information.

7. Susy receives an allowance of £20 a month. She usually spends £9 on clothes and £6 on toiletries. £2 is spent on stationery and she saves the rest. Show this on a pie chart.

8. Usha is a vet. Last week she treated 40 animals. They included 17 dogs, 11 cats, 5 hamsters and 4 lizards. Draw a pie chart to illustrate Usha's week.

9 David draws a pie chart to show the favourite subjects studied by the Year 8 pupils at his school. There are four sectors, labelled Mathematics, English, Art and Other. The largest sector is for mathematics, an angle of 156° representing 52 pupils.
  a) Find the total number of pupils in Year 8.
  b) English is the favourite subject of 37 pupils.
     Find the corresponding angle.
  c) Art is represented by an angle of 81°. Find the number of pupils who named art as their favourite subject.

10 The diagram shows the number of hours spent on sports coverage by a cable TV station last week.
  a) Explain why the use of a 3-D style pie chart appears to distort the information shown in the diagram.
  b) Re-draw the diagram as an ordinary flat pie chart, so that the representation is fair.
  c) What sort of people do you think might wish to use a diagram which deliberately distorts the information?

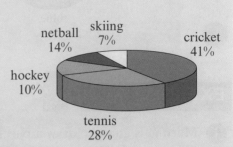

21.3 Harder pie charts

In this section you will practise making pie charts for data which does not always conveniently multiply up to 360°.

Question The 29 pupils in Class 3 are asked to name their favourite type of drink: 11 say it is cola, 9, milk shake, 6, mineral water and 3 name other drinks. Display this information in a pie chart.

Solution There are 29 pupils in total, so multiply by $\frac{360}{29}$ to find the angle in degrees:

Drink	Frequency	Angle
Cola	11	137°
Milk shake	9	112°
Mineral water	6	74°
Other	3	37°

$\frac{11 \times 360}{29} = 136.55 \ldots$
which is rounded to 137°.

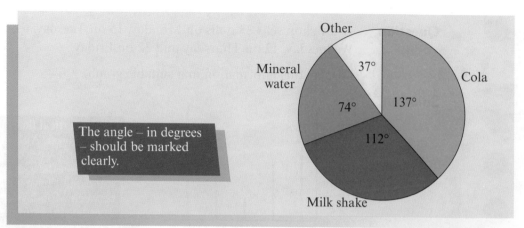

The angle – in degrees – should be marked clearly.

EXERCISE 21.3

1. Forty-four motorists are surveyed and asked to name the country in which their car was built: 21 reply Great Britain, 10, France, 5, Germany and the rest Other countries. Draw up a table of angles, and display this information in a pie chart. ✓

2. Littlewood Farm has an area of 1050 acres. Of this, 450 acres are used for dairy farming, 220 acres for growing cash crops and 120 acres are woodland. The rest of the farmland provides animal feed. Draw up a table of angles, and display this information in a pie chart.

3. Ginnie has a collection of toy animals, made up of 21 puppies, 11 ponies, 18 kittens and 7 rabbits. Display this information in a pie chart.

4. Last August there were 17 sunny days and 9 overcast days; the rest were wet. Display this information in a pie chart.

21.4 Line graphs

In this Section you will be using two quite different types of line graphs.

Vertical line graph
This is rather like a bar chart. It is used when the x-axis consists of categories, e.g. red, green, blue or Monday, Tuesday, Wednesday, with no possibility of any in-between values.

Time series graph (line graph)
This is a continuous line, consisting of several straight segments. It is used when the x-axis is continuous, e.g. a plot of time. In-between values may be estimated from the graph.

Question   A toy shop sells 23 dolls on Monday, 15 on Tuesday, 6 on Wednesday, 12 on Thursday and 32 on Friday.

Display this information in a suitable graph.

Solution

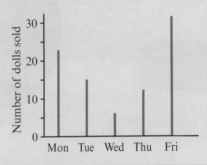

Here a **vertical line graph** is used. Although days of the week are plotted on the *x*-axis you cannot have a value between Monday and Tuesday, for example.

Question   During a busy period on the stock market the share prices of *Easiclean Appliances* change very quickly. The price was 225p at 0900, 275p at 1100 and 295p at 1230. During the afternoon the price peaked at 310p at 1400, then fell to 195p at 1500 before recovering to 240p by 1700.

Display this information in a suitable graph.

Solution

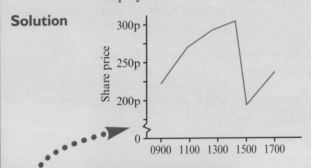

Here a **time series graph** is used. Time is plotted along the *x*-axis, and the straight line segments indicate that there are values in between 0900 and 1100, for example.

This zigzag shows that the *y*-axis has been interrupted.

EXERCISE 21.4

In questions **1–6** decide whether the data should be displayed using a vertical line graph or a time series graph, and then construct the graph.

1   In a survey of pets, seven children say they have 1 pet, twelve children have 2 pets, three children have 3 pets and five children have no pets at all. ✓

2 The depth of water in a river was 10 cm on 1 July, 12 cm on 1 August, 14 cm on 1 September and 15 cm on 1 October. ✓

3 The midday temperature in my garden was 17° on Monday, 19° on Tuesday, 14° on Wednesday, 17° on Thursday and 11° on Friday.

4 Yesterday my pulse rate was 70 at 0900, 75 at 1000, 80 at 1100 and 65 at 1200. It slowed to 55 at 1300 before increasing to 70 at 1600.

5 A shoe shop sold eight pairs of size 44 boots, eleven pairs of size 45, four pairs of size 46 and one pair of size 47.

6 In her summer mathematics examinations Florence scored 84% in Year 7, 72% in Year 8, 66% in Year 9 and 77% in Year 10.

In questions **7** and **8** the graph contains some kind of error. Explain briefly what it is, and draw a corrected version of the graph.

7 The number of words in an eight-page leaflet were counted, to the nearest 25 words. They were:

Page 1	*850 words*
Page 2	*775 words*
Page 3	*800 words*
Page 4	*650 words*
Page 5	*850 words*
Page 6	*800 words*
Page 7	*750 words*
Page 8	*775 words*

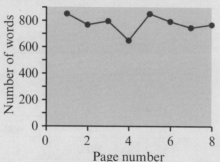

8 The table shows the average rate of spending on health by a new government during the first 400 days after it came to power.

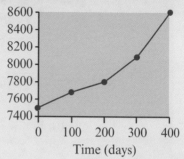

Government Spending on Health

Time (days)	Spending (£ thousands)
0	7500
100	7700
200	7800
300	8100
400	8600

21.5 Frequency tables

When continuous data is recorded it can be rounded off (e.g. to the nearest centimetre) before being written down. Watch out – the data then looks discrete but it is not.

Another method is to record the data using a tally chart (similar to those used for discrete data in Chapter 10). The values are divided into classes, and each class has a corresponding **frequency**.

Question   The heights of 20 indoor plants have been recorded in centimetres, correct to the nearest millimetre, as follows:

32.1 23.6 30.8 34.1 28.0   21.5 27.5 38.3 19.8 22.9

22.7 17.2 25.2 21.6 29.3   27.0 26.1 32.8 28.9 27.0

a) Use a tally method to construct a grouped frequency table.

b) A plant is chosen at random. Find the probability that its height is less than 25 cm.

Solution   a)

Height x (cm)	Tally
$15.0 \leq x < 20.0$	
$20.0 \leq x < 25.0$	
$25.0 \leq x < 30.0$	
$30.0 \leq x < 35.0$		
$35.0 \leq x < 40.0$	

This tally chart contains five classes.

This class includes 15.0 but not 20.0.

This mark corresponds to 32.1.

Height x (cm)	Tally	Frequency
$15.0 \leq x < 20.0$			2
$20.0 \leq x < 25.0$	⊞⊤	5
$25.0 \leq x < 30.0$	⊞⊤ |||	8
$30.0 \leq x < 35.0$	||||	4
$35.0 \leq x < 40.0$			1

b) $P(x < 25.0) = \dfrac{2+5}{20}$

$= \dfrac{7}{20}$

$= 0.35$

EXERCISE 21.5

1 The masses of 25 kittens are measured correct to the nearest gram:

144 122 129 150 155

133 147 138 139 121

103 126 131 135 132

141 130 136 142 151

133 138 121 135 146

a) Draw up a frequency table using classes of $100 \le x < 110$ and so on.

b) What percentage of the kittens have a mass above 140 g?

2 The heights of 30 children are measured correct to the nearest centimetre:

101 125 115 122 136

134 103 120 128 114

126 112 124 105 122

112 127 119 108 139

117 149 118 127 111

141 115 129 121 122

a) Draw up a frequency table using classes of $100 \le x < 110$ and so on.

b) How many children have a height of less than 130 cm?

3 The ages of 24 trees are recorded, to the nearest year: ✓

  2   15   19   15   15

 16   17   19   10   11

 17   17   11   13   2

 14   16   19   2   15

 18   12   13   19

a) Draw up a frequency table using classes of $0 \le x < 5$ and so on.

b) Three of these trees were planted following a storm. How long ago do you think
   the storm took place?

21.6 Histograms and frequency polygons

When continuous data is grouped in classes the frequencies can be
displayed in a number of ways.

A **histogram** looks like a bar chart, but the scale on the x-axis is
continuous, and there are no gaps between the bars. A **frequency
polygon** is obtained by joining the mid-points of the tops of the
histogram columns..

Question

Height x (cm)	Tally	Frequency
$15.0 \leq x < 20.0$	|	2
$20.0 \leq x < 25.0$	卌	5
$25.0 \leq x < 30.0$	卌 |||	8
$30.0 \leq x < 35.0$	||||	4
$35.0 \leq x < 40.0$	|	1

Illustrate this data:
a) with a histogram;
b) with a frequency polygon.

Solution a)

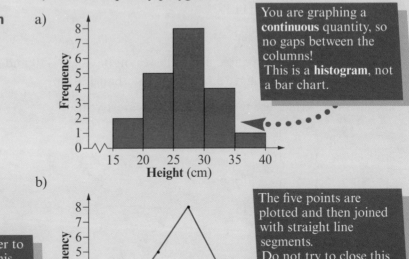

b)

You are graphing a
continuous quantity, so
no gaps between the
columns!
This is a **histogram**, not
a bar chart.

The five points are
plotted and then joined
with straight line
segments.
Do not try to close this
polygon on to the x-axis.

Remember to
include this
zig-zag if the
x-axis does
not extend all
the way back
to zero.

EXERCISE 21.6

In questions **1–6** draw a histogram and a frequency polygon to illustrate the data given in the table.

1

Diameter d (mm)	Frequency
$0 \leq d < 10$	8
$10 \leq d < 20$	9
$20 \leq d < 30$	12
$30 \leq d < 40$	7
$40 \leq d < 50$	1
$50 \leq d < 60$	4

2 ✓

Time t (mins)	Frequency
$15 \leq t < 20$	3
$20 \leq t < 25$	1
$25 \leq t < 30$	3
$30 \leq t < 35$	9
$35 \leq t < 40$	7

3

Mass x (grams)	Frequency
$60 \leq x < 70$	3
$70 \leq x < 80$	6
$80 \leq x < 90$	11
$90 \leq x < 100$	8
$100 \leq x < 110$	7
$110 \leq x < 120$	5

4

Temperature T (°C)	Frequency
$-10 \leq T < -5$	12
$-5 \leq T < 0$	7
$0 \leq T < 5$	5
$5 \leq T < 10$	2
$10 \leq T < 15$	1

5

Speed v (m/s)	Frequency
$20 \leq v < 30$	6
$30 \leq v < 40$	8
$40 \leq v < 50$	7
$50 \leq v < 60$	2

6

Volume V (ml)	Frequency
$160 < V \leq 175$	3
$175 < V \leq 190$	2
$190 < V \leq 205$	3
$205 < V \leq 220$	4
$220 < V \leq 235$	10
$235 < V \leq 250$	3

21.7 Scatter diagrams

A **scatter diagram** shows how two statistical quantities might be related. Points are plotted on a set of (x, y) axes, and any **trend** is observed. Often you will see **positive correlation** or **negative correlation**.

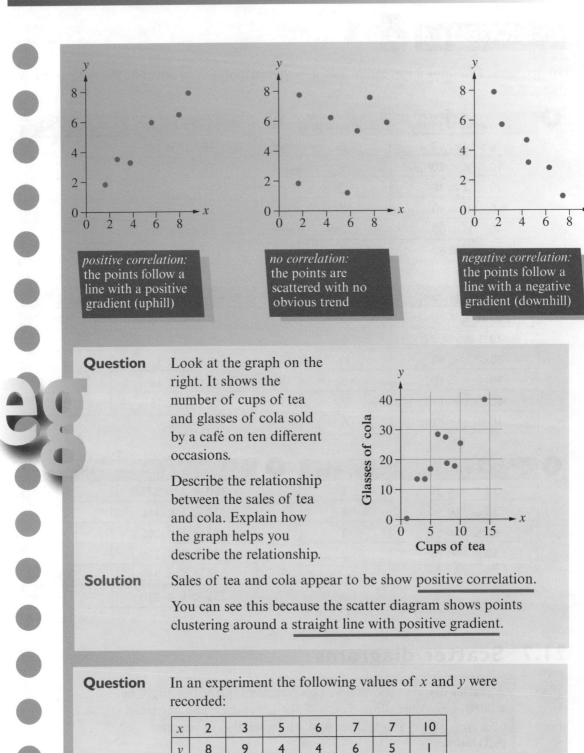

positive correlation:
the points follow a
line with a positive
gradient (uphill)

no correlation:
the points are
scattered with no
obvious trend

negative correlation:
the points follow a
line with a negative
gradient (downhill)

Question Look at the graph on the
right. It shows the
number of cups of tea
and glasses of cola sold
by a café on ten different
occasions.

Describe the relationship
between the sales of tea
and cola. Explain how
the graph helps you
describe the relationship.

Solution Sales of tea and cola appear to be show positive correlation.

You can see this because the scatter diagram shows points
clustering around a straight line with positive gradient.

Question In an experiment the following values of x and y were
recorded:

x	2	3	5	6	7	7	10
y	8	9	4	4	6	5	1

Plot these values on a scatter diagram. Describe the
relationship between x and y.

Solution

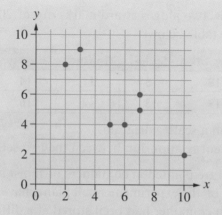

x and y appear to show negative correlation, as the trend line slopes downwards.

EXERCISE 21.7

In questions **1–5** draw coordinate axes and plot the given points. Say whether there is any evidence of correlation between x and y; if so, indicate whether it is positive or negative and whether you think the correlation is strong or weak.

1

x	1	8	4	12	8	9	2	5	7	✓
y	3	6	5	8	9	7	3	4	6	

2

x	2	7	5	3	3	9	6	✓
y	5	2	4	6	1	7	8	

3

x	2	3	3	6	6	10	10	12	✓
y	3	1	4	2	7	9	7	5	

4

x	2	4	4	6	8	9	✓
y	9	6	7	5	3	4	

5

x	2	7	10	5	7	4	9	2	✓
y	2	2	4	5	5	7	8	9	

6 In a 'Dog of the Year Show' two judges award marks out of 20 to each of eight dogs. The marks are given in the table below:

Dog	Fido	Crystal	Spike	Gnasher	d'Arcy	Spot	Lucky
Judge A	11	18	15	11	14	7	5
Judge B	13	19	13	12	16	4	8

a) Illustrate these marks on a scatter diagram.

b) Comment on the apparent relationship between the two sets of marks.

7 In an experiment ten seeds are planted in containers of moist soil and left for a period of time. At the end of the experiment small plants have developed, and their heights are measured. Each container had been stored at a different temperature: ✓

Plant	A	B	C	D	E	F	G	H	I	J
Temperature (°C)	5	10	12	14	16	18	20	22	24	25
Height (mm)	0	8	9	16	16	19	23	29	28	32

a) What do you think happened to Plant A?

b) Plot the results for the other nine plants on a scatter diagram. (Temperature on the *x*-axis and height on the *y*-axis.)

c) Comment on the relationship between height and temperature.

REVIEW EXERCISE 21

1 An outdoor pursuits centre spends £1080 on new equipment. £450 is spent on tents, £270 on rucksacks and £240 on waterproof clothing; the rest is spent on maps. Illustrate this expenditure in a pie chart.

2 A daily newspaper allows 40% of its space to be used for news, 25% for photographs and 35% for advertising. On Sundays the proportions change to 35% news, 15% photographs and 50% advertising. Draw two pie charts to illustrate the use of space in the daily and Sunday editions.

3 On a sports afternoon 42% of the school play hockey, 23% go cross-country running, 20% play squash and the rest swim. Illustrate this information with a pie chart.

4 A packet of coloured beads contains 23 red, 16 blue, 9 green and 14 yellow beads.
   a State the total number of beads in the packet.
   b Calculate the angles required for a pie chart to be drawn, rounding your answer to the nearest degree.
   c Construct the pie chart.

5 Mr Tughard is a dentist. He keeps a note of how many fillings 30 patients need:

```
1  0  0  1  2     1  2  0  0  1     3  0  1  2  1
1  0  1  1  3     0  1  2  1  1     0  0  1  1  0
```

   a Draw up a tally chart and find the total frequencies.
   b Display this data in a suitable type of line graph.

6 Four friends are comparing the number of CDs they own. Annabel has 22, Henrietta has 11, Daniel has 7 and David has 18. Using a key of 1 symbol to 5 CDs, draw a pie chart to show how many CDs the four friends have.

7 In the first three months of the new soccer season City won 3 matches, drew 4 and lost 4, Rovers won 7, drew 3 and lost 5, while United won 4, drew 2 and lost 11. Illustrate this data with a stacked bar chart.

8 Felicity is drawing a pie chart to show land use at a local farm. 40 acres are arable; this is represented by an angle of 30°. Dairy farming has an angle of 120°, and there are 120 acres of woodland.
   a How many acres are dairy?
   b What angle represents woodland?
   c How many acres does the farm have in total?

9 The data below shows the running time of twenty CD tracks, in minutes and seconds. For example, 2:33 indicates 2 minutes and 33 seconds.

2:08   3:00   3:25   2:24   5:22   3:25   2:08   3:13   4:46   3:06

4:50   3:07   2:24   3:15   2:55   3:21   6:57   0:39   2:04   3:47

a Draw up a tally chart, using $0 \leq t < 1$ and so on, where t is the running time in minutes.

b The random play function on my CD player chooses one of these tracks.
What is the probability that the track is over three minutes long?

10 During the last month I have seen 16 sparrows, 13 starlings, 5 blackbirds and 1 robin in my back garden. Illustrate this data with a pie chart.

11 ✳ Fifty-four people are asked how many hours of vigorous exercise they do per week, on average. Their replies are summarised in this table:

Time t spent exercising (hours)	Number of people
$0 \leq t < 1$	18
$1 \leq t < 2$	23
$2 \leq t < 3$	9
$3 \leq t < 4$	3
$4 \leq t < 5$	1

a Explain briefly whether it would be better to display this data in a pie chart or in a frequency polygon.

b Draw the appropriate diagram.

12 The table shows the scores achieved by eight Year 9 students in an algebra test. The test was divided into two parts, Paper 1 and Paper 2.

Paper 1	18	20	11	8	13	9	12	17
Paper 2	14	18	10	9	11	8	10	17

a Plot these scores on a scatter diagram, with Paper 1 scores along the x-axis and Paper 2 scores along the y-axis.

b Describe the relationship between the scores on the two papers.

c Joe scored 11 on Paper 1 but was absent for Paper 2 so he took it at home. Joe's Paper 2 was then marked to give a score of 19. Explain whether this score fits the rest of the data.

13 In an experiment the following results were obtained:

x	10	15	20	25	30	35	40
y	10	12	15	16	21	20	25

   a Plot the data on a scatter diagram.

   b Describe briefly how the quantities x and y appear to be related.

14 Tomi has been conducting an experiment into verbal and numerical skills. She gives two tests to a set of nine friends, with these results:

Verbal skills (x)	60	65	70	75	80	85	90	95	100
Numerical skills (y)	75	65	75	85	75	60	95	70	75

   a Plot the data on a scatter diagram.

   b Write down the conclusion which Tomi might make about how the verbal and numerical skills appear to be related.

15 ✳ The table shows approximate figures for the world's population at intervals of 100 years:

Year	1500	1600	1700	1800	1900
Population (millions)	425	545	610	900	1625

   a Draw a graph with the year plotted along the x-axis and population along the y-axis.

   b From your graph estimate the world's population in i 1550; ii 1750.

   c Explain briefly why it would be unwise to estimate the world's population in 1950 from this graph.

16 ✳ Andrei asks ten adults to tell him their age and shoe size (British units). Their replies are:

Age (years)	21	22	22	25	26	27	29	30	30	35
Shoe size	8	10	6	11	7	7	8	10	6	9

   a Display Andrei's data in a scatter diagram (age along the x-axis).

   b Comment briefly on whether there is any evidence of correlation between age and shoe size for Andrei's data.

   c Naomi asks ten members of her youth club to tell her their age and shoe size. Naomi says: 'There is very clear evidence of strong positive correlation between age and shoe size'.

   d Suggest a reason why Naomi's data shows strong correlation but Andrei's does not.

22 Probability

In this chapter you will learn how to:
- work with mutually exclusive outcomes
- construct tables to show the outcome of two experiments.

22.1 Mutually exclusive outcomes

If an experiment has several different outcomes, none of which can happen at the same time, then the outcomes are said to be **mutually exclusive**.

Question	A fair die is thrown. List all of the mutually exclusive outcomes. Hence find the probability that the score is a prime number.
Solution	There are six mutually exclusive outcomes:

1 2 3 4 5 6

The numbers 2, 3, 5 are prime (remember that 1 is not counted as a prime), so there are three primes out of the six numbers.

The probability of a prime is therefore $\frac{3}{6} = \frac{1}{2}$.

EXERCISE 22.1

1. A fair eight-sided die, marked with the whole numbers from 1 to 8, is thrown.
   a) Make a list of all the mutually exclusive outcomes.
   b) Find the probability that the score is a prime number.
   c) Find the probability that the score is a multiple of 3.

2. A letter is chosen at random from the first ten letters of the alphabet. ✓
   a) Make a list of all the mutually exclusive outcomes.
   b) Find the probability that the letter is a vowel.
   c) Find the probability that the letter is a not a G.

3 A computer selects a whole number at random from 50 to 60 inclusive.
 a) Make a list of all the mutually exclusive outcomes.
 b) Find the probability that the score is an even number.
 e) Find the probability that the score is a multiple of 5.

4 A month of the year is chosen at random.
 a) Write out, in full, the twelve mutually exclusive outcomes.
 b) Find the probability that there is an 'R' in the month.

5 A 20-sided die is labelled with the numbers from 1 to 20, and is then rolled once.
 a) Make a list of all the mutually exclusive outcomes.
 b) Find the probability that the score is a prime number.
 c) Find the probability that the score is a multiple of 10.
 d) Find the probability that the score is not divisible by 3.

22.2 The outcome of two experiments

The idea of listing all the mutually exclusive possibilities can be rather tedious, but is especially useful when you are combining the results of two experiments. A table can be a useful way of organising your work.

Question A spinner marked 1, 2, 3 is thrown and a coin is tossed.

a) Make a list of all six mutually exclusive outcomes.

b) Find the probability that the result is a 1 or 2 on the die and 'Heads' on the coin.

Solution a) The six outcomes are:
 (1, H) (2, H) (3, H) (1, T) (2, T) (3, T).

b) It follows that the probability of (1, H) or (2, H) must be
$\frac{2}{6} = \underline{\frac{1}{3}}$.

EXERCISE 22.2

1 An ordinary six-sided die is thrown, and a coin is tossed.

a) Make a list of the 12 mutually exclusive outcomes.

b) Find the probability that the result is a '3' on the die and a 'Heads' on the coin.

2 In my wardrobe I have three shirts, white, yellow and blue. I also have four ties, pink, purple, yellow and blue. I choose a shirt and a tie at random. ✓

a) Make a list of all the possible choices (there should be 12).

b) Find the probability that I pick a white shirt with a red tie.

c) Find the probability that my shirt and tie are the same colour.

3 Rod is queuing up for lunch at the school canteen. There are three choices of main course, pizza, casserole or salad, and two puddings, crumble or jelly.

a) List all the possible combinations that Rod might choose.

b) Work out the probability that his choice includes pizza.

c) Work out the probability that his choice includes jelly.

d) Find the probability that he chooses pizza and jelly together.

4 Four boys, Alistair, Bart, Clyde and Dipesh, and two girls, Flora and Gerri, go to a party. A dancing competition is announced, and the friends decide to enter a team of one boy and one girl, chosen randomly.

a) Make a list of the possible combinations.

b) Find the probability that Bart dances with Gerri.

5 Mr and Mrs Smith have a newborn baby daughter. They are not sure what to call her, but have narrowed the choice down: her first name will be Bethany, Elizabeth or Jennifer and her middle name will be Anne or Jane.

a) By listing all the possibilities, work out how many different combinations of first and middle name there are.

b) Find the probability that they name the child Bethany Jane. Assume the choice is made at random.

SUMMARY

- In this chapter you have learnt how to make lists of all the mutually exclusive outcomes for a combined experiment, e.g. (1, H) to denote a '1' on a die with a 'Heads' on a coin. This is a powerful way of solving problems based on two experiments, and will help to prepare you for sample space diagrams which you will meet in chapter 33.

REVIEW EXERCISE 22

1 A month of the year is chosen at random. Find the probability that it has 30 days.

2 The numbers from 15 to 30 inclusive are written on discs and placed in a bag for a fairground game. One disc is then chosen at random. An odd number wins a goldfish. A score of 20 wins a teddy bear.
   a Make a list of all the possible numbers.
   b Find the probability of winning a goldfish.
   c Find the probability of winning a teddy bear.

3 A letter is chosen at random from the first fifteen letters of the alphabet.
   a Write out a list of the 15 possible letters.
   b Find the probability that the chosen letter is one of the letters of the word APE.

4 A computer chooses an odd number at random between 90 and 100.
   a Write out a list of all the possible results.
   b Find the probability of getting a result of 91.
   c Find the probability that the chosen number is prime.

5 A six-sided die is thrown and a coin is tossed.
   a Write out all the possible combined outcomes.
   b Find the combined probability that the die shows an odd number and the coin shows a heads.

6 Ice creams are available in four flavours, vanilla, strawberry, chocolate or pistachio. There are also three toppings, nuts, chocolate or hot fudge.
   a Work out how many combinations of ice cream flavour and topping there are.
   b Roz orders a 'Lucky Dip', i.e. a random choice of ice cream and topping. Find the probability that she gets pistachio with hot fudge sauce.

7 The final score in a hockey match was 3–1. List all the possible half-time scores.

8 ✳ A fair coin is tossed three times. Find the probability that 'Heads' is obtained on all three tosses.

End of year review exercises

EXERCISE Y8.1

Do this exercise as mental arithmetic, do not write down any working.

1 Find the value of $(-5) - (-6)$.
2 Find the value of $8 + -3 - 7$.
3 Find the value of $12 - 3 \times 2$.
4 Find the value of $-24 \div -8$
5 Add together 17.56 and 8.74.
6 Work out $57.09 - 28.66$.
7 Find the lowest common multiple of 12 and 18.
8 Express 10 as a fraction of 15.
9 Express 13 as a percentage of 20.
10 Write 0.6 as a percentage.
11 Write 108% as a decimal.
12 Express the ratio $25:15$ in its simplest form.
13 Simplify $15a - 11b + 4a$.
14 Simplify $7 \times y \times y + 11 \times y \times y$.
15 Write down the gradient of the line $y = 3x + 7$.
16 Write down the intercept of the line $y = 2x - 13$.
17 True or false: the number of words on a page of a book is discrete.
18 True or false: the mass of a pencil is discrete.
19 True or false: if you multiply a positive number by 0.8 then it gets bigger.
20 True or false: if you divide a positive number by 0.5 then it gets smaller.

EXERCISE Y8.2

You should show all necessary working for this exercise.

1 Last year my car insurance cost £340; this year it is 20% more. Find this year's cost.
2 Shares which were worth 250 pence each have fallen to 90% of their value. Find the new value of the shares.
3 £24 is to be shared out in the ratio $5:3$. Find the value of the larger share.

4 A triangle has a base of 16 cm and a height of 10 cm. Find its area.

5 A square has sides of length 9 cm. Find its area.

6 A rectangle measures 12 cm by 5 cm. What is its area?

7 A trapezium has parallel sides of lengths 10 cm and 16 cm. The perpendicular distance between them is 10 cm. Find the area of the trapezium.

8 A fair die is rolled. Find the probability that the score is:

 a 6

 b 4, 5 or 6.

9 A card is chosen at random from an ordinary pack of 52. Find the probability that it is an Ace.

10 A spinner has three faces, labelled 1, 2, 3. It is spun twice. By listing all the possible combinations of results, find the probability of getting a score of 3 on both spins.

EXERCISE Y8.3

You should show all necessary working for this exercise.

1 Write 84 as a product of prime factors.

2 Find the highest common factor of 72 and 96.

3 Find the lowest common multiple of 21 and 28.

4 Work out 14.6×3.

5 Work out $177.8 \div 7$.

6 Work out 16.3×4.3.

7 Work out $78.68 \div 1.4$.

8 Find 80% of 500.

9 2 electricians can rewire 3 houses in 5 days. How long will it take 10 electricians to rewire 12 houses?

10 Simplify $5(x + 6)$.

11 Simplify $3(x + 2) + 2(3x - 1)$.

12 Find the missing angles represented by letter in these diagrams. Give a brief reason in each case.

13 Draw a coordinate grid in which x and y can run from 0 to 10.

   a Plot the points (1, 1), (3, 5) and (5, 3), and join them up to form a triangle.

   b Enlarge the triangle by ×2, using the origin as the centre of enlargement.

14 In triangle ABC, AB = 8 cm and BC = 7 cm. The angle ABC between these sides is 55°.

   a Using ruler and protractor, construct an accurate scale drawing of the triangle.

   b Use your drawing to find the length of BC, correct to the nearest 0.1 cm.

15 In triangle PQR, PQ = 12 cm, PR = 8 cm, QR = 7 cm.

   a Using a ruler and compasses, construct an accurate scale drawing of the triangle.

   b Use your drawing to find the values of the angles in the triangle.

16 Using a ruler and pencil, mark two points A and B so that B is 8.5 cm to the right of A. Now, using compasses and a straight edge, construct the perpendicular bisector of the line AB.

17 Using a ruler and protractor, construct an angle of 84°. Now using compasses and a straight edge, construct the angle bisector of this angle. Check the accuracy of your construction by measuring the bisected angle with your protractor.

18 The diagonals of a rhombus are of lengths 24 cm and 10 cm. Find its area.

19 The diagram below shows a sketch of a compound shape. Break it into smaller pieces, and hence find its area.

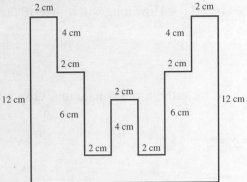

20 The daytime temperature on Mercury reaches 330°C, and at night it falls to −180°C. Find the difference between the daytime and night-time temperatures.

EXERCISE Y8.4

1 Write $4\frac{5}{7}$ as a decimal, correct to 4 decimal places.

2 Write 0.245 as a fraction in its lowest terms.

3 Increase £240 by 23%.

4 A television set costs £528.75 including VAT at 17.5%. What was the price before VAT was added?

5 Last year Janet was earning £1300 a month, and John was earning £1400 a month. This year Janet's pay has increased by 16% and John's has increased by 8%. Find out who is the higher earner this year, and by how much.

6 Find the value of $16a^2 - 11a$ when $a = 2.5$.

7 Draw a set of coordinate axes in which x and y can run from -10 to 10. Plot the graph of $y = 2x + 1$, and give the value of x when y is:

  a 2

  b -2.

8 Prove that the angles in a quadrilateral add up to 360°. (Hint: you may assume that the angles in a triangle add up to 180°.)

9 The diagram shows an object and its image after enlargement. Make a copy of this diagram on squared paper, and use it to find:

  a the coordinates of the centre of enlargement

  b the scale factor of the enlargement.

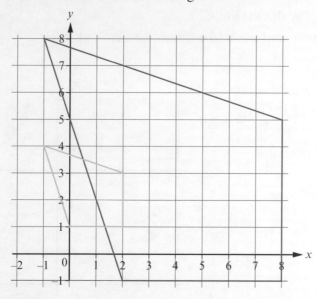

10 A cuboid measures 5 cm by 9 cm by 13 cm.
   a Find its volume.
   b Find the total surface area of all six of its faces.

11 18 children took part in a survey about hair colour. 10 had brown hair, 3 black, 3 blonde and 2 auburn.
   Display this information in a pie chart.

12 A newspaper carries out a survey about watching TV in which 4000 people are asked to state their favourite type of programme. The results are:

   Soaps/sitcoms   35%
   Sports   27%
   News   18%
   Other   20%

   a Display this information in a pie chart.
   b What size angle corresponds to Sports?
   c How many people stated that their favourite type of programme is News?

13 Ted is recording the depth of water at the end of a pier at hourly intervals. Here are his results:

Time	1400	1500	1600	1700
Depth (metres)	4.75	3.8	2.9	2.4

   a Explain whether it is better to draw a vertical line graph or a time series graph to display this information.
   b Construct your graph, and use it to estimate the depth of water at 4:30 p.m.

14 Look at these four scatter diagrams. Write down the letter of the one which shows:
   a strong positive correlation
   b no correlation
   c weak negative correlation.

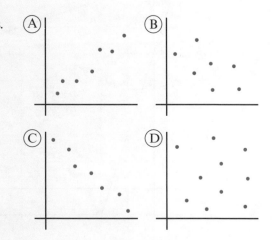

23 Working with fractions

In this chapter you will learn how to:
- add and subtract fractions, using a common denominator
- multiply two fractions, without a calculator
- divide one fraction by another, without a calculator
- perform arithmetic with mixed fractions
- solve problems using fractions.

23.1 Adding and subtracting fractions

Sometimes you will need to add or subtract two fractions. If they already have the same denominator (bottom number) then there is no problem.

Question   Add $\frac{3}{11} + \frac{5}{11}$.

Solution $\frac{3}{11} + \frac{5}{11}$

$= \frac{3+5}{11}$

$= \frac{8}{11}$

> First, check the denominators: 11 and 11. Since they are both the same, you can just add 3 and 5 to get 8 for the final numerator (top number).
> Note that the bottom stays as 11, you don't add the two 11s together.

If the denominators are not the same, you have to use the idea of equivalent fractions, and rewrite them as necessary. This example shows how you might need to rewrite one fraction.

Question   Add $\frac{2}{5} + \frac{3}{10}$.

Solution   First, we have to change $\frac{2}{5}$ into an equivalent fraction with 10 in the bottom.

$\frac{2}{5}$ is equivalent to $\frac{4}{10}$.

Therefore $\frac{2}{5} + \frac{3}{10}$

$= \frac{4}{10} + \frac{3}{10}$

$= \frac{4+3}{10}$

$= \frac{7}{10}$

> You need to change $\frac{2}{5}$ into $\frac{*}{10}$.
> 5 needs to be multiplied by 2 to make 10.
> Therefore 2 is multiplied by 2 as well, to make 4.
> So $\frac{2}{5}$ is equivalent to $\frac{4}{10}$.

In more difficult cases you might have to rewrite **both** fractions, by looking for the **lowest common denominator**. This next example shows you how.

Question   Find $\frac{3}{4} - \frac{2}{7}$.

Solution   First, look at the two denominators. They are 4 and 7.

The smallest number that both 4 and 7 go into exactly is $4 \times 7 = 28$.

So rewrite $\frac{3}{4}$ as $\frac{21}{28}$ and rewrite $\frac{2}{7}$ as $\frac{8}{28}$.

Therefore $\frac{3}{4} - \frac{2}{7}$

$= \frac{21}{28} - \frac{8}{28}$

$= \frac{21-8}{28}$

$= \frac{13}{28}$

Finally, you might find that the answer can be cancelled down. This last example shows how it works, but remember that this won't happen in every question you do.

Question   Find $\frac{5}{6} - \frac{11}{15}$.

Solution   First, look at the two denominators. They are 6 and 15.
The smallest number that both 6 and 15 go into exactly is 30.

So rewrite $\frac{5}{6}$ as $\frac{25}{30}$ and rewrite $\frac{11}{15}$ as $\frac{22}{30}$.

Therefore $\frac{5}{6} - \frac{11}{15}$

$= \frac{25}{30} - \frac{22}{30}$

$= \frac{25-22}{30}$

$= \frac{3}{30}$ This answer can be cancelled down, because 3 goes into both 3 and 30.

$= \frac{1}{10}$

EXERCISE 23.1

1 Work out the value of each of the following. Remember to show all of the steps in your working.

a) $\frac{3}{7} + \frac{2}{7}$ ✓   b) $\frac{5}{13} + \frac{7}{13}$ c) $\frac{10}{11} - \frac{4}{11}$

d) $\frac{5}{12} + \frac{1}{4}$ ✓   e) $\frac{3}{8} + \frac{1}{2}$ f) $\frac{9}{10} - \frac{3}{5}$ g) $\frac{1}{3} + \frac{1}{2}$ h) $\frac{2}{5} + \frac{1}{4}$

i) $\frac{17}{20} - \frac{3}{4}$ j) $\frac{17}{18} - \frac{2}{3}$ k) $\frac{2}{5} + \frac{1}{6}$ l) $\frac{1}{6} + \frac{4}{9}$ m) $\frac{5}{8} - \frac{1}{6}$

n) $\frac{19}{20} - \frac{2}{3}$ ✓   o) $\frac{5}{14} + \frac{4}{21}$

2 Add together four-sevenths and two-ninths.

3 One morning Susie eats one-third of a bag of sweets, and in the afternoon she eats another two-fifths. What fraction of the bag has she eaten altogether?

4 In a youth club one-eighth of the members are boys aged 9 or under, and three-fifths are boys aged over 9. What fraction of the youth club members are boys? ✓

5 During a Duke of Edinburgh expedition Simon has to walk for three days. On the first day he covers two-ninths of the total journey, and on the second day he covers one-third.
a) What fraction of the total journey does Simon cover during the first two days?
b) What fraction needs to be covered on the third day?
c) On which day does he cover the largest part of the journey?

6 In Greenview School there is a Reception Class, an Infants School and a Junior School. Three-tenths of the children are in the Infants school, and one-half are in the Junior School. What fraction are in the Reception Class?

23.2 Multiplying two fractions

To multiply two fractions, you multiply the two top numbers (numerators) and multiply the two bottom numbers (denominators). There is no need to work with common denominators.

Question   Multiply $\frac{3}{4}$ by $\frac{5}{7}$

Solution $\frac{3}{4} \times \frac{5}{7} = \frac{3 \times 5}{4 \times 7}$

$= \frac{15}{28}$

Sometimes the working may be simplified by cancelling a common factor before multiplying. The next example illustrates this.

Question   Multiply $\frac{4}{7}$ by $\frac{5}{8}$.

Solution $\frac{4}{7} \times \frac{5}{8} = \frac{\cancel{4}^{1}}{7} \times \frac{5}{\cancel{8}_{2}}$

$$= \frac{1 \times 5}{7 \times 2}$$

$$= \frac{5}{14}$$

Sometimes you may need to multiply a fraction by a whole number.
You can just write the whole number as a fraction with denominator 1.

Question   Find the value of $\frac{3}{20} \times 5$

Solution $\frac{3}{20} \times 5 = \frac{3}{20} \times \frac{5}{1}$

$$= \frac{3}{\overset{}{\underset{4}{20}}} \times \frac{\overset{1}{\cancel{5}}}{1}$$

$$= \frac{3}{4}$$

EXERCISE 23.2

Work out the value of each of the following, showing your working clearly.

1 $\frac{2}{3} \times \frac{5}{7}$ **6** $\frac{3}{8} \times \frac{2}{3}$ **11** $\frac{1}{4} \times \frac{1}{5}$ **16** $\frac{5}{6} \times \frac{8}{15}$

2 $\frac{3}{5} \times \frac{2}{11}$ ✓   **7** $\frac{5}{6} \times \frac{8}{9}$ **12** $\frac{1}{8} \times \frac{1}{8}$ **17** $\frac{16}{25} \times \frac{5}{8}$

3 $\frac{5}{6} \times \frac{3}{4}$ **8** $\frac{2}{3} \times \frac{3}{10}$ **13** $\frac{4}{15} \times \frac{3}{20}$ **18** $\frac{3}{7} \times \frac{1}{6}$

4 $\frac{5}{9} \times 6$ **9** $\frac{3}{4} \times \frac{14}{15}$ ✓   **14** $\frac{5}{11} \times \frac{3}{10}$ **19** $\frac{5}{12} \times \frac{8}{15}$ ✓

5 $\frac{4}{5} \times \frac{5}{8}$ **10** $\frac{17}{20} \times 10$ **15** $\frac{2}{3} \times \frac{3}{8}$ **20** $\frac{13}{14} \times \frac{4}{5}$

23.3 Dividing one fraction by another

To divide one fraction by another, just turn the second fraction
upside down, then multiply. Any cancelling must be done only after
the second fraction has been turned over.

Question   Divide $\frac{3}{10}$ by $\frac{9}{11}$

Solution $\frac{3}{10} \div \frac{9}{11} = \frac{3}{10} \times \frac{11}{9}$

$$= \frac{\overset{1}{\cancel{3}}}{10} \times \frac{11}{\underset{3}{\cancel{9}}}$$

$$= \frac{11}{30}$$

EXERCISE 23.3

Work out these divisions, without a calculator. Show your working clearly.

1 $\frac{7}{8} \div \frac{9}{10}$ ✓

4 $\frac{5}{8} \div 3$

7 $\frac{9}{16} \div \frac{3}{4}$ ✓

10 $\frac{5}{7} \div 3$

2 $\frac{4}{7} \div \frac{4}{5}$

5 $\frac{4}{7} \div \frac{2}{3}$

8 $\frac{5}{8} \div \frac{5}{6}$

3 $\frac{4}{5} \div 2$

6 $\frac{1}{3} \div \frac{5}{6}$

9 $\frac{1}{4} \div \frac{3}{10}$

23.4 Adding and subtracting mixed fractions

A mixed fraction contains a whole number and a fractional part.
To add or subtract mixed fractions you should try to work with the
whole numbers separately from the fractions, as much as possible.

Question Find $5\frac{3}{4} + 3\frac{2}{3}$

Solution $5\frac{3}{4} + 3\frac{2}{3} = 8 + \frac{3}{4} + \frac{2}{3}$

First of all, add the two whole numbers, 5 and 3, to get 8.

$= 8 + \frac{9}{12} + \frac{8}{12}$

$= 8 + \frac{17}{12}$

Next, add the two fractions, using a common denominator of 12, to get $\frac{17}{12}$.

$= 8 + 1\frac{5}{12}$

$= 9\frac{5}{12}$

$\frac{17}{12}$ is 'top heavy' so it is converted into $1\frac{5}{12}$ before combining with the 8 to finish.

Some subtraction problems require an 'exchange', in which a whole
unit is converted into a fraction. The next worked example shows you
how this is done.

Question Find $7\frac{1}{4} - 2\frac{2}{3}$

Solution $7\frac{1}{4} - 2\frac{2}{3} = 5 + \frac{1}{4} - \frac{2}{3}$

$\frac{1}{4}$ is smaller than $\frac{2}{3}$ so this subtraction cannot be done directly.

$= 4 + 1\frac{1}{4} - \frac{2}{3}$

$= 4 + \frac{5}{4} - \frac{2}{3}$

$= 4 + \frac{15}{12} - \frac{8}{12}$

The trick here is to reduce the 5 to 4, and include the extra 1 in with the $\frac{1}{4}$ to make $\frac{5}{4}$.

$= 4 + \frac{7}{12}$

$= 4\frac{7}{12}$

EXERCISE 23.4

Work out the values of these additions and subtractions.

1 $3\frac{1}{2} + 2\frac{1}{4}$ **6** $3\frac{1}{4} - 1\frac{1}{2}$ **11** $5\frac{5}{9} + 2\frac{2}{3}$ ✓   **16** $5\frac{1}{2} - 1\frac{7}{8}$

2 $1\frac{5}{8} + 1\frac{1}{4}$ ✓   **7** $10\frac{1}{2} + 5\frac{3}{4}$ **12** $4\frac{1}{9} - 1\frac{1}{2}$ ✓   **17** $9\frac{1}{2} + 19\frac{3}{4}$

3 $3\frac{2}{3} + 2\frac{5}{6}$ **8** $2\frac{2}{3} + 1\frac{1}{2}$ **13** $5\frac{1}{3} + 3\frac{2}{3}$ **18** $10\frac{1}{4} - 7\frac{7}{8}$

4 $4\frac{1}{2} - 1\frac{1}{4}$ **9** $5\frac{1}{2} - 3\frac{1}{10}$ **14** $4\frac{3}{10} + 1\frac{1}{2}$ **19** $14\frac{2}{3} + 1\frac{1}{2}$

5 $5\frac{2}{3} - 1\frac{1}{6}$ ✓   **10** $4\frac{1}{10} - 2\frac{1}{2}$ **15** $2\frac{2}{3} - \frac{3}{4}$ **20** $3\frac{1}{4} - 2\frac{9}{10}$

23.5 Multiplying and dividing with mixed fractions

In order to multiply or divide mixed fractions you **must** convert them to top-heavy (improper) fractions first. You may need to convert back to mixed number form again at the end.

Question	Find $1\frac{3}{4} \times 2\frac{2}{3}$
Solution	$1\frac{3}{4} \times 2\frac{2}{3} = \frac{7}{4} \times \frac{8}{3}$
	$= \frac{7}{\cancel{4}_1} \times \frac{\cancel{8}^2}{3}$
	$= \frac{14}{3}$
	$= 4\frac{2}{3}$

EXERCISE 23.5

Work out the answers to these multiplication and division problems.

1 $1\frac{1}{3} \times 1\frac{1}{8}$ **6** $1\frac{1}{2} \div 1\frac{1}{2}$

2 $3\frac{1}{5} \times 1\frac{3}{8}$ ✓   **7** $2\frac{1}{2} \times 1\frac{1}{5}$

3 $1\frac{1}{2} \times 1\frac{1}{2}$ **8** $1\frac{1}{2} \times 2\frac{1}{3}$

4 $1\frac{2}{3} \div 1\frac{3}{7}$ **9** $1\frac{3}{7} \div 1\frac{1}{7}$

5 $2\frac{1}{10} \div 1\frac{2}{5}$ ✓   **10** $2\frac{3}{4} \div 1\frac{1}{8}$

SUMMARY

- In this chapter you have learnt how to carry out addition, subtraction, multiplication and division of fractions, without a calculator. Remember to look for opportunities to cancel when multiplying. When multiplying or dividing mixed fractions, always convert the fractions into top-heavy (improper) fractions first. If the final answer is a top heavy fraction it should then be converted back into mixed fraction form.

REVIEW EXERCISE 23

1 Work out these additions and subtractions.

a $\frac{3}{11} + \frac{4}{11}$ b $\frac{5}{8} + \frac{1}{8}$ c $\frac{3}{4} + \frac{1}{8}$ d $\frac{5}{8} + \frac{1}{2}$ e $\frac{4}{11} - \frac{3}{11}$ f $\frac{3}{4} - \frac{1}{8}$

g $\frac{7}{10} - \frac{1}{2}$ h $\frac{5}{6} - \frac{2}{5}$ i $\frac{9}{10} + \frac{2}{3}$ j $\frac{3}{14} - \frac{1}{7}$

2 Work out these multiplications and divisions.

a $\frac{5}{8} \times \frac{3}{8}$ b $\frac{4}{5} \times \frac{5}{6}$ c $\frac{2}{9} \times \frac{3}{4}$ d $\frac{1}{3} \div \frac{1}{2}$ e $\frac{3}{8} \div \frac{5}{8}$

f $\frac{1}{2} \div \frac{4}{5}$ g $\frac{1}{10} \times \frac{1}{10}$ h $\frac{1}{5} \div \frac{1}{5}$ i $\frac{5}{7} \times \frac{3}{10}$ j $\frac{3}{10} \div \frac{8}{9}$

3 Work out these mixed fraction problems.

a $1\frac{1}{4} + 3\frac{1}{3}$ b $4\frac{2}{3} + 5\frac{5}{6}$ c $8\frac{3}{4} - 2\frac{2}{5}$ d $6\frac{1}{4} - 5\frac{2}{3}$ e $3\frac{1}{3} \times 1\frac{1}{5}$

f $1\frac{2}{7} \times 4\frac{2}{3}$ g $2\frac{1}{2} \div 1\frac{2}{3}$ h $1\frac{5}{7} \div 1\frac{6}{7}$

4 Find the values of each of these.

a $2\frac{5}{7} + 3\frac{2}{7}$ b $4\frac{3}{4} - \frac{9}{10}$ c $1\frac{7}{8} \times 1\frac{1}{5}$ d $4\frac{2}{3} \div 1\frac{1}{6}$ e $1\frac{2}{3} + 2\frac{2}{5}$

f $6\frac{1}{3} - 2\frac{1}{2}$ g $2\frac{1}{2} \times 3\frac{1}{2}$ h $1\frac{1}{9} \div 6\frac{2}{3}$

5 ✳ In the following, the symbol ♣ stands for a missing process – either +, –, × or ÷. Decide which.

a $5\frac{1}{2}$ ♣ $1\frac{3}{4} = 3\frac{3}{4}$ b $2\frac{1}{2}$ ♣ $3\frac{1}{5} = 8$ c $2\frac{2}{3}$ ♣ $3\frac{3}{4} = 6\frac{5}{12}$

d $1\frac{5}{6}$ ♣ $1\frac{1}{5} = 2\frac{1}{5}$

24 Ratio and proportion

OUTLINE

In this chapter you will revise:
- solving problems using ratio.

You will then learn how to:
- solve problems on proportion using ratios
- solve problems on proportion using an algebraic method.

24.1 Ratio

A **ratio** is a set of two (or more) numbers showing how something is divided up into portions. Sometimes ratios may be written in their lowest terms, rather like fractions.

Question   In class 5B at Greenview School there are 14 boys and 18 girls. Write the ratio of boys to girls in its simplest terms.

Solution   The ratio is 14 : 18

= 7 : 9

The symbol 14 : 18 is read as '14 to 18'. Since both 14 and 18 are multiples of 2 you can cancel these numbers down to 7 and 9.

On other occasions ratios are written in the form 1 : *n* or *n* : 1.

Question   An office photocopier can make copies which are larger or smaller than the original. Fiona enlarges a diagram which was 12 cm long; it is now 18 cm long. Write this as a ratio
a) in its simplest form using whole numbers;
b) in the form 1 : *n* where *n* is a decimal fraction.

Solution   The ratio is 12 : 18
= 2 : 3

Now divide both numbers by 2, to get a ratio of 1 : something.
So 2 : 3 = 1 : 1.5

EXERCISE 24.1

1 Write these as ratios in their simplest form, using whole numbers.

   a) 6 : 8   b) 16 : 20   c) 12 : 30   d) 25 : 35   e) 25 : 75

   f) 28 : 35   g) 32 : 40   h) 34 : 51 ✓

2 Write these ratios in the form 1 : n, where n is a decimal number greater than one.

   a) 4 : 5   b) 2 : 7   c) 10 : 17   d) 5 : 9

3 Write these ratios in the form n : 1, where n is a decimal number greater than one.

   a) 7 : 4   b) 11 : 5   c) 21 : 10   d) 5 : 2

24.2 Dividing an amount in a given ratio

Sometimes we need to divide up an amount according to a given ratio. The method is to add up all the parts of the ratio first, and find the value of one 'share'. Then multiply this up to solve the problem.

Question   Josh is 13 years old and Sam is 12. They are given 100 stamps for their collection, and they decide to share them out in the ratio of their ages. How many stamps does each of them receive?

Solution   The ratio is 13 : 12

13 + 12 = 25

Divide 100 up into 25 'shares':

100 ÷ 25 = 4

and so 1 share is equal to 4 stamps.

> The key step is to take the ratio 13 : 12 and work out 13 + 12 = 25. Then divide 25 into the total of 100 stamps, to get 4 stamps.
> Finally multiply 4 stamps by the age of each boy to find out how many stamps each gets.

Therefore Josh gets 13 × 4 = 52 stamps.

Sam gets 12 × 4 = 48 stamps.

EXERCISE 24.2

1 £18 is to be divided in the ratio 5 : 4. Work out the size of each part.

2 A cake weighing 450 grams is to be divided into two parts in the ratio 7 : 8. Work out the weight of each part. ✓

3 253 marbles are to be divided in the ratio 7 : 4. Work out the size of each part.

4 A photographer examines 108 pictures taken at a wedding. The ratio of good pictures to failures is 7 : 2. Work out how many pictures were good, and how many were failures.

5 A factory makes red cars and blue cars in the ratio 3 : 5. Last week it produced a total of 96 cars in these two colours. Calculate the number of cars of each colour which were made last week.

6 Two girls share 60 sweets in the ratio 5 : 7. Work out how many sweets each girl gets.

7 A stick 1 m long is to be cut into two parts so that their lengths are in the ratio 3 : 7. Find the length of the shorter part. ✓

8 Gregory wants to mix three chemicals, A, B, C, in the ratio 2 : 3 : 5. He wants to make 400 grams of the mixture altogether. How much of chemical A does he need?

9 A box of fireworks contains bangers and rockets in the ratio of 5 : 2. If there are 21 fireworks altogether, how many of them are bangers?

10 The books in Greenview School Library are classed either as fiction or non-fiction. The librarian calculates that there are 10 fiction books for every 22 non-fiction.
a) Write this ratio in its simplest form.
b) Calculate the number of each type of book, if the library has 2400 books altogether.

24.3 Direct proportion

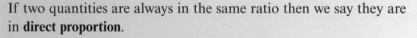

If two quantities are always in the same ratio then we say they are in **direct proportion**.

The rule $y = 2x$ is an example of direct proportion, since y is always twice the size of x. In this case the number 2 is called the **constant of proportionality**.

Question   The cost of a school trip is directly proportional to the number of pupils who attend. If 50 pupils attend the trip then the cost is £80. Find the cost if 90 pupils attend.

This problem can be solved either by a ratio method or by using algebra.

Here is the solution using ratios:

Solution   The ratio of pupils : cost is 50 : 80 = 5 : 8.

We want this to become 90 : something if 90 pupils attend.

Ratio	5	8
$\times 18$		
	90	?

5 must be multiplied by 18 to turn into 90 (that is 90 ÷ 5 = 18).

So 8 must be multiplied by 18 as well.

The cost is 8 × 18 = £144.

Alternatively, here is the solution using algebra:

Solution   Let the cost be c, for a number of pupils n.

Then $c = kn$

When $n = 50$, $c = 80$.

Therefore $80 = k \times 50$, so $k = 80 \div 50 = 1.6$

Since the constant of proportionality is 1.6 we can now write

$c = 1.6n$

Thus for 90 pupils, $n = 90$, giving

$c = 1.6 \times 90$

$= £144$

> The first step is to describe the relationship between c and n using a formula, $c = kn$
>
> Next, use the given numbers to find the value of k.
>
> Finally, now you know the formula, use it to solve the problem.

EXERCISE 24.3

Solve these problems about direct proportion. You may choose to use either a method based on ratios or an algebraic method.

1. The mass of a piece of steel pipe is directly proportional to its length. A piece 80 cm long has a mass of 5 kg. Find the mass of a piece of pipe 200 cm long.

2. The cost of placing an advertisement in a magazine is directly proportional to the number of lines it takes up. An advertisement of 5 lines will cost 80 pence. Find the cost of an advertisement of 12 lines. ✓

3. A tank is being filled with water. The depth of the water is directly proportional to the time for which the tap has been running. Ten minutes after the start the water is 30 cm deep. How deep will it be 25 minutes after the start?

4. A minibus is driving along a stretch of motorway. The distance it travels is proportional to the time for which it has been travelling. In 20 minutes it travels 30 kilometres. How far will it travel in 30 minutes?

5. My video player has a counter. The number of counts showing is proportional to the time for which the tape has been running. After 30 minutes the counter reads 2400. What will be the reading on the counter after 75 minutes?

6. The cost of fitting a new floor to a room is directly proportional to the area of the floor. An area of 10 square metres would cost £250. Find the cost of fitting a new floor to a room whose area is:
   a) 35 square metres
   b) 8 square metres.

7. A photographer copies a photograph measuring 6 inches by 4 inches, and enlarges it until the short side has become 10 inches. Find the length of the long side in the enlargement.

8. Peter claims that the time it takes to do his paper round is directly proportional to the number of papers he has to deliver. Here is some data about his paper round last week:

	Monday to Friday	Saturday
Time taken	2 hours	3 hours
Number of papers delivered	80	120

   a) Explain how the data in the table supports Peter's claim.
   b) On Sunday Peter has to deliver 70 papers. Calculate the time taken, assuming his claim remains true.

- In this chapter you have revised simple problems on proportion, using methods based on ratio.

- You have also solved problems on direct proportion, using algebra. This is a powerful method, and may be very helpful when you come to do an investigational coursework as part of your GCSE preparation.

REVIEW EXERCISE 24

1 Write these ratios in their simplest form, using whole numbers:
   a 14 : 18 **b** 44 : 33   **c** 12 : 30   **d** 14 : 21   **e** 20 : 25   **f** 18 : 21
   g 38 : 57   **h** 95 : 90

2 Write these ratios in the form 1 : *n* or *n* : 1, where *n* is a decimal number bigger than 1:
   a 5 : 8   **b** 2 : 3   **c** 4 : 9   **d** 13 : 10   **e** 11 : 4   **f** 11 : 5
   g 10 : 19   **h** 17 : 2

3 A piece of string 200 cm long is to be divided into two pieces in the ratio 2 : 3. Find the length of each piece.

4 A mathematics exam paper is to be divided into two sections, A and B. The marks available in each section should be in the ratio 4 : 5 and the exam should be out of 45 marks altogether. How many marks should be available for section A?

5 The ratio of boys to girls in a school is 8 : 5. There are 496 boys.
   a Calculate the number of girls in the school.
   b Hence calculate the total number of children in the school.

6 Each day Caspar reckons the ratio of the time he spends asleep to the time awake is 3 : 5. If he is right, how much time does Caspar spend asleep each day?

7 An old cookery book says that the time for which I cook a turkey should be directly proportional to its weight. A turkey weighing 6 pounds should be cooked for 2 hours. How long should I cook a turkey weighing 14 pounds?

8 The time it takes a teacher to mark a pile of exam papers is directly proportional to the number of papers. On Wednesday she marks 25 papers in $2\frac{1}{2}$ hours.

a How long does it take her to mark 42 papers on Thursday?

b On Friday she marks for $3\frac{1}{2}$ hours. How many papers does she mark?

9 The cost of buying a necklace with your name on it is directly proportional to the number of letters in your name. Sarah buys such a necklace and has to pay £2.40. How much does her sister Rosalind have to pay for one?

10 A cereal manufacturer decides that the cost of a packet of cereal should be directly proportional to the amount of cereal inside. A 375 g box costs £1.99. Calculate the price you think they should charge for a 500 g box.

11 ✳ On an orange squash bottle it says, 'Add 1 part of squash to 7 parts of water'. How much water would I need to make up 400 ml of drink?

12 ✳ My television can be set to display a picture in a *widescreen* 16 : 9 format, when the width and height are in the ratio of 16 : 9. If the programme being broadcast is not suitable for widescreen viewing then I select a *standard* 4 : 3 format instead. In either format the height of the picture is unchanged at 36 cm.

a Calculate the width of the picture when I am watching:

i in *widescreen* format   ii in *standard* format.

b Calculate the ratio of the *standard* width to the *widescreen* width, giving your answer as a ratio of whole numbers in its simplest form.

13 ✳ In a certain country the voting system is based on proportional representation. This means that the number of seats for any given political party is proportional to the number of votes they gained in the last election. There are 110 seats available in total.

	People's Party	Democratic Party	New Socialist Party	Raving Monster Party
Number of votes	12 250	16 000	9500	395
Number of seats				

a Copy and complete the table, showing how many seats each party should get.

b Do your answers add up to 110?

25 Rounding and approximation

OUTLINE

In this chapter you will learn how to:
- round numbers off to a number of decimal places or significant figures
- estimate the answers to numerical calculations
- solve problems using trial and improvement methods.

25.1 Decimal places and significant figures

Decimal places are the figures that occur after the decimal point.

Question Write these numbers correct to 3 decimal places:

a) 14.5631   b) 0.205 817   c) 2.009 84

Solution a) 14.563|1
This will round to
14.563 correct to 3 d.p.

> If this figure is 4 or less then we round down and if it is 5 or more we round up.

b) 0.205|817
This will round to
0.206 correct to 3 d.p.

c) 2.009|84
This will round to
2.010 correct to 3 d.p.

> **Warning!** It would be a mistake to write 2.01 as this would suggest that you don't know very much about the third decimal place.

Significant figures are the figures that give information about place value. Significant figures are counted from the left. For whole numbers you stop counting when a final block of zeroes is encountered, but for decimals you must keep counting until the last decimal place, even if it is a zero.

Question Write these numbers correct to 3 significant figures:

a) 19 245   b) 207 740   c) 0.007 087   d) 0.088 966

Solution a) 19 2|45
This will round to
19 200 correct to 3 s.f.

> If this figure is 4 or less then we round down...

b) 207|740
This will round to
208 000 correct to 3 s.f.

... and if this figure is 5 or more we round up.

c) 0.007 08|7
This will round to
0.007 09 correct to 3 s.f.

The zeroes in 0.00 do not count as significant figures, they just make the figures that follow occur in the correct columns. The zero in 708 does count as a significant figure.

d) 0.088 9|66
This will round to
0.0890 correct to 3 s.f.

Do not write 0.089, this would only be 2 s.f.

EXERCISE 25.1

1 Round these correct to two significant figures.

a) 157 ✓   b) 24 677   c) 599   d) 176 206

2 Round these correct to one significant figure.

a) 41 207 ✓   b) 259   c) 1094   d) 108

3 Round each of these numbers to the given number of decimal places.

a) 13.562 (1 d.p.)   b) 104.849 (1 d.p.) ✓   c) 3.0671 (2 d.p.)

d) 88.2219 (3 d.p.)   e) 16.4587 (2 d.p.)   f) 12.204 (2 d.p.) ✓

4 Round each of these numbers to the given number of significant figures.

a) 3.14159 (4 s.f.)   b) 60.2544 (3 s.f.)   c) 17.281 901 (3 s.f.)

d) 46.204 (4 s.f.) ✓   e) 14.2247 (3 s.f.)   f) 0.002 034 (3 s.f.)

25.2 Estimating the answer to a calculation

To obtain an estimate of the answer to a calculation:
round off all the numbers to one significant figure; then do the
calculation using these approximate numbers.

Question   There are 33 coaches on a cross-channel ferry.

Each coach carries 49 passengers. Estimate the total number of
passengers on the coaches.

Solution   The exact calculation is 33×49.

Rounding each of these to one significant figure, the estimate is

$30 \times 50 = 1500$.

> Give the final estimate to 1 or 2 significant figures.

The coaches carry approximately <u>1500 people</u>.

EXERCISE 25.2

Round the numbers to one significant figure, and use the result to estimate the answer to each of these calculations.

1 58×21 ✓   **4** 360×87 **7** $5877 \div 32$ ✓

2 399×31 **5** $4899 \div 46$ **8** 774×773

3 47×22 **6** $377 \div 19$ **9** $1906 \div 44$

Round the numbers to one significant figure, and hence make estimates of the answers to these problems.

10 A confectionery bar weighs 65 grams. Find the total weight of 19 bars. ✓

11 In a lottery 23 people each win £2800. Find the total amount they win.

12 If 354 sweets are shared out between 11 friends how many does each receive?

13 Some wedding guests travel by taxi to the reception. Each taxi can carry 4 people. How many taxis are needed for 77 guests?

14 A star cluster contains about 200 stars. Find the total number of stars in 27 clusters.

15 In a lottery 31 friends win a total of £576 229. How much does each receive?

16 Films cost £4.99 each to process, and I have 11 films. Find the cost of processing all 11 films.

17 A ream (500 sheets) of paper is shared out between 18 students. How many sheets does each receive?

18 If 37 803 letters are sorted into piles of 200 how many piles will there be?

19 It takes me one hour to mark 17 exam scripts. Altogether I mark for 31 hours. How many exam scripts do I mark in this time? ✓

25.3 Checking the reasonableness of an answer

In this section you will be given some calculations followed by a suggested answer. The answer is either exactly right or else it is very wrong. Use the method of estimation to detect the wrong answers, and then correct them by calculator.

Question	Check the calculation $377 \times 244 = 91\,988$
Solution	An estimate is $400 \times 200 = 80\,000$.
	Since this is fairly close to 91 988 the answer looks reasonable.

Question	Check the calculation $3780 \div 18 = 21$
Solution	An estimate is $4000 \div 20 = 200$
	Since this is nowhere near 21 the answer looks wrong.
	Checking on a calculator shows that the answer is 210.

EXERCISE 25.3

Some of these calculations are wrong. Use the method of estimating to check the reasonableness of the answers. If you find any that are badly wrong then use a calculator to obtain the correct exact answer.

1 $87 \times 14 = 1218$ 2 $33 \times 11 = 863$ 3 $16 \times 702 = 1123$ 4 $117 \times 82 = 9594$

5 $365 \times 98 = 35\,770$ 6 $4020 \div 15 = 268$ ✓   7 $10\,570 \div 14 = 155$ ✓

8 $2891 \div 49 = 259$ 9 $23 \times 79 = 1817$ 10 $27\,783 \div 63 = 4411$

25.4 Trial and improvement

Some equations are too difficult to solve by exact methods. In the trial and improvement method you start with a solution that is roughly right, and gradually improve it. You will not usually get an exact solution, but one which is correct to a certain number of figures.

Question	The equation $x^2 + x - 5 = 0$ has a solution between $x = 1$ and $x = 2$. Use a trial and improvement method to find this solution correct to 2 decimal places.

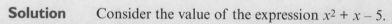

Solution   Consider the value of the expression $x^2 + x - 5$.

When $x = 1$ then $1^2 + 1 - 5 = -3$

When $x = 2$ then $2^2 + 2 - 5 = 1$

> One of these is **positive** and the other **negative**. This change of sign indicates a solution between $x = 1$ and $x = 2$.

When $x = 1.6$ then $1.6^2 + 1.6 - 5 = -0.84$

When $x = 1.7$ then $1.7^2 + 1.7 - 5 = -0.41$

When $x = 1.8$ then $1.8^2 + 1.8 - 5 = 0.04$

> This change of sign shows that the solution is between $x = 1.7$ and $x = 1.8$.

When $x = 1.78$ then $1.78^2 + 1.78 - 5 = -0.0516$

When $x = 1.79$ then $1.79^2 + 1.79 - 5 = -0.0059$

When $x = 1.80$ then $1.80^2 + 1.80 - 5 = 0.0400$

> Now we can see the solution is between $x = 1.79$ and $x = 1.80$.

Since the value of -0.0059 is much closer to zero than is 0.0400 then it seems reasonable to deduce that the solution is $x = 1.79$ correct to 2 d.p.

N.B. If you have access to a computer algebra system package such as *Derive* then you can easily verify that the solution is 1.791 28 correct to 6 significant figures.

EXERCISE 25.4

Solve the equations in the following table by trial and improvement. Remember to show all your working, as in the example above. Stop when you have reached the required level of accuracy.

	Equation	First trial x-value	Find solution correct to	
1	$x^2 + 3x - 7 = 0$	$x = 2$	2 decimal places	
2	$x^2 - 7x - 9 = 0$	$x = 8$	2 decimal places	
3	$x^2 - x - 5 = 0$	$x = 3$	3 decimal places	✓
4	$x^2 + 5x - 5 = 0$	$x = 1$	2 decimal places	
5	$x^2 - x - 10 = 0$	$x = 4$	2 decimal places	
6	$x^2 - 6x + 7 = 0$	$x = 2$	2 decimal places	
7	$x^2 - 10x + 23 = 0$	$x = 6$	2 decimal places	
8	$x^2 + 10x - 120 = 0$	$x = 7$	2 decimal places	
9	$2x^2 - 5x + 3 = 0$	$x = 2$	2 decimal places	
10	$x^2 + 5x - 1 = 0$	$x = 0$	2 decimal places	✓

25.5 Harder problems on trial and improvement

The equations in trial and improvement problems do not always have a convenient '= 0' on the right-hand side, so it may be necessary to rearrange them first. You will not always be told the approximate solution, so you might need to hunt around at first.

Both these aspects are illustrated in the next worked example.

Question   Find a solution to the equation $x^3 = 10x - 4$, giving your answer correct to 1 decimal place.

Solution   First rearrange the equation:

$$\therefore x^3 = 10x - 4$$
$$\therefore x^3 - 10x = -4$$
$$\therefore x^3 - 10x + 4 = 0$$

This equation can now be solved by trial and improvement.

Since no starting value is given, try $x = 1$, $x = 2$ and so on.

When $x = 1$ then $1^3 - 10 \times 1 + 4 = 1 - 10 + 4 = -5$
When $x = 2$ then $2^3 - 10 \times 2 + 4 = 8 - 20 + 4 = -8$
When $x = 3$ then $3^3 - 10 \times 3 + 4 = 27 - 30 + 4 = 1$

This change of sign shows that there is a solution between $x = 2$ and $x = 3$.

When $x = 2.9$ then $2.9^3 - 10 \times 2.9 + 4 = -0.611$
When $x = 3.0$ then $3.0^3 - 10 \times 3.0 + 4 = 1$

This change of sign shows that there is a solution between $x = 2.9$ and $x = 3.0$.

It is a good idea to try 2.95 next.
When $x = 2.95$ then $2.95^3 - 10 \times 2.95 + 4 = 0.172\,375$

Since $x = 2.9$ gives a negative result and $x = 2.95$ gives a positive result then the solution is between $x = 2.9$ and $x = 2.95$.

One solution of the equation $x^3 = 10x - 4$ is $x = 2.9$ correct to 1 d.p.

If you have the use of a computer spreadsheet such as *Excel* or *Works* then you can solve trial and improvement problems very easily. You only need to type the equation in once; the computer can then replicate it for you. Just type the trials down one column, and the result can be seen alongside.

Excel screenshot:

	A	B	C	D	E
1	1	–5			
2	2	–8			
3	3	1			
4	2.8	–2.048			
5	2.9	–0.611			
6	2.95	0.172 375			
7	2.94	0.012 184			
8	2.93	–0.146 24			
9	2.936	–0.0514			
10	2.937	–0.035 53			
11	2.938	–0.019 64			
12	2.939	–0.003 74			
13	2.940	0.091 2184			
14					

The expression $x^3 - 10x + 4$ is typed as '= A1^3–10*A1+4' so that it picks up the *x*-value in cell A1. Then use the mouse to copy down the column.

The change of sign from negative to positive shows that the solution lies between 2.939 and 2.940. By comparing the sizes of –0.003 74 and 0.091 218 4 it looks as if 2.939 is the better answer.

EXERCISE 25.5

In this exercise you may use a calculator or a computer program such as *Excel*.

In questions **1–8** rearrange the equation so that the right-hand side is zero. Then use trial and improvement to find a positive solution for each equation, giving your answer correct to 1 decimal place.

1 $x^3 = 8x - 3$

2 $x^3 = 4x - 1$ ✓

3 $x^2 = 10 - x$

4 $x^3 = 12x - 7$

5 $2x^3 - x = 4$

6 $x^3 - x^2 = 12$

7 $10 - x^3 = 5x$

8 $x^2 = 5x + 17$ ✓

9 The equation $x^3 = 13x - 11$ has two positive solutions. Use trial and improvement to find both of them, giving each answer correct to 2 decimal places. ✓

10 The equation $x^2 = 15x - 11$ has a solution between 0 and 1. Use a trial and improvement method to find its value correct to 3 decimal places.

SUMMARY

- In this chapter you have practised rounding off numbers to one or two significant figures, or to a certain number of decimal places. You have made estimates of the answers to arithmetic problems by working with rounded numbers, and you have detected errors when checking the reasonableness of an answer.

- You have also learnt how to use trial and improvement to solve an equation. This method does not usually yield an exact answer, but it does allow you to obtain a value correct to 1 or 2 decimal places.

- At Key Stage 3 or GCSE you may be asked to 'estimate the value of...'. You must remember to do a calculation based on rounded numbers – do not just guess!

REVIEW EXERCISE 25

1 Round these correct to two significant figures:

   a 54 206   b 1997   c 207

   d 2 539 200   e 7006   f 4502

   g 561   h 7777   i 3333

   j 9999

2 Round these correct to the stated number of significant figures:

   a 64 256 (3 s.f.)   b 386 (1 s.f.)   c 60 801 (1 s.f.)

   d 2996 (3 s.f.)   e 106 277 (3 s.f.) f 4502 (1 s.f.)

   g 11 451 (4 s.f.)   h 186 000 (2 s.f.) i 13 million (1 s.f.)

3 Obtain estimates for the answers to these calculations. Then use your calculator to find the exact answer.

   a 552×21 b $552 \div 23$ c $3102 \div 47$

   d 144×244 e 1.96×615 f 28.1×42.5

   g $33.28 \div 25.6$ h $266.7 \div 3.5$ i 21.05×54.2

4 Show that $x^3 = 64 + x$ has a solution between 4 and 5. Use trial and improvement to find its value correct to 2 decimal places.

5 ✱ Asher and Isabel are trying to solve the equation $x^4 + 4x = 4x^2 + 1$.

  Asher says 'I think the solution lies between 0 and 1'.

  Isabel says 'I think that the solution lies between –2 and –3'.

   a Explain how it is possible for both of them to be right.

   b Find two solutions, giving each correct to 2 decimal places.

6 ✳ The equation $x^2 = 2x + 17$ has two solutions. One of them lies between 4 and 6, while the other lies between −3 and −4.

   a Use trial and improvement to find the positive solution correct to 2 decimal places.

   b Use trial and improvement to find the negative solution correct to 1 decimal place.

7 ✳ Tim, Anwar and Natalie are each trying to find the positive solutions of the equation $x^3 - 11x^2 + 21x + 37 = 0$ by a trial and improvement method.

Tim says 'I think there is a solution between 4 and 5'.
Anwar says 'I think there is a solution between 5 and 7'.
Natalie says 'I think there is a solution between 7 and 8'.

Two of them are right but one is wrong.
   a Which two of them are right?
   b Find the two positive solutions of the equation.

Do questions **8** to **16** using rounded numbers. Do not work out exact answers.

8 ✳ In a clothes shop I buy three items costing £11.99, £13.60 and £25.30. The bill comes to £60.89. Does this seem reasonable?

9 ✳ In a Year 7 end of term test I score 57 in English, 63 in mathematics, 22 in technology and 51 in science. My teacher says I scored 260 altogether. By rounding all the marks to one significant figure show that my teacher is wrong.

10 ✳ Five anglers compare their catches for the month of February: they are 23, 61, 11, 22 and 48 fish respectively. Estimate the total number of fish caught by all five of them.

11 ✳ I have a box file which can hold 800 pages. I wish to store six sets of work in the box file; these contain 210, 35, 79, 112, 21 and 29 pages respectively.
Estimate the total number of pages, and hence say whether the box file is large enough to hold them all.

12 ✳ A pack of butter weighs 225 grams. Estimate the total weight of 18 packs of butter.

13 ✳ A rock band plays a world tour of 39 concerts. They reckon that on average 7900 people watch each concert. Calculate an estimate of the total number of people who watch the concerts. Is this figure more than a million, or less?

14 ✳ One bag of rabbit food lasts my rabbit, Patch, for 12 days. Roughly how many bags would Patch need for a whole year?

15 ✳ A newspaper once claimed that the president of the world's largest computer software company becomes $20 million richer each day. Assuming this claim to be correct, calculate an estimate of how much richer he becomes over a period of three months.

16 ✳ Mrs Green's classroom contains 28 tables, 1 teacher's desk and 29 chairs. There are 26 pupils in class 5B. Estimate the total number of legs of furniture in the room when Mrs Green is teaching class 5B.

17 ✳ The number of seconds in a year can be calculated like this:
$$365 \times 24 \times 60 \times 60$$
a Explain where these numbers come from.
b Calculate an estimate of the answer, using values rounded to one significant figure.
c Obtain the exact answer, using your calculator.

18 ✳ Usha is working with the equation $x^3 - 7x^2 + 13x - 3 = 0$. She knows that it has three solutions, which she calls a, b and c. Only solution a is a whole number.
a Work out the value of the expression $x^3 - 7x^2 + 13x - 3$ when $x = 0$, 1, 2, 3 and 4. Hence state the value of the whole number a.
b Solution b lies between 3.5 and 4. Use a trial and improvement method to find the value of b correct to 3 significant figures.
c From your answers to part a state two whole numbers between which the third solution c must lie. Use trial and improvement to find the value of c correct to 2 decimal places.

26 Linear equations

OUTLINE

In this chapter you will learn how to:
- solve simple linear equations using one operation
- solve more difficult linear equations using several operations
- formulate and solve problems using linear equations.

26.1 Linear equations with one operation

This section looks at techniques for solving equations using the operations of adding, subtracting, multiplying and dividing. Study each example carefully before going on to the Exercise.

Set your working out in detail, just as in the examples.

Question	Solve the equation $x + 5 = 30$.
Solution	$x + 5 = 30$
	$x = 30 - 5$
	$x = 25$

To get the x on its own you need to remove the $+5$. This is done by **subtracting** 5 from both sides of the equation.

Question	Solve the equation $x - 7 = 10$.
Solution	$x - 7 = 10$
	$x = 10 + 7$
	$x = 17$

This time you need to remove the -7. This is done by **adding** 7 to both side of the equation.

Question	Solve the equation $5x = 30$.
Solution	$5x = 30$
	$x = 30 \div 5$
	$x = 6$

$5x$ means 5 times x. To get the x on its own you must **divide** both sides by 5.

Question	Solve the equation $\frac{x}{3} = 4$.
Solution	$\frac{x}{3} = 4$
	$x = 4 \times 3$
	$x = 12$

$\frac{x}{3}$ means $x \div 3$.

To get the x on its own you must **multiply** both sides by 3.

Note: Always copy the question as the first line of your working. Set out the lines that follow so that the = signs are aligned.

EXERCISE 26.1

Solve these linear equations, showing all your working.

1 $x + 4 = 19$ **2** $x + 6 = 23$ **3** $x + 11 = 4$ ✓   **4** $x - 3 = 29$

5 $x - 11 = 5$ **6** $x - 4 = -5$ **7** $3x = 24$ **8** $8x = 56$ ✓

9 $4x = 22$ **10** $\frac{x}{3} = 9$ **11** $\frac{x}{11} = 3$ ✓   **12** $\frac{x}{6} = 13$

13 $x - 14 = 9$ ✓   **14** $x + 9 = 14$ **15** $\frac{x}{7} = 13$ **16** $6x = 18$

17 $x + 2 = 1$ **18** $x - 9 = 9$ **19** $\frac{x}{3} = 4$ **20** $9x = 45$

26.2 Linear equations with two operations

In this section two operations will be used. Study each example carefully before going on to the Exercise.

Set your working out in detail, just as in the examples. Do not try to solve the equation in one line – the key is to break the problem down into small steps.

Question   Solve the equation $2x + 5 = 31$.

Solution
$$2x + 5 = 31$$
$$2x = 31 - 5$$
$$2x = 26$$
$$x = 26 \div 2$$
$$x = 13$$

First of all, treat this as a problem to find $2x$.

Then finish off by finding x.

Question   Solve the equation $4x - 7 = 17$.

Solution
$$4x - 7 = 17$$
$$4x = 17 + 7$$
$$4x = 24$$
$$x = 24 \div 4$$
$$x = 6$$

First of all, treat this as a problem to find $4x$.

Then finish off by finding x.

Question   Solve the equation $5x = 30 + 2x$.

Solution
$$5x = 30 + 2x$$
$$5x - 2x = 30$$
$$3x = 30$$
$$x = 30 \div 3$$
$$\underline{x = 10}$$

$5x$ appears on one side of the equation, and $2x$ on the other side. The first step is to subtract $2x$ from both sides of the equation. This leaves a simple one-operation problem to finish off.

Question   Solve the equation $3x = 15 - 2x$.

Solution
$$3x = 15 - 2x$$
$$3x + 2x = 15$$
$$5x = 15$$
$$x = 15 \div 5$$
$$\underline{x = 3}$$

$3x$ appears on one side of the equation, and $-2x$ on the other side. The first step is to add $2x$ to both sides of the equation. This leaves a simple one-operation problem to finish off.

EXERCISE 26.2

Solve these linear equations, showing all your workings.

1. $5x + 1 = 31$
2. $4x + 9 = 45$
3. $7x + 2 = 51$ ✓
4. $3x - 1 = 8$
5. $7x - 9 = 12$
6. $11x - 7 = 59$
7. $7x = 60 + 2x$
8. $4x = 18 + x$
9. $11x = 21 + 4x$ ✓
10. $3x = 72 - 3x$
11. $5x = 28 - 2x$
12. $4x = 63 - 5x$
13. $6x - 7 = 29$ ✓
14. $2x + 17 = 9$
15. $8x = 15 - 2x$
16. $14x = 55 + 3x$
17. $9x + 5 = 41$
18. $2x - 3 = 2$
19. $4x = 15 - 2x$ ✓
20. $35x = 48 + 29x$

26.3 Harder linear equations

These equations are a little harder. Once again, the key is to break the problem down into small steps.

Question   Solve the equation $7x + 6 = 41 + 2x$.

Solution
$$7x + 6 = 41 + 2x$$
$$7x - 2x + 6 = 41$$
$$5x + 6 = 41$$
$$5x = 41 - 6$$
$$5x = 35$$
$$\therefore x = 35 \div 5$$
$$\underline{x = 7}$$

The first stage is to subtract $2x$ from both sides. This makes the equation much simpler.

The next stage is to subtract 6 from both sides. This makes the equation even simpler.

The final step is simply to divide by 5.

Question   Solve the equation $5x + 7 = 42 - 2x$.

Solution
$$5x + 7 = 42 - 2x$$
$$5x + 2x + 7 = 42$$
$$7x + 7 = 42$$
$$7x = 42 - 7$$
$$7x = 35$$
$$\therefore x = 35 \div 7$$
$$\underline{x = 5}$$

This time, begin by adding $2x$ to both sides.

Next, subtract 7 from both sides.

Finally, divide both sides by 7.

Question   Solve the equation $5x + 7 = 31 + 9x$.

Solution
$$5x + 7 = 31 + 9x$$
$$5x - 9x + 7 = 31$$
$$-4x + 7 = 42$$

You might begin by subtracting $9x$ from both sides …

… but this will lead to a **negative** number of xs.

To avoid this situation, begin again and collect the x-terms on the **right-hand side** of the equation.

$$5x + 7 = 31 + 9x$$
$$7 = 31 + 9x - 5x$$
$$7 = 31 + 4x$$
$$7 - 31 = 4x$$
$$-24 = 4x$$
$$-24 \div 4 = x$$
$$\therefore \underline{x = -6}$$

The first stage is to take $5x$ from both sides.

Next, subtract 31 from both sides.

The final step is simply to divide by 4.

EXERCISE 26.3

Solve these linear equations, showing all your working. You will need a calculator for some of the later ones, where the answers are not whole numbers.

1 $6x + 4 = 20 - 2x$

2 $3x + 5 = 37 - x$ ✓

3 $2x + 3 = 11 + x$

4 $2x - 1 = 8 - x$

5 $7x - 4 = 2x + 31$

6 $4x + 21 = 3 - 2x$

7 $9x + 7 = 63 + x$ ✓

8 $3x + 7 = 2x + 7$

9 $x - 4 = 17 - 6x$

10 $6x + 3 = 23 + x$

11 $15x - 4 = 9x + 23$

12 $6 - x = 20 - 4x$

13 $7x + 4 = 4x - 3$

14 $8x + 5 = 3x + 23$

15 $15x - 37 = 15 - x$ ✓

16 $17 - 2x = 51 - 7x$

17 $28 - x = 17 + 3x$

18 $5x + 11 = 20x - 64$

19 $45x + 11 = 20x - 54$

20 $21 + 2x = 35 + 12x$ ✓

26.4 Setting up and solving equations

Sometimes you will meet a problem given in words, or in a diagram.

Turn the problem into an equation, then solve it using the methods you have practised.

Question	I think of a number and multiply it by 6, then I add 5 to the answer. I end up with 59. What number did I first think of?
Solution	Let the number I think of be x. When I multiply by 6 it becomes $6x$. When I add 5 it becomes $6x + 5$. $6x + 5 = 59$ $\quad 6x = 59 - 5$ $\quad 6x = 54$ $\quad\ x = 54 \div 6$ $\quad\ \underline{x = 9}$

Question	The length of a rectangle is 6 cm more than its breadth. The perimeter is 40 cm. Find the dimensions of the rectangle.
Solution	Let the breadth be x cm. Then the length is $x + 6$ cm.

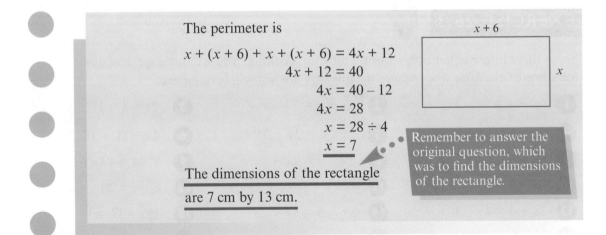

The perimeter is

$$x + (x + 6) + x + (x + 6) = 4x + 12$$
$$4x + 12 = 40$$
$$4x = 40 - 12$$
$$4x = 28$$
$$x = 28 \div 4$$
$$x = 7$$

The dimensions of the rectangle

are 7 cm by 13 cm.

Remember to answer the original question, which was to find the dimensions of the rectangle.

EXERCISE 26.4

Write equations to describe each of these problems, then use the equation to solve the problem.

1. I think of a number and multiply it by 3, then add 11. The answer is 59. What number did I think of?

2. The length of a rectangle is 9 cm more than its breadth. The perimeter is 70 cm. Find the dimensions of the rectangle.

3. Rana likes to collect toy dogs. If she had 84 more dogs then she would have four times as many as she actually has. How many does she have? ✓

4. I think of a number and multiply it by 6, then add 7. The answer is 61. What number did I think of?

5. Tim and Gavin are the same age. If you multiply Tim's age by 5 and then add 7 you get the same answer as if you had multiplied Gavin's age by 10 and taken away 43. How old are Tim and Gavin?

6. Flora, Natalie and Usha are playing a numbers game. Flora whispers the same number to Natalie and to Usha.

   Natalie multiplies the number by 7, then adds 4.
   Usha takes the number away from 100.
   They both end up with the same number.

   What number did Flora whisper to the other two girls? ✓

SUMMARY

- In this chapter you have solved linear equations involving one or more processes. Remember to write down the given equation, and then solve it in a number of small steps rather than trying to do everything all in one go.

- In harder problems you have usually collected the x-terms together on the left-hand side of the equation, or on the right-hand side if this helps to avoid difficulties with negative numbers.

- You have also practised setting up and solving equations from information given in words: this will become an increasingly important skill as your knowledge of mathematics develops.

REVIEW EXERCISE 26

1 Solve these equations, showing all your working clearly.

   a $x + 3 = 31$ b $x - 2 = 11$ c $x - 8 = 0$ d $x + 17 = 12$

   e $3x = 96$ f $\frac{x}{4} = 17$ g $11x = 121$ h $\frac{x}{11} = 3$

2 Solve these equations, showing all your working clearly.

   a $3x - 7 = 17$ b $5x + 6 = 51$ c $11x = 16 + 3x$

   d $4x = 77 - 3x$ e $2x + 17 = 9$ f $4x = 25 + 9x$

   g $8x + 5 = 79$ h $7x = 55 - 3x$

3 Solve these equations, showing all your working clearly.

   a $13 + 3x = 21 + x$ b $33 + 7x = 23 + 2x$ c $3x + 23 = 7x - 1$

   d $2 + 8x = 57 - 3x$ e $8 - x = 18 - 3x$ f $2x + 12 = 5x - 12$

4 One side of a square is labelled $(3x + 4)$ cm and another side is labelled $(28 - x)$ cm.

   a Write this information in an equation.

   b Solve the equation, and hence find the perimeter of the square.

5 I think of a number and multiply it by 7, then I add 13 to the result. The final answer is 69.

   a Write this information in an equation.

   b Solve the equation, to find the number I thought of.

6 John has been counting his marbles, which are either red, blue or yellow.

He has n red marbles.

He has two more blue marbles than he has red.

He has twice as many yellows as he has red.

In total he has 62 marbles.

a Write down, in terms of *n*, the number of blue marbles he has.

b Write down, in terms of *n*, the number of yellow marbles he has.

c Write down an equation for the total number of marbles, and solve it.

d Write down how many marbles of each colour John has.

7 ✶ Séan is told 'Think of a number, multiply it by 3, then add 8'.
By mistake he multiplies it by 8, then adds 3. He ends up with the
number 75. If he had followed the instructions correctly what number
would he have ended up with?

8 ✶ Two of the sides of an equilateral triangle are labelled $(4x - 7)$ mm
and $(33 - x)$ mm.

a Find the value of x.   **b** Find the perimeter of the triangle.

9 ✶ I asked my grandma to tell me how old she was. She replied 'If you
multiply my age by 3 and then subtract 100 you get the same answer as
if you took my age and added 34'.

a Write this information in an equation, using x to represent grandma's age.

b Solve the equation, to find grandma's age.

10 ✶ Richard and Ben went shopping. They each began with the same
amount of spending money.

Richard says: Ben says:

'I bought seven
pencils. I have
17p left.'

'I bought five
pencils. I have
55p left.'

a Express this information in an equation.

b Solve your equation, to find the cost of a pencil.

11 ✶ The diagram shows an isosceles triangle ABC.
The sides AB and AC are equal in length.

a Set up an equation in x and solve it.

b Hence state the lengths of the three sides.

c Find the perimeter of the triangle.

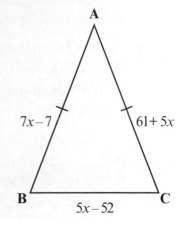

27 Number patterns

In this chapter you will learn how to:
- extend number patterns, describing them in words
- use position-to-term and term-to-term rules
- find an algebraic rule for a given linear number pattern.

27.1 Number patterns

Here are some of the more widely used number patterns:

1	3	5	7	9	...	**odd** numbers
2	4	6	8	10	...	**even** numbers
1	4	9	16	25	...	**square** numbers
1	8	27	64	125	...	**cube** numbers
2	3	5	7	11	...	**prime** numbers
1	2	4	8	16	...	**powers of 2**
1	3	6	10	15	...	**triangular** numbers

It is often a good idea to look at the differences between terms in a number pattern. This can help to unlock the pattern so that you can generate more terms.

Question   Describe in words the number pattern 4, 7, 10, 13, 16 ... and find the next two terms.

Solution   Here are the terms and their differences:

The pattern starts at 4 and goes up 3 at a time.

The next two terms are 19 and 22.

Each number is called a **term**. This example gives you five terms to start with.

EXERCISE 27.1

Describe each of these number patterns in words, and find the next two terms.

1   5, 7, 9, 11, 13, ...

2   11, 16, 21, 26, 31, ...

3   16, 19, 22, 25, 28 ... ✓

4   11, 9, 7, 5, 3, ... ✓

5   40, 36, 32, 28, 24 ...

6   1, 2, 4, 8, 16, ...

7   1, 3, 6, 10, 15, ... ✓

8   45, 54, 63, 72, 81, ...

9   11, 22, 33, 44, 55, ...

10   100, 99, 97, 94, 90, ...

27.2 Position-to-term and term-to-term rules

The terms in a number pattern are often written algebraically. The symbol u_1 represents the first term, u_2 the second term and so on.

A **position-to-term** rule tells you how to find each term if you know its position.

$u_n = 2n + 5$ is an example of a position-to-term rule.

Question   Find the first five terms of the number pattern described by the position-to-term rule:
$u_n = 2n + 5$

Solution   For the first term, set $n = 1$.
$u_1 = 2 \times 1 + 5 = \underline{7}$

For the second term, set $n = 2$.
$u_2 = 2 \times 2 + 5 = \underline{9}$

For the third term, set $n = 3$.
$u_3 = 2 \times 3 + 5 = \underline{11}$

Similarly $u_4 = 2 \times 4 + 5 = \underline{13}$ and $u_5 = 2 \times 5 + 5 = \underline{15}$.

The first five terms are $\underline{7, 9, 11, 13, 15}$

A **term-to-term** rule tells you how to find each term if you know the one before. You also need to know the value of the first term.

$u_{n+1} = 2u_n + 3$ and $u_1 = 4$ is an example of a term-to-term rule.

Question   Find the first five terms of the number pattern described by the term-to-term rule:
$u_{n+1} = 2u_n + 3$ and $u_1 = 4$

Solution   The first term is given: $u_1 = 4$
For the second term, set $n = 1$ so that $n + 1 = 2$.
$$u_2 = 2u_1 + 3 = 2 \times 4 + 3$$
$$= 11$$

For the third term, set $n = 2$ so that $n + 1 = 3$.
$$u_3 = 2u_2 + 3 = 2 \times 11 + 3$$
$$= 25$$

Similarly $u_4 = 2u_3 + 3 = 2 \times 25 + 3 = 53$ and
$$u_5 = 2u_4 + 3 = 2 \times 53 + 3 = 109$$

The first five terms are 4, 11, 25, 53, 109

EXERCISE 27.2

1 Find the first five terms of the number patterns given by these position-to-term rules.
a) $u_n = 2n + 3$ b) $u_n = 5n + 9$ c) $u_n = 4n - 2$ ✓   d) $u_n = 3n - 2$
e) $u_n = n + 100$ f) $u_n = 10 - 2n$ ✓   g) $u_n = 30 + n$ h) $u_n = 10(n + 2)$
i) $u_n = n \times (n - 1)$ j) $u_n = n^2$ ✓

2 Find the first six terms of the number patterns given by these term-to-term rules.
a) $u_{n+1} = 2u_n$ and $u_1 = 1$ b) $u_{n+1} = 2u_n + 1$ and $u_1 = 1$ ✓
c) $u_{n+1} = 3u_n - 2$ and $u_1 = 3$ d) $u_{n+1} = 3(u_n - 2)$ and $u_1 = 4$
e) $u_{n+1} = 3(u_n - 2)$ and $u_1 = 3$ f) $u_{n+1} = 10 - u_n$ and $u_1 = 4$
g) $u_{n+1} = u_n - 10$ and $u_1 = 4$ h) $u_{n+1} = u_n + n$ and $u_1 = 1$ ✓
i) $u_{n+1} = 2 \times u_n$ and $u_1 = 32$ j) $u_{n+1} = \frac{1}{2} \times u_n$ and $u_1 = 32$

27.3 Finding a position-to-term rule for a number pattern

A **linear** pattern is one which goes up in equal steps: 5, 8, 11, 14, 17 ...

Question   Find a position-to-term rule for the number pattern whose first
five terms are:
5, 8, 11, 14, 17

Solution   Here are the terms and their differences:

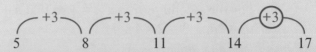

As the difference is always 3, try the position-to-term rule
$u_n = ③n$.
This rule gives:

3   6   9   12   15

in which all the numbers are 2 less than those in the
pattern, so 2 must be added on to the suggested rule.

The position-to-term rule is $\underline{u_n = 3n + 2}$

Question   Find a position-to-term rule for the number pattern whose first
five terms are:
25, 23, 21, 19, 17

Solution   Here are the terms and their differences:

As the difference is always –2, try the position-to-term
rule $u_n = -2n$.

This rule gives:

–2   –4   –6   –8   –10

> When the numbers
> go **down** like this you
> will always have a
> **negative** number here.

in which all the numbers are 27 less than those in the
pattern, so 27 must be added on to the suggested rule.

The position-to-term rule is $\underline{u_n = 27 - 2n}$

EXERCISE 27.3

① In the following, find the next two terms in the number pattern. Find also the
position-to-term rule.
a) 11, 13, 15, 17, 19, ...   b) 10, 13, 16, 19, 22, ... ✓   c) 6, 7, 8, 9, 10, ...
d) 10, 15, 20, 25, 30, ...   e) 50, 45, 40, 35, 30, ...   f) 10, 12, 14, 16, 18, ...
g) 20, 23, 26, 29, 32, ...   h) 10, 7, 4, 1, –2, ... ✓   i) 4, 11, 18, 25, 32, ...
j) 100, 89, 78, 67, 56, ...

2 In the following you are given the first five terms of a number pattern. Say whether each one is linear or not. For those that are linear, find a position-to-term rule. For those that are not linear, describe the pattern in words.

a) 21, 23, 25, 27, 29, ... b) 21, 23, 26, 30, 35, ... ✓ c) 21, 24, 27, 30, 33, ... ✓
d) 21, 24, 29, 36, 45, ... e) 2, 4, 8, 16, 32, ... f) 8, 5, 2, –1, –4, ...
g) 8, 18, 28, 38, 48, ... h) 2, 3, 5, 7, 11, ... i) 60, 80, 100, 120, 140, ...
j) 1, 8, 27, 64, 125, ...

REVIEW EXERCISE 27

1 Copy down the given number pattern, and continue it for three more terms.
   a 122, 116, 111, 107, 104, ... b 7, 12, 17, 22, 27, ...
   c 13, 14, 16, 19, 23, ... d 22, 20, 18, 16, 14, ...

2 In the following you are given a rule describing a number pattern. Say whether it is a term-to-term rule or a position-to-term rule, and find the first six terms in the number pattern.

   a $u_n = 3n - 3$ b $u_{n+1} = u_n + 3$ and $u_1 = 1$ c $u_n = n^2 + 1$
   d $u_n = 5n - 11$ e $u_n = n^2 + n + 1$ f $u_{n+1} = 3u_n$ and $u_1 = 1$
   g $u_n = 18 + 2n$ h $u_n = 3u_{n-1} + 2$ and $u_1 = 20$

3 In the following you are given the first few terms in a number pattern. If the pattern is linear then find a position-to-term rule for the pattern; if it is not linear then find a term-to-term rule instead.

   a 60, 63, 66, 69, 72, ... b 10, 30, 90, 270, ... c 80, 40, 20, 10, 5, ...
   d –7, 3, 13, 23, ... e 1, 5, 25, 125, ... f 8, 6, 4, 2, ...
   g 10, 16, 22, 28, ... h 243, 81, 27, 9, 3, ...

4 ✳ At my local library there is a system of fines if books are overdue. In the first week the fine is 40p, in the second week it is 70p, in the third week £1 and so on.

a Write down the fines, in pence, for each of the first six weeks.

b Find a rule for the fine, in pence, in the nth week.

c Rewrite your answer to b so that it is now in pounds.

5 ✳ **a** Find the first five terms of the number pattern generated by the rule $u_{n+1} = u_n + 2$ and $u_1 = 1$.

b What name is given to this set of numbers?

c Without working out any more terms, describe carefully the sets of numbers which are generated by each of these rules:

   i $u_{n+1} = u_n + 2$ and $u_1 = 2$ **ii** $u_{n+1} = u_n + 1$ and $u_1 = 1$

   iii $u_{n+1} = u_n + n + 1$ and $u_1 = 1$

6 ✳ Richard is investigating linear number patterns, and writes down this example: **8 14 22 26 32** ...

Unfortunately Richard has made one mistake in this list.

a Write out the list with the mistake corrected.

b Find a term-to-term rule connecting the terms u_{n+1} and u_n.

c Find a position-to-term rule for the nth term u_n.

7 ✳ Rosemarie is going on a long car journey. She looks at the number of kilometres recorded on the car's distance meter at the start of the journey, and at regular half-hourly intervals during the first part of the journey. Here are the first four readings:

      33 576   33 618   33 660   33 702

a Find a position-to-term rule for these numbers, and check that $u_{11} = 33\ 996$.

b Explain why this value of u_{11} is likely to be meaningless in reality.

8 ✳ The mathematician Leonardo of Pisa used this number pattern:

$u_{n+2} = u_{n+1} + u_n$ and $u_1 = 1$, $u_2 = 1$

a Work out the first ten terms of the pattern.

b Calculate the values of $\frac{u_8}{u_9}$ and $\frac{u_9}{u_{10}}$, as decimals correct to 3 decimal places. What do you notice?

c Now continue the pattern until you are able to find $\frac{u_{14}}{u_{15}}$. What do you notice?

d Look in a reference book about mathematics, and see if you can find the nickname by which Leonardo of Pisa is better known.

28 Functions and graphs

In this chapter you will learn how to:
- rearrange linear expressions and sketch their graphs
- plot the graphs of simple quadratic functions
- draw graphs to describe real world behaviour.

28.1 Rearranging linear expressions

You are already familiar with linear expressions such as $y = 2x + 3$. It is easy to plot the corresponding graph, since it will be a straight line with gradient 2 and intercept 3.

Sometimes the linear equation will be disguised, however, and you need to rearrange it into the $y = mx + c$ form first, in order to be able to make a sketch.

Question   Rearrange $y - 3x - 2 = 0$ into the form $y = mx + c$. Hence write down the gradient and intercept of the line, and sketch its graph.

Solution
$$y - 3x - 2 = 0$$

Therefore $y - 3x = 2$

and so $\underline{y = 3x + 2}$

The gradient is 3 and the intercept is 2.

The graph therefore crosses the y-axis at $(0, 3)$ and goes up 2 units for each 1 unit across, so the graph must look like this:

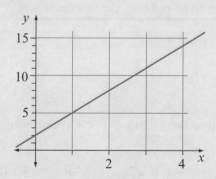

Question   Rearrange $2x + 3y - 5 = 0$ into the form $y = mx + c$. Hence write down the gradient and intercept of the line, and sketch its graph.

Solution
$$2x + y - 5 = 0$$

Therefore $2x + y = 5$

and so $y = -2x + 5$

The gradient is –2 and the intercept is 5.

The graph therefore crosses the y-axis at $(0, 5)$ and goes down 2 units for each 1 unit across, so the graph must look like this:

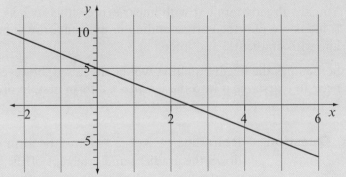

Question   The graph of the equation $\frac{y}{4} - x = 0$ is a straight line. Find its gradient and intercept.

Solution
$$\frac{y}{4} - x = 0$$

Therefore $y - 4x = 0$

and so $y = 4x$

The gradient is 4 and the intercept is 0.

EXERCISE 28.1

1 Rearrange these equations into the form $y = mx + c$, and write down the gradient and intercept in each case.

a) $y - 3x - 4 = 0$ ✓   b) $\frac{y}{3} - x = 0$ ✓   c) $y + 4x - 2 = 0$ ✓

d) $3y - 6x = 4$ ✓   e) $4y - x + 3 = 0$ f) $2y + 3x = 12$

2 Rearrange each of these equations into the form $y = mx + c$. Find the gradient and intercept, and hence sketch each line.

a) $x + y = 12$ ✓   b) $3x - 4y + 5 = 0$ c) $\frac{y}{5} - 2x = 0$ d) $4x + 3y - 1 = 0$

28.2 Graphs of curves

Functions of the form $y = ax^2 + bx + c$, for example $y = x^2 + 2x + 3$, do not have straight line graphs. They are non-linear functions.

To draw a graph of a non-linear function, work out the coordinates of **many points**, then join them up with a smooth curve. You may need to compute extra points where the curve bends most.

Question   Draw the graph of $y = x^2 + 2x + 3$ for values of x from –2 to 4.

Solution   First, choose whole number x-values throughout the range from –2 to 4.

x	–2	–1	0	1	2	3	4
y							

When $x = -2$, $y = (-2)^2 + 2 \times -2 + 3 = 4 - 4 + 3 = 3$

When $x = -1$, $y = (-1)^2 + 2 \times -1 + 3 = 1 - 2 + 3 = 2$

When $x = 0$, $y = (0)^2 + 2 \times 0 + 3 = 0 + 0 + 3 = 3$

When $x = 1$, $y = (1)^2 + 2 \times 1 + 3 = 1 + 2 + 3 = 6$

When $x = 2$, $y = (2)^2 + 2 \times 2 + 3 = 4 + 4 + 3 = 11$

When $x = 3$, $y = (3)^2 + 2 \times 3 + 3 = 9 + 6 + 3 = 18$

When $x = 4$, $y = (4)^2 + 2 \times 4 + 3 = 16 + 8 + 3 = 27$

Now write the y-coordinates in the table.

x	–2	–1	0	1	2	3	4
y	3	2	3	6	11	18	27

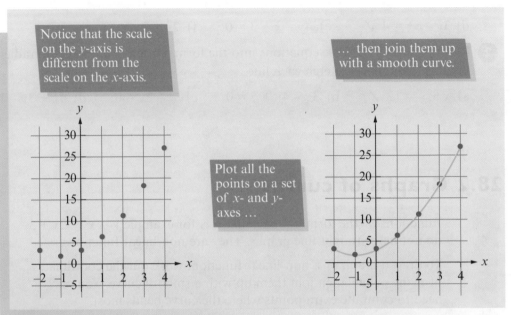

Notice that the scale on the y-axis is different from the scale on the x-axis.

... then join them up with a smooth curve.

Plot all the points on a set of x- and y-axes ...

Sometimes it can be helpful to break the formula up into several steps in order to calculate the values of y in the table. The next example illustrates this.

Question   Draw the graph of $y = 10 + 2x - x^2$ for values of x from -3 to 3.

Solution

x	-3	-2	-1	0	1	2	3
10							
$+2x$							
$-x^2$							
y							

First, draw up this table.

x	-3	-2	-1	0	1	2	3
10	10	10	10	10	10	10	10
$+2x$							
$-x^2$							
y							

Fill in the 10s ...

x	-3	-2	-1	0	1	2	3
10	10	10	10	10	10	10	10
$+2x$	-6	-4	-2	0	2	4	6
$-x^2$							
y							

... then the $+2x$ ...

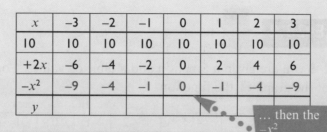

x	-3	-2	-1	0	1	2	3
10	10	10	10	10	10	10	10
$+2x$	-6	-4	-2	0	2	4	6
$-x^2$	-9	-4	-1	0	-1	-4	-9
y							

... then the $-x^2$ ...

Finally, add the three parts in each column to get the value for y.

x	-3	-2	-1	0	1	2	3
10	10	10	10	10	10	10	10
$+2x$	-6	-4	-2	0	2	4	6
$-x^2$	-9	-4	-1	0	-1	-4	-9
y	-5	2	7	10	11	10	7

Plot all the points on a set of x- and y- axes ...

... then join them up with a smooth curve.

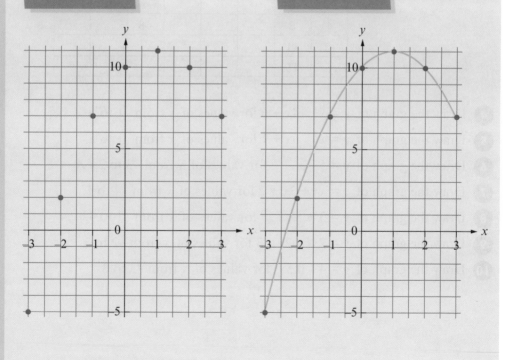

EXERCISE 28.2

In questions **1–3** you are given a function and a table of values. Copy and complete the table, then plot the graph of the function.

1 $y = x^2 + 4x - 3$ ✓

x	−4	−3	−2	−1	0	1	2	3
x^2	16	9		1	0		4	
$+4x$	−16	−12	−8		0	4		
−3	−3	−3	−3	−3	−3	−3	−3	−3
y	−3	−6						

2 $y = 10 + 2x - x^2$

x	−3	−2	−1	0	1	2	3
10	10	10	10	10	10	10	10
$+2x$		−4	−2			4	
$-x^2$	−9	−4				−4	
y		2					

3 $y = 2x^2 - 4x - 1$

x	−2	−1	0	1	2	3	4
$2x^2$	8					18	
$-4x$	8				−8		
−1	−1						
y	15						

4 Draw the graph of $y = x^2 - 4x + 6$ for values of x from −1 to 5.

5 Draw the graph of $y = x^2 - 6x + 1$ for values of x from −1 to 5.

6 Draw the graph of $y = 5 - x - x^2$ for values of x from −3 to 2. ✓

7 Draw the graph of $y = x^2 + 3x + 2$ for values of x from −4 to 1.

8 Draw the graph of $y = 3 + 3x - x^2$ for values of x from −1 to 4.

9 Draw the graph of $y = 2x^2 - 2x - 3$ for values of x from −2 to 3.

10 Draw the graph of $y = 4 - 0.5x^2$ for values of x from −3 to 3.

28.3 Obtaining information from other graphs

Not all graphs are generated by mathematical formulae like linear or quadratic functions. In this section you will meet other types of graphs from which information can be obtained by reading from one axis onto the graph and then across to the other axis.

Question   The growth chart shows how an average baby girl's weight will increase throughout her first year. Using the graph, find approximate values for:

a) the weight of an average baby girl, at age 32 weeks

b) the age of an average baby girl, whose weight is 6 kilograms

c) estimate the weight at birth of an average baby girl.

Solution   Reading on to the graph below as shown:

a) The average weight at 32 weeks is 8.3 kilograms.

b) The age of a baby girl weighing 6 kilograms is about 13 weeks.

c) The graph shows an average birth weight of 3.5 kilograms.

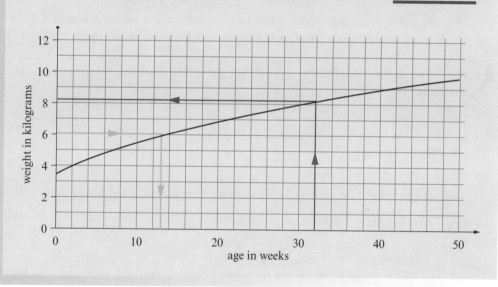

EXERCISE 28.3

1. A bank publishes this table to show how much an investment of £100 would be worth after up to 20 years:

Years	2	4	6	8	10	15	20
Value (£)	110	121	134	147	162	207	265

   a) Draw a graph to illustrate this information.
   b) Use your graph to obtain the value of the investment after 12 years.

2. A stone is dropped over the edge of a high cliff. The table shows its velocity during the next six seconds: ✓

Time (seconds)	0	1	2	3	4	5	6
Velocity (metres per second)	0	5	20	45	80	125	0

   a) Illustrate this data on a graph, with time along the x-axis and velocity on the y-axis.
   b) Use your graph to estimate the velocity after 4.5 seconds.
   c) Use your graph to estimate the time at which the velocity reaches 40 m/s.
   d) How many seconds after being dropped does the stone land?

3. The table shows the number of pupils on the roll of Greenview school at 10-year intervals:

Year	1950	1960	1970	1980	1990
Number of pupils	44	292	311	329	351

   Greenview School opened in 1950. An oak tree was planted when there were 300 pupils on the roll, and a swimming pool was opened when there were 340 pupils on the roll.

   a) Display the information in the table on a graph.
   b) Use your graph to estimate the year in which the oak tree was planted.
   c) Use your graph to estimate the year in which the swimming pool was opened.

4. The graph shows the progress of two athletes in a race. The time for which they have been running is shown along the x-axis, and the distance covered is on the y-axis. They both started running at time 0.

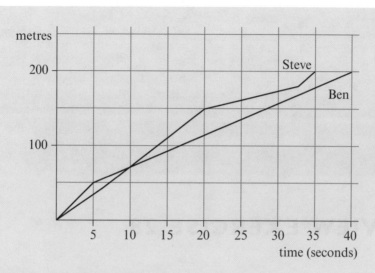

a) What distance was the race run over?

b) Who won the race?

c) Who was in the lead after 20 seconds?

d) At what time were the athletes level?

e) Steve put in an extra burst of speed near the end. How long did this last for?

5 A tap delivers water at a steady rate into a cone-shaped container which looks like this:

Which one of these graphs best describes how the container fills?

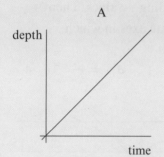

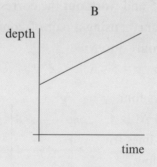

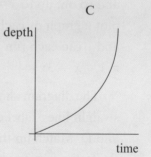

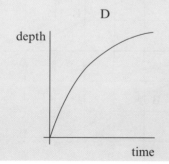

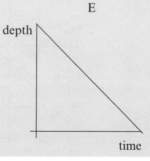

- In this chapter you have practised rearranging equations of straight lines into the form $y = mx + c$. The gradient is m and the intercept is c, so this information can help you sketch the graph of the line.

- You have plotted the graphs of quadratics and cubics. These are curves, so a table must be set up, and as many points as possible plotted. They are then joined up with a smooth curve.

- Finally, you have solved problems using a variety of graphs, including distance–time graphs.

REVIEW EXERCISE 28

1   Find the gradient and intercept of each of these straight lines. You may need to do some rearranging first.

a $y = 5x + 3$ b $2x + y = 6$ c $\frac{y}{3} - 5x = 0$ d $2x + 3y + 4 = 0$

e $x + y = 10$ f $x - y = 0$

2   Rearrange these equations into the form $y = mx + c$, and make a sketch of each one.

a $4x + y = 2$ b $x + y + 1 = 0$ c $\frac{x}{5} - 2y = 0$ d $3x + 2y = 12$

3   For parts a, b, c and d you need to draw up a table of values for $x = -5, -4$ and so on, up to $x = 5$ and work out the corresponding y-values. Then plot a graph of each curve, using a pair of coordinate axes in which x and y can each run from -5 to 5.

a $y = x^2 - 3x - 4$ b $y = 5 - x^2$ c $y = x^2 - x - 1$ d $y = x^2 - 3x - 4$

4   ✳ The diagram shows four straight lines, labelled A, B, C and D. Match up the lines to the four equations below.

a $y = x + 2$

b $y = 2x - 1$

c $y = -x - 1$

d $y = 6 - x$

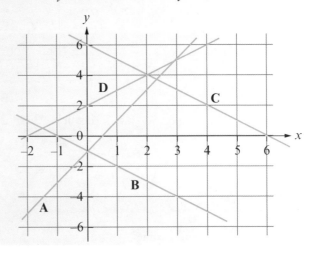

5 ✳ Temperatures can be measured either in degrees Fahrenheit (F) or degrees Celsius (C). A temperature of 0°C is equivalent to 32°F, while 100°C is the same as 212°F.

   a Draw coordinate axes in which x represents °C and y represents °F. Make sure that x can run from 0 to 100 and y from 30 to 220.

   b Plot the points (0, 32) and (100, 212) on your graph, and join them up with a straight line to make a conversion graph.

   c Use your graph to convert 30°C into °F, and 180°F into °C.

   d Does your conversion graph indicate that y is proportional to x?

6 ✳ The table shows approximate figures for the world's population at intervals of 100 years:

Year	1500	1600	1700	1800	1900
Population (millions)	425	545	610	900	1625

   a Draw a graph with the year plotted along the x-axis and population along the y-axis.

   b From your graph estimate the world's population in
      i 1550; ii 1750.

   c Explain briefly why it would be unwise to estimate the world's population in 1950 from this graph.

7 ✳ The diagram shows four curves, labelled A, B, C and D. Match up the lines to the four equations below.

   a $y = x^2 + 2$
   b $y = x^2 - 6$
   c $y = -2 + 8x - 2x^2$
   d $y = \frac{1}{2}x^2$

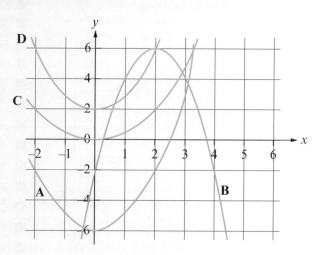

29 Quadrilaterals, polygons and angles

OUTLINE

In this chapter you will learn how to:
- classify quadrilaterals by properties
- use vertically opposite, interior, alternate and corresponding angles
- use angle sum properties of general polygons
- use equations to solve angle problems.

29.1 Types of quadrilateral

A **quadrilateral** is a 2-D geometric shape with four straight sides.

The properties of some special quadrilaterals are summarised in the table below.

Quadrilateral		Properties
Square		■ Four equal sides ■ Opposite sides are parallel ■ Four equal angles of 90° ■ Rotational symmetry of order 4 ■ Four lines of symmetry
Rhombus		■ Four equal sides ■ Opposite sides are parallel ■ Two pairs of equal angles ■ Rotational symmetry of order 2 ■ Two lines of symmetry
Rectangle		■ Two pairs of equal sides ■ Opposite sides are parallel ■ Four equal angles of 90° ■ Rotational symmetry of order 2 ■ Two lines of symmetry
Parallelogram		■ Two pairs of equal sides ■ Opposite sides are parallel ■ Two pairs of equal angles ■ Rotational symmetry of order 2 ■ No line of symmetry

Quadrilateral		Properties
Kite		■ Two pairs of equal sides ■ One pair of equal angles ■ One line of symmetry
Arrowhead		■ Two pairs of equal sides ■ One pair of equal angles ■ One line of symmetry
Trapezium		■ One pair of parallel sides ■ Some trapeziums have a line of symmetry, others do not

Question

Draw a pair of coordinate axes in which x and y can each run from 0 to 10.

Plot the points A (2, 5), B (7, 3), C (9, 5) and D (7, 7) and join them up, in order, to form a closed quadrilateral. Name the type of quadrilateral that is obtained. Mark any line(s) of symmetry on your diagram.

Solution

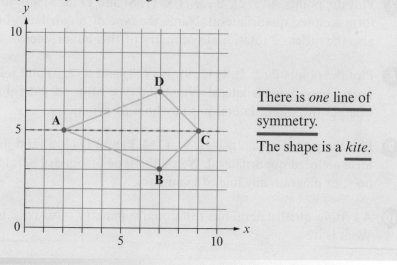

There is *one* line of symmetry.

The shape is a *kite*.

EXERCISE 29.1

In each of these questions you will need to draw a coordinate grid in which x and y can range from 0 to 10.

1. Plot the points A (2, 2), B (8, 3), C (8, 7) and D (2, 6) and join them up, in order, to form a closed quadrilateral. Name the type of quadrilateral that is obtained. Mark the angle DAB on your diagram, and mark another angle which is equal to it. ✓

2. Plot the points P (1, 6), Q (5, 4), R (9, 6) and S (5, 8) and join them to form the quadrilateral PQRS. Name the type of quadrilateral that is obtained. Mark any line(s) of symmetry on your diagram.

3. Plot the points A (5, 2), B (8, 7), C (3, 10) and D (0, 5) and join them up, in order, to form a closed quadrilateral. Name the type of quadrilateral that is obtained.

4. Plot the points P (2, 2), Q (8, 2), R (7, 7) and S (5, 7) and join them up, in order, to form a closed quadrilateral. Name the type of quadrilateral that is obtained. ✓

5. Plot the points A (6, 9), B (2, 7), C (5, 1) and D (9, 3) and join them up, in order, to form a closed quadrilateral. Name the type of quadrilateral that is obtained. Find also the coordinates of the point X at the centre of the quadrilateral.

6. Plot the points P (7, 5), Q (6, 1), R (1, 5) and S (2, 9) and join them up, in order, to form a closed quadrilateral. Name the type of quadrilateral that is obtained. State whether the quadrilateral has any lines of symmetry.

7. Plot the points A (3, 2), B (2, 7), C (7, 8) and D (8, 3) and join them up, in order, to form a closed quadrilateral. Name the type of quadrilateral that is obtained. State also the order of rotational symmetry of this quadrilateral.

8. Plot the points P (2, 2), Q (2, 9), R (8, 8) and S (8, 3) and join them up, in order, to form a closed quadrilateral. Name the type of quadrilateral that is obtained. State whether this quadrilateral has any lines of symmetry.

9. Plot the points A (2, 2), B (2, 9), C (4, 7) and D (3, 3) and join them up, in order, to form a closed quadrilateral. Name the type of quadrilateral that is obtained. Mark on your diagram any line of symmetry.

10. A certain quadrilateral has rotational symmetry of order 2 but no line of symmetry. What is it?

29.2 Angles and parallels

The angles inside a quadrilateral add up to 360°.

Question   Find the missing angle a.

Solution $80 + 123 + 105 + a = 360$
$308 + a = 360$
$a = 360 - 308$
$\underline{a = 52°}$

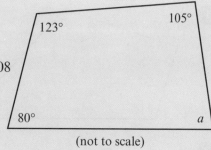

(not to scale)

In the next Exercise you will need to use the fact that angles in a quadrilateral add up to 360°. You will also need to know the following properties of angles and parallel lines:

Angles at a point add up to 360°.   Z-angles (alternate angles) are equal.

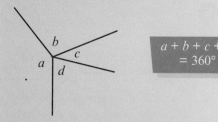

$a + b + c + d = 360°$

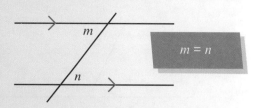

$m = n$

Angles on a straight line add up to 180°.   F-angles (corresponding angles) are equal.

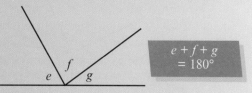

$e + f + g = 180°$

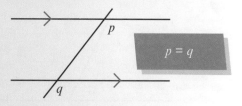

$p = q$

Vertically opposite angles are equal.   Interior angles add up to 180°.

$h = j \quad i = k$

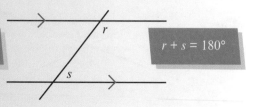

$r + s = 180°$

EXERCISE 29.2

Find the angles represented by letters in these diagrams. Give a brief reason in each case.
(*The diagrams are not drawn to scale.*)

1

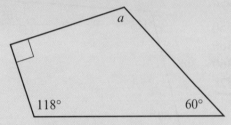

2 ✓

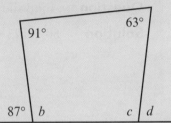

3 ✓

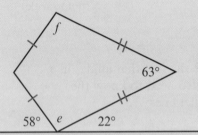

4

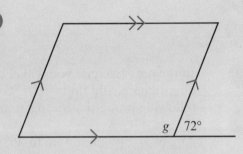

5

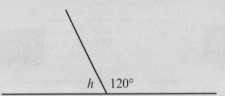

6

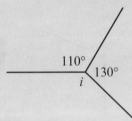

7

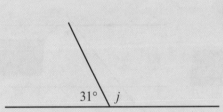

8

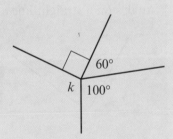

9

10

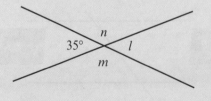

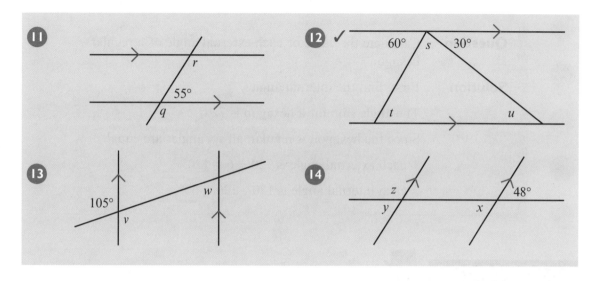

29.3 General polygons

You have been using the result that the angles inside any quadrilateral must always add up to 360°. As you add another side the angle sum goes up by 180°, so the five angles in any pentagon must add up to 540°, the six angles in a hexagon add to 720° and so on.

At each vertex, or corner, of a polygon there is an **internal angle** and an **external angle**:

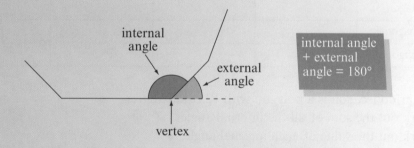

internal angle
+ external
angle = 180°

Question	Calculate the value of each internal angle inside a regular pentagon.
Solution	The angle sum in any pentagon is 540°.
	If the pentagon is regular, all five angles are equal.
	∴ each angle is 540 ÷ 5 = <u>108°</u>

Question   Calculate the value of each external angle of a regular hexagon.

Solution   First, find the internal angles.

The angle sum for a hexagon is 720°.

Since the hexagon is regular, all six angles are equal.

∴ each external angle is 720 ÷ 6 = 120°.

∴ each internal angle is 180 − 120 = 60°.

EXERCISE 29.3

1   Copy and complete this table, to show the properties of some basic regular polygons.

Name of regular polygon	Number of sides	Sum of internal angles	Value of each internal angle	Value of each external angle
Square	4	360°	90°	90°
Pentagon	5	540°	108°	72°
Hexagon	6	720°		
Heptagon				
Octagon				
Nonagon				
Decagon				

2   A regular dodecagon is a polygon with 12 equal angles.
   a) Work out the sum of all the internal angles. ✓
   b) Work out the value of each internal angle. ✓
   c) Work out the value of each external angle. ✓

3   A certain regular polygon has a total of 14 sides.
   a) Calculate the value of each internal angle.
   b) Calculate the value of each external angle.
   c) Check that all of the external angles add up to 360°.

4   A regular polygon has 36 sides.
   a) Find the value of each external angle, using the fact that they all add up to 360°.
   b) Hence find the sum of the interior angles.

29.4 Using equations to solve angle problems

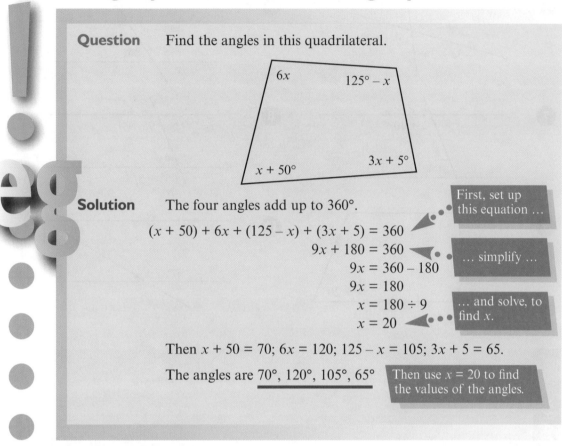

Question   Find the angles in this quadrilateral.

$6x$

$125° - x$

$x + 50°$

$3x + 5°$

Solution   The four angles add up to 360°.

First, set up this equation ...

$(x + 50) + 6x + (125 - x) + (3x + 5) = 360$

$9x + 180 = 360$

... simplify ...

$9x = 360 - 180$

$9x = 180$

$x = 180 \div 9$

... and solve, to find x.

$x = 20$

Then $x + 50 = 70$; $6x = 120$; $125 - x = 105$; $3x + 5 = 65$.

The angles are 70°, 120°, 105°, 65°

Then use $x = 20$ to find the values of the angles.

EXERCISE 29.4

Find the values represented by letters. You should set up and solve an equation where possible.

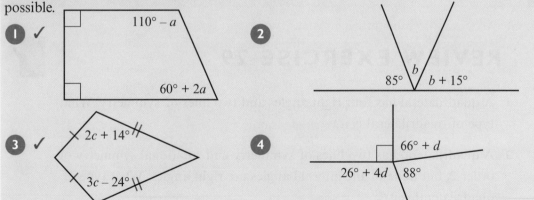

1 ✓ $110° - a$ $60° + 2a$

2 $85°$ b $b + 15°$

3 ✓ $2c + 14°$ $3c - 24°$

4 $66° + d$ $26° + 4d$ $88°$

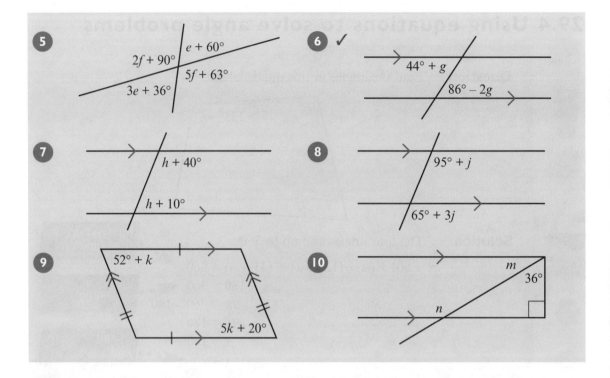

5 $2f + 90°$ $e + 60°$ $5f + 63°$ $3e + 36°$

6 ✓ $44° + g$ $86° - 2g$

7 $h + 40°$ $h + 10°$

8 $95° + j$ $65° + 3j$

9 $52° + k$ $5k + 20°$

10 m $36°$ n

SUMMARY

- In this chapter you have used symmetries to classify types of quadrilateral, including square, rhombus, rectangle, parallelogram, kite, arrowhead and trapezium.

- You have revised Z-angles and F-angles, and you have learnt that vertically opposite angles are equal, while interior angles (between two parallel lines) add up to 180°.

- Angles in any quadrilateral add up to 360°; in a pentagon 540°, and a hexagon 720° and so on – each extra side increases the angle sum by 180°. An internal angle and its matching external angle always add up to 180°.

- You have practised using these principles to solve problems, including algebra problems with angles.

REVIEW EXERCISE 29

1 A quadrilateral has four right angles and two lines of symmetry. What type of quadrilateral is it?

2 A quadrilateral has two lines of symmetry and rotational symmetry of order 2, but none of the internal angles are right angles. What type of quadrilateral is it?

3 Sanjay says: 'Any quadrilateral with four equal sides must be a square'.
Is he right or is he wrong?

4 Gita says: 'Any quadrilateral with rotational symmetry of order 4 must
be a square'. Is she right or is she wrong?

5 Make a copy of this table in your exercise book:

Four lines of symmetry	Two lines of symmetry	One line of symmetry	No line of symmetry

Put the words 'arrowhead, kite, parallelogram, rectangle, rhombus,
square and trapezium' in the correct columns.

6 In parts **a**–**h** find the angles represented by letters.

a

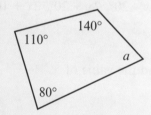

b

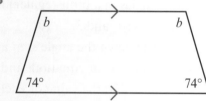

c

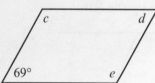

d

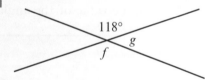

e

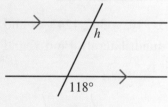

f

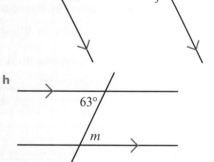

g

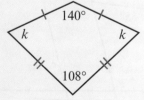

h

7 **a** Write down the sum of the angles in a pentagon.

   b Four of the angles in a (non-regular) pentagon are 120°, 110°, 95° and 92°. Find the fifth one.

8 In parts **a–d** set up and solve an equation to find the value of each letter.

  a

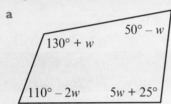

  b

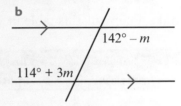

  c

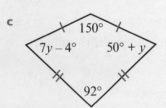

  d

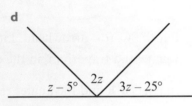

9 The angles in a (non-regular) hexagon are $3x - 20°$, $2x + 20°$, $2x + 10°$, $2x$, $4x - 80°$ and $3x - 10°$.

  a Write down the angle sum as an equation.

  b Simplify your equation, and solve it to find the value of x.

  c Hence find the value of each angle.

10 ✳ Find the value of the angle represented by the letter a.

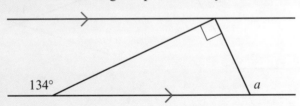

11 ✳ The four angles in a quadrilateral are $5x$, $10x - 30°$, $124° - x$ and $3x + 28°$ (in order, as you go around the quadrilateral). Find x, and hence decide what type of quadrilateral it is.

12 ✳ Find the values represented by letters in this diagram:

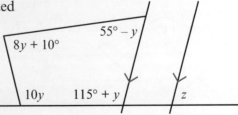

30 Transformations

In this chapter you will learn how to:
- draw shapes in different orientations on grids
- translate objects using a given translation vector
- reflect objects in a given mirror line
- rotate objects about a given centre of rotation
- recognise congruent shapes.

30.1 2-D shapes and grids

Sometimes you will need to take a 2-D shape drawn on a grid and move it to a different orientation. The shape might need to be translated (moved) or rotated (turned), or it could be reflected in a mirror line.

Question   The diagram shows a complete 2-D shape, labelled with a letter **A**. An incomplete copy of it has been made elsewhere on the grid, labelled **B**.

a) Finish off the incomplete copy.

b) Explain how the shape **A** has been moved to **B**.

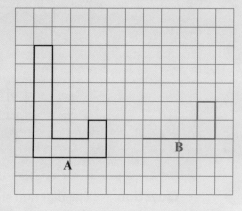

Solution   a)

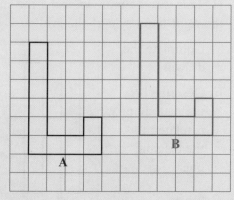

b) The shape A has been translated to produce shape **B**.

Question The diagram shows a 2-D shape **P** and an incomplete copy of it, **Q**.

Finish the drawing for **Q**, and explain how **P** and **Q** are related.

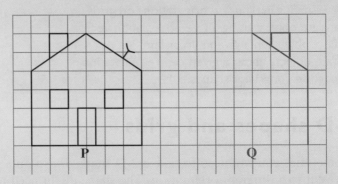

Solution The shapes **P** and **Q** are mirror images, or reflections, of each other.

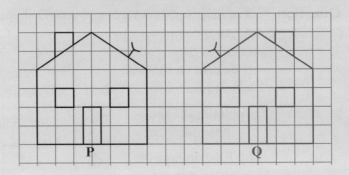

Question The diagram shows a complete pattern in the shape of a letter H. This is to be redrawn using the small 'registration marks' on the right-hand side of the grid.

a) Complete the drawing.

b) Describe how the new shape is related to the original one.

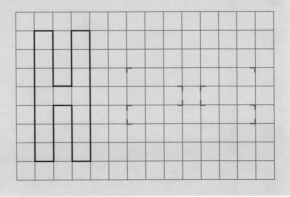

Solution a)

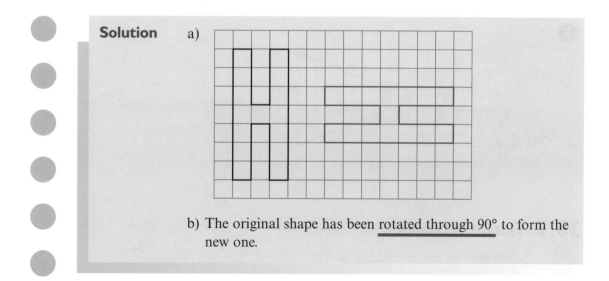

b) The original shape has been rotated through 90° to form the new one.

EXERCISE 30.1

Copy each of these diagrams onto squared paper, and complete the new pattern. Describe how each new pattern is related to the original one.

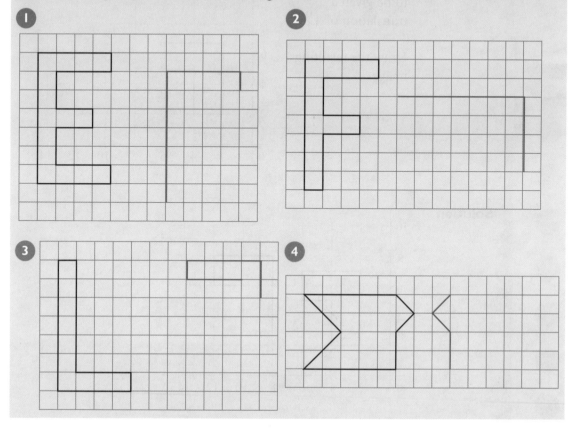

1

2

3

4

5

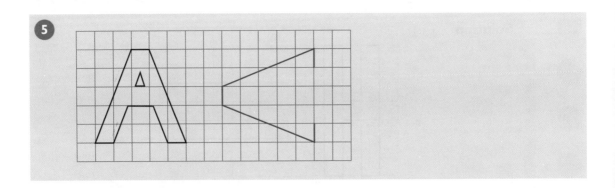

30.2 Translations

A **translation** is often written as a column vector, e.g. $\binom{6}{1}$.
The top number (6) tells you how many units to move
to the right (in the x direction), and the bottom number (1) tells you
how many units to move up (in the y direction).

Question   The object below is
to be given a
translation of $\binom{6}{1}$.

Draw the resulting
image.

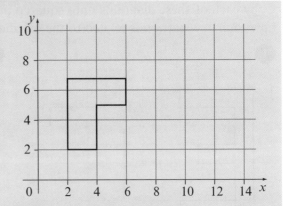

Solution

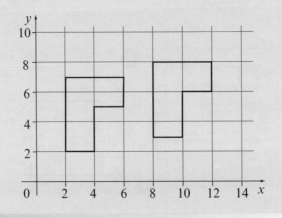

Negative numbers in the translation vector indicate that you move left (instead of right) or down (instead of up).

Question The object shown is to be given a translation of $\begin{pmatrix} -5 \\ 2 \end{pmatrix}$.
Draw the image.

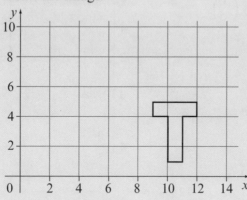

Solution

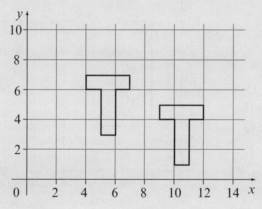

EXERCISE 30.2

① Make a drawing of this grid and the given object (shape). Then draw the resulting images for each of these three translations:

a) $\begin{pmatrix} 4 \\ 2 \end{pmatrix}$ b) $\begin{pmatrix} 3 \\ -3 \end{pmatrix}$ c) $\begin{pmatrix} -5 \\ -2 \end{pmatrix}$.

(Each translation is applied to the **original object**.)

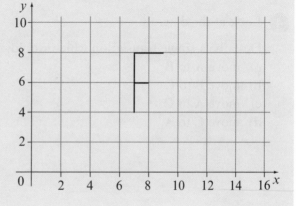

2 Make a drawing of this grid and the given object (shape). Then draw the resulting images for each of these three translations:

a) $\binom{5}{3}$ b) $\binom{-4}{2}$ c) $\binom{0}{-5}$.

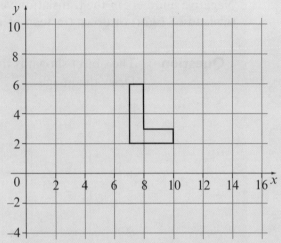

3 Make a drawing of this grid and given object. Label the object **P**.

a) Translate **P** using the vector $\binom{5}{2}$.

Label the result **Q**.

b) Now using **Q** as the object, translate **Q** using the vector $\binom{7}{-2}$.

Label the result **R**.

c) Describe a single transformation which would move **P** directly to **R**.

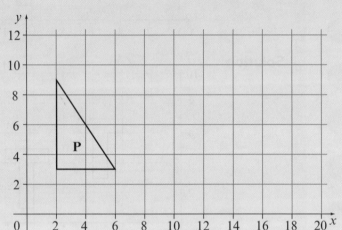

4 Look at the diagram.

Describe a single translation which would:

a) move **A** to **B**

b) move **B** to **C**

c) move **A** to **C**

d) move **C** to **A**.

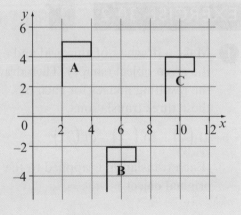

254

30.3 Reflections

Reflections are fully described once you give the location of the mirror line. This is often done for grid problems by writing an equation, like $y = 5$ (a horizontal line) or $x = 3$ (a vertical line).

Question The shape below is to be reflected in the mirror line $x = 7$. Draw the mirror line, and show the result of the reflection.

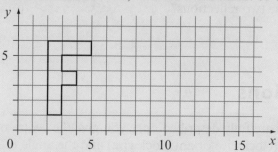

Solution

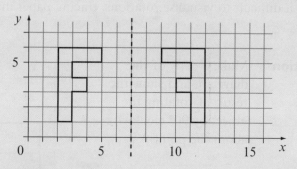

EXERCISE 30.3

1 Make four separate copies of the diagram below, then carry out the reflections in questions a) to d).

a) Reflect the shape in the line $x = 2$.

b) Reflect the shape in the line $y = 2$.

c) Reflect the shape in the line $x = 0$ (i.e. the y-axis).

d) Reflect the shape in the line $x = -1$.

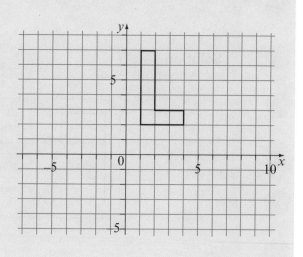

2 Make an accurate copy of the
diagram onto squared paper.

a) Reflect the object in the line $x = 4$
to form an image.

b) Now reflect this image in the line
$x = 2$.

c) What can you say about the combined
result of the two reflections?

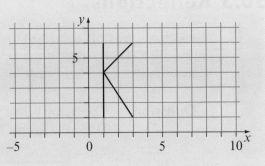

30.4 Rotations

Rotations are fully described once you give the centre of rotation, the
direction (clockwise or anticlockwise) and the angle of rotation. If
you find it difficult to visualise rotations, tracing paper may be very
useful.

Question Make a copy of the
diagram, and show the
result of rotating the
object by 90° clockwise
about the point A.

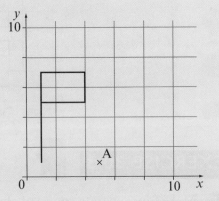

Solution

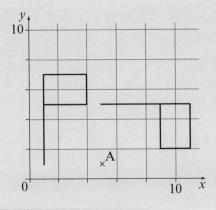

256

EXERCISE 30.4

1 Make a copy of this diagram. Then draw the
result of rotating the object:
a) through 90° anticlockwise about O
b) through 90° clockwise about O
c) through 180° about O.
Explain why no direction of rotation is needed
in part c).

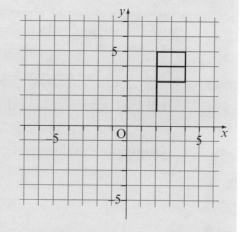

2 Draw a coordinate grid in which x and y can run from −10 to 10.
a) Plot the points (3, 3), (7, 3) and (3, 9), and join them up to form a triangle.
b) Rotate the original object by 90° clockwise about O.
c) Rotate the original object by 90° anticlockwise about (1, 0).

3 Draw a coordinate grid in which x and y can run from −10 to 10.
a) Plot the points (3, 3), (9, 3), (7, 8) and (5, 8), and join them up in order, to form a
quadrilateral.
b) What type of quadrilateral is this?
c) Rotate the quadrilateral through 180° about (1, 1).

4 Samir has been told to rotate an object through 90° clockwise about the origin. By
mistake, he rotates it through 90° anticlockwise about the origin instead. Explain
carefully what Samir needs to do to his image in order to move it to the right place.

5 Draw a coordinate grid in which x and y can run from
−10 to 10.
a) Plot these points shown on the grid opposite to form
an object in the shape of a letter F. Label it (1).
b) Rotate the original object (1) through 90° clockwise
about (4, 0). Label the result (2).
c) Now rotate this image (2) through 90° anticlockwise
about (0, −8). Label the result (3).
d) Describe a single transformation which would take
you straight from object (1) to image (3).

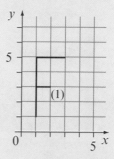

30.5 Congruent shapes

Two shapes are said to be **congruent** if they are the **same shape and size**. Translations, reflections and rotations all produce images which are congruent to the original object.

Two shapes are **congruent** if they are exactly the same shape and size. The two shapes do not have to be the same way round – one could be a reflected version of the other.

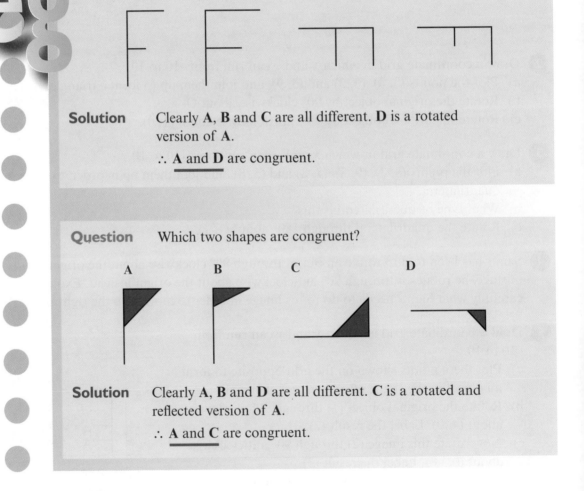

Question   Which two shapes are congruent?

A   B   C   D

Solution   Clearly **A**, **B** and **C** are all different. **D** is a rotated version of **A**.

∴ **A** and **D** are congruent.

Question   Which two shapes are congruent?

A   B   C   D

Solution   Clearly **A**, **B** and **D** are all different. **C** is a rotated and reflected version of **A**.

∴ **A** and **C** are congruent.

EXERCISE 30.5

1 Which two triangles are congruent?

A   B   C   D

2 Which two shapes are congruent?

A   B   C   D   E

 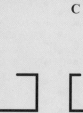 

3 Name the shape which is congruent to:
a) A   b) F   c) E   d) D

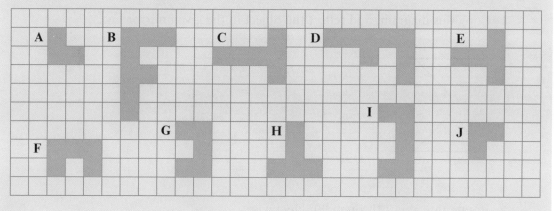

REVIEW EXERCISE 30

1 The shape labelled **P** has been drawn using isometric dotty paper. The shape labelled **Q** is the result of rotating **P** through 180°. The drawing of **Q** is incomplete.

a Copy the diagram onto isometric dotty paper.

b Finish the drawing, so that the shape **Q** is complete.

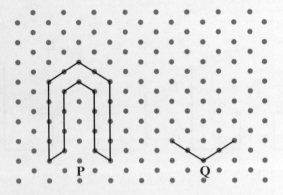

2 Copy this diagram, and reflect the object in the given mirror line.

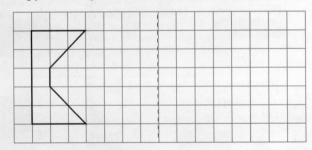

3 Rotate this object through 90° clockwise.

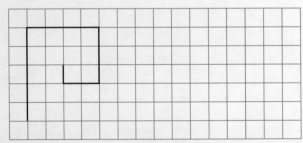

4 Make a copy of this diagram.
Then draw the result of transforming
the object by:

a a translation of $\begin{pmatrix} -5 \\ 2 \end{pmatrix}$

b a reflection in
the line $x = 6$

c a rotation of 90° anticlockwise
about the origin.

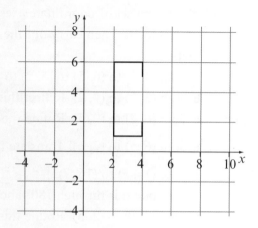

5 Yasmin draws an isosceles triangle. Amy also draws an isosceles triangle.
Yasmin says: 'Both triangles are isosceles, so they must be congruent'.
Is Yasmin right? Explain your reasoning.

6 You will need to work with one or two friends for this activity. You will
also need some square dotted paper, and some scissors.

On dotted paper draw two congruent shapes
and cut them out.
For example, you might make these:

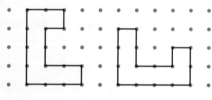

Now fit them together to make a
single shape:

Finally, copy the outline of the
combined shape onto a fresh sheet
of dotted paper:

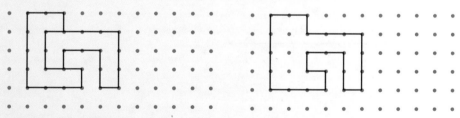

Challenge a friend to find out how to divide the complete shape into two
congruent parts.

7 ✳ Draw a set of coordinate axes in which x can run from 0 to 20 and y from 0 to 10. Then carry out the following constructions, to make a picture.

a Join (3, 5) to (6, 5) to (3, 2) to (6, 2). Translate this shape by $\binom{8}{5}$.

b Join (3, 7) to (7, 7). Reflect this shape in the line $x = 7$.

c Join (6, 2) to (9, 5). Rotate this line through 180° about (16, 7).

d Join (6, 5) to (7, 6). Translate this by i $\binom{3}{0}$ and ii $\binom{-4}{1}$.

e Join (14, 5) to (16, 7).
i Rotate this through 180° about (16, 7) and ii translate it by $\binom{0}{2}$.

f Join (2, 6) to (2, 5). Rotate this line through 90° clockwise about (2, 5).

g Join (9, 5) to (12, 5). Translate this by $\binom{2}{0}$.

h Join (16, 9) to (17, 9). Reflect this in the line $x = 17$.

8 ✳ The map below shows two points A and B. A horse is at point A, and wishes to walk to point B. He is thirsty, however, and must stop for a drink in the river on the way. The river flows along the x-axis.

a Make a copy of this diagram on squared paper.

b Find the shortest path the horse might take.
[*Clue: it is helpful to draw the reflection of point B, using the river as a mirror line.*]

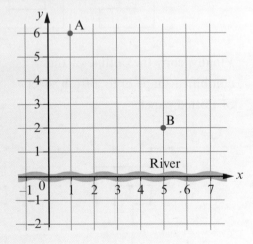

31 The circle

In this chapter you will revise:
- the definition of a circle and the naming of its parts.

You will then learn how to:
- find the circumference of a circle, using $C = 2\pi r$ or $C = \pi d$
- find the area of a circle using $A = \pi r^2$
- solve inverse problems to find the radius or diameter.

OUTLINE

31.1 Circle vocabulary

A circle has a **centre**, which is often labelled with the letter O.

The circle is constructed by joining all the points which are at a fixed distance from the centre. This fixed distance is called the **radius**.

The points around the edge of the circle are said to lie on its **circumference**.

A straight line joining any two points on the circumference is called a **chord**.

The longest possible chord must pass through the centre of the circle; it is then called a **diameter**.

A chord divides the interior of the circle into two unequal regions, called **segments**. The smaller one is the **minor segment**, the larger is the **major segment**.

When an arc is connected to the centre of the circle a wedge-shaped region is formed. This is called a **sector**.

If the sector occupies less than half a circle it is a **minor sector**; if more than half, it is a **major sector**.

If the sector occupies exactly half the circle it is a **semicircle**.

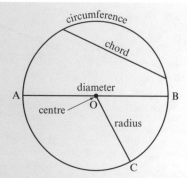

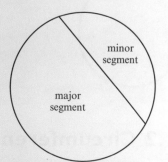

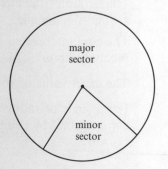

EXERCISE 31.1

Look at the ten drawings below. For each one, write down the word that matches the highlighted line or area.

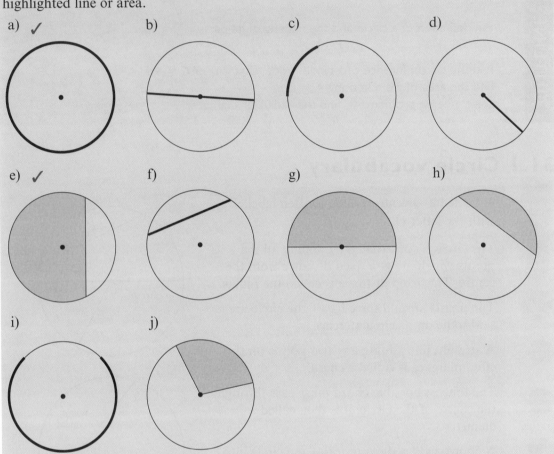

a) ✓ b) c) d)

e) ✓ f) g) h)

i) j)

31.2 Circumference of a circle

The length of the **circumference** of a circle is the distance all the way around the outside.

The circumference is just over three times the diameter; more precisely, about 3.142 times.

The exact value of this decimal ratio is called 'pi' and is written π.

For a circle of radius r or diameter d the length of the circumference can be found by using either of these results: $C = 2\pi r$
$$C = \pi d$$

Question A circle has radius 12 cm. Find its circumference.

Your calculator should have the value of π stored in it, probably to 10 significant figures. Just use this key sequence:

$$2 \times \pi \times 1 \; 2 =$$

Solution $r = 12$.
Using the result
$C = 2\pi r$ we have

$C = 2\pi r$
    $= 2 \times 3.141\,592\,6 \times 12$
    $= 75.398\,222\,4$ (by calculator)
    $= \underline{75.4 \text{ cm}}$ correct to 3 s.f.

Question A circle has diameter 11 cm. Find its circumference.

Solution $d = 11$. Using the result $C = \pi d$ we have

$C = \pi d$
    $= 3.141\,592\,6 \times 11$
    $= 34.557\,518\,6$ (by calculator)
    $= \underline{34.6 \text{ cm}}$ correct to 3 s.f.

It is a good idea to write down several figures...

...and then round them off to 3 significant figures.

EXERCISE 31.2

1 Find the circumference of each of these circles, correct to 3 significant figures.

a) $r = 8$ cm   b) $r = 18$ cm   c) $r = 5$ km ✓   d) $d = 20$ cm   e) $d = 28$ mm

f) $r = 12$ mm   g) $d = 14$ km   h) $d = 19$ m ✓   i) $r = 6$ cm   j) $d = 2$ cm

2 Find the circumference of each of these circles, correct to 4 significant figures.

a) $d = 2.9$ m   b) $r = 1.5$ cm   c) $d = 42.8$ mm ✓   d) $r = 4.1$ cm

e) $r = 15$ cm   f) $d = 62.5$ mm   g) $d = 0.9252$ km   h) $r = 12.25$ km ✓

i) $r = 1255$ mm   j) $d = 1.008$ km

31.3 Area of a circle

For a circle of radius r or diameter d the area A can be found by using the result $A = \pi r^2$

Question   A circle has radius 12 cm. Find its area.

> You can use the square key x^2 on your calculator. This sequence will work well:
>
> $\boxed{\pi}$ $\boxed{\times}$ $\boxed{1}$ $\boxed{2}$ $\boxed{x^2}$ $\boxed{=}$

Solution $r = 12$. Using the result $A = \pi r^2$ we have

$A = \pi r^2$
$= 3.141\ 592\ 6 \times 12 \times 12$
$= 452.389\ 334\ 4$ (by calculator)
$= \underline{452\ \text{cm}^2}$ correct to 3 s.f.

Question   A circle has diameter 11 cm. Find its area.

Solution $d = 11$ so $r = 11 \div 2 = 5.5$.

> For area problems you cannot work with diameter, you **must** find the radius straight away.

Using the result $A = \pi r^2$ we have
$A = \pi r^2$
$= 3.141\ 592\ 6 \times 5.5 \times 5.5$
$= 95.033\ 176\ 15$ (by calculator)
$= \underline{95.0\ \text{cm}^2}$ correct to 3 s.f.

> Remember to write **cm²**, not just cm.

EXERCISE 31.3

1 Find the area of each of these circles, correct to 3 significant figures.

  a) $r = 8$ cm   b) $r = 18$ cm   c) $r = 5$ km ✓   d) $d = 20$ cm   e) $d = 28$ mm

  f) $r = 12$ mm   g) $d = 14$ km ✓ h) $d = 19$ m   i) $r = 6$ cm   j) $d = 2$ cm

2 Find the area of each of these circles, correct to 4 significant figures.

  a) $d = 2.9$ m   b) $r = 1.5$ cm   c) $d = 42.8$ mm ✓   d) $r = 4.1$ cm

  e) $r = 15$ cm ✓ f) $d = 62.5$ mm   g) $d = 0.9252$ km   h) $r = 12.25$ km

  i) $r = 1255$ mm j) $d = 1.008$ km

31.4 Inverse problems

Sometimes you are given the circumference or area of a circle, and you find the radius by working backwards.

Question   A circle has area 125 cm². Find its radius.

Solution   Using the result $A = \pi r^2$ we have

$$\pi r^2 = 125$$
$$r^2 = \frac{125}{\pi}$$

Concentrate on finding r^2 first, then square root it to find r.

$$= 39.788\ 735\ 77\ldots$$
$$r = \sqrt{39.788\ 735\ 77\ldots}$$

Once again, rounding is done only at the very last stage.

$$= 6.307\ 831\ 305\ldots$$
$$= \underline{6.31\ \text{cm correct to 3 s.f.}}$$

Question   A circle has circumference 16.5 cm. Find its diameter.

Solution   Using the result $C = 2\pi r$ we have

The question says 'find its diameter' but it is usually best to find the radius first. This can simply be doubled at the end, to obtain the diameter.

$$2\pi r = 16.5$$
$$r = \frac{16.5}{2\pi}$$
$$= 2.626\ 056\ 561\ldots$$

$$d = 2 \times r$$
$$= 2 \times 2.626\ 056\ 561\ldots$$
$$= 5.252\ 113\ 122\ldots$$
$$= \underline{5.25\ \text{cm correct to 3 s.f.}}$$

Beware of rounding too early! The full calculator values are used until the very last line, when the answer is rounded to 3 s.f.

EXERCISE 31.4

Find the radius of each of these circles.

1 Circumference 35 mm

2 Circumference 20 inches ✓

3 Area 35 mm² ✓

4 Area 4.56 m²

5 Circumference 235 mm

6 Area 865 cm²

7 Circumference 11 m

8 Area 24 cm²

9 Area 1.035 mm²

10 Circumference 8500 km

REVIEW EXERCISE 31

1   A circle has radius 19 cm. Find its circumference.

2   A circle has diameter 29 cm. Find its area.

3   A circle has diameter 48 cm. Find its circumference.

4   A circle has radius 1100 mm. Find its area.

5   A circle has radius 27 cm. Find its circumference and area, each correct to 4 significant figures.

6   A circle has diameter 93 mm. Find its circumference and area, each correct to 2 significant figures.

7   A circle has area 975 cm^2. Find its radius.

8   A circle has circumference 1185 mm. Find its diameter.

9   Find the diameter of a circle whose area is 75 cm^2.

10   Find the radius of a circle whose circumference is 99 m.

11   ✳ Richard measures the circumference of two tree trunks. The smaller one is 2.35 m and the larger one is 3.77 m.

    a   Calculate the radius of the smaller tree trunk.

    b   Calculate the radius of the larger tree trunk.

    c   Richard says '2.35 goes into 3.77 about 1.6 times, so the radius of the larger trunk is about 60% bigger than the radius of the small trunk'. Is Richard right or is he wrong?

12 ✱ In 1893 the American engineer G W G Ferris built a 'Big Wheel' for the Chicago Exposition. It could carry 36 cabins, each holding 60 people. This Ferris wheel was 76 m in diameter.

    a Calculate the total number of people who could travel on the Ferris wheel when it was full.

    b Calculate the circumference of the Ferris wheel.

13 ✱ A circular paddling pool has a circumference of 24.5 m.

    a Find the radius, correct to 3 significant figures.

    b Hence find the area of the surface of the pool, also correct to 3 significant figures.

14 ✱ A machine marks sheets of plastic into small squares measuring 6 cm by 6 cm. A circular disc of radius 3 cm is pressed from each square, and the plastic left over is discarded.

    a Calculate the area of one circular disc.

    b Write down the area of one small square.

    c Find the percentage of plastic which is discarded.

15 ✱ The Earth travels around its orbit once each year. The Earth's orbit is approximately circular, with a radius of about 93 million miles.

    a Taking this information as exact, calculate the distance that the Earth travels during one year. Give your answer in miles, correct to 2 significant figures.

    b Rewrite your answer to part a so that it is in kilometres. (1 mile = 1.609 kilometres)

16 ✱ A scientist is studying a colony of penguins. She notices that during a blizzard they huddle together in a circle of circumference 11.2 m.

    a Calculate the radius of the circle.

    b Calculate the area of the circle.

    c Calculate the number of penguins in the colony, assuming that each penguin takes up 0.04 m^2 of ground space.

17 ✱ Damian has two circular discs. One is red; it has an area of 121 cm^2. The other is blue and has a circumference of 52 cm. Which of Damian's discs is larger?

18 ✳ The front wheel of my bicycle has diameter 64 cm.

   a Find the circumference of the wheel, in centimetres.

   b Write down the number of centimetres in 6 km.

   c Find out how many times the front wheel turns when I cycle a
distance of 6 km.

19 ✳ Tammy has cut out a circle of radius 12 cm, and Simon has cut out a
circle of radius 6 cm. Simon says to Tammy:

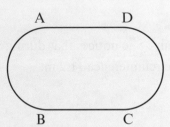

*'Your circle is twice the
size of mine, so it should have twice
the circumference and twice the
area … but something doesn't quite
seem right.'*

   a Find the circumference and area of Simon's circle.

   b Find the circumference and area of Tammy's circle.

   c Write down a correct statement that Simon should have made about
the circumference and area of Tammy's circle.

20 ✳ A sports centre is marking out a new running track. The diagram
shows the outline design for the track:

A D	AB is a semicircular arc.
	BC is a straight section of length 65 m.
	CD is a semicircular arc.
	DA is a straight section of length 65 m.
B C	The length of the whole track is 200 m.

Calculate the radius of each semicircular arc.

32 Surveys and sampling

OUTLINE

In this chapter you will learn how to:
- design a survey to collect data
- consider the effect of sample size
- construct and improve data collection sheets.

32.1 Statistical surveys

A **statistical survey** is one way of gathering information about a **population**. The questions to be asked are assembled into a **questionnaire**.

Sometimes the entire population take part in the survey; it is then called a **census**. A national census happens in Great Britain once every 10 years.

Usually it is too time-consuming to survey the entire population, however, so a representative group, or **sample**, of people is selected. This can be a very efficient method, but the sample must be chosen carefully, otherwise the results could be inaccurate. Samples which deliberately distort the picture are said to suffer from **bias**.

Question

Jasmine is carrying out a survey about the amount of pocket money that children in her school receive. She decides to ask 10 children from each year group to take part in the survey. The school contains 5 year groups, each containing 200 pupils.

a) Explain how Jasmine has tried to choose her sample to be free of bias.

b) Do you think Jasmine's chosen sample size will produce an accurate result?

Solution

a) Each year group contains the same number (200) of people, so Jasmine chose equal numbers of people (10) from each year group to form her sample.

b) The school contains 1000 pupils, but Jasmine has sampled only 50 of them. This is probably too small a sample for the result to be very accurate.

Questionnaires have to be designed carefully so that they are easy for someone to answer. **Tick boxes** are often useful. Take care to avoid vague questions like 'How much TV do you watch?' A better question is 'How many hours of TV do you watch during a normal school week?'

Question   Pedro is designing a questionnaire about food. Here is one of his questions:

What foods do you eat? _____

Suggest two ways of improving Pedro's question.

Solution   The question is too vague, he should say, 'What foods do you eat each day?' for example.

Also, the question is difficult to answer, he should use tick boxes.

So, the improved question would look like this:

Which of these foods do you eat each day?

(You may tick more than one option)

☐ meat   ☐ fish   ☐ fruit   ☐ cheese

☐ bread   ☐ veg   ☐ other

EXERCISE 32.1

1   Questions a) to f) describe statistical surveys. In each case the sample is likely to suffer from bias. Explain why.

a)   Doris is in year 7 at secondary school. She wants to investigate how much pocket money the children at her school get, so she surveys all the children in her class.

b)   Rupinder wants to find out whether people in England think that the Internet is a good thing or not. To do this, he sets up a web page and asks the people who visit it to answer five short questions. ✓

c)   Gary wants to find out the average age at which couples in England get married. He asks the local vicar for details of all the church weddings in his district for the last five years.

d)   In Deepdale College there are 250 boys and 450 girls. Martina wants to find out what the students think about plans to introduce a new Dance course, and she decides to ask 70 students their opinions. Martina chooses 35 boys at random, and 35 girls at random. ✓

e) Annis is investigating the fitness of the year 11 students at her school. She waits at the finish of the year 11 annual cross-country race, and records the pulse rate of the first 20 people to finish the race.

f) Bob wants to estimate the average midday temperature in Britain yesterday. He decides to look in the newspaper, and finds the midday temperatures for 50 seaside towns from around Britain. He chooses 25 of these, at random, as his sample.

2 Hugh has designed a simple questionnaire about alcohol abuse. It contains six questions. Decide whether each question is a good one or not; if not, suggest an improvement.
a) State your sex   ☐ male   ☐ female
b) State your age   ☐ under 16   ☐ 16 – 19   ☐ 19 – 21   ☐ 21 or over
c) How much do you drink? _____
d) Are you a smoker?   ☐ Yes   ☐ No
e) Do you play sport?   ☐ Never   ☐ Sometimes   ☐ Often
f) Have you ever had an accident as a result of drinking?   ☐ Yes   ☐ No

32.2 Data collection sheets

Statistical surveys can generate a lot of paper! One way of keeping things compact is to use a **data collection sheet**. This is a single form on which you record the responses to all the various questions you are asking.

Question Martha is carrying out a survey about how children travel to her school. Design a suitable data collection sheet.

Solution

Name	Class	Age	Method of travel	Distance	Time of leaving home	Time of arrival at school	Duration of journey

EXERCISE 32.2

1 Here are the titles of six GCSE statistics investigations. Design a suitable data collection sheet for each one.

a) What time do people get up in the morning?

b) What do teenagers spend their pocket money on?

c) Saturday jobs, is it better to work in food or clothes shops?

d) The types of videos that people watch today.

e) Electrical gadgets in the house.

f) Where do people go on holiday?

SUMMARY

- In this chapter you have used the basic vocabulary of statistical sampling, and you have looked for bias in a sample.

- You have also given some thought to the design of questionnaires, and the construction of data collection sheets.

- Remember to use tick boxes where appropriate, as they can make the questions much easier to answer.

REVIEW EXERCISE 32

1 In questions **a**–**d** explain briefly whether you think the suggested sample is likely to suffer from bias.

a Isobel is collecting information about the shopping habits of local people. She carries out a telephone survey, choosing names randomly from a telephone directory, and ringing the selected people up between 7.00 and 8.00 p.m.

b James is investigating how much his year group at school know about sport. He writes the name of each student in his year group on a slip of paper, and puts all the names in a hat. He then pulls out 30 names at random, to form the sample.

c Jamila wants to see what school students think about the new lunch canteen. She asks the first 50 people in the lunch queue to fill out a questionnaire.

d Kwabena is carrying out a survey of attendance at Premiership football clubs. He decides to record data about all the clubs in the Premiership.

2 Design a simple questionnaire about a topic that interests you, for example, animal welfare.

   a Write at least four questions.

   b Try out your questionnaire on a small sample of people. (This is called a *pilot survey*.)

   c Consider improving your questions as a result of the pilot. Then ask a larger number of people to answer the questions, and record their answers on a data collection sheet.

   d Describe your population, and say whether you think the sample is biased or not.

3 ✳ Marcus is wanting to find out about music CDs owned by his year group at school. He decides to ask 20 of his friends to answer these three questions:

How many CDs do you own? _____

How often do you listen to your CDs? _____

Do you spend a lot on CDs each week? _____

   a Explain briefly why each question is unsuitable as it stands.

   b Write an improved version of each question.

   c Design a suitable data collection sheet for the three improved questions.

   d Explain why asking 20 of his friends will probably result in a biased sample.

33 Probability

33.1 Mutually exclusive outcomes

If an experiment has several different outcomes, none of which can happen at the same time, then the outcomes are said to be **mutually exclusive**. For example, when a die is thrown, the outcomes 'the score is 4' and 'the score is 5' are mutually exclusive.

If a set of mutually exclusive outcomes covers all possibilities, then they are said to be **exhaustive**. The values of these probabilities will add up to 1.

Question   The probability that a rat can find its way out of a maze in a timed test is 0.3. Find the probability that it does not find its way out of the maze.

Solution   The two outcomes are mutually exclusive and exhaustive, so
probability(rat does not find its way out) $= 1 - 0.3$
$$= \underline{0.7}$$

Question   When Sang plays chess against Christine he wins, draws, or loses. The probability that Sang wins is 0.3 and the probability that he draws is 0.1. Calculate the probability that Sang loses.

Solution   Let the probability that Sang loses be p. Win, draw and lose are three mutually exclusive and exhaustive outcomes, so they add up to 1.

$$0.3 + 0.1 + p = 1$$
$$0.4 + p = 1$$
$$p = 1 - 0.4$$
$$= 0.6$$

The probability that Sang loses is $\underline{0.6}$

EXERCISE 33.1

1. The probability that my lottery ticket will win a prize this weekend is 0.02. Calculate the probability that it will not win a prize.

2. In a Mathematics test, Timothy reckons there is a probability of 0.3 that he will get full marks. Calculate the probability that he will not get full marks. ✓

3. When I send a letter by first class post there is a probability of 0.85 that it will arrive the next day. Find the probability that it does not arrive the next day.

4. The probability that a toy rocket will launch successfully is 0.77. Find the probability that it does not launch successfully.

5. The probability that I am on time for school each day is 0.82. Find the probability that I am late.

6. A bag contains a mixture of red, green and blue balls. The probability of choosing a red ball is 0.34, and the probability of choosing a green ball is 0.56. Find the probability of choosing a blue ball. ✓

7. A large drawer contains a mixture of loose socks. The socks are grey, blue or black. When I choose a sock at random, the probability of getting a grey one is 0.24 and the probability of getting a blue one is 0.33. Find the probability of getting a black sock.

8. In a board game I have to choose a letter out of a bag. The probability of getting a vowel is 0.45. Find the probability of getting a consonant.

9. My CDs are all either pop, jazz or classical. One tenth of my CDs are pop, and I have twice as many jazz as I have pop CDs. When a CD is chosen at random, find the probability that it will be a classical one.

10. The probability that a local hockey team wins any particular game has been estimated at 0.4. Kieron says:

> 'If that is true, then the probability that they lose must be 0.6.'

Explain carefully whether Kieron is right or wrong.

33.2 Sample space diagrams

A **sample space** diagram is a way of showing the combined probability of the outcomes of two experiments. It usually takes the form of a table.

Question   Two fair dice are thrown, and the scores are recorded. Find the probability that the total of the two scores is 9.

Solution   We begin by drawing up a table:

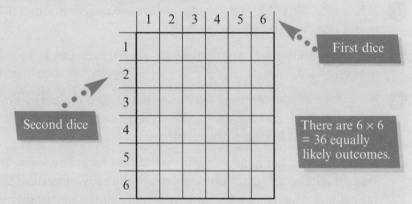

First dice

Second dice

There are 6 × 6 = 36 equally likely outcomes.

Now write in the totals:

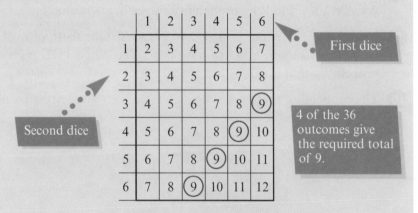

First dice

Second dice

4 of the 36 outcomes give the required total of 9.

P(total of 9) = $\dfrac{\text{number of ways of getting a total of 9}}{\text{total number of equally likely outcomes}}$

$= \dfrac{4}{36}$

$= \dfrac{1}{9}$

You could give the answer as a decimal: 0.111 111 ... but it is usually easier to write it as a fraction.

EXERCISE 33.2

Draw up a sample space diagram for each of these situations, and use it to answer the question. Answers should be left as fractions, cancelled down where possible.

1. Two fair dice are thrown and the total is recorded.
   Find the probability that the total is:
   a) odd b) prime c) five.
   What is the most likely total?

2. A spinner has four equal sectors, labelled 1, 2, 3, 4. It is spun twice. Find the probability that the total score is 6.

3. A spinner has six equal sectors, labelled 1, 2, 2, 3, 3, 6. It is spun twice. Find the probability that the total score is 6. ✓

4. Two coins are tossed. Find the probability that the result is:
   a) two heads b) two tails c) one head and one tail.

5. One spinner has three equal sectors labelled 1, 2, 3; another spinner has five equal sectors labelled 1, 2, 3, 4, 5. Each spinner is spun, and the total score is obtained. Find the probability that this total is 6. Find also the most likely total.

6. I have four coins in my left pocket: they are 2p, 5p, 5p and 10p. I have three coins in my right pocket: they are 2p, 5p and 20p. Two coins are chosen at random, one from each pocket. Find the probability that: ✓
   a) both coins are 5p
   b) the total value of the coins is 7p.

7. My top drawer contains 3 red socks and 2 black socks, while my second drawer contains 2 red socks and 4 black socks. In the dark I take one sock from each drawer. Find the probability that I end up with:
   a) two red socks
   b) two socks of the same colour.

8. A pack of cards is shuffled, and one card is chosen at random; its suit is recorded. From a second shuffled pack another card is chosen, and again its suit is noted. Find the probability that the cards are:
   a) both diamonds
   b) both black.
   [*There are two red suits (hearts, diamonds) and two black suits (clubs, spades).*]

9. Lenny is in a hurry to order some fast food, so he chooses randomly from beef burger, chicken burger or veggie burger. This is accompanied by either jacket potato, French fries or salad, again chosen randomly. Find the probability that Lenny's chosen meal includes French fries but not a veggie burger.

10 Two fair dice are thrown and the two scores are multiplied to form a product, which is then recorded. For example, when one die shows 4 and the other shows 3 then a product of 12 is recorded.
Find the probability that the product is:
a) 12✓   b) 15✓   c) odd✓   d) prime.✓

33.3 Tree diagrams

A **tree diagram** is used when there are two or more stages to a problem, each with only two or three outcomes. Probabilities are written on the branches, and multiplied to obtain the final total.

Question   The probability that I buy a lottery ticket on a Saturday is 0.3, and the probability that my wife does is 0.4. Draw a tree diagram, and use it to find the probability that:

a) we both buy tickets   b) only one of us does.

Solution

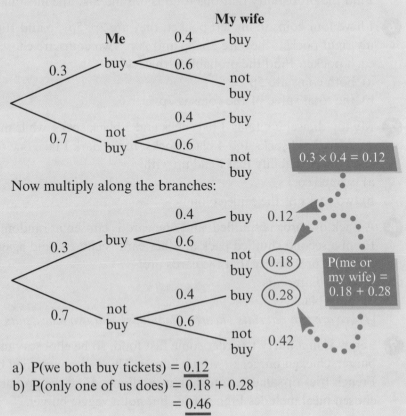

Now multiply along the branches:

a) P(we both buy tickets) = <u>0.12</u>
b) P(only one of us does) = 0.18 + 0.28
                          = <u>0.46</u>

Warning!

Make sure that you understand when to multiply and when to add probabilities. You **multiply** along the branches, e.g. 0.3×0.6 to get 0.18 at the end.

You **add** in order to combine alternative end points, e.g. $0.18 + 0.28$.

We can multiply the probabilities in this case because we have assumed that my decision about whether to buy a ticket is **independent** of my wife's decision.

EXERCISE 33.3

Solve each of these problems with the aid of a clearly labelled tree diagram. You can assume that the events are independent.

1 The probability that Usha can finish the crossword in her daily newspaper in under half an hour is 0.6. Calculate the probability that, on two randomly chosen days, Usha is able to finish both crosswords in under half an hour each. ✓

2 The probability that Tom forgets to bring his calculator to a mathematics lesson is 0.25. Find the probability that, in two successive lessons, Tom forgets his calculator:
a) on both occasions   b) only once.

3 When Boris goes shopping he visits the baker's with probability $\frac{3}{20}$ while the corresponding figure for Doris is $\frac{7}{20}$. They are both going shopping tomorrow. Calculate the probability that at least one of them will visit the baker's.

4 The probability that a Christmas cracker detonates successfully is 0.8. Three crackers are chosen at random. Calculate the probability that exactly two of them detonate properly. ✓

5 On my journey to work I have to drive through two sets of traffic lights. The probability that I find the first set on red is 0.2, but the probability that the second set is red is 0.7. Find the probability that, on a randomly chosen journey:
a) both sets are red   b) only the first set is red   c) exactly one set is red.

6 A cereal manufacturer places a plastic toy inside each cereal packet. When a packet is chosen at random the probability that it contains a submarine is 0.3, while the probability of an aircraft is 0.45. The only other possibility is that the toy is a tractor.
a) Calculate the probability of obtaining a tractor.
b) Two packets are chosen at random. Calculate the probability of obtaining exactly one submarine.
c) Three packets are chosen at random. Calculate the probability of obtaining at least one aircraft.

7 A newspaper reckons that a quarter of the voters in a certain area support the Progressive Party. Four people are chosen at random and asked which party they support. Calculate the probability that exactly one of them supports the Progressive Party.

8 When a certain type of rocket is used to launch a satellite there is a 5% chance that the launch will be unsuccessful.
a) Express the probability 5% as a decimal.
b) Four launches are planned. Find the probability that only three of them are successful.

9 In a multiple-choice test there are five suggested answers to each question. Only one answer is right. I decide to guess the answers to the last three questions.
a) Explain why the probability of guessing an answer correctly is 0.2.
b) Find the probability that I guess all three correctly.
c) Find the probability that I guess only one of the answers correctly.

10 When United play a match at home they reckon to win, draw or lose with probabilities 0.5, 0.3 and 0.2 respectively. United are due to play their next two matches at home. Find the probability that they will: ✓
a) win both matches   b) win only one of them, and draw the other
c) lose both matches.

SUMMARY

- In this chapter you have learnt how to deduce the value of a missing probability, by using the principle that the probabilities describing all the alternative outcomes to an experiment must always add up to 1.

- You have used sample space diagrams for the probability of a combined event, and a tree diagram for a sequence of events. In using tree diagrams, remember to multiply the probabilities as you work along the branches.

REVIEW EXERCISE 33

1 When I play chess against a certain friend the result is that I either win, draw or lose. I win a game with probability 0.4 and draw with probability 0.

a Calculate the probability that I lose a game.
b Calculate the probability that I lose three games in a row.

2 In a game of Paper, Scissors, Stone I am equally likely to win, draw or lose. I play two games. Find the probability that:

a I win the first game

b I win both games

c I do not win either game.

3 Two fair dice are thrown. Draw a sample space diagram to show the 36 equally likely outcomes, and use your diagram to find:

a the probability that the total is 10

b the probability that the total is less than 5

c the probability that at least one of the dice shows a 6.

4 One bag contains a red ball, a blue ball and a yellow ball, while a second bag contains two red balls and one yellow ball. Two balls are randomly chosen, one from each bag. Draw a sample space diagram, and use it to find the probability that:

a both balls are red

b at least one ball is red

c both balls are the same colour.

5 A computer game produces letters which I have to arrange to make a word. The letters are classed as either vowels or consonants. When a letter is chosen the probability of getting a vowel is 0.3.

a Write down the probability of getting a consonant.

b Draw a tree diagram to show the results of choosing two letters.

c Find the probability that when two letters are chosen, the first one is a vowel and the second is a consonant.

d Find the probability that when two letters are chosen, one is a vowel and the other is a consonant.

6 Two ordinary dice are renumbered so that they each carry the values 1, 1, 1, 1, 1, 6 on their faces. Both dice are thrown together.

a Draw a sample space diagram to show the possible outcomes.

b Find the probability that the total is 7.

c Find the probability that the total is even.

7 ✳ Three coins are tossed. One of the possible outcomes is heads on the first coin, heads on the second and tails on the third. This is written HHT.

First coin	Second coin	Third coin
H	H	T

a Copy and complete this table to show all the possible outcomes.
b Find the probability of getting three heads.
c Find the probability of getting two heads and one tail (in any order).

8 ✳ When I throw a dart at a board the probability that I hit the bull is 0.1. I throw three darts altogether. Draw a tree diagram to show the three throws, and use it to find the probability that I obtain:
a no bull . b three bulls c exactly one bull.

9 ✳ A ball is chosen at random from a bag, and then replaced. A second ball is then chosen at random. The probability that **both** balls are red is 0.36.
a Calculate the probability that the first ball is red.
b The bag contains 20 balls in total. Each ball is either red or green. How many green balls must there be in the bag?

10 ✳ A drawer contains six socks, of which two are blue. Peter decides to pick two socks out without turning the light on. He takes out one sock and puts it on, then takes out a second sock and puts it on. Peter reckons that the probability of getting a pair of blue socks is

$$P = \frac{2}{6} \times \frac{2}{6} = \frac{4}{36} = \frac{1}{9}.$$

Unfortunately Peter's calculation is wrong.
a Explain briefly why Peter's calculation is wrong.
b Work out the correct answer to this problem.

End of year review exercises

EXERCISE Y9.1

Do this exercise as mental arithmetic – do not write down any working.

1   Write the ratio 15:24 in its simplest form.

2   Write the ratio 15:12 in the form 1 : *n*.

3   £500 is to be shared out in the ratio 5:3:2. Find the value of the smallest share.

4   Write 3.141 592 6 correct to 4 decimal places.

5   Write 76.031 correct to 3 significant figures.

6   Sheets of stickers cost 99 pence each. Roughly how much would it cost for 21 sheets?

7   Find *x* if *x* + 11 = 7.

8   Find *y* if 2*y* + 1 = 19.

9   Find the next two numbers: 5, 8, 11, 14, __, __.

10 Find the next two numbers: 5, 6, 8, 11, __, __.

11 A quadrilateral has four equal sides but no right angles. What type of quadrilateral is it?

12 How many mirror lines does a kite have?

13 What name is given to a 2-D mathematical shape with six straight edges?

14 Six cans of drink cost £1.50. How much will 15 cans cost?

15 Three of the angles in a quadrilateral add up to 295°. State the size of the fourth angle.

16 The angles in a certain quadrilateral are 140°, 100°, 20°, 100° (in order as you go around it). Gary says, 'This shape must be a kite'. Is Gary right?

17 The angles in a certain quadrilateral are 80°, 100°, 80°, 100° (in order as you go around it). Lucy says, 'This shape must be a parallelogram'. Is Lucy right?

18 The perimeter of a square is 20 cm. Find its area.

19 True or false: angles in a pie chart must always add up to 360°.

20 True or false: 2.5 kilograms is exactly the same as 250 grams.

EXERCISE Y9.2

You should show all necessary working for this exercise.

1. Add $\frac{3}{10}$ and $\frac{1}{5}$.

2. Take $\frac{3}{4}$ away from $\frac{11}{12}$.

3. Find the value of $\frac{13}{20} \times 5$.

4. Multiply $\frac{7}{8}$ by $\frac{4}{5}$.

5. Workout $\frac{5}{8} \div \frac{15}{22}$.

6. In a cafe, the cost of a glass of orange juice is proportional to the volume of juice it contains. A 125 ml glass costs 35 pence. Find the cost of a 200 ml glass.

7. Burger meals cost £2.88 plus another 30 pence to 'go large'. Roughly how much would it cost for 19 people to purchase 'go large' burger meals?

8. Find x if $\frac{x}{4} = 5$.

9. Find y if $20 = 3y - 1$.

10. Find the first three terms in the number pattern described by $u_n = 3_n - 1$.

11. Find the first three terms in the number pattern described by $u_{n+1}, = 3u_n - 1$ and $u_1 = 1$.

12. Write the equation $y - 5x + 3 = 0$ in the form $y = mx + c$. Hence state the gradient of the line.

13. Write the equation $2y - 5x = 12$ in the form $y = mx + c$. Hence state the intercept of the line.

14. What name is given to a 2-D mathematical shape with eight straight edges?

15. What name is given to a 3-D mathematical solid with eight flat faces?

16. Copy these two sentences and complete the missing words:
    A str□ig□t line formed by joining two points on the cir□□□□□□□□□ of a circle is called a ch□□□. If, in addition, the ch□□□ passes through the c□n□□ of the circle then it is called a d□□□□□er.

17. Find the total number of days in the months from August to December inclusive.

18. Every day the number of bacteria in a colony doubles. Today there are 6000. How many will there be in three days' time?

19. A fair die is thrown twice. Find the probability that the total score is at least 7.

20 The probability that a set of traffic lights shows red is 0.2. I approach these lights on two different occasions during the week. Find the probability that the lights show:

    a red both times

    b red on one occasion only.

EXERCISE Y9.3

You should show all necessary working for this exercise.

1 Work out $1\frac{2}{3} + 3\frac{3}{4}$.

2 Find the value of $6\frac{1}{2} - 3\frac{9}{10}$.

3 Work out $2\frac{2}{3} \times 1\frac{5}{16}$.

4 Find the value of $3\frac{1}{2} \div 1\frac{1}{4}$.

5 A local multi-storey car park charges these prices:

Duration of stay, hours	Cost, pence
1	50
2	80
3	110
4	140

    a Is there a linear relationship between duration of stay and cost?

    b Is the cost proportional to the duration of stay?

6 In the old Imperial system of measures, one fathom is equal to six feet.

    a Roughly how many centimetres are there in half a fathom?

    b Roughly how many fathoms are there in 200 feet?

7 Harsha is calculating the area of a rectangle. It measures 14.1 cm by 10.5 cm. He uses a calculator, and says that the answer is 14.8 cm^2, to 3 significant figures. Harsha's answer is not correct.

    a Make a rough estimate of the area, showing your working carefully.

    b Explain briefly what mistake you think Harsha might have made.

8 Solve the equation $5x + 3 = 3x + 11$.

9 Solve the equation $7x - 2 = 68 - 3x$.

10 Find a formula for the nth term of this number pattern: 6, 10, 14, 18, … .

11 Find the missing angles represented by letters:

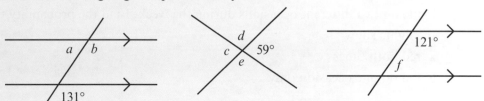

12 Draw a set of coordinate axes in which x and y can run from 0 to 10.
   a Plot the triangle whose vertices are at (1, 1), (4, 1) and (1, 5). Label it A.
   b Plot the triangle whose vertices are at (6, 2), (9, 2) and (6, 6). Label it B.
   c Describe a transformation which moves triangle A to triangle B.

13 Draw a set of coordinate axes in which x and y can run from –10 to 10.
   a Plot the triangle whose vertices are at (2, 2), (9, 2) and (3, 8). Label it A.
   b Reflect triangle A in the x-axis. Label this new triangle B.
   c Reflect triangle B in the y-axis. Label this new triangle C.
   d Describe a single transformation which moves triangle A to triangle C.

14 A local primary school wants to collect information about the ages of its pupils and how they travel to school. Design a suitable data collection sheet.

15 Jamila, who is aged 13, wants to find out what teenagers at her school think about the importance of fashion.
   She designs a questionnaire, and asks 10 of her friends to fill it in.
   a Suggest two ways in which Jamila's sample is likely to be biased.
   b State briefly whether you think her sample is of a suitable size.

EXERCISE Y9.4

1 The equation $x^2 - 9x + 4 = 0$ has a solution between $x = 8$ and $x = 9$.
Use trial and improvement to find its value correct to 1 decimal place.

2 The equation $x^3 + x - 4 = 0$ has a solution between $x = 1$ and $x = 2$.
Use trial and improvement to find its value correct to 2 decimal places.

3 The four angles in a quadrilateral are $x + 5$, $2x + 15$, $3x + 10$ and $5x$, all angles being in degrees. Set up an equation, and solve it to find the value of x. Hence find the sizes of all four angles.

4 Copy and complete this table, in which x and y are related by the formula $y = x^2 + 3x - 1$.

x	-3	-2	-1	0	1	2	3
x^2	9	4			1		
$3x$	-9		-3		3		
-1	-1	-1		-1		-1	-1
y	-1	-3			3		

Draw coordinate axes in which x can run from -3 to 3 and y can run from -3 to 17. Plot the points, and join them up with a smooth curve. Use your graph to obtain a value of x when $y = 0$.

5 Water is poured into an unusual shaped container at a steady rate. Here is a sketch of the container.

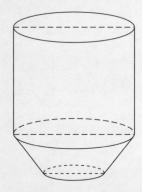

Draw a sketch graph to show how the depth of water changes over time. You should mark time along the x-axis and depth up the y-axis.

6 Here is one vertex of a regular polygon.

144°

Calculate the number of sides which this polygon must have.

7 Explain why the diagram below could not represent one vertex of a regular polygon.

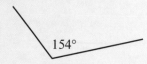

154°

8   A circle has a diameter of 16 cm. Find its circumference.

9   A circle has a radius of 21 cm. Find its area.

10   A circle has an area of 45 cm². Find its diameter.

Answers to Self-check Questions

Chapter 1
Working with numbers

Exercise 1.1
2 13 593
9 20 003
14 Sixty-three thousand, two hundred and seven
20 Thirty-two thousand and sixty-seven

Exercise 1.2
3 96 615
8 2808
14 Twenty-one thousand, eight hundred and four
17 Nineteen thousand, two hundred and seventeen

Exercise 1.3
5 637 000
6 2390
15 Eighty-three thousand
16 Six thousand four hundred

Exercise 1.4
1 32 8 24

Exercise 1.5
1 c) 9, 18, 27, 36
   i) No
   n) Yes
2 d) 1, 2, 4, 8, 16

Exercise 1.6
5 Prime
6 59
7 41, 43, 47
8 Composite

Chapter 2
Long multiplication and long division

Exercise 2.1
2 15 228
8 31 744
17 243 873
19 50 625

Exercise 2.2
1 b) 5284
   i) 275
2 i) 999

Chapter 3
Working with decimals

Exercise 3.1
1 c) 1.9
2 a) 2.9
   d) 4.3
3 c) 6.39
4 a) 5.67

Exercise 3.2
1 b) 3.003, 3.01, 3.209, 3.21, 3.3
2 a) 0.42, 0.415, 0.4, 0.37, 0.365

Exercise 3.3
4 62.8
5 3.5
13 54.19
14 33.24
20 £16.99

Exercise 3.4
1 135.6
11 2.1
20 8.6 kilometres

Chapter 4
Working with fractions

Exercise 4.1
3 $\frac{5}{9}$ 10 $\frac{5}{16}$

Exercise 4.2
3 $\frac{8}{18}$, $\frac{12}{27}$, $\frac{16}{36}$ 6 44

Exercise 4.3
2 $\frac{2}{3}$ 10 $\frac{1}{5}$

Chapter 5 Fractions, decimals and percentages

Exercise 5.1
2 132

9 93
12 305

Exercise 5.2
2 60%

Exercise 5.3
1 630
7 $420
11 324
18 108

Exercise 5.4
6 62.5%
8 36.4%
10 71.4%
17 14%

Exercise 5.5
1 $\frac{8}{25}$ 7 $\frac{1}{40}$
14 $\frac{3}{20}$ 19 $\frac{1}{6}$

Exercise 5.6
2 0.9 9 $\frac{13}{20}$, 0.65

Chapter 6
Introducing algebra

Exercise 6.1
1 c) $4x + 7$
2 b) $5(y - 4)$

Exercise 6.2
1 b) $2x - 5$
2 c) $21, 9 + 2x$
   g) £1100, $£1500 - 50t$

Exercise 6.3
1 14
2 11
12 77
16 51.9

Exercise 6.4
1 c) 53
   f) 20
2 c) 62
3 d) −1

Chapter 7
Graphs of straight lines

Exercise 7.1

1

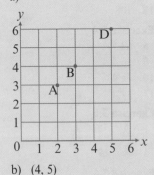

A square

4 a)

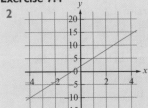

b) (4, 5)

Exercise 7.2

2 A square

3 A trapezium

Exercise 7.3

1 P (6, 4) Q (–4, 5) R (4, –3)
S (–7, –7) T (3, –6) U (–9, 3)

Exercise 7.4

2

8

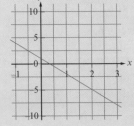

Chapter 8 Lines and angles

Exercise 8.1

1 L1 and L3, also L4 and L6

2 L1 and L5, also L3 and L4

5 Lines L1 and L3 are parallel
(or possibly coincident)

Exercise 8.2

1 Acute

2 Obtuse

3 Right-angled

Exercise 8.3

1 53°

3 105°

5 348°

Exercise 8.4

1 80°

3 135°

Exercise 8.5

1 $a = 29°$

5 $e = 50°$

Exercise 8.6

1 48°

4 101°

Chapter 9 Metric units

Exercise 9.1

1 15 cm 5 mm

7 2.5 litres

Exercise 9.2

1 c) centimetres
  j) kilometres

2 f) grams

Exercise 9.3

1 6.6

3 10.4

4 5.75 $(5\frac{3}{4})$

Chapter 10 Averages and spread

Exercise 10.1

2 8.375

4 8.05

12 0.5

20 66.8 grams, yes, as 66.8 > 65

Exercise 10.2

1 5, 7

7 6.5, 3

Exercise 10.3

1 6

7 11

Exercise 10.4

3 a) 30 throws
  b) the mode is 2

Exercise 10.5

1 The two stations have a
similar average (median)
temperature, but station B
has a greater range.

4 The range is similar for each
group, but the trainees earn
about £16 000 less than the
fully qualified accountants.

Chapter 11 Introducing probability

Exercise 11.1

3 uncertain

9 certain

Exercise 11.2

2 a) likely
  b) impossible
  c) unlikely
  d) even chance

Exercise 11.3

1 $\frac{1}{10}$

2 $\frac{3}{10}$

6 $\frac{1}{4}$ (or $\frac{3}{12}$)

Chapter 12 Working with whole numbers

Exercise 12.1

1 d) –7.5, –7.33, 14.05, 14.66

2 b) –11
  d) –7
  j) 16

Exercise 12.2

2 –18

8 45

21 16

Exercise 12.3

2 $2 \times 3 \times 11$

4 $2^2 \times 3^2$

18 $2^4 \times 3^2$

Exercise 12.4

3 9

8 70

16 24

Exercise 12.5

1 b) 208

o) 165

Chapter 13 Working with decimals

Exercise 13.1

1 c) 10.006

2 a) Sixty-nine point two five

3 e) 63.59

l) 424.19

Exercise 13.2

5 484.5

7 90.07

Exercise 13.3

1 1.02

10 4.375

18 2.25

Exercise 13.4

1 6.5

7 14.4

14 887

Chapter 14 Percentages, ratios and the unitary method

Exercise 14.1

1 c) $\frac{19}{24}$

j) $\frac{1}{2}$

2 a) 80%

g) 37%

Exercise 14.2

1 a) 0.375

j) 4.6429

2 c) $\frac{22}{25}$

e) $3\frac{16}{25}$

Exercise 14.3

1 b) 70%

f) 620%

2 a) 0.333

h) 0.075

Exercise 14.4

1 £18

9 a) 252

b) 108

Exercise 14.5

1 b) 371

e) £936

5 a) 1.12

b) £18.50

Exercise 14.6

1 b) 3:4

h) 20:13:11

3 a) 3:5:12

b) 45 minutes

Exercise 14.7

2 120 minutes

9 150 minutes

Chapter 15 Algebra

Exercise 15.1

3 c) $4m + 6n$

6 a) $7y^3$

c) $9b^2 + 7b$

Exercise 15.2

1 a) $2x + 8y$

2 a) $9x + 14$

3 c) $22x + 19y$

Exercise 15.3

1 $A = 22$

5 $Q = 50$

Chapter 16 Gradient and intercept of a straight line

Exercise 16.1

1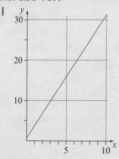

Exercise 16.2

1 $y = x + 3$

2 $y = 2x$

6 $y = 2$

Chapter 17 Lines and angles

Exercise 17.1

2 $a = 110°$ (alternate to 110°), $b = 70°$ (angles on a straight line), $c = 70°$ (alternate to b)

Exercise 17.2

2 $a = 103°$ (corresponding to 103°), $b = 77°$ (angles on a straight line)

Exercise 17.3

(there are no check answers for this exercise, since the questions are on proof)

Chapter 18 Enlargement

As these questions are extended drawings there are no key answers to this chapter.

Chapter 19 Geometric constructions

As these questions are extended drawings there are no key answers to this chapter.

Chapter 20 Area and volume

Exercise 20.1

1 a) 156 cm²

f) 71.5 cm²

3 319 cm²

4 219 cm²

Exercise 20.2

2 Rectangle, 98 cm²

4 Rhombus, 108 cm²

5 Trapezium, 35 cm²

8 Parallelogram, 100.75 cm²

Exercise 20.3

1 184 cm²

3 408 cm²

Exercise 20.4

1   560 cm³   412 cm²

4   570.18 cm³   419 cm²

Chapter 21 Graphs and charts

Exercise 21.1

1   Discrete

7   Continuous

8   Discrete

Exercise 21.2

4

■ Books 180°
■ Photocopying 96°
■ Classroom equipment 54°
■ Staff Training 15°
□ Other 15°

Exercise 21.3

1

Country	Great Britain	France	Germany	Other
Angle	172°	82°	41°	65°

■ Great Britain
■ France
■ Germany
■ Other

Exercise 21.4

1   Line graph

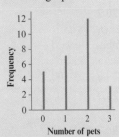

2   Time series graph

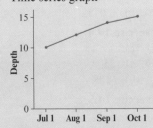

Exercise 21.5

3   a)

Age	$0 \le x < 5$	$5 \le x < 10$	$10 \le x < 15$	$15 \le x < 20$
Frequency	3	0	7	14

   b)   The storm probably took place 2 years ago.

Exercise 21.6

2

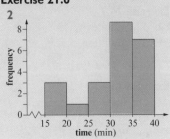

Exercise 21.7

1   Strong positive correlation

2   No correlation

3   Weak positive correlation

4   Strong negative correlation

5   Weak negative correlation

7   a)   Plant A probably died.

   b)

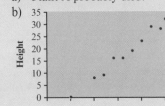

7   c)   The height and temperature show strong positive correlation.

Chapter 22 Probability

Exercise 22.1

2   a)   A, B, C, D, E, F, G, H, I, J

   b) $\frac{3}{10}$

   c) $\frac{9}{10}$

Exercise 22.2

2   a)   (white, pink), (yellow, pink), (blue, pink), (white, purple), (yellow, purple), (blue, purple), (white, yellow), (yellow, yellow), (blue, yellow), (white, blue), (yellow, blue), (blue, blue)

   b) $\frac{1}{12}$

   c) $\frac{2}{12}$ (or $\frac{1}{6}$)

Chapter 23 Working with fractions

Exercise 23.1

1   a) $\frac{5}{7}$

   d) $\frac{2}{3}$

   n) $\frac{17}{60}$

4   $\frac{29}{40}$

Exercise 23.2

2   $\frac{6}{55}$

9   $\frac{7}{10}$

19   $\frac{2}{9}$

Exercise 23.3

1   $\frac{35}{36}$

7   $\frac{3}{4}$

Exercise 23.4

2 $2\frac{7}{8}$

5 $4\frac{1}{2}$

11 $8\frac{2}{9}$

12 $2\frac{11}{18}$

Exercise 23.5

2 $4\frac{2}{5}$ 5 $1\frac{1}{2}$

Chapter 24 Ratio and proportion

Exercise 24.1

1 h) 2 : 3

Exercise 24.2

2 210 grams, 240 grams

7 30 cm

Exercise 24.3

2 £1.92

Chapter 25 Rounding and approximation

Exercise 25.1

1 a) 160

2 a) 40 000

3 b) 104.8

   f) 12.20

4 d) 46.20

Exercise 25.2

1 $60 \times 20 = 1200$

7 $6000 \div 30 = 200$

10 $70 \times 20 = 1400$ grams

19 $20 \times 30 = 600$ scripts

Exercise 25.3

6 $4000 \div 20 = 200$ so this looks about right.

7 $11\,000 \div 10 = 1100$ so this looks wrong. By calculator, the answer is 755.

Exercise 25.4

3 2.792

10 0.19

Exercise 25.5

2 1.9

8 7.3

9 0.90 and 3.07

Chapter 26 Linear equations

Exercise 26.1

3 $x = -7$

8 $x = 7$

11 $x = 33$

13 $x = 23$

Exercise 26.2

3 $x = 7$

9 $x = 3$

13 $x = 6$

19 $x = 2\frac{1}{2}$

Exercise 26.3

2 $x = 8$

7 $x = 7$

15 $x = 3.25$

20 $x = -1.4$

Exercise 26.4

3 28 dogs

6 12

Chapter 27 Number patterns

Exercise 27.1

3 Start at 16, go up 3 at a time. 31, 34.

4 Start at 11, go down 2 at a time. 1, –1.

7 Start at 1, go up 2, then 3, then 4 etc. 21, 28.

Exercise 27.2

1 c) 2, 6, 10, 14, 18

   f) 8, 6, 4, 2, 0

   j) 1, 4, 9, 16, 25

2 b) 1, 3, 7, 15, 31, 63

   h) 1, 2, 4, 7, 11, 16

Exercise 27.3

1 b) 25, 28. $u_n = 3n + 7$

   h) –5, –8. $u_n = -3n + 13$

2 b) Not linear. Start at 21, go up 2, then 3, then 4 etc.

   c) Linear. $u_n = 3n + 18$

Chapter 28 Functions and graphs

Exercise 28.1

1 a) $y = 3x + 4$
      gradient = 3, intercept = 4

   b) $y = 3x$
      gradient = 3, intercept = 0

   c) $y = -4x + 2$
      gradient = –4, intercept = 2

   d) $y = 2x + \frac{4}{3}$
      gradient = 2, intercept = $\frac{4}{3}$

2 a) $y = -4x + 12$
      gradient = –1, intercept = 12

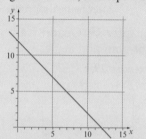

Exercise 28.2

1

x	–4	–3	–2	–1	0	1	2	3
x^2	16	9	4	1	0	1	4	9
$+4x$	–16	–12	–8	–4	0	4	8	12
–3	–3	–3	–3	–3	–3	–3	–3	–3
y	–3	–6	–7	–6	–3	2	9	18

6

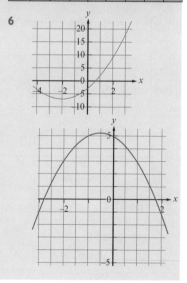

Exercise 28.3

2 a)

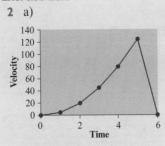

b) 101 m/s
c) 2.8 sec
d) It lands between 5 and 6
   seconds
   after being dropped.

Chapter 29 Quadrilaterals, polygons and angles

Exercise 29.1

1

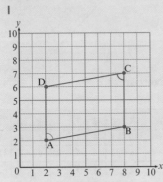

A parallelogram

4

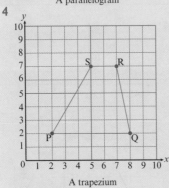

A trapezium

Exercise 29.2

2 $b = 93°$ (angles on a straight
   line add up to 180°)
   $c = 113°$ (angles in a

quadrilateral add up to 360°)
$d = 67°$ (angles on a straight
line)

3 $e = 100°$ (angles on a straight
line)
$f = 100°$ (opposite angles of
a kite, symmetric with e)

12 $s = 90°$ (angles on a straight
line)
$t = 60°$ (Z-angles)
$u = 30°$ (Z-angles)

Exercise 29.3

2 a) 1800°
  b) 150°
  c) 30°

Exercise 29.4

1 $a = 10°$
3 $c = 38°$
6 $g = 14°$

Chapter 30 Transformations

As these questions are extended
drawings there are no key
answers to this chapter.

Chapter 31 The circle

Exercise 31.1

a Circumference
e Major segment

Exercise 31.2

1 c) 31.4 km
  h) 59.7 m
2 c) 134.5 mm
  h) 76.97 km

Exercise 31.3

1 c) 78.5 km²
  g) 154 km²
2 c) 1439 mm²
  e) 706.9 cm²

Exercise 31.4

2 3.18 inches
3 3.34 mm

Chapter 32 Surveys and sampling

Exercise 32.1

1 b) Since Rupinder is doing
     a web-based survey, only
     people with Internet
     access will be able to
     respond.
  d) There are more girls than
     boys in the population,
     so Martina should have
     chosen 25 boys and 45
     girls, not 35 of each.

Chapter 33 Probability

Exercise 33.1

2 0.7
6 0.1

Exercise 33.2

3 $\frac{1}{9}$

6 a) $\frac{1}{6}$

  b) $\frac{1}{4}$

10 a) $\frac{1}{9}$

   b) $\frac{1}{18}$

   c) $\frac{1}{4}$

   d) $\frac{1}{9}$

Exercise 33.3

1 0.36
4 0.384
10 a) 0.25
   b) 0.3
   c) 0.04

Index